Frontiers *of* Possession

Frontiers *of* Possession

SPAIN AND PORTUGAL IN EUROPE
AND THE AMERICAS

Tamar Herzog

Harvard University Press

Cambridge, Massachusetts
London, England   2015

Second Printing

Library of Congress Cataloging-in-Publication Data
Herzog, Tamar.
    Frontiers of possession : Spain and Portugal in Europe and the
Americas / Tamar Herzog.
        pages   cm
    Includes bibliographical references and index.
    ISBN 978-0-674-73538-5 (alk. paper)
    1. Spain—Foreign relations.   2. Spain—Territorial expansion—
History.   3. Portugal—Foreign relations.   4. Portugal—Territorial
expansion—History.   5. Spain—Colonies—America—History.
6. Portugal—Colonies—America—History.   7. Imperialism—
History.   I. Title.
DP84.H47   2015
946.0009'03—dc23   2014009292

Contents

INTRODUCTION   1

PART I

Defining Imperial Spaces: How South America
   Became a Contested Territory   17

  1. European Traditions: Bulls, Treaties, Possession,
     and Vassalage   25

  2. Europeans and Indians: Conversion,
     Submission, and Land Rights   70

PART II

Defining European Spaces: The Making of Spain
   and Portugal in Iberia   135

  3. Fighting a Hydra: 1290–1955   149

  4. Moving Islands in a Sea of Land: 1518–1864   191

     Conclusion   243

ABBREVIATIONS   269

NOTES   273

ACKNOWLEDGMENTS   375

INDEX   377

Frontiers *of* Possession

Introduction

T HIS BOOK ANALYZES the territorial formation of Spain and Portugal in both Europe and the Americas. Rather than being determined by treaties or military confrontations, as historians have asserted, the shape both countries acquired in the early modern period was the end result of multiple activities by a plethora of agents who, while they went about accomplishing different tasks, also defined the territories of their communities and states. Situated on islands of occupation and surrounded by a sea of land they considered open for their expansion, farmers, nobles, clergymen, friars, missionaries, settlers, governors, municipal authorities, and military men in both the Old and the New Worlds explored, settled, and used different spaces. They vocally and often violently rejected claims by neighbors who wanted to do the same, arguing that they had a preferential right. Resembling a cacophony rather than a dialogue, these exchanges sometimes involved agents who were perhaps authorized to speak for their community or king—as was the case with governors, town councils, and military commanders—but they mostly called for the participation of many others who were not. Conducted in multiple sites by different actors, on various occasions, and for different ends, territorial confrontations were mostly unplanned and uncontrolled. They occurred spontaneously when the situation so required—when the various interested parties wanted to travel, collect fruits, built huts, let their animals pasture, or convert and control the local population— yet their persistence and change over time ended up restructuring both territories and rights. In Europe, these debates confronting neighbors lasted for centuries, acquiring the topography of shifting sands that appeared immutable yet in reality constantly metamorphosed while discussants, their objects of desire, and their arguments profoundly mutated. They featured ancient rights and entitlements that were compared and contrasted to evolving social, political, cultural, and economic conditions whose meaning slowly transformed as a result of changes in contemporary understandings regarding how land could be acquired and maintained. In the Americas, debates as to who could do what, where it could be done, and thus how communal terrain would be defined were shorter, yet they took a dramatic turn because the territory was huge and most contemporaries assumed it harbored great promises. Also in the New World, territorial conflicts involved the presence of indigenous peoples and thus required a constant effort to integrate (or eliminate) individuals and groups whom the Spaniards and the Portuguese considered were part of a horizon that could, indeed must, become their own.

Historians studying territorial conflicts in the past have tended to define them as disputes over boundaries. Resorting to a series of opposites, they distinguished between borders according to whether they were linear (defined by a line) or zonal (including an amorphous area), internal (vis-à-vis domestic yet nonsubjected peoples and territories) or external (vis-à-vis foreign powers), natural (as dependent on natural accidents, or as emerging "naturally" over time) or artificial (imposed from the outside). Linking the appearance of modern boundaries with the consolidation of states, they suggested that preoccupation with defining political spaces came from above, as kings, who were previously concerned mainly with personal subjugation, sought to territorialize their control.[1] These processes, transpiring after local communities had expanded to hinterlands that were considered empty and had undergone processes of territorialization, took shape as monarchs contracted with one another and negotiated with local authorities who could resist these developments, collaborate with them, or even initiate and encourage them. As a consequence of these exchanges between a "center" and a "periphery" that were sometimes at odds but sometimes collaborated, local communities were "nationalized."[2] Thereafter, a territory made of a multiplicity of communities and different jurisdictions (military, fiscal, customs administration, sanitary, ecclesiastical, and so forth) came to be constructed as a single, national space that could give birth to present-day structures. The peace of Westphalia (1648) authorized these developments by recognizing the existence of a system of states, each with its own territorial sovereignty.

These narratives, mainly focused on the genealogy of states and nations, rarely asked which were the precise mechanisms and processes that countless individuals and groups embraced to establish territorial claims for themselves, their communities, and their monarchs. Neither were they interested in understanding what was involved in carving out territory in the early modern period or how rights to land were constructed, negotiated, and remembered by both locals and outsiders. Insisting that several types of distinct jurisdictions existed, most authors studied them separately, often ignoring the ways by which they dynamically interacted. Also under-analyzed was the question of how, in the process of claim making, identities changed not only on the level of states (and nations) but also on the local scene, where individuals defined themselves (or were classified by others) as members or nonmembers. It was as if the question of *how* claims were actually made and defended and *how* they were understood was nonimportant because it was sufficient to argue either that disagreement among locals invited the intervention of states or that states embraced "possession" as the basis for defending their rights. In these narratives, local communities were often presented as timeless and ahistorical entities, while states were portrayed as active promoters of change. Law, when it was introduced at all, had the caricature presence of something that diplomats and statesmen sometimes used but that even they did not take seriously. How contemporaries understood possession and what it led them to do was barely ever discussed. The neglect to examine the link between private actors on the one hand and the formation of territorial divisions on the other was particularly odd given that natural law discussants, so abundant all over Europe at that time, were contemporaneously obsessed with precisely this question, namely, how communal and private property were formed over time as a result of agreements and disagreements among individuals and groups. Was not their obsession telling? Were they not reproducing at least partially what they observed was unfolding around them?

If historians of Europe insisted on straightforward genealogies that linked present to past and gave primacy to royal actions on the one hand, economic interests that led local actors to pursue certain goals on the other, colonial historians suggested instead that while European borders were "natural" because they gradually emerged by autochthonous processes, colonial borders were "artificial" because they were unilaterally imposed by colonial powers ignorant of local realities in a relatively short time span.[3] Many argued that, unlike in the Old World, in the New World external frontiers vis-à-vis neighbors appeared before internal frontiers of occupation were possessed and integrated. According to these accounts, the hardest task postcolonial states faced therefore was not the need to battle neighbors from the outside but the obligation to control peoples and territories that were purportedly internal to them yet hardly formed part of their polities.

These metanarratives were largely followed by historians of Spain, Portugal, and their overseas domains. They presented the territorial formation of Spain and Portugal in Iberia as the by-product of the process by which Christian communities gradually becoming states expanded southward, eliminating the last vestiges of Muslim presence (the so-called Reconquest).[4] Among other things, these developments allowed for the creation of a small territory that came to be identified as Portugal. The separation between it and the rest of the peninsula was defined in a series of bilateral agreements that, after a long military and political struggle in the eleventh, twelfth, and thirteenth centuries, recognized the independence of Portugal and distinguished it from Castile, from which it originally descended. The Treaty of Alcañices (1297) signed by the kings of Portugal and Castile and which defined the border between the two kingdoms was an important step in this direction because, according to most scholars, it consolidated a separation that thereafter suffered no major modifications.[5] For historians of Portugal, this narrative affirmed the individuality of that country and its right to an independent existence.[6] For Spaniards, it was mainly a lamentable episode that was neither foretold nor mandated.

But whatever role the emergence and affirmation of Portugal played in modern, often nationalistic narratives, because the border between it and Spain (Castile) was generally considered a medieval affair concluded in 1297, historians of fifteenth-, sixteenth-, seventeenth-, and eighteenth-century Iberia tended to care about territorial divisions only when they were violated (in war or by contraband) or when they were useful to the construction of transfrontier histories that allegedly demonstrated that the separation between Castilian and Portuguese territories was imposed by states at the displeasure of the local inhabitants, who preferred to ignore it. Proposing a history of the border either from above (the result of royal agency) or from below (the way local communities undermined it) but rarely joining both visions, Iberian historians thus suggested an opposition between a center and a periphery with the occasional consensus emerging when local interests so demanded. They were rarely interested in asking how the theoretical division coined in 1297 was implemented or how early modern individuals living in both Spain and Portugal and their communities understood, constructed, and defended their right to land, thus also contributing to the formation of the border.[7] Neither did they analyze how evolving conceptions regarding the use of land changed the nature of territorial debates as well as their consequences on the ground or how memory and forgetfulness helped in these processes. The pervasiveness and persistence of conflicts between residents and villages belonging to both states along their emerging frontier were simply ignored or classified as inconsequential.

While historians of Iberia in Europe insisted on the agency of kings and the longevity of a medieval border, historians of Iberia in the Americas ascertained that the penetration of Spaniards and Portuguese into the New World was governed by a series of formal documents, most famous among them the Treaty of Tordesillas, signed in 1494. Although acknowledging that these accords (also including the Treaty of Madrid in 1750 and San Idelfonso in 1777, among others) failed to solve the question of who was authorized to take over which part (see Part I), most scholars nonetheless considered that in their aftermaths, there was a border that the parties could respect or ignore.[8] Converting the past into a moral tale in which there were "good" and "bad" actors as well as clear entitlements, historians proceeded to adopt either the Portuguese or the Spanish stand, rarely observing the controversy as it was experienced on both sides. They implicitly suggested that the question of who had rights to which part of the Americas was clear (when it never was) or that there was an evident rule that could be adopted (which there was none). Limiting their questioning mostly to what happened in European courts or to military operations, most historians also failed to describe how the activities of individuals and groups residing in the New World contributed to the formation of territorial divides. Some mentioned expeditions that roamed the interior of the American continent, but almost none followed these through to observe how they were used by both locals and kings to argue for rights. Very few were willing to engage with the complexity of the processes that led to occupation or to examine the plethora of agents and interests that were responsible for them.[9] And although in recent years many have ascertained that interaction with natives was an important factor in these territorial debates, most scholars nevertheless continued to distinguish between a so-called exterior frontier (vis-à-vis other Europeans) and a so-called interior frontier (vis-à-vis the native population) as if both did not coincide in the same place and time and did not affect one another.[10] Considering law as mostly irrelevant because "reality" rather than "norms" directed what would happen, neither they nor their colleagues working on Iberia were willing to engage with legality in meaningful ways. The question of what territorial conflict between Spaniards and Portuguese on one side of the ocean could tell us about what simultaneously happened on the other was simply never posed.

In what follows, I ask how territorial divisions in both Iberia and the Americas came into being by studying the interactions among many actors who represented varying interests and spoke from different places. I argue that, rather than preexisting entities clashing or people who had rights defending them against voracious enemies, claim making was the most common means for appropriating and thus constructing and reconstructing communal spaces.[11] Bilateral treaties might have framed these conflicts, but on both sides of the ocean of equal structural importance were contemporary notions regarding how domination over land (and people) could be achieved and maintained. Armed conquests might have allowed Spaniards and Portuguese to occupy certain sites, but more dangerous than war was peace, because it allowed for gradual penetration that would be impossible in times of military confrontation. For that reason, rather than solving the territorial conflict, the union of Spain and Portugal (1580–1640) exacerbated it, because in its aftermath it was difficult, perhaps even impossible, to decide what had been achieved by whom. Historical evidence also suggests that contemporaries did not ask whether borders were linear or zonal, internal or external, artificial or natural. Instead, they mostly cared about the extension and nature of their usage rights. Depending on who was asking, when, and for what end, the space contemporaries sought to appropriate could be linear or zonal, commonly used or exclusively maintained, consist of moving islands of occupation that followed, for example, the itinerary of nomad allies or resemble corridors that allowed transiting between different sites of possession immersed in a sea of unoccupied land.[12] Expanding their territories according to where they wanted their animals to graze, where they collected fruit, cultivated the land, built a hut, explored a mine, collected taxes, or established a mission, an internal frontier of occupation (meant to take hold of the land and its inhabitants) coincided with an external frontier (against "foreign" neighbors). In the process, rather than being predetermined and fixed, the meaning and extension of both "internal" and "external" were constantly reelaborated. Territorial entitlements involved not only identifying action (what was done) but also classifying actors (who they were). They thus led to frequent debates as to who was Spanish and who Portuguese and (in the New World) when Indians became one or the other. As a result, the territorial definition of Spain and Portugal in both Europe and the Americas was not the consequence of their subjects expanding the sovereignty of their states or empires (as most authors have assumed) or of locals trying to associate their interests with the state (as others have sustained) but the outcome of much more multifaceted procedures that allowed actors to define themselves and at the same time make claims to the territory.[13]

In these dynamics, law mattered a great deal. Often ignored by historians who mostly sought to explain the economic or political interests that motivated disputes, the question of how communities could acquire (or loose) their entitlements was nevertheless essential to these debates because it served as a matrix allowing those who wished to collect fruits or cultivate a certain area to interpret what both they and their rivals were doing. The way juridical perceptions ruled over daily interactions was clear, for example, when coming to interpret the use of violence. Aggression, which was typical of many territorial confrontations, could express an emotional or irrational reaction that disrupted communication among neighbors. However, it was also mandated by a legal logic that suggested that silence implied consent and reaction implied opposition (see Part I). Under this guise, aggression was not necessarily a "senseless" (albeit natural) reaction. It was, on the contrary, performative because it transmitted a clear juridical response to what contemporaries believed were legal challenges. Paradoxically, archival documents suggest that the closer communities were and the stronger the ties linking their inhabitants, the more likely they were to engage in brutality.

If this portrait is correct, then territorial divisions in both Europe and overseas were the end result of complex processes of appropriation that were carried out by hundreds of individuals in thousands of daily interactions.[14] Conflict manifested itself mostly in minute struggle rather than great wars, individual actions rather than formal treaties or diplomatic negotiations. It was expressed in acts, words, and attitudes that required interpretation that was seldom consensual but that, over time, established certain facts both on the ground and juridically. Even when kings were unaware of what their vassals were doing, could not fix their activities on maps, or believed divisions were inexistent or unclear, locals generally knew that if they roamed in certain territories they were likely to be left alone but that if they penetrated others they might (although not always) suffer repercussions. For them, the distinction between what was theirs and what was not did not depend on formal documents conserved in archives, on treaties, or even on the existence of border stones. These may have been crucial for outsider observers who did not know the territory well, but for those who did, partitions were a daily experience, a habitus of sorts. Asked to explain in 1500 where divisions between Villarinho (in Portugal) and La Tejera (in Galicia) lay,

Alvaro Pires said that he "had always seen Portugal in possession of that territory" *(porque sempre viu estar Portugal de pose).*[15] Pedro Rodrigues explained that his father had told him where once upon a time they were located and that thirty or thirty-five years earlier, when he took his cattle to the other side of the river, he was attacked and his animals sequestered. Joham Alvares was told that he should not cross the river, and he also saw other people obeying this rule. Gonçalo Annes was informed by other community members where the divisions were, and he experienced them personally when several of his animals crossed the river without his knowledge or consent. Joam Fernandes confessed that he was the first to labor on the other side and that the inhabitants of La Tejera immediately came and protested against his activities. During these proceedings, Castilian witnesses equally affirmed what they had heard, what they knew, and what they had experienced. They also asserted that while some of their actions were not contested, others provoked the opposition of their neighbors. Thus, although most witnesses declared that they knew nothing of a formal demarcation or a separation between Spain and Portugal, they all concurred that locally, divisions, even if contested, could be well known. Part of a reality with which *fronterizos* cohabited, they expected that if they limited their activities to certain terrains they were likely to be alright and that if they penetrated others they could be harassed, punished, or assaulted, their animals could be sequestered, and they could be fined or jailed. They watched others obeying these rules or they were told by their parents, relatives, and neighbors what they meant. Most testimony collected by rivals reproduced these local narratives which, on the one hand, allowed witnesses to insist they knew nothing of a border and had absolutely no proof where it could be located but, on the other, described in detail where inhabitants could graze, roam, and cultivate and where not. This was true regardless of whether their versions coincided with or contradicted those of their opponents. Because such was the case, claims made by kings to territory in both Europe and the America were only the tip of an iceberg. Below it was a far more complex story in which individual and communal action directed at obtaining possession, invoking prescription, and resorting to both memory and forgetfulness played a major role.

On most occasions, the hardest task individuals and communities faced was not to win over their adversaries but to recruit the king and his officers to their cause. In order to guarantee their success, many adopted arguments likely to carry favor with the monarch. They suggested that royal sovereignty, justice, and pride were at stake, they threatened that small conflicts could light a huge fire and degenerate into a major war, or they invoked the need to imprison smugglers or reform the territory. But whatever their excuse for involving the king was, monarchs intervened (or not) according to an equally complex set of considerations. Rulers mostly justified their response by referring to their obligation to preserve the peace (*sossego* or *sosiego*), act as judges, or protect their vassals. On occasions, they and their officers might have believed what they were told or felt committed to a certain individual or community by virtue of clientage. In the Americas, they might have considered the territory important and might have hoped it would bring them great riches. But even when they were willing to intervene, kings often hoped to impose by mere presence or expected that procrastination would lead the conflict to die of its own. They were, even in the Americas, distant figures, not particularly attentive to local developments or partial to them. They certainly had no recollection of past events nor necessarily a particular vision of what the future should be.

In order to provide a fully integrated account of what was involved in carving out territory in early modern Iberia, I consulted dozens of archives and manuscript collections on both sides of the Atlantic Ocean, in both Spain and Portugal and in their present-day successor states in Latin America.[16] As I processed the information, I decided to part from the customary narrative and strategically begin my story with the New World, not the Old. Historians of Latin America traditionally have referred to Europe as the motherland and considered its history a "precedent" that explained how colonialism developed. Mostly interested in medieval history, they implicitly suggested that developments in Spain and Portugal ceased being relevant thereafter, either because nothing important transpired or because it no longer affected overseas developments. Meanwhile, historians of Spain and Portugal generally ignored colonialism altogether or relegated it to a marginal, even eccentric place, within

European history. What would happen, I asked, if we artificially reversed the existing narratives, if we began with America in order to discern what it can teach us about Europe? If we considered that Iberia coexisted on both sides of the ocean for hundreds of years rather than assuming that one shore ceased to matter after the other came into being? After all, suggesting that medieval Iberia chronologically preceded early modern Spanish and Portuguese America is natural; arguing that Europe continued to be the source of all things and received nothing thereafter is not. Placing Europe first, I reasoned, was a convention that could not be easily sustained if we wished to observe what transpired in the Old World in the sixteenth, seventeenth, eighteenth, and nineteenth centuries. The intuitive order that placed Europe first was perhaps the logical result of the genealogical predicament of history, but it had hidden costs. It obscured our vision because it set us up to argue that Europe affected the Americas, while forgetting the inverse. It encouraged us to think about the particularities of the New World while enabling us to ignore those that characterized the Old. The motherland–offspring paradigm also produced a tendency toward comparative history that more often than not stereotyped Europe as an orderly, natural space and portrayed the colonies as chaotic, artificial, and exploitative. Although some of these conclusions might have been justified by what transpired in the New World, many of them were also built into the way historians have set up the equation. But if we reversed the narrative, perhaps we could use both sides of the ocean to reflect one another as skewed mirrors, making them both participants in a unified space that existed contemporaneously. Looking at Europe would force us to consider the effect of change over time more dramatically than in the Americas, yet the Americas would enhance the sense of urgency and immediateness. Both would equally suggest that the dynamic between crown officials and local actors was immensely complex, but they would each propose a different vision of how that transpired. As for law versus chaos, placing the Americas first would have us consider the degree to which on both sides of the Atlantic peace and violence coexisted interdependently rather than alternatively. Thus, while it sometimes sacrificed chronology, placing the Americas first had the potential of freeing us from many conventions too often taken for granted and could serve to illuminate ways in which individuals and groups in both worlds engaged with similar questions and searched for similar answers, though sometimes in intensely different ways.[17]

Starting with America was therefore a means to accentuate, even dramatize, the effort to think about the Old World and the New World as a single space and, distancing ourselves from existing metanarratives, consider them both as vibrant entities that coexisted rather than were chronologically arranged. Combining these concerns with attention to presentation and scale, I make the Americas not only precede Europe but also introduce many of the basic questions I seek to study. I describe my findings regarding the New World in wide brushstrokes, assembling my material thematically according to actors and arguments rather than place or chronology. Examining American conflicts, I ask why treaties failed to resolve it, interrogate the meaning of possession, and analyze the extension and consequences of the union and rupture between Spain and Portugal. Responding to the usual affirmation that treaties were important, I explain their juridical futility and sustain their complete incapacity to solve the questions at hand. Responding to the theoretical assertion that possession became the main guideline for the acquisition of overseas territories, I unpack its significance and implications by asking how contemporary actors understood it and how it affected what they said or did. Because possessing required classifying actors as members of communities, I discuss how individuals and groups came to be identified as Spanish or Portuguese and what happened during the sixty years in which both countries were subjected to the same monarch. Having examined in Chapter 1 how the Spanish and the Portuguese argued their rights to the land with one another according to their European traditions, in Chapter 2 I move on to analyze their relationships with American natives. Rather than making the frontier vis-à-vis Indians a separate affair from the territorial dispute between Spain and Portugal, I demonstrate that because religious conversion also lead to civic conversion, it influenced the territorial ascription of indigenous land and justified the massive involvement of missionaries in what was purportedly a secular political affair. I argue that the right to land could also be secured by alliance making and war. Here I assert that both violence and peace were strategies used by the Spanish and the Portuguese in order to subject the indigenous peoples and that this subjection in turn had territorial implications. Whether these developments implied that the Spanish and the Portuguese recognized the indigenous right to land is another question. Juxtaposing the theoretical debate on native right to what actually happened on the ground, I suggest that, rather than a distinction between law and its application, what transpired in the American interior was an ideologically motivated divide between an internal and an external frontier, allowing actors to apply different criteria when dealing with rival Europeans and when facing natives.

Having observed the Americas, in Part II I move to the Iberian Peninsula and ask how what we have learned about the New World can illuminate what we know of the Old. After a short introduction that examines the emergence of Portugal and the territorial questions it generated, I analyze several individual conflicts in the *longue durée*. I interpret them by closely observing who the parties were, what the coveted object was, and how claims were made. In Chapter 3 I describe border conflicts that included multiple parties, some across the forming border, some not, who fought over different territories for a diversity of reasons. I demonstrate that their struggle might have been affected by the border that gradually separated the kingdom of Castile and Spain from Portugal but that it was also greatly modified by changing economic practices, demographic growth, and the gradual discrediting of common pastures. In Chapter 4 I observe conflicts that involved natural changes, scientific observations, historical memory, and a constant reimagining of both present and past. I ask how private, ecclesiastical, military, and political jurisdictions supported or contradicted one another, how the uncertainty of the past led to the search for "reasonable" solutions, and how contemporary changes in perceptions modified what was acceptable and what had to be rejected. All these cases, I argue, exemplified the impossibility of classifying territorial conflicts as "simply" confronting Spaniards and Portuguese or rival kings against one another.

Mostly interested in a chronological unearthing of territorial conflicts, in this part concerned with the Iberian Peninsula I argue that

the "European traditions" identified in the Americas also worked in
Europe but that their operation was different because persevering
for centuries, European territorial conflicts experienced important
mutations related to both memory and forgetfulness as well as public perceptions and law. I also suggest that the American point of
view is helpful in reconsidering the role of different actors and,
most particularly, the way European peasants could be imagined as
natives, even barbarians, who were external rather than internal to
the state. If the American case is meant to serve as an introduction,
the Iberian case is meant to expose even more fully the uncertain-
ties of the past. Each actor and group, I argue, had their own reading
of what transpired, and neither their contemporaries nor we can truly
judge who was right and who wrong. Locals constantly referred back
to a status quo that they all believed existed, but each had a different
recollection of what it contained. The passing of information from
one generation to the other and the constant appeal to experience,
therefore, were both mechanisms for preservation and instruments
for change. Under the guise of continuity, the territories controlled
by the Portuguese and the Spaniards in Iberia and the definition of
who their members were mutated over time. Read together, the
American and Iberian parts should illuminate not only the histories
of Spain and Portugal and their overseas domains, and not only the
historiography on border formation, but also the question of how we
write history. In the conclusion, therefore, I refer to some of these
issues by observing the division of Iberian history into Spanish and
Portuguese narratives, the juxtaposition of a European to a colonial
history, the conventional narrative that distinguishes Anglo from
Spanish colonization, the tradition of border studies, the role of law
as a structure of meaning, and the (in)ability of the past to supply
solutions to present-day territorial conflicts.

   In what follows, I refer to Spain and Portugal, Spaniards and Portuguese, even though I am well aware that these entities and identities
were in flux and they often included sites, individuals, and communities to whom we would deny these categorizations today. I do so
by way of convention. Faithful to contemporary usage, rather than
adopting designations such as Spanish American or Portuguese
American, in most cases I utilize the same terms (Spanish and Por-

tuguese, Spain and Portugal) to refer to individuals and entities in both the Old and the New Worlds. I also refer to the Americas generically, though it is clear to me that according to present-day terminology my study is limited to the southern part of the continent. In the narrative, I often attribute agency to municipal bodies. Although this may sound odd in English, this was the way early modern Iberian communities that were legally defined as corporations were perceived and indeed acted. I also deliberately avoid studying the case of Olivença/Olivenza, a territory that in 1801 was conquered by Spain and was never returned. Many in Portugal still resent this development, and there are plenty of associations that demand its devolution.[18] Yet, from my point of view, this episode—pertaining to the nineteenth and twentieth centuries—occurred too late to be included in this study. It was also highly atypical, indeed, the only recorded case of a military conquest that had persisted despite diplomatic agreement to end it. For practical ends and in order to facilitate the reading, I use a standardized English translation of names and titles in the text but conserve the original (often chaotic) spelling in the notes. I also modernized citations in Spanish, Portuguese, French, and Italian to make them more accessible and easily understandable to readers.

PART I

Defining Imperial Spaces: How South America Became a Contested Territory

THE TERRITORIAL CONFLICT between Spain and Portugal regarding the extension of their overseas domains was as ancient as the European expansion. In 1493, shortly after Columbus returned from his first voyage, the Catholic monarchs secured two papal bulls *(Inter Caetera)* that entrusted them with the duty to convert Native Americans in return for certain rights in territories discovered west of a meridian passing one hundred leagues off the islands "vulgarly called the Azores and Cabo Verde" (two island groups in the Atlantic). Because at that time Spain's only viable rival for maritime expansion was Portugal, the following year the monarchs signed the Treaty of Tordesillas, confirmed by the pope in 1506, in which they agreed that a different meridian (this time passing 370 leagues to the west of the Cabo Verde Islands) would separate their respective zones of influence.[1] Lands not belonging to Christians that were already discovered or that would be discovered to the east of this meridian would be Portuguese; to the west, Spanish.

Although this agreement seemed clear, in the decades and centuries following its adoption, its implementation provoked constant debate. The first time the issue was seriously tested was in the early sixteenth century, when the two monarchs disagreed as to who had the right to discover and possess the Moluccas, a group of islands in

the Pacific Ocean (presently in Indonesia).[2] At stake was the factual
question of who discovered and possessed these islands first, but the
conflict also required determining (1) whether the meridian set in
Tordesillas encircled the globe, thus establishing the rights of Spain
and Portugal not only in the Atlantic but also in the Pacific; and (2)
if this was the case, whether the Moluccas were located east or west
of the meridian and were thus in Spain's or Portugal's sphere of expansion.[3] The decision to extend the treaty to the Pacific provoked
no conflict, but the question of whether these islands were east or
west of the meridian proved impossible to resolve. Juridically, the
parties would have to agree on how to interpret the term "the Cabo
Verde Islands," coined in Tordesillas. Did the signing parties intend
to measure the meridian from the most central point of this archipelago (as Spain would eventually claim) or from its most westward
point (as Portugal would insist)? But even if the parties could settle
this point (which they did not), they still needed to identify the exact location of the Moluccas in relation to this line. This, too, was a
highly debated scientific issue at a time when neither the shape nor
the size of the earth, nor the location of territories, was consensual.

In 1524, experts summoned to examine these questions and give
their opinion as to whether, according to Tordesillas, the Moluccas
should be Spanish or Portuguese failed to agree. In the Treaty of
Zaragoza (1529), the Spanish king consented to sell the Moluccas,
which he insisted were his, to the Portuguese, who continued to
consider them their own.[4] Although the conflict ended in a compromise, the questions it raised remained unresolved. Both sides continued to argue that the Moluccas were theirs, and both were aware of
the fact that this affirmation was important. After all, at stake was
not only, not even mainly, what happened in the Pacific but what
would transpire in the New World.

The question of how Tordesillas would be interpreted and implemented arose again in the 1530s, when the two courts disagreed
whether the territory known as River Plate (present-day Argentina
and Uruguay, perhaps even Brazil) was to be Spanish or Portuguese.[5]
This conflict, which was highly theoretical at this stage because neither Spain nor Portugal was capable of capitalizing on its claims, died
on its own. Nonetheless, it was a bitter reminder that nothing was

settled and nothing agreed. Hopes for a peaceful solution reemerged in 1580, when Philip II of Spain became king of Portugal. In the aftermath of this "union," many believed that the conflict between the two powers was resolved automatically because the same monarch ruled both countries. This, at least, was the a posteriori Spanish version, which insisted that, because the right to land and jurisdiction were royal, as long as the two kingdoms shared the same ruler, confrontation was impossible.[6] Whether this analysis was juridically correct or not (I will return to this point), in the eighteenth century Spaniards insisted that during the sixty years in which Spain and Portugal were united (1580–1640), the Treaty of Tordesillas was "forgotten," perhaps even annulled.[7] Some even claimed that, as a result, during that period the respective rights of Spain and Portugal could be determined only according to the *Inter Caetera*, the 1493 papal bulls that set a meridian, which was more favorable than Tordesillas to Spain. Others asserted instead that the territories of both countries were de jure separated but de facto indistinguishable. These claims were rejected by those who argued that during the union the Treaty of Tordesillas remained in force and Spain and Portugal remained separate. According to this last version, mainly upheld by Portuguese interlocutors, because the risk for confusion was greater during the union, it was particularly important for contemporaries to determine which territory belonged to whom.[8] But regardless of who was right and who wrong, it is clear that the dispute reemerged as soon as the kingdom of Portugal separated from Spain (in December 1640). According to Spanish complaints, as early as 1641, Portuguese troops invaded Spanish holdings in Omaguas (present-day Peru). In the Amazon region, the seventeenth century saw Portuguese soldiers and settlers attacking Spanish missions, arguing they were established illegally on Portuguese soil. In the River Plate, Spaniards conquered the Portuguese settlement of Colonia de Sacramento (in present-day Uruguay) which, according to them, was located on Spanish ground.[9] As in the 1520s, experts convened in 1681 and 1682 to decide whether Colonia was to the east or the west of the meridian set in Tordesillas disagreed, thus leaving the question of how to implement Tordesillas open while also encouraging both sides to attempt to gain by force what they could not gain by consensus.[10]

Thereafter, the heartland of South America became a battleground. Portuguese from the east, Spaniards from the west, and ecclesiastics from both sides penetrated the interior with the aim of taking hold of both territory and its resources, people included. Because over time European penetration became more intense, by the late eighteenth century the dispute expanded dramatically to include territories that are presently part of Brazil, Paraguay, Uruguay, Argentina, Venezuela, Colombia, Ecuador, Peru, and Bolivia. The Treaty of Utrecht (1715), the Treaty of Madrid (signed 1750, canceled 1761), the Treaty of Paris (1763), and the Treaty of San Idelfonso (1777) all attempted to settle these differences.[11] However, the issues they raised remained unsolved until the end of the colonial period, and they continued to haunt Latin American states long after their independence.

The question of which territory belonged to whom concerned European courts. It called for diplomatic negotiations and the signing of successive treaties, as well as the occasional war. Yet, while the story of courts has been studied extensively, most historians rarely asked how individuals and groups challenged one another in continuous and quotidian discussions over the extension of their land. These debates, focusing not on the rights of kings or even countries but instead directed at knowing who could take which routes and where fruits could be collected, huts constructed, mines discovered, and Indians subjugated, took place on the contested territory as contemporaries sought to accomplish certain tasks. Engaged in them were settlers, ecclesiastics, military men, governors, and natives who, confronted with the need to justify their activities, found themselves involved in affirming both who they were and what were the rights of their communities. Why they were required to engage in such conversations, when these took place, and what they said is the subject of the first part of this book, in which I argue that historians and politicians who looked to the past too often and too quickly assumed that the allegations made by early modern rivals represented the truth rather than claim making. Those favoring the Spanish stand (or wishing to benefit from it) reproduced the reports Spaniards sent to Madrid in order to convince the monarch to assist them in their quarrels, in which local actors portrayed themselves as passive observers of a continual Portuguese advance into Spanish territories.[12] Spaniards, they suggested, may have discovered many areas in the sixteenth century, but their failure to settle them allowed the Portuguese, who were better equipped and manned, to take hold of most. The Portuguese lived intrusively on the land. They deliberately ignored the commitments in the (many) treaties they had signed, and their behavior was treacherous, disloyal, and unacceptable. Since the seventeenth century, ambition had led them to appropriate vast regions in the American interior with an ultimate goal of creating a "powerful empire" *(poderoso imperio)* that would embrace the entire continent, including the rich mining districts of Peru.[13] "Wishing to imitate the glory of Spain" *(los portugueses siempre émulos de las glorias de España)*, their expansion was made possible by Spanish neglect *(indolencia)* and the insufficient attention Spaniards gave to territorial issues.[14]

These accusations, which were meant to capture royal attention rather than necessarily to represent the truth, also reflected Spanish bewilderment at Portuguese expansion, which was indeed short of spectacular. Having begun in the sixteenth and early seventeenth century with a few settlements along the Atlantic coast, the Portuguese gradually came to control (or pretend to control) a huge territory, dozens of times larger. Even if they were following their own interpretation of Tordesillas or the law, as they would often assert, how were they able to achieve what Spaniards could not? Yet, as historians justifying Portugal would remark, while the Spaniards accused the Portuguese of misbehaving, Portuguese interlocutors writing to their king presented Spain as an extremely powerful party that was likely to control soon the entire continent.[15] According to them, Spaniards constructed new fortifications and missions in Portuguese territories, they controlled river navigation, and, alongside their Indian allies, they attacked Portuguese forts on Portuguese territory. Portraying Spaniards as violent intruders *(intrusos)*, the Portuguese accused them of having "astute customs" *(costumadas astúcias)* and of displaying arrogance *(soberbos)*. They also contended that Spanish claims to American territories were as malicious and ambitious *(maliciosa ambição)* as their pretension to rule Portugal. All attempts to reason with Spaniards failed because they either refused to listen or to be convinced. They gave peace treaties absurd interpretations and were violent, uncivil, and cruel. While Spaniards advanced into the interior, the Portuguese emulated crabs refusing to leave the shoreline.[16]

This exchange of accusations reached such a point that some Spaniards were willing to argue that the Portuguese were not only liars and traitors but also barbarians. Their lack of civility was clear in their refusal to observe the pacts they had made and to obey royal orders. Because of their behavior, they could be compared to infidels. Contravening the laws of human correspondence and ignoring Christian precepts, they conducted their affairs like the Ottoman muftis who "inculcated in the renegades of our faith [the] insane resolution of turning against their origin" or, even worse, they followed the teachings of Machiavelli.[17] While Spanish interlocutors accused the Portuguese of infidelity, Portuguese correspondents suggested Spaniards were heretics.[18] Like the Dutch, Spaniards attempted to take over territories belonging to Portugal and, also like the Dutch, they distorted known truths and their actions were both uncivil *(incivil)* and ambitious. They violated Christian precepts that instructed the faithful against coveting the property of another. Accusing each other of unruly behavior, both Spaniards and Portuguese presented themselves as vassals who respected the "law of nations" *(derecho de las gentes/direito das gentes)* and the treaties. Any other insinuation was slander or libel *(calumnia* or *injuria)* as they had always acted with "justice, equity and moderation" *(justicia, equidad y moderación).*[19] Because the conquest of the Americas was achieved at great cost, it would be against natural law *(derecho natural)* as well as royal rights *(regalía)* not to defend it.[20]

Linking incorrect political behavior to a faulty civility, as well as heresy, formed part of a repertoire that early modern individuals and communities employed to discuss legal violations. Though ordinary in some respects, it testified to the degree to which already in the early modern period the conflict between Spain and Portugal in the Americas was fashioned as a tale of right and wrong, good and bad. Reproducing the information archival sources included and adopting contemporary allegations as their own, historians and politicians writing in the nineteenth and the twentieth centuries assumed that these documents reflected what was actually happening on the ground, never suspecting that they recorded instead juridical and political (sometimes phantasmagorical) assertions that were often problematic even as they were pronounced.

Rather than taking this road or attempting—as other historians have done—to describe the "proper" or "true" divisions between the two powers, in what follows I analyze how the legal and political situation forced itself on contemporaries who, in the process of legitimizing their particular activities, also created a space that they identified as their own. Their understanding of what was theirs, I argue, was perhaps structured by treaties or wars, but it depended principally on European traditions that assigned to them certain entitlements and on their relationship with the indigenous peoples.

1 European Traditions: Bulls, Treaties, Possession, and Vassalage

ALTHOUGH THE CRITERIA making a territory Spanish or Portuguese could vary by author, place, and time, most contemporary narratives mentioned two types of questions. The first involved several formal documents that suggested that in 1493 the pope gave Spain certain rights, that in 1494 the Treaty of Tordesillas endorsed these (with some changes), and that subsequent treaties (1681, 1715, 1750, 1761, and 1777) either confirmed or undermined these arrangements. The second invoked legal doctrines which, originating in Roman law and developed in the Middle Ages and the early modern period, determined that title depended on possession.[1] How these two vastly distinct criteria—formal documents versus a juridical doctrine—interacted with one another was often unclear. Most parties of course claimed that their rights were based on bulls, treaties, and possession, but they disagreed on what happened, for example, when the bulls indicated a different solution than the treaties or when the treaties and occupation contradicted one another. The options as to how to treat such conflicts were diverse. Some argued that entitlements granted by bulls and treaties gave absolute title. Territories mentioned in them were Spanish or Portuguese if they were "discovered," that is, founded and reached, no other action being required to make the land Spanish or Portuguese.[2] Others suggested instead that bulls and treaties only delineated spheres of potential expansion and that possession was always required to obtain title.[3] This second interpretation called for additional questions, namely, what would happen when possession was taken in lands outside the boundaries of the legitimate sphere of expansion? Was such possession void? Also unclear was the status of territories that were Spanish according to the bulls but Portuguese according to the Treaty of Tordesillas. Could royal sovereignty, even royal agreement to renounce certain rights, modify what the pope, a higher authority, had determined?

Inability to agree on criteria allowed discussants to choose one solution over the other according to their interests. Rather than a clear chronology that described how legal arguments changed over time, theories were adopted and abandoned according to place, period, and need. Because the Portuguese relied heavily on possession, Spaniards were often induced to argue that the occupation of territories beyond the legitimate sphere of expansion had no legal validity.[4] On occasions, they even went so far as to affirm that papal donation was sufficient to acquire title and that no other act such as discovery or possession was required.[5] Spaniards also suggested at times that the bulls, which gave Spain a larger territory in the Americas than all other arrangements, were preferable because they originated in a higher authority. Yet, when it suited their interests, Spaniards also could advance contrary claims, for example, arguing that possession taken outside the legitimate sphere of expansion could be valid if sufficient time had elapsed.[6] Following similar strategies, the Portuguese sometimes insisted on the implementation of Tordesillas (as, for example, in the case of Colonia de Sacramento); on other occasions they privileged possession.[7] They could also suggest that their rights depended on bulls and that the duty to convert could not expire.[8] No one could take possession of a land that the pope had set aside so that the Portuguese could convert its natives, even if they had failed to do so. Both Spaniards and Portuguese were acutely aware of this instrumentalization, and they accused one another of invoking Tordesillas or forgetting it according to convenience.[9]

While debate persisted as to whether territories should be assigned according to papal bulls, the Treaty of Tordesillas, other treaties, or possession, the implementation of each one of these options provoked equally complicated confrontations. Both papal donation and the Treaty of Tordesillas required determining where the meridian they established passed, that is, which point of the Azores and Cabo Verde Islands (mentioned in the bulls) or the Cabo Verde Islands (mentioned in Tordesillas) would be the focal point and how the meridian would be measured and delineated. Implementing the bulls and treaty also entailed knowing if the disputed territories were east or west of this meridian. Similarly, to draw a border line, the parties had to agree how to interpret the other treaties they signed, most particularly the Treaty of Madrid and the Treaty of San Idelfonso. Intepretations varied because of lack of information regarding the geography of the continent and the location of different rivers, settlements, and mountains, but also because there was a continuous debate as to what the parties knew, what they wished to establish, and what the treaties actually determined.

Applying the Roman doctrine of possession was no less difficult. The decision as to who had possession of which territory depended on information that was often difficult to gather or outright lacking. At stake was not only the question of who arrived first but also what transpired thereafter. Possession also set off legal debates regarding what it required and how it could be established and maintained. It implied the need to classify actors as members of the community and suggested that Indians had to be integrated into European polities if their territories were to be subjected to European control. The bulls, treaties, and doctrines, in short, did not include answers, only questions, and their implementation called for legal interpretation, scientific determination, and data collection.

Contemporaries were overwhelmed by the enormity of these tasks. Experts employed by both parties recognized that the issues at stake were difficult (dificultoso) and uncertain (falible). They explained in the seventeenth century that, in order to draw the meridian established in Tordesillas, they needed to agree on the shape and size of the earth (which they did not) and that, in order to know whether certain territories were to the east or west, they required a trustworthy system indicating their exact location (which was still lacking).[10] Practitioners who were asked what the situation on the ground was were just as hesitant. Responding to questionnaires, they constantly explained that they were familiar with only some areas, and only partially. Attempts to find authorities that would

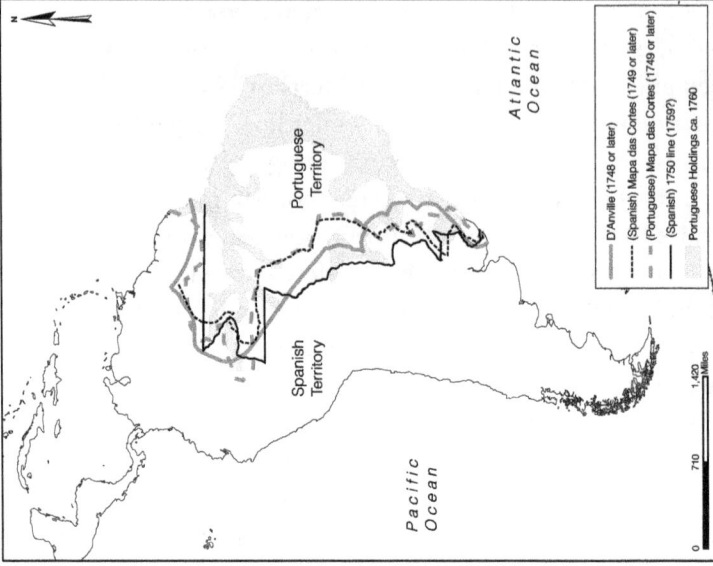

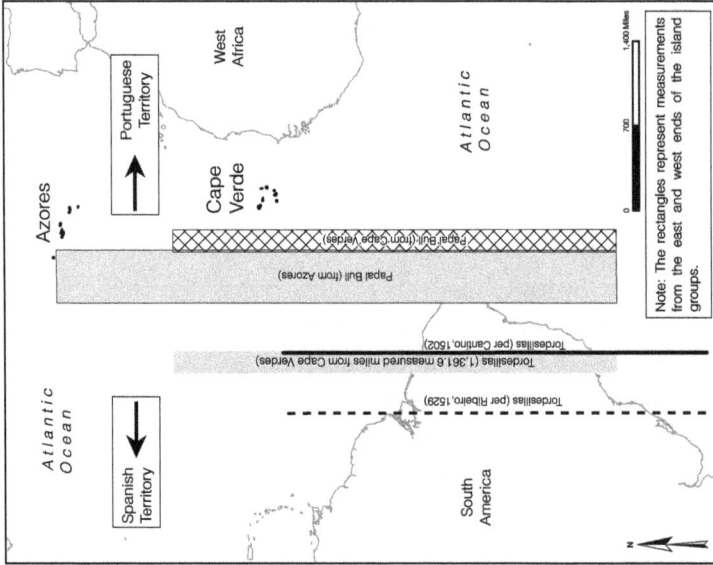

Contested Claims in South America

Several of the possible contemporary interpretations as to where the division between Spain and Portugal should be according to the Papal Bulls (1493), the Treaty of Tordesillas (1494), and the Treaty of Madrid (1750). In the case of the bulls and Tordesillas, the answer depended on whether measurement would be from the east, center, or west of the Azores or Cape Verde. In the eighteenth century, the parties often used the same map (for example, the Mapa das Cortes) but they drew on it different lines, whose authorship and date are difficult to verify.

settle these questions once and for all mostly failed. There were plenty of maps and many suggestions regarding where the meridian should pass, but their visions of the world's and the region's geography were so diverse that it was unclear which should be given preference. There were plenty of documents, too. In 1681, the secretary of the Spanish team negotiating with Portugal produced a long list of citations that confirmed Spanish rights to the River Plate.[11] Yet, while it was clear that some backed the Spanish position, others did not. During the same period, Portuguese experts also concluded that several interpretations were possible and agreed that additional information was required to solve the issue fully.[12] If at stake was what was known and what ignored, also important was the question of which criteria should be applied and how to discern which sources and authorities were most trustworthy. Some interlocutors argued that the best proof for entitlement was a Portuguese writer admitting the rights of Spain or vice versa; others sustained that authors belonging to neutral parties were more reliable. For some, older information was more accurate than newer. Others believed, on the contrary, that modern measuring and recording techniques produced better results than ancient narratives. Also debated was the question of whether repetition was a sign of correctness or simply the consequence of the tendency for authors to copy one another. Should one adopt the opinion of the majority or the solution that found less opposition? The nature of the appropriate expertise was also questioned. Should the opinion of geographers be preferred to the advice of pilots who knew how to navigate?[13] Which information and which opinion, in short, would "win the day" (*levou a vitória*) and remain "victorious and without dispute" (*ficou vitoriosa e sem contenda*)?[14]

By the eighteenth century, the quantity of material that had accumulated was such that contemporaries complained it was virtually impossible to handle. Those discussing the rights of their country had to consider the Treaty of Tordesillas (1494), the agreement reached in Zaragoza (1529), succeeding treaties (1681, 1715, 1750, 1761, 1763, and 1777), the writings of chronicles and historians, travel narratives, and multiple maps, as well as a wide array of administrative, judicial, economic, and diplomatic documentation.[15] In the 1770s, this material could include as many as twenty large boxes, dozens of books, and

over thirty maps. Committees who studied this information heard
the testimony of experts and collected written opinions from geographers and jurists. Their members also considered eyewitness accounts
that reported on the whereabouts of rivers, the character of the indigenous inhabitants, and the location of different sites. Because the
right to land involved matters of conscience, they sometimes consulted with theologians and friars. This accumulation led Viceroy
Nicolás Arredondo to protest in 1795, in Buenos Aires, that he was
forced to consult "an infinite number of papers."[16] In Mato Grosso,
the Portuguese authorities complained as well, suggesting that there
was simply too much to consider.[17] Contemporaries thus struggled
not only with the need to obtain the necessary information but also
with how to summarize and process it, comparing its components
or translating them into a single vision.[18] Many hoped that scientific
progress eventually would clarify most, if not all, of the pending issues.[19] They suggested that what was practically unsolvable in the
sixteenth century, when Tordesillas was signed, could be resolved,
for example, in an eighteenth century that prided itself on progress
and enlightenment. Yet, while some had faith in science, which they
believed would serve as an antidote to chaos, others placed their
trust in the law. They harbored the illusion that the territorial conflict could be terminated by reaching yet another understanding and
signing yet another treaty. Bilateral agreements, they argued, would
create "a hindrance and a wall that would make sovereignty unquestionable" by manifesting "the limits of one domination and the
other, a matter until the present unverifiable." They would solve a
disagreement that for more than 250 years had agitated both royal
courts, "cutting the roots that allowed the bad branches of so much
dissension to grow and that made vassals experience the fatal effects
of discord."[20] Treaties, in short, would end "past storms" *(borrascas
pasadas)* and ensure tranquility. They would form a division *(raya)*
that would make both dominions "safe and secure" *(cobertos e seguros)*. Conceived of as methods to guarantee peace, not as instruments
for legal innovation, as many historians have attested in the past,
contemporaries suggested that treaties were practical solutions that
included "concessions of common utility" *(algunas cesiones de común
utilidad)*.[21] Growing belief that a scientifically abstract imaginary
line as in Tordesillas (1494) was impractical led the parties to give

preference in the 1750 Madrid treaty to possession. Yet this solution also proved unworkable because the two powers could not agree on who possessed what and on how to demarcate on the ground what was spelled out in the formal agreement. In 1777, consequently, Spaniards and Portuguese adopted yet another method, which combined Tordesillas with possession, also separating the territories of the two powers by a belt of "neutral land" *(campos neutrales)* that no one could own or penetrate. Yet this, too, led to disagreement. The constant discord drove some to advocate the adoption of "natural" rather than "artificial" borders.[22] Such borders, they hypothesized, would not only physically limit human action, they would also be fixed on the ground in ways that no party could ignore or contest. Yet, the wish to find a magic solution produced a juridical nightmare. As treaties accumulated and as criteria changed, so did the legal complication. Thus, while scientists and practitioners continued to disagree about facts and figures, jurists became entangled in debates regarding meaning and precedence. Increasingly, one of the most difficult questions they faced was whether the treaties subsequent to Tordesillas were meant to clarify or replace it. Some accords, for example, the 1750 Madrid treaty, made direct reference to this question, but most others did not.[23] What happened to Tordesillas after the accords were signed? This question was asked regarding the Treaty of Utrecht (1715), which stipulated that Spain would return Colonia de Sacramento to Portugal, also ceding to it "all rights and actions, without ever again disturbing this possession."[24] Did this agreement mean that Spaniards also implicitly renounced the Treaty of Tordesillas, which according to them placed Colonia under their control? And, in the Treaty of San Idelfonso (1777), the abandonment of Tordesillas was mentioned only with regards to the Philippines. Given that the Treaty of Madrid (1750), which explicitly "canceled" Tordesillas, was annulled in 1761, did this mean that in all other respects Tordesillas was still alive, even after the signature of the new treaty in 1777?[25]

Because answering this question was important—if the treaties upheld Tordesillas they had to be read in conjunction with it, not as a replacement for it—jurists working for Spain and Portugal disagreed about their correct interpretation.[26] They also differed as to whether newer treaties were meant to preserve the territorial status quo or modify it. If the first interpretation was correct, then a treaty that stated that certain areas were Portuguese could also serve as a proof that the parties consented that they were thus even before the agreement was signed. But if the treaty was meant to change the existing situation, then inclusion among Portuguese territories proved nothing or sustained the inverse: that the territory was not theirs before the agreement was signed. This question was particularly poignant, for example, after the Treaty of Madrid (1750) was annulled in 1761. Did territories included in Portugal according to the treaty also belong to it before the treaty was signed, and they should therefore remain in Portuguese possession after it was annulled, or were they ceded to Portugal in the treaty and therefore should be returned to Spain after the treaty ceased to exist? Questions were also asked regarding the relations between treaties and territories acquired in war. Did the Treaty of Utrecht, for example, mandate a return to the prewar status quo? If so, what was the nature of that status quo and who had the authority to decide on what it included? Rarely in agreement, the Spaniards and the Portuguese thus endlessly debated whether certain territories were ceded, conquered, or possessed and who their rightful owner was.

But even if the parties could agree which criteria should be given preference and how treaties should be interpreted, they still needed to demarcate on the ground what they decided on paper. This exercise proved just as difficult because treaties often mentioned rivers, settlements, and mountains that never existed or were not located where the parties had imagined.[27] Others had a different name in Spanish and Portuguese. Because the territory was not only huge but also unknown, experts sent to the Americas in the 1750s, 1770s, and 1780s to demarcate the divisions described in the 1750 and 1777 treaties disagreed, their work degenerating into endless debates regarding where rivers flowed and where mountains were located.[28] Like those wishing to implement Tordesillas, these experts thus failed to reach concord on how a theoretical, imaginary line described in a European document would become a concrete, material reality in the Americas.

As a result of these difficulties, while some insisted on nominating yet another set of experts to examine the rights of the parties, or on signing yet another treaty, others suggested that only "action on the ground" could lead to the acquisition of rights. Proponents of both positions existed in Spain and Portugal, Spanish and Portuguese America. The territorial conflict between Spain and Portugal, in short, included not only confrontation between neighbors but also an internal discussion regarding what was just and what was possible. It placed in opposition those who trusted that scientific progress would solve all the pending issues and those who believed that deciding the border by using "uncertain geographical principles" *(principios inciertos geográficos)* was impossible; those hoping that treaties would end the debate and those who suspected they could not; those who promoted scientific knowledge and those who believed in practical information; those who wanted to be right and those who wanted to establish facts on the ground.[29]

While debate raged regarding the meaning of terms and the implementation of treaties, local actors also waged daily struggles to obtain, enlarge, and preserve possession. Whether they did so in observance of Roman law, because they understood that unless you exercised rights you had none, or because this best suited their interests (or a combination thereof), we will never know. What we do know is that from the seventeenth century, and intensifying in the eighteenth century, attention was geared toward justifying possession. Contemporaries understood possession as a very wide phenomenon that allowed the acquisition of rights through almost any type of activity.[30] Although most agreed that forming a settlement along with performing jurisdictional acts such as granting offices, collecting taxes, or persecuting criminals was the best way to take possession of land, many argued that using land in other ways also could constitute possession. For example, while some suggested that possession required working the land permanently, others argued it was sufficient to perform seasonal activities such as letting one's cattle pasture, collecting wood, or hunting and fishing. Because pasturing was an activity that constituted possession, they even suggested that occupation could be achieved without direct human intervention. According to them, all it took was for unsupervised animals to roam an area, and the only condition required was to demonstrate ownership over them.[31] Routes taken by cows, their multiplication, and their survival could thus serve to claim land, and the struggle over animals could be interpreted as involving a territorial debate. For many, discovery and penetration also constituted possession. Others argued that so did ceremonial acts such as the drawing of the arms of Portugal on a mountain.[32] Many agreed that river navigation and commerce with natives could establish rights to both the river and the riverbank. The same happened with land routes: roads discovered or carved out in the jungle were both markers of and mechanisms to constitute possession. This meant that those who roamed the American interior searching for slaves and gold could thereafter be identified also as conquerors. Because such activities, as well as commerce with natives, potentially generated territorial rights, contraband, for example, could have implications much wider and more important than its economic significance. It could, in fact, lay grounds for territorial claims.[33] Because the legality of the action was irrelevant, even expeditions enslaving Indians (when enslavement was prohibited by law) or attacking Spanish settlements (in times of peace) could generate rights. For this to happen, there was no need for a formal expedition led by a person of authority or licensed by the king because territorial penetration, it was generally agreed, could be performed by any vassal at any time.[34]

As if they had read Pufendorf, contemporary discussants thus consented that the question of which activity could produce title could vary from place to place, time to time.[35] They also concluded that possession could not depend only on an "act of mind" but required that others would understand the intention to appropriate and, by extension, the wish to exclude all others from doing so. Implying that at the center of possession was the idea of "communication," contemporaries equally insisted that protest against the taking of possession should be manifested "by outward, visible, acts." Silence, they suggested, would be interpreted as consent unless it could be proved that ignorance, fear, or other pressing circumstances hindered protest. They thus concluded, similarly to Grotius, that "if a person knows his property to be in the possession of another, and allows it to remain so for a length of time, without asserting his claim, unless there appear sufficient reasons for his silence, he is construed to have entirely abandoned all pretentious to the same."[36]

As a result of these convictions, and despite disagreeing in the concrete as to which activity constituted title in which case (and usually adopting the interpretation that best suited their interests), all discussants consented that (1) the activity constituting possession had to be performed with the intention to acquire rights; (2) it must meet no opposition (the lack of opposition equaled consent); and (3) it had to be performed by people who were authorized to take possession for the king or community either because they had contracted with the crown or because they were its vassals.[37]

Replicating what were originally Roman law doctrines that, by this time, had greatly mutated and were considered part of the law of nations, perhaps even natural law, local interlocutors thus asserted that the first condition for possession was the requirement that the acts undertaken would be accompanied by the wish to appropriate. Following this understanding, they proceeded to distinguish between activities that desired to expand territories (and could thus constitute possession) from all others, which were conducted for other ends such as economic benefit, or religious pursuits (and gave no territorial rights). This required that they imagine (or juridically construct) what their rivals intended to do by observing their behavior, listening to what they said, or remembering previous encounters. However, because they believed that "transit in a foreign territory without urgent necessity . . . always gave way to a bad presumption" *(siempre este tránsito es de mala presunción siendo por dominios ajenos y esto sin urgente necesidad)*, in the Americas, at least, they generally concluded that all presence must be interpreted as directed at establishing occupation. Those who wished to argue otherwise, they suggested, carried the burden of proof; they had to demonstrate that they roamed the territory with another intention in mind.[38] Such claims, however, often met with resistance, as both Spaniards and the Portuguese accused one another of lying.[39] They argued that those pretending to be merchants were in reality spies or explorers. Individuals who claimed to have arrived at the territory because they had quarreled with their wives, wanted to defect or avoid criminal prosecution, or had lost their way were thus told that their intentions were different. Those catching turtles or collecting cacao were censured for violating territorial rights despite their claims that all they wanted to do was survive. The same thing happened with friars who were suspected of harboring intentions other than finding refuge or converting natives or with military commanders whose explanation that they chased violent natives or runaway slaves were similarly rejected. Because distinguishing "good" from "bad" incursions *(distinguir os bons dos maus)* was so difficult, Spaniards concluded—and the Portuguese would have probably agreed—that "a large volume was needed" to describe all the "ridiculous titles and pretexts" that their rivals used to disguise their activities.[40]

Although these suspicions might have been on occasions unjustified, evidence suggests that on others troops sent to accompany Jesuit friars could secretly be told that their true mission was to take possession of the land.[41] Military commanders could instruct their men to pretend that they were in the area collecting fruits when in earnest they were observing the territory and its inhabitants. In 1768, a Portuguese commander caught in the area of Iguatemi assured Spaniards that he was sent by the governor of São Paulo to explore the "deserts of its hinterland" *(los desiertos de sus campañas)* and "destroy" the "infidel nations" *(naciones infieles)* who had attacked the Portuguese.[42] Excusing his presence and assuring locals that he had no intention to harm them or injure their rights or those of Spain, he received the answer that, because his activities contravened the "laws of good faith and reciprocal union" *(las leyes de buena fe y de la recíproca unión)*, he must immediately leave the region. His Spanish interlocutors were fortunate to have responded in this way, as later they found out that after the expedition left São Paulo its members were told that their true mission was to build a settlement on the Iguatemi River.

Whereas the original intentions of those roaming the territory were important, so was their change over time. Take, for example, the activities of the residents of São Paulo (Paulistas, often also called, rightly or wrongly, Bandeirantes) who, along their native allies, journeyed in the American interior in the late sixteenth, seventeenth, and eighteenth centuries. In the eighteenth century, the members of such expeditions were vindicated by some Portuguese as the true conquistadors of Brazil.[43] Despite this image (that persists to date), historical records suggest that until the eighteenth century Paulistas might have cared very little about territory.[44] According to available sources, during the seventeenth century they were mainly interested in capturing Indians for slavery and in establishing commercial routes.[45] This activity was censured by both the Spanish and the Portuguese authorities because it was illegal, not because it violated territorial rights. It was only in the late seventeenth century and during the following one that Paulistas focused their activities on discovering and possessing mines.[46] It was during that period that some Portuguese authors started to herald them as heroes. They suggested that their attacks on Spanish missions, mainly inspired by the wish to obtain slaves, were also motivated by patriotic zeal. After all, Jesuit missions were allegedly established on Portuguese territory.

If the first condition for possession was penetration with intention to appropriate, the second condition was that possession must be taken with no opposition because, according to the legal doctrine, under normal circumstances people protested against actions that jeopardized their rights. Failure to protest—that is, silence—could thus be interpreted as consent. Because even the smallest, unauthorized, and illegal act could have territorial significance and silence could be interpreted as consent, people living on the border had to be extremely vigilant. They had to make sure that no penetration occurred and that, when it did, response in the form of protest would immediately follow. Those inhabiting the American interior were acutely aware of these requirements.[47] Though they were laymen untrained in law, they constantly asserted that their main duty was to conserve the territory and that the best way of doing so was to control what their neighbors were doing and to react immediately and violently when a protest was required. Yet, the practical difficulty in knowing what was happening on the ground (and with what intention) was often insurmountable. The question of whether rivals penetrated or settled certain areas haunted contemporaries, and rumors constantly circulated as to who was where, doing what. Forces sent to verify these reports often failed to gather sufficient information.[48] They easily mistook one river for the other or searched for the newly established settlement where it did not exist. It sometimes took months before they discovered the whereabouts of their opponents, and success was often tied to persistence or chance. Returning reports could also indicate that rivals might have been present on the terrain but that they had already abandoned the territory or continued on to another location.[49]

In their effort to gather information, both parties resorted to routine interrogation of ecclesiastics and merchants who traveled between Spanish and Portuguese settlements. They also collected the declarations of settlers, natives, soldiers, deserters, slaves, and criminals whose opinion was considered important despite the fact that many of them were socially marginal, their loyalty questionable, and their testimonies compromised by complex processes of translation and mediation.[50] Individuals delivering letters from one authority to the other, who waited for a response, or who accompanied returning prisoners or deserters were also questioned, and efforts were made to intercept and read mail.[51] Information could be voluntarily given, extracted by force, or rewarded by payment. The use of undercover agents was sufficiently common to allow the governor of Colonia de Sacramento (Portugal) to boast in the 1770s of having a network of informants in Buenos Aires, Montevideo, and "other parts belonging to Spain."[52] According to his version, he even had confidential sources among persons closest to the new Spanish commander of the city. Collection of news, however, did not only happen in the Americas. It continued on the Iberian Peninsula and could involve informants in Seville and Madrid.[53]

Because rumors circulated and because the presence of rivals was often deduced from indirect evidence, such as finding Spanish or Portuguese tools among natives, there were always more forces to look for, more settlers to expel, more forts to demolish. The degree of hysteria was such that, fearing espionage in the 1770s, a Spanish commander did not allow a Portuguese letter carrier to enter his camp.[54] Although the Portuguese protested that this behavior contradicted the laws of urbanity, on that occasion the Spaniard was right: the delivery was indeed an excuse to send an observer. Yet the Portuguese concluded that if Spaniards reacted in this way, they had something to hide. Soon after, the Portuguese commander took the same measure of prohibiting Spaniards in his camp. While the governor of Paraguay (Spain) concluded that this change necessarily meant the Portuguese were planning "something," the commander explained to his superiors that he wanted to keep secret the poor state of his troops, manned mainly by "naked blacks and mulatos." To excuse his behavior, he told Spaniards that he did not allow their entry because he feared disorder. Small incidents, he argued, could sometimes light a great fire. Common-sense conclusions also prevailed. For example, contemporaries reckoned that if deserters were well received in the enemy camp, they must be spies; if they returned to the establishment they had fled, they were informants and their desertion a mockery.

Despite great efforts at information gathering, contemporaries were under the impression that these mostly failed. Both Spanish and Portuguese interlocutors complained that they lacked "verifiable news" and that the reports they received were often contradictory, leaving them with "affliction" and "confusion."[55] They asserted that the great distances, the inaccessibility of the terrain, insufficient familiarity with it, and bad communications were all to blame. They also stressed that the activities of rivals were "clandestine" and that it was therefore impossible to protest against them in a timely fashion.[56]

If it was difficult to identify what the other party was doing, deciding if it deserved protest was even more complicated because it required knowing whether these activities infringed on one's rights. Answering this question involved scientific and juridical criteria and forced local interlocutors—most of whom were not policymakers, diplomats, experts, or jurists but instead soldiers, commanders, governors, settlers, ecclesiastics, merchants, or native inhabitants—to engage in long and complicated debates regarding which territory belonged to whom. Whether they were protecting their own interests or representing an authority, they needed to know what they and others could legally do, but mostly it was urgent that they establish what could be tolerated by silence and what required protest.[57] This necessity compelled virtually everyone living on the territory because, according to contemporaries, a "supreme law" authorized even particular individuals to defend themselves and their king against territorial aggression.

Adopting the policy of better-safe-than-sorry, both the Spanish and the Portuguese tended to protest as often as they could, even when they were unsure about the correctness of their allegations. In 1731, for example, the president of Quito (present-day Ecuador) informed the Council of Indies that the governor of Pará (present-day Brazil) had contravened the peace treaties by building a fort on Castilian territory. It was only after he protested that he began an investigation aimed at discovering why and how the territory was Spanish.[58] That rejecting territorial incursions implied identifying

what was yours was also clear in 1775, when the Portuguese captain
of Rio Negro first captured Spaniards, whom he accused of settling
in Portuguese territory, and then conducted an inquiry meant to "justify and prove the possession and dominion that your majesty has"
in that area in order to "authenticate" (autenticar) Portugal's claims.[59]
However, rather than confirming Portuguese entitlements, the data
collected from witnesses established that, despite claims by virtue of
a century-long discovery, navigation, and commerce, no specific
person could be cited as having roamed these parts before 1736. The
inquiry also clarified that Spaniards were present in the area since at
least 1744 and that, as a result, the Portuguese might have preceded
them by only eight years. Evidence also affirmed that Spaniards
possessed that territory until 1631, when their missions were destroyed by the Portuguese, and that they had attempted to return to
the area since.[60]

It is therefore fair to conclude that, rather than proving certitude,
as most historians have assumed, most protests obeyed a legal rationale that suggested that unless you objected your silence would be
interpreted as consent. Under this guise, the certainty expressed in
contemporary records was not necessarily the reflection of an inner
belief but instead was the product of a legal requirement. It is therefore not surprising that, although on occasions those facing such
challenges lamented their ignorance, confessed their confusion, or
requested instructions from their king as to how they should proceed, in most cases, they immediately vindicated their rights.[61] Indeed, they even protested against the presence of rivals in territories
that they knew and admitted were (still) undecided (duvidosos).[62]

Debates regarding possession not only forced the parties into action. They also encouraged the production of a paper trail aimed at
proving who was where and doing what. Often elaborated by individuals who sought privileges or rewards in exchange for their efforts at exploring, conquering, dominating, converting, settling, or
otherwise using the territory, the writing down and safeguarding of
these pieces of evidence were also encouraged by the crowns, who
wished to use them to establish territorial rights. Royal interest
in proving that royal subjects explored, conquered, transited, and
subjugated thus coincided with the private interests of those who

sought reward. Mutually supporting one another, these testimonies, prevalent in the archives, nevertheless mostly revealed the frailty of the possession they sought to document. Many described successive expeditions, each celebrating its success but barely producing tangible results.[63] Nonetheless, they could on occasions become formidable tools. The fear that the production of documents could lead to territorial acquisition was clear in the correspondence that took place in 1770 between Spanish and Portuguese military commanders after the Portuguese proclaimed himself governor of Río Grande de San Pedro instead of Viamont, as he had called himself before. To this challenge, his Spanish correspondent answered with determination.[64] Expressing doubt as to whether the change was innocent, he suggested it might allow the Portuguese to claim in the future that they possessed San Pedro (which they did not). After all, for expansion to happen, the Spaniard sustained, there was no need for troops, not even settlers; it would be sufficient to do what the Portuguese did, namely, write a document pretending to be where one was not. As far as the Spanish commander was concerned, therefore, at stake was not a discussion about an honorary title. What the Portuguese commander was doing by signing his letters and orders as if he were in San Pedro was to take possession of the land.

If, on the one hand, contemporary understanding of the law encouraged actors to protest even when they were unsure about their rights or when violations happened only on paper but not on the ground, on the other, it also pushed them into a competition as to who would arrive to which territory first. Most clearly acknowledged in the eighteenth century, both the Spaniards and the Portuguese argued that unless they acted fast, those on the other side would precede them and acquire rights.[65] Referring to the need to "act de facto" (obrar de fato), they suggested that this policy, as well as defending one's territory, were part of a natural law (direito natural), which bound both parties.[66] The end result was the emergence of a repetitive pattern. When kings, their officials, or local actors considered it profitable, new areas were explored, penetrated, used, or settled. Because according to contemporary understanding these actions implied asserting rights, rivals could respond in one of two ways: either they agreed to this expansion by remaining silent or they objected to it by protesting. The parties could then enter into "negotiations," which led either to "conventions," in which the expanding power extracted a "confession" from its opponents that its activities were justified, or to further protest.[67] Read against one another, contemporary testimonies thus suggest that, rather than unauthorized settlers penetrating territories belonging to Spain or Portugal, as historians have argued in the past, what mainly happened in the American interior was the gradual incursion of Europeans into areas whose ascription was uncertain, perhaps not yet debated, let alone decided. That is, Spanish and Portuguese territories were not "lost" because rivals penetrated them. Instead, areas that were once ignored—because they were considered too remote, economically useless, or hostile—gradually became a valid destination to both Spaniards and the Portuguese at around the same time. Occupation by one power tended to attract the attention of the other, often making possession contemporaneous or without a clear genealogy of who came first and who second. It is therefore not surprising that both the Spaniards and the Portuguese considered peace a potentially more important time for territorial acquisition than war. While war forced military commanders to defend their territory, during peace they were mandated to conserve and augment their jurisdiction (sempre no tempo de paz a sua conservação e aumento de terreno e no da guerra a defesa).[68]

Because rights hinged on possession, which depended on activity, the territory that resulted was often discontinuous. Rather than consisting of a line or a front or even an amorphous area, it was made of fields, farms, woods, and settlements and their hinterland, thus taking the form of an archipelago, with "islands" of occupation surrounded by a "sea" of "unoccupied land."[69] What happened to the territory in between (the sea) was one question; how contemporaries defined the islands of occupation was another. The nuclear nature of the territory Europeans possessed came to light, for example, during the discussion about Colonia de Sacramento. Colonia was built, destroyed, rebuilt, taken again, and returned on several occasions during the late seventeenth and eighteenth centuries. While discussants in Europe referred to it as a solid, clear unit, precision dissipated in the Americas. What did it mean to cede or receive Colonia? Was

Colonia the territory of its fort? Did it include a hinterland? How would this hinterland be defined? Did ceding it to Portugal imply that the territory between Colonia and the nearest Portuguese settlement was also Portuguese? These questions, which haunted contemporaries, required interpreting the treaties signed between the two powers, but they also depended on judicial doctrine, as well as on questions of possession: Did those establishing Colonia in 1681 take possession only of its site or also of the fields around it? What did a site consist of? How should its fields be defined?

What Colonia meant was debated from as early as 1701 (the treaty of alliance among Portugal, France, and Spain), in which Spain recognized Portugal's rights to the settlement "as it presently was" (*como en el presente es*—art. 14). According to the governor of Buenos Aires and the viceroy of Peru, this expression included the built site but not its surrounding areas. The Portuguese, on the contrary, argued that the treaty recognized Portuguese claims to all the territory north of the River Plate, including Montevideo and Maldonado (presently in Uruguay), and the Jesuit missions of Paraguay.[70] Although no formal agreement was reached at that stage (1701), in practice, the construction of a Spanish garrison nearby forced the Portuguese into conforming to the Spanish interpretation. The Treaty of Utrecht (1715) again failed to define what Colonia (which Spain was to cede to Portugal) meant. While the Portuguese insisted on the old reading, their Spanish interlocutors admitted that various interpretations were possible. Nonetheless, they argued for the prevalence of a restricted reading that equated Colonia with its fort. What should be returned to Portugal, they asserted, was the territory protected by the fort's cannons (*tiro del cañón*). Yet even this was insufficiently clear, because measuring what the cannons covered depended on the type of cannon, their position, the amount of gunpowder, the angle at which they would be shot, and so forth.[71] Considering such questions important, Spanish commanders asked the governor of Colonia to allow their experts to participate in the firing that would lead to demarcation. The commander (of course) refused. Thus, while in their bilateral agreements and in their correspondence with local authorities both the Spanish and Portuguese kings insisted there was no need to define what Colonia included, locals constantly lamented their inability to agree.[72] Discord continued into the 1740s, with both monarchs instructing their vassals to preserve the status quo and delimit the territory accordingly and both ignoring local complaints that, given the questions at stake, this task was impossible. In practice, the Spaniards continued to blockade Colonia until the 1770s, thus ensuring by force the preeminence of their interpretation, which they could not achieve by negotiation.

The cumulative effect of all these factors was that although large-scale war was rare in the American heartland, struggle between Spaniards and Portuguese occurred daily. These conflicts were triggered by questions such as who sent their horses to pasture where, who built a hut, and who collected fruit. Confrontations were aggravated by contemporary inability to verify rumors or to act efficiently against what they perceived as territorial aggressions. Because kings instructed their vassals to keep harmonious relations with their neighbors while also ordering them to guard closely royal rights, "defending the terrain stubbornly," tension was continuous. Vigilance was particularly important in times of peace because, "as experience had demonstrated, even during peace and transgressing the treaties, the Portuguese attempted to take possession of the land without previous declaration while they orally and in written form assured Spaniards of their good intentions."[73]

As a result of these dynamics, the Spanish–Portuguese territorial conflict was characterized less by constant violence than by a tedious interplay of action and reaction, challenges and responses. Individuals who did not necessarily have the right training or the correct will were thus forced into involvement with what today we would identify as a political and a juridical debate. In order to live in the interior, in order to collect fruit or conduct commerce, in order to convert natives, in order to govern and protect the territory, they needed information not only about what was happening on the ground but also, and mainly, about what it meant. These individuals sometimes confessed that territorial rights were matters for cabinets *(negocios de gabinete)* and that they were not authorized to discuss them. But more often than not, they proceeded to debate and defend the rights of their country. Structured as a dialogue, these conversations were nevertheless a multi-logue, perhaps even a cacophony that encompassed many parties speaking from different places and involving different sites and diverse interests. Often expressed in oral communication, it was also reproduced in the exchange of letters between individuals and authorities in Mato Grosso, Santa Cruz de la Sierra, Colonia de Sacramento, Buenos Aires, Belém do Pará, Quito, Mainas, Quixos, Chiquitos, La Plata (present-day Sucre in Bolivia), São Paulo, Rio de Janeiro, Asunción de Paraguay, Lima, Madrid, and Lisbon, to name just a few locations. And, although words were the main instruments of this battle, their meaning and significance depended not only on what was said but also on how it was said. Each gesture, each action, and each word counted. So did every inch and every foot of land.

Learning as they went, some interlocutors achieved a fairly astounding degree of expertise. Exchanges of letters between eighteenth-century Spanish and Portuguese military commanders, for example, habitually distinguished between occupation in times of war and possession in times of peace. They appealed to the laws of nations, statutes of limitation, and the legal presumption that converted silence into consent.[74] These letters also differentiated violations that were against natural law (*direito natural*) from others that were not. Laymen involved in these discussions thus acted as jurists, but they also took part in what today we would identify as diplomatic negotiations. For example, the Spanish and the Portuguese military commanders of Rio Grande signed a convention in 1763 regarding their bilateral relations.[75] Authorized by their superiors, this treaty "determined and clarified the extension of their respective jurisdictions in this frontier until another decision is taken by the monarchs" (*conferir y declarar los términos de una y otra parte en esta frontera mientras nuestras respectivas cortes, enteradas de este convenio, ni dispusieren otra cosa con el fin de evitar todo motivo de discordia*). In addition to the usual clauses promising compliance, peace, and good relations, the accord also included provisions for a common cause against thieves and vagabonds and it fixed the limits of each nation [*sic*] in a farm called La Tratada. It also consented, "without creating a precedent," to the use of the river, considered a Spanish monopoly, by the Portuguese. In the years following this convention (*convención*), which both promised to observe (*observar inviolablemente*), both commanders

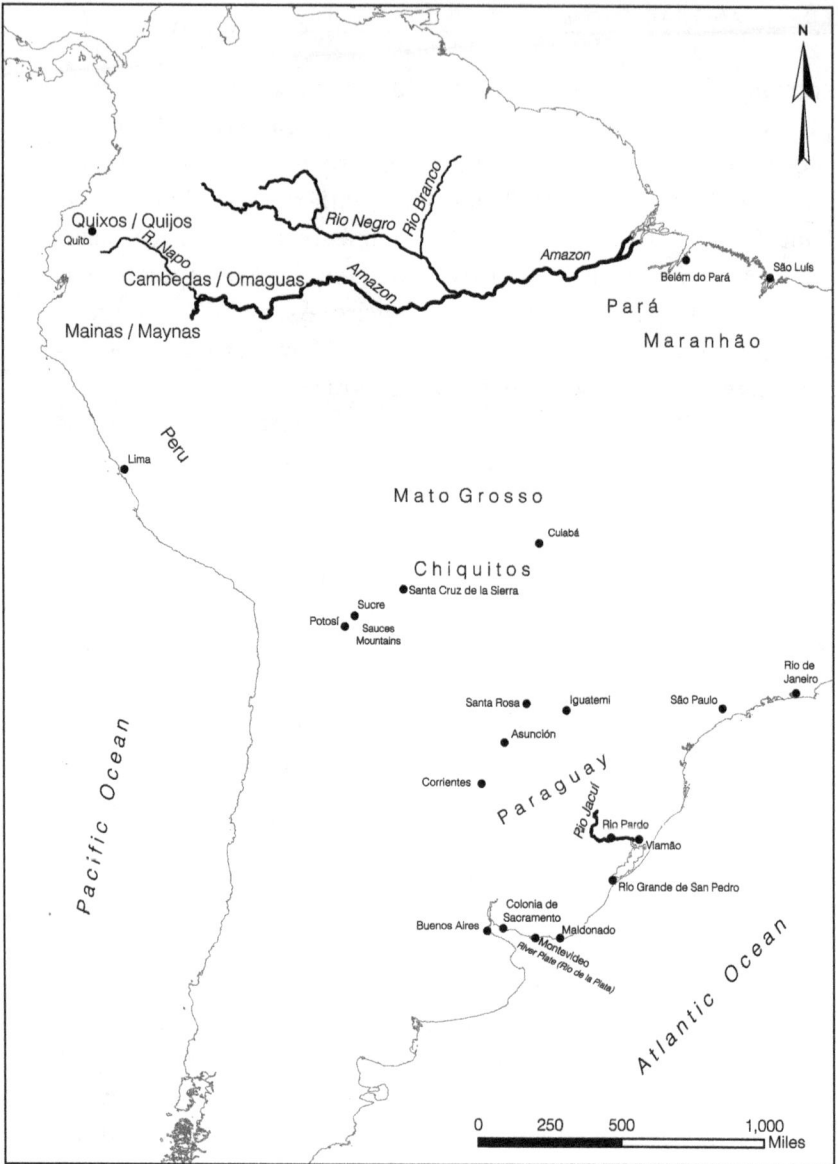

South America

Contested localities, rivers, and areas in South America. Not all the contested territories are
included, only those specifically cited in the text.

considered the border they had set as a real division, complaining whenever it was breached yet also constantly arguing about what precisely had been decided and how it was to be interpreted.[76] And although initially adopted as a working rather than a permanent solution, the convention became performative. Because it had allowed both countries to use the river, by 1770 the commanders of both agreed that the frontier between their respective posts now passed in the middle of that river, which they now shared.[77]

The involvement of laymen in these legal, political, and diplomatic negotiations was necessary but dangerous. Not only could it modify the attribution of territories, as happened in Rio Grande in 1763, it could also lead to confusion. For example, the Spanish commander of Rio Pardo exchanged in 1765 several letters with his Portuguese counterpart commanding the post at Rio Jacuy, in which he protested against Portuguese clandestine penetration into territories that were Spanish according to the "law of nations."[78] Suggesting that these actions could not have been ordered by the Portuguese monarch, who wished to observe peace with Spain, the Spanish commander requested that the Portuguese retreat so as to avoid new disturbances (*nuevos disturbios*). The Portuguese commander refused because, he explained, the Portuguese settlers whose presence was detected had penetrated the region during wartime, that is, at a time when entering enemy territory was legitimate. Until his king instructed him otherwise, he had to observe the status quo. Paradoxically, the Spanish commander concluded that this response included a confession of guilt, among other reasons, because it clarified that the rights of Spain to the territory were never under dispute before the war. Rejecting the Portuguese juridical interpretation, he suggested that if war allowed foreign settlers to enter new territories, peace mandated their retreat. His aim, he declared, was not to provoke confrontations, only to protect the rights of his king. During the exchange, however, the Spanish commander made several important mistakes, such as acknowledging to the Portuguese—violating Spain's official position—that Spain had no rights to the territory of Colonia de Sacramento. The Portuguese commander joyfully seized on his error, thanking him for a confession that Madrid refused to make. Alarmed, the Spanish commander recanted: he had only expressed his opinion on the situation after 1715 (the Treaty of Utrecht) and, at any rate, his remarks, he argued, had no juridical value because they were part of "historical conversations" *(conversación histórica)* that examined the origin of the conflict and its development and were not meant to establish (or deny) rights. Somewhat similarly, in 1775, the Spanish governor of Paraguay requested the commander of the Portuguese post of Iguatemi to agree to peaceful relations between the inhabitants of both provinces. The Portuguese consented, yet in the aftermath of this exchange it became clear that each side understood the agreement differently. For the Portuguese, the accord included a recognition that the Iguatemi River served as the dividing line *(raya)* between the two dominions; for the governor of Paraguay, it did not affect the extension of the territory but was only a means to stop further Portuguese incursions.[79] While for the Portuguese it included a license to use "their side of the river," for the Spaniards it implied that the Portuguese could not extend beyond their existing settlement nor could they penetrate the hinterland.

If the first condition for possession was the intention to take the territory and the second the lack of opposition, the third condition determined that only actions carried out by vassals or individuals commissioned by the crown could produce title. Because of this requirement, struggle over land often translated into disagreement regarding the membership status of actors, who had to be classified as vassals of one power or the other for their countries to obtain possession.[80] These issues were already present in the sixteenth century when the conflict between both countries surfaced. However, the union of the crowns of Spain and Portugal (1580–1640) made them even thornier because conversations now entailed defining what the union was and how it affected vassalage and territory. From a juridical point of view, it was unclear whether the Treaty of Tordesillas continued to operate during the union or whether it was implicitly annulled.[81] Also debated was the status of Portugal during this period. Was it integrated into Castile, thus ceasing its independent existence and separate territorial demarcation, or was it attached to the monarchy yet nonetheless conserving its structures and territory? The answer to this question depended on whether Philip II of Spain in 1580 conquered or inherited Portugal for, according to the law, conquest resulted in integration, whereas inheritance did not. This was a matter of great controversy.[82] Philip claimed Portugal by inheritance, but he imposed his legal (and moral) vision through military might. This combination of factors produced long debate. Initially, Portugal was given autonomy and its institutions and laws were respected (thus indicating inheritance), and in 1579, 1581, and 1582 Philip ceremoniously pledged allegiance to this interpretation. Nonetheless, in the following years, he and his counselors insisted on occasions that this treatment was the result of "royal grace," not royal duty, implying that Philip could have chosen another route (i.e., conquest). This complexity was evident to contemporaries, who criticized Philip for his lack of coherence. If he inherited Portugal, why did he conquer it? If he conquered it, why did he conserve its rights? And how could a theory of conquest be sustained when Portugal had not defended itself militarily?[83]

Because the answer to these questions was not clear, as early as 1619, the Portuguese parliament (Cortes) asked the king to ensure that Portuguese overseas territories liberated from Dutch occupation would be considered Portuguese.[84] Avoiding a direct confrontation, the king's advisers proposed that he respond that at the moment he had no other choice but to make them Spanish because he depended on Castilian military might. Without Spanish forces, neither Spain nor Portugal would be able to conserve them. The king's advisers also recommended that he remind the Cortes that even if these territories were ruled by a different crown, they would not change a master because, whether Portuguese or Spanish, they would still belong to the same monarch. Only when the Dutch ceased their presence in these areas would it be possible to discuss to whom they should thereafter belong. In the aftermaths of this exchange, the question of what would happen to Portuguese overseas territories thus remained unresolved. Thereafter, the status of districts discovered, conquered or reconquered, or possessed or repossessed during the union plagued bilateral relations. Particularly acute in the Americas, where territorial expansion acquired spectacular dimensions during the union, it required deciding whether this advance was made for the crown of Portugal, for the crown of Castile, or in the name of both.[85] If the juridical situation was unclear, circumstances on the ground were even murkier. As long as the union lasted, Portuguese subjects were sent to discover and possess territories within the allegedly Spanish part of the Americas and vice versa. They could be acting for their king in his capacity as monarch of Spain and they could receive backing from authorities in both Spain and Portugal. How could one know who should benefit from their activities?

One example for such discussions was the legal and political confusion caused by an expedition that roamed the interior of the Amazon basin in the 1630s. Its story began a few decades earlier, when the royal court *(audiencia)* of Quito contracted the services of a Spaniard to conquer that region. When he failed to accomplish this task, the court first commissioned a Portuguese and then ordered the governor of Maranhão and Pará (in Portugal) to take care of the exploration.[86] Nothing happened until 1636, when a group of Spanish soldiers accompanied by native allies and two Spanish Franciscans arrived in Belém, in Portuguese territories. When the local governor, who was already commissioned to explore the area by Quito (Spain), realized that they had traveled from the Pacific to the Atlantic, he organized an exploratory force that was to take this route on the inverse. This expedition, led by the Portuguese Pedro Teixeira and manned by Portuguese soldiers, native allies, and Spanish friars, left Pará soon afterward, arriving in Quito in 1638, where it was received with great joy and public celebration.[87]

This story was of little consequence until the 1690s, when Portuguese and Spaniards confronted one another in the territory between the Napo and the Amazon Rivers, each claiming it as its own. While the Spaniards based their claims on a succession of Spanish expeditions and on the Treaty of Tordesillas, the Portuguese made reference to a "discovery and possession" allegedly carried out by Pedro Teixeira in the 1630s. Reaching its zenith in the eighteenth century, the debate as to whether by virtue of the said expedition Portuguese territories extended to the Napo River involved local actors as well as interlocutors in both courts. To support their claims, the Portuguese produced copies of what they considered a formal act of possession taking and argued that (1) it covered the territory in contention and (2) it was taken for the crown of Portugal.[88] They also added that Teixeira was specifically commissioned to discover and take possession of the territory and that the Spanish authorities of Quito and Lima were aware of his powers and consented to his activity. According to some Portuguese sources, he explicitly asked and received the *audiencia*'s approval to take possession of the land. The *audiencia* may have thought it was licensing a discovery for the crown of Castile—after all, Teixeira brought with him letters to the viceroy of Peru, and the territory was Spanish according to Tordesillas—but such was not the case. Even if Teixeira took possession "for king Philip" without specifying whether in his capacity as king of Spain or of Portugal, his act should benefit Portugal because he was Portuguese.[89] The peace treaty of 1668 that recognized Portuguese independence determined as much because it adjudicated to Portugal all the territories it possessed before the uprising of 1640. In order to demonstrate that the territory up to the Napo River was theirs, Portuguese interlocutors also proceeded to identify the place where the alleged ceremony of possession took place, situating it on the banks of that river.

Late seventeenth- and eighteenth-century Spaniards rejected these claims.[90] They explained that even if Teixeira had explored the land and had taken possession of it—a claim they dismissed—his activities necessarily benefited the crown of Castile. The fact that he was Portuguese was irrelevant because during the union many Portuguese operated for Castile and vice versa. The territory Teixeira allegedly discovered was within the Castilian sphere of expansion according to both papal bulls and the Treaty of Tordesillas, and it was initially discovered by friars working for Spain. The hypothesis that the *audiencia* of Quito allowed Teixeira to take possession for the crown of Portugal was preposterous. It was unthinkable and, furthermore, illegal as neither the president of the *audiencia* nor the viceroy could alienate royal property. The only way this territory could become Portuguese was by royal concession, yet such grant was never given nor was it likely, as by the time news of the discovery reached Madrid (1641) Portugal had already rebelled. At any rate, even if possession did take place and even if its legal implications could be ascertained (which they could not), it had transpired much further to the east than the Portuguese claimed, indeed much nearer to Pará than to Quito, and it was restricted to a small territory, not the entire Amazon basin, as the Portuguese argued. Spanish interlocutors also pointed out that if this expedition had any importance at all, it was because it confirmed Spanish rights to the territory. After all, the person who truly discovered it first was Father Cristóbal Acuña, the Franciscan who arrived at Belém and then returned with Teixeira to Quito.

These a posteriori reconstructions of what happened in the 1630s were highly problematic. It was unclear whether the formal act of possession presented by the Portuguese was authentic. Its copies were discovered when convenient, and they describe one of the very few occasions in which a formal act of possession was pursued in Portuguese America. Acuña's narrative of the expedition—an otherwise extremely detailed account—and the report submitted by Filipe de Matos Cotrim, a Portuguese who participated in it, did not mention such an act. Yet, even if the ceremony did take place, in the eighteenth century no one knew, or had ways of knowing, where it had transpired. But whatever one wishes to believe, the eighteenth-century debate over what the mid-seventeenth-century Teixeira expedition might have achieved mainly exposed how something that initially was of little consequence could become incredibly crucial later on.[91] Clues for this dramatic transformation are abundant. Documents produced in the 1630s reveal that the *audiencia* of Quito, rather than distinguishing Spaniards from Portuguese, celebrated the arrival of an expedition that proved that the Amazon connected the Atlantic with the Pacific.[92] Unlike other Europeans, the court did not consider the Portuguese a threat.[93] The only concern the *audiencia* expressed was against Portuguese settlement in the region, which it considered dangerous not because of the possible transfer of territory from Castile to Portugal but out of fear that settlers would engage in contraband trade.[94] These concerns, however, were not sufficiently troubling to justify the expulsion of the Portuguese who came to Quito with the expedition, many of whom remained in the jurisdiction permanently. The viceroy of Peru, who instructed Teixeira to return immediately to Pará where he was most needed in the struggle against the Dutch, was more preoccupied with the security of the Atlantic than with issues of possession.[95] He might have also been alarmed by the discovery of a route connecting east and west because he suspected that it might enable some Portuguese to attack the Jesuit missions in order to enslave their inhabitants. The viceroy might also have objected to the Portuguese presence in an interior still dominated by indigenous, nonconverted nations, because he suspected the Portuguese of religious unorthodoxy. The Council of the Indies that studied the case in 1640 was alarmed that the new route might enable the Portuguese to trade enslaved Indians in Spanish territories, thus contravening both the legal prohibition against Indian slavery and Spain's commercial monopoly in the Americas.[96] Acuña's report addressed similar issues. As a Franciscan friar who had joined the expedition with the hope of discovering infidel Indians to convert, he complained that on their way back to Pará (1640), Portuguese soldiers quarreled with their Spanish counterparts over whether the expedition should pass through Rio Negro, where it was believed that plenty of Indians could be captured for servitude.[97] Acuña was interested in affirming not only that the interior of the continent could be penetrated by navigating its rivers but mainly that many native nations, with many potential converts, resided there.[98] Portuguese documentation equally suggested that issues of possession were either absent in the 1630s or were very low in a long list of priorities. Most Portuguese interlocutors hoped to discover a route linking the Pacific to the Atlantic and to pacify the natives inhabiting its immediate surroundings.[99] Many were especially enthusiastic about reports of the discovery of gold mines.[100] Portuguese documentation also revealed that the five Spanish friars who accompanied the expedition on its way back to Quito and then Belém joined it at the request of the Portuguese, who, far from concerned with the presence of Spaniards, requested their company. They even suggested that they would remain in Belém and tend to the spiritual well-being of local residents. As had happened in Quito with the Portuguese, their arrival in the city was celebrated, and they were allowed to found a convent and train novices.[101]

The reinterpretation that late seventeenth- and eighteenth-century discussants gave to what had transpired in the 1630s was therefore not mandated by what actually happened during the expedition but by what had occurred thereafter, namely, the separation of Spain and Portugal. This transformation was already evident, for example, in the way the Spanish authorities considered these events in the 1640s. The viceroy of Peru, who was concerned that Luso-Americans might join the Portuguese rebellion, asked in 1648 why Spanish friars and soldiers had engaged in discovering a road without royal permission; why the Portuguese had repeated it; and why the authorities of Quito had allowed the Portuguese to return using the same route.[102] Criticizing the decisions taken by Alonso Pérez de Salazar, who was president of the *audiencia* of Quito at that time, the viceroy rejected his explanation that the Portuguese were simply too numerous to be detained at the city. The viceroy admitted, however, that the damage *(daño)* the expedition caused could not have been predicted because the meaning of what had transpired had completely changed because of the way "things have developed" *(y fue mayor para el estado en que se han ido poniendo las cosas)*, that is, because of the uprising of Portugal. Other documents reveal that until the late seventeenth century, the discovery of a route from the Atlantic to the Pacific was the most common explanation of why the expedition first took place. João Felipe Bettendorff, a German Jesuit belonging to the Portuguese province of the order who was rector of the college in Belém and superior of the missions in the Amazon, insisted on this point in 1698, suggesting that the matter was of extreme importance because this road offered a safer, alternative itinerary for exporting silver from Potosí (where the main silver mines of Upper Peru were located) to Spain.[103] Yet, reflecting a mutation already under way, Bettendorff toward the end of his analysis, well aware that Spain and Portugal disagreed regarding the extension of their holdings in the Amazon, also mentioned that Teixeira had taken possession of the land for the crown of Portugal. The emergence of a territorial explanation for why the expedition took place might also have had other explanations. For example, in the 1690s it allowed the authorities of Pará to argue that their municipal jurisdiction covered all the territory up to the Napo River, where a demarcation allegedly placed by Teixeira still existed.[104] Responding to local needs—mainly the presence of other Portuguese in the region and the wish to subjugate them to that city—this interpretation affirmed the control of Belém, rather than the sovereignty of Portugal, over that territory. But whatever the causes for the transformation were, by the mid-eighteenth century, only a few traces were left of the older interpretations of why the expedition took place. By that time, contemporaries assumed that it was always and only about territorial expansion.[105]

Yet the wish to recruit the past to justify the present called for a long and arduous effort at reinterpretation. One of the basic requirements it elicited was the construction of a clear distinction between Spaniards and Portuguese, Spain and Portugal, because only that could clarify which of the two powers could benefit from what had transpired. But whereas such a distinction might have been evident to eighteenth-century discussants, its retroactive application was extremely hazardous.[106] That in the eighteenth century Portuguese independence seemed natural and evident was one thing; that in the 1630s contemporaries thought it was, was another. Despite a posteriori reconstructions, until 1640 no one knew, perhaps did not even suspect, that Spain and Portugal would ever separate again. In the preceding period, the relations between the two Iberian polities and their inhabitants were still a matter of controversy. Forming part of a larger debate regarding who Spaniards were and what Spain consisted of, during this period contemporaries all over the Iberian peninsula engaged in clarifying and thus also building the relations between their various kingdoms. They explored the ability, wish, or possibility to envision this ensemble as a single political unit or on the contrary as a fractured entity, divided into more or less independent parts (kingdoms), each with its own constitution, regime, laws, inhabitants, and rights. Choosing one option over the other had important legal ramifications that could greatly affect individual actors. For example, if all natives of the Iberian Peninsula were members of a single community, they all had identical rights and obligations; if they were members of separate communities, they each had a different set.[107] Alarmed by the prospects of unity, in the late fourteenth and fifteenth centuries most Iberian parliaments adopted rules that defined their natives and distinguished them from all other Iberians by instituting local monopolies on office-holding and ecclesiastical benefices. But if protectionist policies were initially adopted, in the sixteenth century, perhaps influenced by the promises of overseas expansion or by the confrontations provoked by the Reformation and the wars it unleashed, significant political and legal gestures were made toward the construction of a unified Spain. These began with a series of decisions that legally defined those individuals who would be allowed to emigrate to and trade in the New World. Rather than restricting this right to Castilians (as could be expected because the New World was considered a Castilian territory), the colonial monopoly instead allowed "all natives of our kingdoms" to enjoy these privileges. In the aftermaths of its institution, who formed part of this group became a contested question. First asked with respect to the natives of the crown of Aragon, who insisted on their inclusion in order to enjoy the benefits associated with maritime expansion, it was then raised and settled with regards to the kingdom of Navarre, whose natives, like the Aragonese before them, were also classified as "natives of Spain."[108] Whereas consequently the Aragonese and the Navarrese (and, of course, all Castilians) became legally "Spanish" at least with respect to emigration and trade in the New World, the Portuguese were formally declared foreign in the *Recopilación de Indias* that reproduced a decision dated 1596 and confirmed in 1614. This decision was contested by several among them who, like the Aragonese and the Navarrese did, insisted that they too were Spaniards. Describing Spain as a body made of several kingdoms, they argued that "because Portugal was part of Spain and the Portuguese as native and as true Spaniards and as native and loyal vassals of his majesty, they should not be in Peru and other parts of Spanish America be considered or included in the condition of foreigners." After all, "were not the Portuguese as Spanish as those of Navarre, Guipúzcoa, Vizcaya, Aragon, Valencia and Catalonia? Although the latter are Spanish, they, like us, the Portuguese, are not Castilian. Is it thinkable that they are more Spanish and more loyal vassals of Your Majesty than the Portuguese?"[109] This narrative presented Portugal as a full and equal participant in the Hispanic monarchy, and it argued that Spain as a community comprised three equal parts: Castile, Aragon, and Portugal; inhabiting it were "Portuguese Spaniards," "Castilian Spaniards," and "Aragonese Spaniards."[110] These formal allegations found echo in petitions that merchants of Portuguese extraction living in Spanish American advanced affirming that, because they were Portuguese, they should not be included among "foreigners" whose residence and trade were prohibited.[111]

Such claims were sometimes supported by the Spanish authorities who, on occasions and most particularly after the union ended, authorized these interpretations, determining, for example in 1683, that a Portuguese who had emigrated to Spain before 1640 was "Spanish" rather than foreign.[112] Even as late as 1704 and in the midst of a war with Portugal (the War of the Spanish Succession), some Spanish authorities were still willing to follow this understanding and classify the Portuguese who reached the Spanish Indies before 1641 as nonforeigners.[113] Unlike other Portuguese who arrived after the union ended, these pre-1641 Portuguese were entirely Spanish.

Although many of these allegations were voiced by interested parties who strove to legitimize their presence and commerce in Spanish America or who sought other rewards, they nevertheless found support in a literature that claimed that Portugal was part of Spain. In 1580, the bishop of Coria, for example, asserted that Spaniards and Portuguese were so similar in culture, language, and commerce that only malice would distinguish them into separate nations or groups.[114] In 1581, a Spanish Jesuit pointed out that a war between Castile and Portugal would entail a struggle of "Christians against Christians, Catholics against Catholics, and Spaniards against Spaniards."[115] In 1616, the Portuguese Pedro Barbosa de Luna suggested that Portugal was more Spanish than Aragon, and in 1628 Manuel Faria y Sousa equally insisted both on the antiquity of Portugal as on its Spanish essence.[116] To the Portuguese Gabriel Pereira de Castro writing in 1621, the union with Castile and Aragon reestablished the "old Hispanic crown" *(antiqua Corona Hispaniae)*.[117] Writing in Aragon, Martin Carrillo affirmed in 1620 that Philip II had been the "first king and master of all of Spain" *(primer rey y señor de toda España)* because, for the first time, Spain also included Portugal.[118] Vestiges of a united Spain persisted over time. During the peace negotiations with Portugal in the 1660s, Spaniards suggested that their king maintain superiority over the Duke of Braganza because, while the former would be emperor of Spain, the duke would become king of Portugal.[119] The two countries would continue to be associated on other levels too, the Spanish emperor having powers to name individuals to posts in Portugal and its overseas domains, and natives having certain privileges in both jurisdictions. Such a construction made sense, these interlocutors suggested, because nature itself sanctioned such a union between Portugal and "the other kingdoms of Spain."[120] After all, Portugal was not separated from the rest of the peninsula by mountains, rivers, or even seas, and attempts to unify the peninsula were constant. Their failure with regards to Portugal was an accident, not a purposeful result. Even as late as 1706, some Portuguese still considered their kingdom "one of the most notable of Spain," and in 1768 some Spaniards insisted Portugal was a "property that, against the rights of blood and possession" *(una propiedad que contra el derecho de la sangre y posesión)*, had been lost in 1640.[121]

Debates as to who Spaniards ("natives of Spain") were included discussions regarding the advantages and disadvantages of constructing an Iberian polity in which all kingdoms would be equally included. These debates, which arose particularly in periods of political, economic, and social crises, pitted those who rejected the prospects of unification against those who embraced it, believing it would advance their individual goals and perhaps also the well-being of their kingdom.[122] Both sectors existed in Castile and Aragon, but they also were evident in Portugal, where supporters of complete integration of Iberia competed with others who, fearing such developments, insisted it was vital to maintain a separate Portugal. Stances depended on economic imperatives and personal gain but were also conditioned by what was at stake, that is, which privileges or duties were being debated.[123]

The place Portugal would occupy became particularly contested in the 1640s, after the Duke of Braganza declared himself king of an independent state. Historians have long suggested that it was natural that the Portuguese would support the independence of their kingdom by backing Braganza and that Spaniards would resist it by continuing their allegiance to Philip. Nevertheless, we now know that such was not necessarily the case. Rather than depending on nativeness or pitting Portuguese against Spaniards, response to developments in 1640 was mainly guided by perceptions of what was just and what was possible.[124] Instead of comprehending the crisis as "national" (as many historians would do since), contemporaries asked themselves which position they should choose.[125] Believing that the rebellion would be short-lived, motivated by personal loyalty to Philip, or concerned with access to a wider set of administrative, religious, and military posts or a larger network of commercial entrepôts, in the 1640s, 1650s, and 1660s many Portuguese emigrated to or remained in Spain and Spanish America, voting with their feet against the uprising. In Ceuta, Tangier, and Macao, doubts were expressed by local garrisons whether to join the uprising or negotiate with Philip.[126] In Angola, after Portuguese troops survived Dutch attacks (1641), their commanders debated whether to accept Dutch sovereignty, remain loyal to Philip, or side with Braganza. But if the response of the Portuguese was not automatic, neither was the position of all Castilians. Perhaps because many of its richest inhabitants were of Portuguese extraction and their livelihood depended on the Portuguese maritime system, Buenos Aires was rumored to be considering joining the uprising. Some even suggested that Colonia de Sacramento might have been established by the Portuguese in 1679 and 1680 at the petition of these Bonarenses who sought to ensure their enduring contacts with Brazil.[127] But even in peninsular Spain some individuals believed that their interests would be best served by joining the Braganza uprising. Most famous among them was the Duke of Medina Sidonia. In 1641, the duke confessed that he had decided to support João, believing such a move would guarantee the continuation of the "ties that linked him and his vassals" to their "relatives in Portugal." As brother-in-law of João (who had married the duke's sister) and as the owner of an estate that included much of southern Spain, the duke hoped this move would guarantee him control of his estates and relieve him of taxes.[128] In order to elicit the support of locals, he planned to distribute pamphlets stressing the advantages of joining Braganza. The Marquis of Ayamonte, governor of the coast of Andalusia, who also backed João, was suspected of plotting to create an autonomous "Republic of Andalusia" under the protection of Portugal. These decisions were encouraged by the Duke of Braganza, who actively attempted to recruit adherents among Spaniards, promising them in return different rewards and suggesting that by joining him they would free themselves of the tyranny, tributes, taxes, and other impositions to which they were subject and which "transformed them into slaves, not vassals."[129]

Implicit in these promises was a vision of a united peninsula; only this time it would be constituted by Portugal, not Spain, and led by João, not Philip.

The decision whether to back the uprising and a separate Portugal (perhaps heading a pan-Spanish polity) or remain loyal to Philip (and a unified monarchy led by Castile and Aragon) was thus extremely complex. It involved questions of personal loyalty to a monarch but also implied a certain gamble regarding how the crisis would be resolved. Fears of repression might have also played a role.[130] The new Portuguese monarch put those who failed to back him on trial, accusing them of lèse-majesté and rebellion and punishing them with expulsion from the military orders, confiscation of property, and even death.[131] While Braganza pressured his subjects, so did Philip. As soon as news of the uprising reached Madrid, the Spanish royal favorite (valido), the Count-Duke of Olivares, called the Portuguese nobility and clergy residing in the court for a meeting.[132] He informed the some eighty people present of the "detestable treason" (detestable traición) committed by the Duke of Braganza and requested their help in ensuring its suppression. Presenting the duke as an ungrateful subject who had risen up against a "pious and just king" who had favored him continuously, the count-duke expected these Portuguese to help Philip, and he was willing to reward those who would. Until 1668, when a definitive peace treaty was signed between Spain and Portugal, the promotion of loyal Portuguese (i.e., those who backed Philip) continued, as did the existence in Madrid of a royal council responsible for managing Portuguese affairs. This continuation was in part a strategic move to show that the Spanish king was willing to trust and honor those Portuguese who were loyal to him, encouraging others in doubt to do the same.[133]

The complex set of considerations that might have caused certain individuals and groups to back the Braganzas or the Habsburgs, a unified Spain or a separate Portugal, was particularly clear in the Americas, where the governor of Rio de Janeiro consulted with local dignitaries on how he should proceed. Rumors indicated he might have checked with the authorities of Buenos Aires on whether they would support the city in the event it decided not to follow the uprising and that he continuously reconsidered his position, on occasions offering to reunite with Philip's monarchy in return for certain benefits.[134] In São Paolo it is possible that, rather than choosing between the Braganzas and the Habsburgs, locals might have wished to crown a prince of their own.[135] Strong personal ties to Castile and Spain justified these developments—by that time, Luso- and Spanish Americans were so internally mixed that it was hard to divide them into two distinct groups—but there were also strong economic imperatives that could explain why southern Brazil, mainly Rio and São Paolo, might have wanted to remain within the Spanish commercial sphere. But the question of whether to follow the Portuguese uprising or remain loyal to Philip could also depend on speculation about which of the two monarchs would be, for example, friendlier to the Indian slave trade. Believing that support for the union continued in some parts of Portuguese America, in the 1640s and 1650s Philip sent emissaries to different Portuguese American ports in the hope of ensuring their loyalty. He also wrote to local dignitaries requesting their support and promising to authorize even a closer union by allowing direct communications between Spain and Brazil. Philip also considered other methods, including a propaganda war and the organization of a Luso-American uprising against the Duke of Braganza. These connections suggest that, de facto although perhaps not de jure, Brazil continued to form part of the Spanish monarchy until the 1660s, perhaps even the 1680s, when the foundation of Colonia de Sacramento made it clear that the interests of its inhabitants no longer coincided with those of Spain.[136]

In the mid-seventeenth century, therefore, individuals and groups had to choose whether they should favor Philip and the gradual building of a single Spain or follow Braganza and guarantee, at least for a while, an independent Portugal. Because contemporaries were aware that this decision did not hinge on one's origin, nativeness, or even previous loyalties, tension was particularly high, placing "everything under suspense, between suspicion and hope."[137] Rather than distinguishing Spaniards from Portuguese and automatically assuming the former would back Philip and the latter João, contemporaries proceeded to classify individuals as loyal or disloyal, obedient or disobedient. Such deliberations were particularly clear in Spain, where in 1640 the Council of the Indies debated whether it should take measures against natives of Portuguese living in Spanish territories.[138] Stressing that there was no reason to assume they were all partners in crime *(cómplices)*, the council suggested it would be unfair to treat them as anything other than royal vassals. Its members also stated that after so many years of union, it was practically impossible to distinguish Spaniards from Portuguese. Efforts to identify those who supported the uprising (and merited retaliation) from those who did not continued thereafter.[139] They sometimes produced unjustified suspicion and the persecution of possibly loyal Portuguese. Yet, if these developments gave expression to popular fear, perhaps even hatred, they also testified to the degree of mixing that already existed, with natives of Portugal residing, trading, and otherwise extremely integrated in Spanish enclaves. As the governor of Puerto Rico asserted in 1641, by that time most Portuguese in his jurisdiction had become so rooted in the territory that they could be considered naturalized.[140] In Lima, the viceroy explained that it was essential to distinguish the Portuguese whose presence was worrisome from all others who had rendered services to the king, were employed in local tribunals, were born in Castile, were the sons of Castilians, or were married to Castilians and well rooted in Lima *(arraigados en esta tierra)*.[141] He also confessed that, had he done differently, expelling all the Portuguese, commerce at the port of Lima (Callao) would immediately cease. "No one abhorred the Portuguese nation, only its guilt," he asserted.[142] Others suggested that in Spanish America there were as many "Creole Spaniards from Portugal" *(españoles criollos de Portugal)* as "Portugues-ed Spaniards" that could not be trusted.[143] It is therefore not surprising that most attempts to tell apart the Portuguese occurred in Buenos Aires, an enclave that featured a particularly numerous Portuguese population, which was tightly connected to southern Brazil and whose members not only were extremely affluent but also dominated the local town council.[144]

If the loyalty of individuals could not be asserted by referencing their nativeness, neither could the honesty of their choice be easily ascertained. In the 1640s and 1650s, defections from one side to the other were extremely common. Ships on their way to Portuguese stations in Africa with newly nominated officials or Portuguese nobles on their way to European capitals as emissaries of the Braganza could end up in Spain protesting their loyalty to Philip.[145] An example of such a dramatic "conversion" was the case of Raymundo, Duke of Aveiro, who excused himself from attending the Cortes of 1641 that pledged allegiance to the new Braganza dynasty by arguing he was indisposed. Accompanied by his mother, sister, and wife, in 1660 he fled to Madrid, thereafter openly declaring his loyalty to Philip. While his change of heart was openly declared, others were suspected of harboring loyalty to the enemy even in the absence of direct proof. The viceroy of Brazil, for example, immediately supported Braganza yet, because it was well known that two of his sons and his wife remained loyal to Philip and because it was feared that he might be playing both sides, he fell under suspicion and was sent to Portugal in chains.[146] It is therefore not surprising that during this period the Count of Linhares (of Portuguese extraction) insisted that his loyalty to Philip was genuine as "he did not sell himself for any price but instead had clean faith, void of interests" *(yo no me vendí a ningún precio, sino mostré una fe limpia de todo interés).*[147] It was nevertheless clear that he too might have hoped that the rebellion would be short-lived and that he would soon be reinstituted to his titles and properties now sequestered in Portugal.

Changes in allegiance were not the monopoly of elites. According to some witnesses, in 1652, two Spanish majors helped the Portuguese plan their attack on Badajoz, on the Spanish border.[148] In 1655, the sergeant major of the fort of Salvaterra (Portugal), who secretly backed Philip, aided Spaniards. In 1659, similar suspicions arose against another Portuguese captain who, relieved of his military post, moved to Spain with his family. Convinced that he had made a bad choice, he returned to Portugal in 1663 and rejoined the army. Municipal bodies might also have followed similar patterns. Concerned with survival rather than with abstract loyalties and perhaps favoring the union because of their geographic location on the border, in 1662, the inhabitants of Monforte (Portugal) were classified by the Braganza propaganda as traitors because they welcomed the Spanish forces that invaded their village. Similarly, in 1662, the inhabitants of Cabeço de Vide (Portugal) declared their loyalty to Philip as they received his (invading) army with demonstrations of joy. In 1663, some complained that Elvas (Portugal), also on the border, was "full of traitors" who "showed bad will" toward João. The same year, the Évora city council, cathedral chapter, and Inquisition welcomed the Spanish forces that occupied them.[149] Spanish enclaves may have been equally indecisive, with parts of Extremadura (on the border) backing João and some of their residents even pledging allegiance to him in return for privileges.[150]

The political crisis of the 1640s, 1650s, and 1660s, in short, forced individuals, families, institutions, and communities to make difficult choices. Rather than following a nation, they backed the prince to whom they felt personally tied, whom they believed would best defend their interests, and who would lead them to a unified Spain or a separate Portugal.[151] A civil, perhaps political, even economic dispute, it did not confront two kingdoms, nor did it pit Portuguese against Spaniards. Instead, it ran through both countries, in the process also redefining what Spain and Portugal were. It is nevertheless clear that in the aftermath of the breakup, an enormous effort was invested, mainly on the Portuguese side, to legitimize these events by adopting a narrative that transformed Spaniards into voracious foreigners and the union into an illegitimate occupation.[152] Whereas from the Spanish perspective Portugal remained Spanish—indeed there was great difficulty in Madrid to accept it had stopped being thus (Portuguese independence was recognized only in 1668, and even then with hesitation[153])—from the Portuguese point of view Portugal was and had always been different. It was during this period— from the 1640s into the early eighteenth century and beyond—that a vast literature in the form of pamphlets, essays, and books appeared, explaining why the rebellion was justified. These materials mainly insisted on the separate existence of Portugal. They responded to the need to legitimate Dom João internationally (to use an anachronism) but, more important, they were directed at the home audience, for whom these developments—the rebellion and the independence— may not have been necessarily justified or wise.

Thus, while eighteenth-century discussants could imagine that the discovery by Teixeira was done either for Spain or for Portugal, it is quite possible that from the perspective of actors operating in the 1630s it was done for both simultaneously. Yet what might have been evident while the union lasted could no longer be maintained after it was broken. By the eighteenth century, the campaign to legitimize Portuguese independence had achieved such a success that even Spaniards no longer questioned it. By that time they too, like their Portuguese interlocutors, dismissed the possibility of a united Spain, automatically assuming that in the 1630s both kingdoms were clearly separated, as were their residents, and each pursued its own territorial agenda.

The question of who was Spanish and who Portuguese and whether possession was taken for one country or the other, which was often invoked during the union and in its aftermath, continued to haunt contemporary imagination until the early nineteenth century. This was particularly evident with regards to the status of the residents of São Paulo who roamed the interior of the continent in search of slaves, mines, and, commerce. Were they Portuguese? Could the extensive geographical projection of their activities benefit Portugal? In the eighteenth century, Spanish interlocutors answered these questions negatively.[154] They explained that during the seventeenth and the early eighteenth centuries, São Paulo was not truly subject to Portugal. Established by criminals sent from Europe to Brazil and populated by Dutch pirates, Jews [sic], heretics, and other delinquents belonging to a great variety of nations, many of its residents were also Spanish.[155] The expeditions they organized might have had Portuguese captains, but their members were not Portuguese. Rather than subjected to one crown or populated by the vassals of a single lord, São Paolo was "an independent republic." Changing sides as they wished, its residents recognized Philip II of Spain in 1583 as their king, in 1630 they were ruled by several lords (señores particulares), and in 1641, when Portugal rebelled against Spain, they hesitated as to whether to remain loyal to Philip IV of Spain or swear allegiance to the new Braganza dynasty. It was not until the mid-eighteenth century that São Paulo became truly Portuguese, and it was only after this date that the activities of its residents could generate rights for Portugal.

Although eighteenth-century Portuguese discussants protested that what Paulistas had achieved in the seventeenth and early eighteenth centuries could and must benefit the crown of Portugal, it is nevertheless clear that contemporary sources justified some of the claims made by Spaniards. They mentioned, for example, that the city was theoretically subject to Rio de Janeiro, yet they admitted that during the seventeenth century it was populated by individuals whose loyalty was uncertain. Many among them were New Christians, whose relationship with the Netherlands was stronger than their ties to Portugal. These sources also cited complaints, such as those voiced in 1740 by the intendant of Cuiabá, according to which Paulistas involved in contraband drank to the health of King Philip V of Spain, whom they publically supported. The intendant concluded that Paulistas could not be trusted because they were either "Portuguesed Castilians" *(castelhanos aportuguesados)* or a mixture of Portuguese, Spanish, and native elements.[156]

The argument that some Portuguese sources made suggesting that locals were rebels who did not obey the orders of the king was perhaps a means to justify why successive governors failed to control them and why they contravened royal orders by enslaving Indians and attacking Spanish missions. But however instrumental these claims might have been, many of them contained information that historians have since verified.[157] Thus, although in twentieth-century Brazil, São Paulo and its *bandeirantes* were portrayed as national heroes responsible for the expansion of their patria, many historians now affirm that during the sixteenth and seventeenth centuries São Paulo functioned mainly as a native enclave, with only a limited European presence.[158] It was populated by many Spaniards, and it looked to Spanish, rather than Portuguese, territories for inspiration, aid, and commerce. Historians have also concluded that most *bandeirantes* were involved not in slaving expeditions aimed at territorial expansion but in commercial activities that followed more or less fixed routes linking the Atlantic with Paraguay and Peru. The members of such expeditions were Portuguese, Spaniards, and Italians, and their enterprise was backed by the local authorities on both sides. During the union of the crowns and even in its aftermath, São Paulo flourished because of its position as a strategic site between two connected empires. The local elites of Paraguay, who also sought to play the same role and, in the process, broaden their jurisdiction in the same direction as Paulistas, resented this success and complained about it. But the most powerful enemies Paulistas confronted were the Jesuits. As members of that order gradually extended their missionary activities to the regions mediating between Paraguay and São Paulo, and as they strove to establish a territory that would be independent of both, they came into conflict with Paulistas. When Spanish policies that initially encouraged communication between the Atlantic and the Pacific changed and Spanish kings moved to separate the mines of Upper Peru from Paraguay and the Atlantic, these regional conflicts escalated. The identification of *bandeirantes* with "Portuguese slave traders" interested in territorial acquisition that many historians have automatically reproduced since dated from this period. It first appeared in Jesuit narratives that, starting in the 1620s, insisted that Paulistas were not loyal merchants extending their activities by linking the Atlantic to the interior following royal design (as most of them were) but instead disobedient subjects who endangered royal sovereignty.[159] Jesuits also portrayed Paulistas as heretics who allied with the Dutch and the Jews, the monarchy's worse enemies. These images were intended to drum up royal support for the Jesuit missions in Paraguay and allow the order greater control over the native population. They intentionally downplayed the more serious tensions in the area, those that confronted settlers with ecclesiastics and ecclesiastical with royal jurisdiction. Justifying on the Spanish side the growing independence and militarization of the Jesuit missions in Paraguay, on the Portuguese side they pushed for the creation of a diocese in Rio de Janeiro. They also converted what was essentially a regional conflict into a "national" one, theoretically opposing Spaniards with Portuguese and involving the demarcation of their respective territories. By the eighteenth century, this new interpretation became useful not only to the Jesuits but also to Paulistas and the Portuguese crown. The former adopted it to justify denying other Portuguese the right to explore and use the interior of the continent. From the discovery of mines in 1694, Paulistas thus argued that (1) they were Portuguese and (2) they should receive a monopoly on these newly discovered regions. While Paulistas insisted on their "Portuguese-ness" in order to secure privileges for themselves, the Portuguese crown used their "Portuguese-ness" in order to make claims to territories vis-à-vis Spain.

EUROPEAN TRADITIONS THUS REQUIRED Spanish and Portuguese discussants to evaluate the relative weight and the possible interpretations of papal bull and treaties but also sent them to Roman doctrines and occupation. Because scientific knowledge and accumulated experience were insufficient and because the juridical situation itself was highly complex and volatile, neither bulls, nor treaties, nor occupation gave them definite answers. Uncertainty unleashed a competition as to who would occupy which part, but it mainly forced the parties into vigilance as it was equally important, perhaps even more important, to make sure that rivals would not attempt to change the status quo. This requirement explains the involvement of individuals who had no training in law, nor were necessarily commissioned by the king, in lengthy debates regarding territorial rights. In their interactions with one another, these individuals often expressed a certainty they did not necessarily possess, and they made claims that they could not necessarily back. Their daily engagement with questions of territorial extension, mainly geared to justify where they could collect fruits, establish a settlement, or navigate, resulted in a cacophony, in which there were multiple voices, some more authorized than others, some more knowledgeable than others, some more motivated than others. It ensured a constant debate and questioning, but it also encouraged the occasional employment of violence, meant to demonstrate disproval and disagreement. And, because only actions taken by vassals could lead to the acquisition of rights, these dynamics also forced contemporaries to identify who they and their rivals were and to which community they belonged. But knowing who was a Spaniard and who was a Portuguese was a highly complicated issue, certainly during the union of the crowns (1580–1640) but even more so in its aftermath.

The question of which country had rights where and which crown could claim what was therefore a highly multifaceted and deeply intricate affair for which there were (and still are) no clear answers.

Rather than subjects extending the jurisdiction of their community or neighbors coveting the property of one another, the penetration of Europeans to the American interior was much more chaotic, hazardous, and lacking a firm juridical basis (because all allegations were open to reinterpretation and all ideas and doctrines could be upheld or dismissed) than contemporaries (and historians and politicians following them) had led us to believe.

2 Europeans and Indians: Conversion, Submission, and Land Rights

THE QUESTION OF WHO was vassal of which country (and therefore which activity could benefit whom) involved not only Europeans but also the indigenous population living in the American interior. Contemporaries believed that religious conversion implied civic conversion and that, in the process, natives were transformed into both Christians and vassals of the power that had evangelized them. Considering this conclusion consensual and evident, they barely ever discussed or justified it. Instead, they suggested in passing, for example in 1652, that Indians who had collaborated with the Dutch were traitors because, having been baptized by the Portuguese, they now owed them their allegiance.[1] Or, assimilating conversion to military conquest, they suggested that overwhelming Indians "by arms had always been impossible, because by moving from one place to the other and entering into the densest mountains, as they have done when we searched for them, all efforts are frustrated, expenses lost, and many lives exposed to illnesses. The only hope is that they admit missionaries and that these, using flattery and other efforts, might win them over. That is how we have managed to resettle them. Conquest by a missionary would be greater than that of a numerous army, but this is the work of God, not men."[2]

An excellent example of how religious and civic conversion operated together could be found in 1659, when Portuguese troops accompanied by the Jesuit António Vieira met with a group of hostile Indians, whom they hoped to pacify.[3] The ritual began when native leaders entered Vieira's canoe and presented him with an image of Christ, which they had received four years earlier from European missionaries. It continued later that day, with the celebration of a Mass on a richly ornamented altar outside a church in the presence, on the right, of Christianized indigenous groups, clothed and armed; on the left, of leaders of not-yet-pacified groups in their "barbarian cloths and bows and arrows"; and, in the middle, the Portuguese. Vieira spoke to the not-yet-submitted natives, and using the services of interpreters, he informed them of their obligation to answer with "clean hearts" and without deceit (com limpo coração, sem engano) to the questions he would thereafter pose and to fulfill inviolably what they had promised. Taking turns, each native leader was asked whether he wanted to receive the true faith and be a vassal of the king of Portugal like the Portuguese and the natives of nations already Christianized and vassalized (avassaladas). To explain what this implied, the converted Indians and Portuguese declared together that the obligation of vassals was to obey the king. Vassals also had to submit to royal laws and have perpetual and inviolable peace with all other royal subjects. They were to be friends of those who were in royal allegiance and enemies of those who resisted the king. In return, vassals enjoyed freely their properties and benefited from all agreements and privileges that the laws gave them. Answering affirmatively, each native leader approached the altar and, placing his bow and arrow on the ground, put his hands in Vieira's and swore, "I, named so and so, leader of such and such nation, in my name and that of all my subjects and descendants, promise to God and the king of Portugal, in the faith of our lord Jesus Christ, to be (as I am already) from now on, vassal of his Majesty and to keep perpetual peace with the Portuguese, being the friend of all their friends and the enemy of all his enemies, which I promise to guard and comply with entirely for always."[4] Kissing Vieira's hands, the leader then hugged the Jesuits, the Portuguese, and the already-converted Indians present at the ceremony. A Te Deum followed, and while the newly accepted Indians threw their bows and arrows away, the Portuguese and their indigenous allies did the same with their weapons. The entire ceremony was accompanied by the sounds of trumpets, horns, and drums, and the "continuous cries of infinite number of voices" *(um grito contínuo de infinitas vozes)* by which the multitude expressed its joy in "multiple languages." A juridical document was then drawn up testifying to all that had transpired. An exchange of gifts followed, as did music and dances. In celebration, a great cross was built and was adored by both "Christians and pagans" *(gentio)*. The entire ceremony took three days to complete, and it may have involved as many as fifty Indian leaders and some forty thousand of their followers.

The doctrine that related religious and civic conversion, which was widespread among both Spaniards and Portuguese, was also taken up by the religious orders in the American interior. It allowed them to argue that they had "augmented the royal treasury" *(aumentos de los reales haberes)* by conquering *(conquistar)* numerous indigenous nations, founding villages, and making natives both political and Christian beings.[5] Thereafter, missionaries claimed that Indians who had friendly relations with the Portuguese implicitly changed their political adhesion when they chose to reside in a Jesuit mission sponsored by Spain. Referring to converted Indians not only as vassals but on occasions also as "Spaniards," friars insisted they should be considered as such because their fidelity and love to the king and obedience to his orders made them worthy of this treatment.[6]

The tying of religious and civic conversion was such that, on occasions, missionaries even sustained that this method was the only legitimate means for making Indians vassals. The Portuguese António Vieira was particularly eloquent on this point, explaining that captivity and forced immigration did not change the political adhesion of those vanquished because if Spanish captives in Algeria continued to belong to their nation, so did Indians captured by the Portuguese.[7] By the second half of the eighteenth century, the association between conversion and vassalage gave rise to new theories that claimed that the rights of Spain and Portugal to certain territories sanctioned by papal bulls or the Treaty of Tordesillas persisted only as long as the Indians were pagans. They authorized Europeans to subject natives and their territory to both God and state, yet, after the indigenous converted, these rights expired because the territory and its people were already domesticated, indeed Europeanized.[8] Voiced by Spanish Jesuits (and their sympathizers) in the 1750s and 1760s, this theory was developed in order to prove that Portugal had absolutely no rights to the territory east of the Uruguay River because, aside from the question of whether this land was Portuguese according to the Treaty of Tordesillas or whether the king had voluntarily ceded it in the Madrid treaty he signed in 1750, after the Indians inhabiting the region converted to Christianity and became vassals of Spain, they were no longer in Portugal's legitimate expansion zone. Other interlocutors also argued that after Spanish Jesuits converted the Indians, the Portuguese could no longer conquer or "possess" (poseer) them.[9] Imagining natives as a no-man's-land, eighteenth-century discussants thus held that before Europeans arrived and natives were subjected to them through missionary work, they belonged to no one and any European could take possession of them as a "vacant" property. Yet, they also asserted that after Indians were "taken," indeed possessed, Indians became part of the political commonwealth and could no longer be incorporated by other Europeans. Implying that in their case conversion was a form of agriculture, by the end of this process the Spanish and the Portuguese asserted that conversion could give grounds to territorial claims in much the same way as English "improvement" did.[10]

The theories linking conversion to vassalage ensured competition between Spain and Portugal as to which power would convert the Indians first, and they forced missionaries to persuade Indians not only to change their religious beliefs but also to choose Spanish or Portuguese missionaries as their guides. Promising natives better conditions, mainly the continuous presence of missionaries in their settlements, according to Spanish complaints the Portuguese managed to persuade several nations to submit themselves to Portugal. In response, Spanish Jesuits insisted in 1735 that the Portuguese were not authorized to pursue such policies because Spain had preferential rights to Indians by virtue of the bulls that charged it with their evangelization. They also suggested that, as was well known, although the Portuguese were Catholics, they were not truly interested in saving souls, only in territorial domination and economic profit.[11] As if answering these allegations, the Portuguese governor of Mato Grosso complained in 1751 against Spanish pretention to have a monopoly over the conversion of natives. By which divine or positive law, by which right or papal bull, he asked, were the Indians living in these parts the property of Spain?[12] If the Portuguese were heretics, such a claim would make sense, but given that they were not, and that they also sought to convert the Indians as they were now doing, why should they not be allowed to do so? If Spain could "conquer Indians for God" *(conquistar indios para dios)*, so could Portugal, and if Spain could gain vassals and territories and extend its domains by establishing missions, so could it.

Instrumental in making Indians Spanish or Portuguese, friars were also important in converting native land into European territory. Arguing that their activities constituted possession, Jesuits insisted that the territory of their missions was Spanish or Portuguese not only because of what papal bulls or the Treaty of Tordesillas mandated but mainly because they, the ecclesiastics, took possession of it for the kings of Spain or Portugal.[13] Spanish Franciscans equally boasted on occasions that certain rivers were discovered and possessed by their friars, and Portuguese Carmelites asserted that they had "conquered" territories for Portugal.[14] Contemporary authors agreed with this analysis, identifying Jesuits as "conquistadors" and arguing that they were perfectly suited to subject the territory to Spain.[15] Jesuits' contribution to the expansion of Spanish territories was openly recognized in 1776, when the Marquis of Valdelirios informed the Spanish foreign minister that because Jesuits working for Spain had been present in Paraguay since the 1630s and because they behaved as if the territory belonged to them, Spain had also acquired rights there.[16] In 1751, the Portuguese king suggested too that the activities of Portuguese Jesuits confirmed the conquest and possession that he already had or was in the process of completing because their missions "augmented the Christianity of Indians as well as conserved the dominions of the king."[17]

If missionaries and their activities were a reason and a justification to claim vassals and land, their presence in the American interior was also instrumental in other ways. Because they lived in the
contested area and had close contacts with the native population,
missionaries were in a perfect position to supply information regarding the whereabouts of potential enemies.[18] They sent reports
to their superiors and informed the authorities about territorial violations. Coloring this information according to their needs and desires, Spanish Jesuits often portrayed the Portuguese as individuals
motivated by greed *(codicia)*, who acted as pirates *(piratas)* and behaved like bad neighbors. Because their activity contravened not
only the rights of Spain but also papal and divine law, the Portuguese,
Spanish Jesuits argued, were also perverse Catholics. The Portuguese attacked Jesuit missions in the seventeenth century, thus
seriously undermining the conversion effort by forcing Jesuits to
relocate their villages and by provoking the flight of many natives
who feared subjection to Portugal, removal to Pará, and subsequent
enslavement. Because Jesuits knew that the Portuguese justified
their activities by arguing that Jesuits had penetrated their jurisdiction, Spanish Jesuits insisted that such was not the case. On the one
hand, the Portuguese did not care about land and jurisdiction; on the
other, the rights of Castile to the region were clear because they were
based on papal bulls, the Treaty of Tordesillas, discovery, and possession. Portuguese claims to rights by the passage of time were false
because the territory was discovered by Spain and because there was
no statute of limitations when the injured party protested, as Spain
did. Spanish Jesuits thus affirmed that although they did not care
who owned the land, the future of their missions depended on their
belonging to Spain because Spain, not Portugal, cared about the
salvation of indigenous souls.

As expert witnesses who knew the territory well and cared about
who would control it, Spanish Jesuits were also involved in giving
council, including legal and political advice. From the 1670s, they
participated in debates about whether certain territories were Spanish or Portuguese, and in 1680, after Colonia de Sacramento was
established by the Portuguese in an area that Spaniards considered
their own, Jesuits instructed the Council of Indies (dealing with

American matters at the court) as to how to respond.[19] Opposing the treaty that ceded the city (conquered by Spanish forces) to Portugal in 1681, Spanish Jesuits explained that this move was dangerous politically because it encouraged Portuguese territorial ambitions.[20] Jesuits also wrote tracts about Spanish rights to the territory and drew maps of the region that became useful instruments in the bilateral negotiations between the courts.[21]

If on occasions Jesuit involvement seemed fortuitous, even accidental, on others it took on a much more deliberate and continuous form. Because he believed in the connection between Spanish territorial claims and conversion, for over twenty years Father Samuel Fritz, a native of Bohemia who arrived in Spanish America in 1685 and became superior of the Jesuit missions in the Amazon region in 1704 and who continued to reside in the territory until his death in 1725, constantly informed authorities in Quito, Lima, and Madrid and the Spanish ambassadors in Lisbon and Rome about territorial issues.[22] Fritz acknowledged that the matter was not his to argue or decide and he insisted that he was not interested in land, only in the salvation of souls, yet he persistently engaged in defending the territorial rights of Spain. He gave his opinion on the correct interpretation of the treaties and classified certain Portuguese activities as violations. He authored "notes" on the demarcation between the two countries that analyzed lines of longitude and where they passed, interpreted the 1681 provisional treaty, and rejected Portuguese claims to territories possessed against formal agreements or without formal license. Fritz also criticized the Portuguese for engaging in indigenous slavery and affirmed the rights of Jesuits to the territories that they had conquered (conquistado). In his frequent reports to his superiors, Fritz described his success at establishing missions, as well as the hostility of the Portuguese who, according to him, were interested only in capturing slaves, engaging in commercial activities, and collecting cacao. Fritz's involvement depended on firsthand information that he acquired by exploring and living in the territory, but he also cited historians, geographers, and jurists. His contribution to the defense of Spain's territorial rights became a legend among his contemporaries. Some considered him not only a missionary but also a cosmograph because, while he enthusiastically converted the natives, he also registered and recognized the Amazon River, searching for its origin, measuring distances, describing the other rivers that joined it and the mountains along it, and eventually (in 1706) drawing a map of the region.[23] This map was sent to Madrid and became extremely helpful in negotiations with Portugal in the 1730s and 1740s.

The involvement of Spanish Jesuits in the border conflict extended to questions of strategy. For example, in the 1730s and 1740s, Spanish Jesuits expressed their opinion on whether the confrontation would be best resolved by sending troops or by attempting (yet another round of) negotiations, and they advocated in favor of establishing settlements in the interior and arming mission Indians.[24] It is also possible that in 1761 Spanish Jesuits were instrumental in convincing Spanish authorities to annul the Treaty of Madrid. Records indicate that, besides the allegation that they had encouraged "their" Indians to disobey the order to evacuate the territory that was to be handed to Portugal (I will return to this episode below), they also appeared before both local and metropolitan authorities to insist on the practical difficulties and the political impossibility of implementing the treaty.[25] Because they accused the Portuguese of wanting to conquer the entire continent, the Jesuits also argued that Portugal's coveting of the territory of the missions was only a prelude to what it truly attempted to do.

Jesuits belonging to the Spanish province of the order may have been particularly active, yet Portuguese Jesuits probably fulfilled similar roles. At the request of the king or of their own volition, they wrote manuscripts defending the rights of Portugal to Colonia de Sacramento and the Amazon basin. Lamenting that royal ministers were often ignorant of Portugal's rights, Portuguese Jesuits instructed them as to what these were, explaining where the line of Tordesillas lay and assuring them that Spanish Jesuits were in the wrong. Like their colleagues working for Spain, Portuguese Jesuits suggested that their duty to aid the natives spiritually forced them to engage in matters "more proper for soldiers than for priests."[26] If Fritz, native of Bohemia, was particularly active among Spanish Jesuits, Aloísio Conrado Pfeil, his contemporary, friend, and admirer, a native of Switzerland, fulfilled the same role in Portugal.[27] Not only did he write various manifestos regarding the rights of this country vis-à-vis both France and Spain, he also drew maps that, sent to Lisbon, became particularly influential during bilateral negotiations between the courts.

Friars got involved in the territorial conflict because, like settlers, natives, military commanders, and governors, they wished to pursue certain activities without suffering competition or facing challenges. They wrote and received missives, corresponded with one another as well as with the authorities of both sides, and, on occasions, even risked their liberty or lives defending their cause. The activities of Fritz can serve again as an example. While convalescing in Belém do Pará (Portuguese territories) in 1690, he was accused of spying for Spain and of having established missions in Portuguese territory. According to Aloísio Conrad Pfeil, who reported on this incident to the Jesuit superior in Rome, as soon as Fritz—whom he called a saintly man, clearly in a sign of his admiration—arrived in the city, rumors circulated that he had illegally occupied Portuguese territory.[28] Taking measures that, according to Pfeil, had "never been seen or heard of before and contravened the law of nations, customary and Portuguese law, and royal interests," the governor of Pará prohibited Fritz from leaving the city until the king could be consulted. Pfeil expressed uncertainty over why this had happened, that is, whether the governor truly considered Fritz an explorer for Spain or whether his decision expressed more general hostility toward the Jesuits. Pfeil criticized Jódoco Peres, the superior of the order in Belém, for siding with the governor without consulting with the other friars. He reasoned that the superior was perhaps frightened by the reaction of the governor; that he perhaps believed that by obeying the governor he was defending the jurisdiction of the king; but Pfeil concluded that Peres acted against the interests of both the Jesuit order and its vassals, namely, the Indians of Cambedas, who depended on Fritz. Pfeil said that all local Jesuits agreed with this analysis and believed that Peres had committed a mistake that gravely offended both the Jesuit general in Rome and the Catholic king of Spain. Because his attempts to change the governor's decision failed, Pfeil recommended that Fritz write to the Portuguese monarch, who he trusted would order his release. Summarizing his argument, Pfeil expressed concern not only with saving indigenous souls but also with the reputation of his order. He feared Spaniards might follow this (bad) example and imprison Jesuits working for Portugal who, following royal orders, also engaged in expanding their missions in the American interior. Was it not better, he asked, to allow Jesuits to work peacefully without involving them in territorial issues? This question, he insisted, was not "mere metaphysics." It required a clear and immediate answer.

When news of Fritz's ordeal arrived in Lisbon, the Portuguese monarch ordered his release. What happened next remains unclear. According to Fritz's diary, the local governor ordered that he be taken back to his mission by Portuguese troops sent allegedly to ensure his safe conduct but in reality to protest against Castilian penetration into an area that the Portuguese considered their own, also taking possession of it. According to Portuguese narratives, Fritz prohibited the soldiers from following him because he wanted to avoid Portuguese presence on what he argued was Spanish soil. According to yet a third version, Fritz convinced the Portuguese commander that Portuguese claims were unsound. According to a fourth, he responded to Portuguese claims by arguing that there was no point in protesting to him against illegal Castilian occupation because, as a friar working for the church, he was not a party to the discussion. But whatever might have happened on the return journey, there were abundant indications that Fritz was well aware of what was at stake in making one allegation or the other. Fearing Portuguese interference with his missions (present and future), he traveled to Quito in order to convince the authorities that his missionary work, as well as the rights of the crown of Castile to the territory, should be actively defended.[29] Because the governor of Mainas, whom he met on his way, suggested it would be better to go to Lima rather than Quito, he made his entry into the vice-regal capital in July 1692, creating a true spectacle. Tall and red-headed, dressed as a pilgrim and accompanied by Indians, he was ceremoniously un- and re-dressed by the Jesuit provincial despite his protests that he wanted to remain in his old, humble, and ragged cloths. The Count of Moncloa, viceroy of Peru, confessed to be a great admirer of Fritz's work, which involved "liberating single-handedly so many people

from the ancient tyranny of the devil," but he nevertheless refused
to give Fritz true assistance. Each time Fritz brought up the Portuguese and their expansionist policies, the viceroy responded that
they, too, were Christians and Catholics. The Portuguese, he explained to Fritz, were belligerent people *(gente belicosa)*, and the Indians to whom he preached did not offer any of the financial profits
that other provinces whose defense was also necessary did *(aquellos
bosques en lo temporal no fructifican al rey de España como otras muchas
provincias)*.[30] At any rate, the Americas were enormous and had
sufficient space for both crowns to expand as they wished. Disap-
pointed, Fritz submitted to the viceroy a formal petition, in which
he explained that Jesuits had succeeded in conquering the Amazon
River but that, although their success was spectacular, they now
faced the Portuguese in Rio Negro and required help in the form
of soldiers and financial support. The protector of royal interests
(fiscal) agreed, yet in the spring of 1693 the viceroy decided to supply
Fritz with only very limited, one-time financial support and practically no men.

This was to become the most common answer Spanish authorities gave to Jesuit appeals. In 1711, the *audiencia* of Quito responded
so halfheartedly to similar requests that the Jesuit provincial concluded that there was no hope that it would support the mission fi-
nancially or militarily.[31] All it was willing to do was to order the
governor of Mainas and Quijos, the Spanish province closest to the
area in contention, to defend the Napo River with his Indians, imprisoning, if he could, any Portuguese roaming the territory. Yet
the governor, who in 1694 did engage in exploration and conquest,
was no longer interested in subjugating Indians, let alone confronting the Portuguese.[32] The Council of the Indies criticized him in
1719 for failing to do so, but contemporaries understood that the
commission he received was impossible. Many of them also knew it
was less than innocent. The year he was sent to stop the Portuguese
(1711) was precisely the time in which the magistrates of the royal
court *(audiencia de Quito)* had refused to give his firstborn and successor (Juan Bautista Sánchez de Orellana) possession of his office
as royal judge *(oidor)* on the grounds that he lacked juridical training and was too young.

The confrontation between Fritz and the Portuguese degenerated in the following years in part because of the growing Portuguese interest in the territory and partly because in 1693 this area,
once the responsibility of Portuguese Jesuits, was assigned to the
Calced Carmelite order *(carmelitas calzados)*. As early as 1697, Portuguese Carmelites, accompanied by troops, tried to take possession
of their newly assigned mission territory, immediately coming into
conflict with Spanish Jesuits who argued that the area was Spanish
and Jesuit rather than Portuguese and Carmelite. Fritz, who again
understood what was at stake, requested that Carmelites and their
companions delay possession taking so that he could exchange letters with their superiors regarding the respective rights of both
countries. By that stage, Fritz's familiarity with the judicial jargon
and formulas of his period was astounding. During the 1697 encounter, he formally announced to the Portuguese commander (by
way of *requerimiento*) who he was ("Father Samuel, a Jesuit, missionary of the crown of Castile in this river"), why he protested ("because you, by order of the governor of Pará, with armed company,
have come to these provinces more than 800 leagues from Pará to
Peru, where I, from 1688, for the crown of Castile without prejudice
to Portuguese conquests, or controversy, have worked peacefully
until now as a missionary, and now you come with Carmelite friars
to introduce them here as missionaries and in this way expel me
from this mission") and what he requested ("I demand that you do
not introduce any innovations that would harm my work until the
two crowns decide on their respective limits").[33] Fritz then demanded that the Portuguese commander certify in writing that he
had received the admonition. The Portuguese officer, no less knowledgeable in the etiquette of protest and counterprotest, responded
to him that he had been sent by the governor to give the Carmelites
possession of their assigned missions. He also declared that although
the courts should decide on the limits of both states, an ancient demarcation that was established during the union of the crowns (the
Teixeira expedition) convinced him that the territory was Portuguese. The Carmelites also engaged in the debate.[34] They explained
to Fritz that his allegations were frivolous and designed to enlarge, rather than safeguard, Spanish territories. They argued that

his interpretation of the degrees of longitude and the direction of the demarcation set in papal bulls was mistaken and that the Portuguese had already taken possession of that territory in 1639, when Teixeira placed a demarcation stone, dividing both crowns. The Carmelites were not attempting to proselytize outside their limits; rather he, Fritz, was some 300 leagues inside Portuguese territory. If the Portuguese had agreed to his presence this far, it was mainly because they did not want to deprive natives of spiritual guidance (*pasto espiritual*). But now that the Carmelites were in place and were willing to do the same, Jesuit help was no longer necessary. At any rate, because Fritz was in Portuguese territory with Portuguese knowledge and consent, his activities could not constitute occupation for Spain. After all, it would be as if by living in Pará he claimed rights to that city. Thus, while the Carmelite superior reprimanded Fritz, reminding him that missionaries should convert people, not preach about degrees and demarcations, he also engaged in these discussions and warned Fritz that he would be imprisoned if he continued in his (illegal) activities. He reported to Fritz that the Jesuit superior of Pará sided with the Carmelites and even produced a letter to that effect, in which the superior told Fritz of his duties as a Jesuit. Portuguese Carmelites also sent emissaries to Quito to discuss their allegations, and their representative there, Wenceslao Braer, was well received and heard by the *audiencia*. Yet, while the Carmelite superior argued that Fritz acknowledged that he was in the wrong and left the territory so that the Portuguese could establish missions on it, in his diary Fritz told a completely different story about a false Portuguese claim that the Indians had chosen to ally with and to convert under them as well as about Portuguese aggression that violently forced his evacuation.

In 1702, Fritz met again with the Carmelites and Portuguese officers and soldiers "in order to discuss the limits of these missions."[35] The meeting apparently ended in an understanding that allowed for peace during the following years. Hostilities, however, reinitiated in 1707, when the Carmelites complained to the governor of Pará and the Portuguese king that Spanish Jesuits had once again invaded their missions. While the Carmelites demanded that the monarch build a fort because only the presence of soldiers could halt the

Spanish (in the form of Jesuit) advance, the king responded that Carmelites must settle these differences alone because, on the basis of what his advisers suggested, he believed the problem was generated not by territorial debates but by rivalries among orders. Precisely for that reason, Portuguese royal officials also maintained that it would have been much easier to reach an understanding had Portuguese Jesuits, rather than Carmelites, been in charge of these missions. Following the same rationale, the Portuguese Overseas Council (Conselho Ultramarino) concluded by asserting that though territorial questions were important, the salvation of indigenous souls was more so. As a result, it was better to allow Spanish Jesuits to work in the region than to have no friars there at all. Nonetheless, while both courts suggested moderation, in the heartland of South America, Jesuits imprisoned Carmelites, Carmelites imprisoned Jesuits, and missions were fortified, abandoned, and destroyed. Portuguese and Spanish troops roamed the territory, exchanging prisoners and looting churches.

Best known for his (frenetic) activities, Fritz was not the only friar involved in these exchanges. In 1707, the Spanish Jesuit Juan Bautista received in his mission Portuguese troops accompanied by a Carmelite friar.[36] The captain in charge argued that the party was only looking for fugitives who had escaped the Carmelite mission, yet Juan Bautista responded by insisting on Spanish rights. The Indians they were looking for, he stated, were Spanish, as was the territory. The captain disagreed, arguing that they were Portuguese, as was the land. The conflict escalated in the following years after the governor of Pará gave orders to evacuate all (Spanish) Jesuits from missions allegedly founded on Portuguese territory and return (restituir) their Indians to Portugal.[37] The Jesuits answered by informing the governor about the rights of Spain and by writing to their superiors and the Quito royal authorities. In response, the president of the *audiencia* corresponded with the Portuguese, while the Council of Indies, also informed of what had transpired, instructed the Spanish ambassador in Lisbon to lodge a formal protest.[38] As debate continued in the courts, so did negotiations in the American interior. The Jesuits sent missives to the Portuguese governor to protest that their missions were not where he had imagined and assuring him that they had never accepted Indians who were vassals of Portugal.[39] The Jesuits even offered the governor a truce: though the father superior acknowledged that he could not discuss the rights of Spain and though he was certain he was right, he was nevertheless willing to stop Jesuit penetration in the area until he received orders from Madrid. He expected Portuguese Carmelites to do the same. At his request, the Portuguese governor of Pará sent a "capable person" to the Jesuit mission where the superior resided to discuss the rights of both powers.[40] The individual selected, Belchior Mendes y Moraes, was a sergeant major with "capacity, valor and practice." He arrived at the Spanish mission in 1732 with "authentic documents" (*instrumentos autênticos*) demonstrating the rights of Portugal to the territory extending from Pará to the Napo River. His instructions, he explained, were to "adjust the limits [between the two crowns], ending the disturbances that for some time now have confronted the vassals of the two monarchies."[41] If his claims were accepted, he would immediately proceed to build a fort on the banks of the Napo, thus visually demarcating the territory as Portuguese. The Jesuits, however, rejected these plans. In a letter to the Portuguese governor of Pará, their superior agreed that it would be preferable to settle these matters once and for all, but he also said, "there was no authorized person here to perform this investigation regarding the division and legitimate demarcation of these lands for the crown of Castile."[42] He, father superior, could not take part in such debates because he was but a "poor ecclesiastic" (*pobre religioso*) who lacked understanding (*capacidad corta*) and was not empowered to speak for Castile. Having said that, the Jesuit addressed the territorial question directly. He also warned the Portuguese sergeant-major against building the fort and began arming the mission Indians. At this stage, the president of the *audiencia* of Quito reentered the conversation.[43] Accusing Portuguese officials and Carmelites of "wanting to reverse and confuse the limits already fixed for the jurisdiction of both monarchies" (*invertir y confundir los determinados lindes de las jurisdicciones de ambas monarquías*), he mocked the governor of Pará for wishing to become a "legislator of domains that the wise judgment of the apostolic seat has determined" (*a constituirse legislador de unos dominios que tiene determinados el sabio juicio de la silla apostólica*). Backing the position already taken by the Jesuits and invoking both bulls and possession, the president argued that Spain and the Jesuits had legitimate rights in the region and requested that the governor of Pará control "his" Carmelites. The courts were interested in preserving the peace and would certainly want an alliance rather than a confrontation. In a second letter to the Portuguese governor, the president of Quito also formally objected to the construction of a fort on the banks of the Napo. In 1737, when the new Jesuit superior received word of a possible Portuguese attack against Spanish missions, he rushed to the contested area and awaited the arrival of the Portuguese, arms in hand.[44] The troops that arrived, however, claimed that their sole intention was to verify whether Jesuits were indeed penetrating Portuguese territories, as had been rumored. The superior requested that they define what "Portuguese territories" were, but the sergeant refused to do so because, according to him, he was not authorized to engage in such debates. The Jesuit interpreted his answer as an excuse: it allowed the Portuguese, he said, to modify constantly what they claimed as their own. Taking advantage of their presence in the mission, the superior protested against the occupation of "Jesuit territories" by (Portuguese) Carmelites. The territories of Castile, he argued, were much wider than the Portuguese pretended. Indeed, they reached all the way to Belém. This time, the governor of Pará answered with sarcasm. It was not his duty to dispute the status and meaning of the papal bulls upon which Jesuits argued their case, but he observed that for the last 240 years Spaniards had never based their claims on the bulls.[45] Why were the Jesuits taking this road now? Mocking their allegations, the Portuguese governor also asked whether Spanish ministers and ambassadors knew about these bulls; how could the pope, who could not even appropriate for his own family a portion of Italy, give so freely half the world to Spain? The inability of the crowns to arrive at a compromise in conversations in Badajoz and Elvas in the 1520s and 1680s, as well as in subsequent meetings and conquests, demonstrated that the bulls had been de facto and de jure overridden. The Jesuits should not complain against the Portuguese because, if it were not for the latter, the Jesuits could not have proselytized in the region at all, because it would have fallen under Dutch (heretic) sovereignty. The

Portuguese governor concluded his letter arguing that what he and his predecessors suggested as a division was a moderate solution, indeed a compromise. The Portuguese could lay claim to a much wider territory than they had so far, but they refrained from doing so because they wanted to maintain peaceful relations with Spaniards. He also suggested that the problem was not how the Portuguese or Spaniards behaved but the ambitions of the Jesuits. Because what was at stake were missionary activities, not territorial rights, the governor offered yet another solution: he would be willing to allow the presence of Jesuits "all the way to Pará" if such a presence were not used to make territorial claims.

Theories linking conversion to subjugation and missions to possession not only intensified the race to win over natives, they also constantly raised the question of which was the higher cause: salvation of the souls or territorial domination. As the viceroy of Peru suggested to Fritz in 1692, the Portuguese Overseas Council asserted in 1709, and the governor of Pará argued in 1737, in theory what mattered most was to support the evangelization process independently of the question of who carried it out. Yet, in practice, the political implications of establishing missions were far too important to ignore, and they justified a growing confrontation between royal officials and missionaries, who often were perceived as worse enemies than rival European powers. Because Spanish Jesuits were particularly successful in penetrating the American interior, the Portuguese were especially vehement in presenting them as their true antagonists.[46] Arguing that Jesuits rather than Spaniards were intruding on their territories and presenting their quarrel with them not as a religious issue—which order under which power would convert natives—but as a political contest for land, the Marquís of Fronteira, a member of the Portuguese council of state, stated in the 1680s that in the seventeenth century Italian Jesuits had violently occupied Portuguese territories without title or permission, to the displeasure of both crowns.[47] For the Portuguese, classifying Jesuits as agents of the Spanish state justified taking military action against them. It even enabled the Portuguese to argue that Paulistas, who roamed the interior searching for slaves, commerce, and mines and who attacked and destroyed Jesuit missions, were in reality patriots moved by the wish to defend Portuguese territory against Spanish (in the form of Jesuit) aggression.[48] Because the Jesuits' presence was interpreted as a territorial incursion by a foreign power, the Portuguese could also argue that compatriots who helped these friars could be accused of the crime of lèse-majesté.[49] While useful to the Portuguese, the confrontation also aided the Jesuits, who could advocate successfully the militarization of their missions. As a result of these developments, from as early as the 1630s, the Jesuits organized, trained, supplied, and commanded native troops. Initially charged with defending their settlements against Portuguese attacks, these forces by the mid-seventeenth century also participated in military engagements elsewhere, for example, in Paraguay, Santa Cruz de la Sierra (present-day Bolivia), Colonia de Sacramento, and Montevideo (present-day Uruguay), to name just a few.[50] Native troops also explored the interior, patrolled the countryside, and arrested criminals.[51]

The involvement of missionaries in converting natives, bringing about their vassalage on the one hand, defending territorial rights on the other, gave rise to controversy. Were missionaries loyal to the state and willing to defend its territorial rights, or were they interested only in conversion?[52] Did they indoctrinate Indians to love their monarch? These debates formed part of a more generalized questioning, which was particularly acute in the case of the Jesuit order. Common in Europe and the Americas long before the order was expelled (1759 and 1767) and disbanded (1773), from the early seventeenth century Jesuits were routinely accused of wanting to form a republic of their own. According to the allegations, they subjected "their" Indians not to the king but to their order. Instead of training natives to resist enemies, they habituated them to oppose royal demands, making friars, not the monarch, the true masters of the land.[53] These charges became so frequent that by the second half of the seventeenth century, the Jesuit representative (*procurador*) in Madrid complained it was impossible to answer them all.[54] Motivated by conflict with other religious orders (over how to convert natives and who would do so best) and fueled by concerns regarding control over native labor and taxation (which settlers wanted to impose), these debates and cross-accusations placed Jesuits in confrontation with other friars, local ecclesiastical powers, local and royal authorities, as well as society at large. As a result of these tensions, not only were the Portuguese opposed to the Spaniards, not only did they each confront the Indians, but both also had to deal with social, political, economic, and religious pressures favoring or censuring the different religious orders that were alternately presented as the best allies or the worst enemies.

The events following the Treaty of Madrid (1750) were perhaps the best demonstration of how these tensions could overlap, mutually aggravating one another. The execution of this treaty between Spain and Portugal required the evacuation of seven Spanish Jesuit missions from a territory now ceded to Portugal. On that occasion, many Indians—perhaps backed by Jesuits, perhaps not (the debate still continues[55])—refused to abandon their settlements, which they defended against a mixed Spanish–Portuguese military force. Those criticizing the Jesuits were convinced that their "long hand" was behind indigenous protests and, eventually, indigenous armed resistance to the evacuation of the missions; those favoring the Jesuits (and Jesuits themselves) answered that these accusations were absurd. But whatever the case might have been, in the decades following the signature of the treaty, Indian resistance, echoes of which reached Europe, became symbolic of the danger of allowing missionaries to represent the state in the interior vis-à-vis the native population and foreign powers. Did Jesuits encourage their Indians to disobey royal orders? Did they join them in resisting expulsion? Jesuit involvement with the Treaty of Madrid began long before it was adopted. From the late 1740s, Jesuits sent missives to the Spanish king and his confessor, first asking him not to sign the treaty and then criticizing him for ignoring their plea. Jesuits appealed to the king's conscience, arguing that converted Indians would return to their pagan ways if missions were dismantled or handed over to the Portuguese.[56] They also said the king could not unilaterally abandon Indians who were his vassals. According to their rivals, Jesuits not only claimed that the treaty was prejudicial, they also suggested that the king was fooled by the Portuguese into signing it and argued that he had no true dominion of the Americas and no right to cede the territory (*negándole a su majestad el verdadero do-*

*minio de esta América y el derecho y facultad para ceder y enajenar aquel-
las tierras)*, which was indigenous rather than royal.[57]

Discussion regarding the legality and wisdom of the treaty took place in Paraguay (the area most affected), in various American capitals, and in Europe. It involved the participation of natives who verbally protested the evacuation order, discussed the justness of their cause with the military commanders and priests who came to implement it, and sent missives to the authorities in Buenos Aires insisting that because the land was theirs, it could not be given to Portugal without their consent.[58] Yet the discussions also included a great variety of other actors who were not directly affected by what had been agreed upon. Evidence suggests, for example, that debates regarding the 1750 treaty took place in Buenos Aires when friends met to discuss the news of the day, during and after Mass, and among office holders.[59] Pamphlets and counter-pamphlets circulated, discrediting or defending the Jesuits, supporting or criticizing the king. The controversy might have been so widespread and involved so many individuals that it undermined the authority of government. Such, at least, was the impression of the incoming governor of Buenos Aires, who in 1767 argued that the city was infested with people who openly questioned the behavior of the king *(llena de inquietudes y de muchas especies sediciosas)*.[60] In Europe, the debate, which produced a vast literature in France, the Low Countries, Italy, and Spain, portrayed the Jesuits as a paradigm for infidelity and disloyalty.[61] According to some historians, these visions were at least partially responsible for the decision first to expel the Jesuits (from Portugal in 1759; France in 1764; and Spain, Austria, and the Two Sicilies in 1767) and then to disband the order altogether (in 1773).[62] Jesuits' bad reputation persisted thereafter. The former governor of Buenos Aires in 1770 accused his counterpart of Paraguay of willfully allowing Portuguese settlement on Spanish territory, imitating what the Jesuits, his mentors and sponsors, had done in the past.[63] The very same year and hundreds of miles away, a Portuguese captain, wishing to convince "Spanish Indians" that they would be better off under Portugal, hoped to enlist fugitive (imaginary?) Jesuits to his cause by writing them letters asking for their support.[64] Indian resistance and the role Jesuits may have played in promoting it also generated speculation as to what would happen in the region next. Would Jesuits incite the Indians again? Would they attempt to build another republic? In the 1750s and 1760s, constant rumors circulated that Indian armies, led by Jesuits, might invade Portuguese territories.[65] In 1767, Portuguese officials in Lisbon feared that some Spanish Jesuits might penetrate Portuguese domains and attempt to influence their natives. Other pieces of news pointed to the possibility that Jesuits were again gathering Indian troops or that they might join forces with the Portuguese in order to fight nonconverted Indians.[66] These rumors continued even after the expulsion of the Jesuits from Spain and Spanish America, suggesting that some Jesuits might have remained in the territory and might be living among natives, even acting as native chiefs (caciques).[67] Becoming increasingly fantastic over time, these stories described Jesuits married to multiple native wives, procreating many children, and accumulating many vassals. Attempts to verify this information in 1772, for example, proved it could be based on mere suppositions. In that case, it originated in the report of an acculturated Indian (indio ladino) who had seen a white man who might have been Spanish leading a group of infidel Indians. Because these Indians called him "partiro," which in their language meant "father," the witness assumed the leader was a Jesuit. But even if rumors were unfounded, it is nevertheless clear that even after their expulsion and disbandment, the Jesuits continued to serve as experts and were asked for their opinion on how to conserve the missions they had left, which indigenous nations should be subjected next, which roads and settlements were necessary, and how to organize resistance to the Portuguese who "as neighbors wished to introduce themselves into the territory or perhaps already had."[68] Fears of friars controlling Indians and encouraging insubordination persisted into the 1800s.[69]

The territorial conflict between Spain and Portugal thus also involved the struggle over the right, presented as privilege, to convert Indians. Conversion was useful for the state—which received in return new vassals and territories—but it also confronted rival orders and rival provinces of the same order over people and land. Because of their location in a particularly troublesome site, Jesuits working for Spain and Carmelites working for Portugal became entangled in discussions that often degenerated into bitter accusations.[70] These led the Jesuits to complain that the Carmelites violently infringed on their jurisdiction by attacking their missions, capturing their Indians, and causing sufficient panic among natives as to encourage many of them to seek refuge in the woods.[71] Whereas Jesuits had no weapons other than their speech *(su sagrado instituto y predicación evangélica)*, Carmelites were the armed chiefs *(caudillos)* of Portuguese troops. The Jesuits also asserted that the Carmelites did not care about the salvation of souls; they only pursued commercial profit. The Carmelites responded that their missionary activity was constantly harmed by the Jesuits, who penetrated Portuguese and thus "Carmelite" territories.[72] The Jesuits, they argued, convinced "their" Indians to flee and join Jesuit settlements by telling them that the Portuguese did not protect their Indians. Indeed, rather than Carmelites attacking Jesuits, the inverse was true: the real aggressors were the Jesuits, who constantly sought to expand their territories and thus the territories of their state. Because the confrontation pitted Jesuits against Carmelites, both Spaniards and the Portuguese suggested on occasions that the conflict between both countries would immediately cease if the Amazon basin were missionized by Jesuits and Jesuits alone. Nonetheless, although collaboration across provinces and countries did exist—Jesuits from Lima, for example, recruited the help of their Brazilian counterparts to missionize Indians whose language those friars spoke—it was infrequent. Furthermore, on occasions, it seemed to harm rather than advance missionary goals because, suspecting that Portuguese Jesuits might be informing their Spanish brethren of Portuguese plans to attack them, the Portuguese authorities often considered them a fifth column. They thus preferred not to seek their support, believing that they spied for Spain or even supported its territorial claims.[73] Cross-provincial rivalries were, on the contrary, frequent. They were clear, for example, when in the late seventeenth century Fritz was arrested in Belém do Pará by the Jesuit superior against the protests of some (but not all) of his brethren. And if not all Jesuits were necessarily friends, neither were all Carmelites necessarily their enemies. In 1746, a (Spanish) Jesuit recommended to the Carmelite superior in Lisbon the person of Domingo de Santa Teresa, who was a missionary in the village next to his.[74] Describing him as "one of the many suns that the Carmelite order provided the world, illuminating it with the light of their sanctity, knowledge, doctrine, and zeal," he explained that in the eleven years in which Domingo resided in the Amazon region, he had enlarged the territories of his mission by converting many natives and rebuilding abandoned settlements. Expressing a pan-missionary vision that rejoiced at the salvation of souls rather than worried about territorial expansion, the Jesuit described his frequent visits to Carmelite territory and the mutual admiration and hospitality that both friars enjoyed.

Given the importance of conversion and the tensions it generated, it is surprising that contemporary records hardly ever mentioned the well-known fact that most Jesuits and many Carmelites working for Spain and Portugal in the American interior were foreigners, at times even Portuguese in Spanish territories, or Spaniards in Portuguese lands.[75] Downplaying such factors, the Portuguese identified foreign friars—for example, Samuel Fritz—as "Castilian" because of their loyalty to Spain.[76] The Jesuits played into this game, too, referring to themselves as barriers to Portuguese excursions and explaining that natives have not seen "any other governor or Spaniard" except for them (*no han visto estos indios más gobernador ni español que a mí*). Both Fritz (a native of Bohemia) and Juan Bautista (a native of Germanic territories) followed this route, referring to the Catholic monarchs as "their" monarchs and identifying themselves as "missionaries for Castile."

Rather than being "national" (avant la lettre) or purely territorial, the conflict between Spain and Portugal thus also involved rivalries between different religious orders. It provoked debates over whether conversion was more important than extending royal sovereignty and territory, and it required determining how Indians (and their lands) could be subjected to Europeans and who would accomplish it first. Missionaries got involved in such discussions because their activity depended on royal permission but also because they hoped to recruit financial and military support to the conversion effort. Unauthorized to discuss who should be expanding where, friars frequently ended up elaborating on the rights of the monarch and country that sponsored or allowed their activities, in the process becoming not only conquerors and pacifiers but also councilors, diplomats, jurists, and military men.

The participation of friars in discovering, conquering, overpowering, and converting Indians continued into the late 1810s. However, over time, the nature of clerical involvement was somewhat modified. Vital in the first period, in which the "state" was almost completely absent in the American interior, by the mid- to late eighteenth century, religious efforts at conversion coincided with attempts to take hold of the territory and its people in other ways. During this period, the presence of soldiers, scientists, settlers, and civic authorities in the American interior substantially increased.[77] Many penetrated the region with the hope of improving their living conditions. Others were sent there in order to implement the treaties signed in 1750 and 1777 by the Spanish and Portuguese monarchs. Yet a third group manned the fortifications, which Spain and Portugal constructed as a means to address both Indian and European hostility. Members of a fourth group arrived in the New World in order to engage in "enlightened" projects, motivated by the wish to improve the local economy or to gather scientific information. This growing presence was also accompanied by reforms whose declared goal in Portuguese territories at least was to transform the missions into state-run settlements by removing them from the religious orders and placing them under secular authorities.[78] The "secularization of the missions," as these efforts were labeled, involved a formal integration policy that would make natives both vassals and Portuguese, but it also produced the (relatively) massive penetration of administrative and military personnel in areas where their presence had been scarce. Because of all these factors, by the mid- to late eighteenth century, religious control gave way to a new type of conversion that instead stressed indigenous political allegiance and acculturation.

As with other contemporaries, many of the individuals who arrived in the interior in the eighteenth and early nineteenth centuries might have not cared for territorial issues, yet their presence greatly affected the conflict. If, once upon a time, friars were the best but also practically the only informants on what was happening in the interior, by the mid- to late eighteenth century, information also flowed from many other directions. Military men, settlers, administrators, promoters of economic activities, and scientists gradually became major actors on the political and diplomatic scene. As the friars had done before them, they informed the courts and local authorities about how to proceed, collected information, and negotiated with rival parties. Their activities, including exploring and using the land, were also means by which to press additional territorial claims.[79] This growing involvement led to the proliferation of a new type of literature. Many of the individuals who had been to the American interior wrote memoirs and diaries in which they recounted their personal experiences and described the region.[80] They reported on the character and behavior of Indians, the movements of enemy troops, and routes that might be opened and territories that might be discovered. They drew maps, which communicated the message that the interior was not only known and reachable, it could even be subdued, as could its inhabitants. Some such experts became so notable as to be appointed formal advisers to kings, their opinions being solicited not only on practical but also on juridical matters. In 1747, for example, Jorge Juan and Antonio Ulloa—who were sent to the Americas to accompany a French scientific mission mainly interested in studying the shape of the earth—wrote an essay analyzing the rights of Spain and Portugal.[81] Beginning their survey with the history of the conflict reaching back to the papal donation and the Treaty of Tordesillas, Juan and Ulloa proceeded to investigate, validate, or deny the scientific interpretations proposed by the experts of both sides. Concluding that, contrary to what had happened before, the scientific conflict could be settled now that both parties had enough information regarding the region and science had sufficiently advanced, Juan and Ulloa nevertheless mainly addressed the question of right by possession, citing the many authors who had confirmed the discoveries and occupation by Spaniards. Although favorable to the Spanish cause, because of its highly detailed nature this essay was kept secret for over two decades. It was picked up in the 1770s by the Spanish negotiators and was only then made public.[82] Similarly, in 1780 Francisco Xavier Mendes de Morais, a slave trader living in the interior since 1725 who had already in 1775 provided testimony regarding the legitimacy of Portuguese claims to Rio Branco, wrote at the request of the governor of Rio Negro a report concerning the territory and its river system that supported, and thus became part of, Portuguese claims to that territory.[83] A well-known *sertanista* who was considered a "very practical man in these interiors" *(homem muito prático destes sertões)*, he also suggested in his essay others who could be asked for their opinion and who among Indians, settlers, and Portuguese knew the territory best. Similar to advice given by missionaries, documents elaborated by these "experts" became extremely influential, supplying the crowns and local authorities with scientific and factual information with which to support their claims. They became a new weapon, secular and scientific, in the struggle to affirm rights. Yet, although "science" was said to be impartial and universally true, it is nevertheless clear that in all these cases it was conceived as an instrument servicing the state and benefiting the patria *(al servicio del estado y al mayor beneficio de la patria)*.[84]

If, on the one hand, during the mid- to late eighteenth century the nature of European presence in the American interior was greatly modified, on the other, during this period treaties with not-yet-subjected Indians substantially grew in number. In part a response to theories that natives had "natural freedom" to choose whether they wanted to submit to Europeans and that only a reciprocal convention, not force nor even conversion, could determine personal and territorial subjection, in part the result of geopolitical considerations, the passage from conversion to pacts allowed monarchs to obtain greater control over developments in the American interior. It also led to the elaboration of new theories that sustained that after Indians contracted with Europeans rather than becoming partners or allies, both they and, most important, their lands became the property of that crown. Contemporaries referred to this reality when they asserted that by subjecting himself to Spain, the local Indian chief "gave this territory, where he lived, to us" *(la entrega de este territorio a nosotros)*.[85] Similarly, when the indigenous captain Mariano Camaydevena requested in 1784 submission to Spain rather than Portugal *(quería estar bajo la dominación española y no portuguesa)*, the Spanish local authorities responded with enthusiasm.[86] His adherence to Spain, they suggested, was of no small consequence because after Mariano became Spanish, so did his territory. Portuguese reforms granting Indians subjecthood in 1755 as a result might have not had indigenous well-being as their focal point. Instead, they might have implied that now that Indians living in the former missions were Portuguese, so was their land. Because changes in indigenous political adhesion had territorial effects, it is also possible that the Portuguese so-called conquest of the seven Paraguayan missions in 1801 was not truly a military enterprise. Historians now argue that it consisted instead of a series of negotiations with local residents who were dissatisfied with conditions under Spain and who decided to become Portuguese.[87] This was, in short, a pacific conquest that changed the allegiance of local residents rather than took over land.

Because submission to Europeans granted land rights, on many occasions in the 1770s, 1780s, and 1790s, Spanish commanders accused their Portuguese counterparts of "taking" *(extraer)* or "stealing" *(robar)* "their" Indians.[88] Calling these activities "piracy," Spaniards argued that the Portuguese invaded native villages belonging to Spain, captured their inhabitants and moved them, sometimes en masse, to Portugal. Upset by the prospects of losing Indian laborers and settlers, Spaniards who protested these actions were also aware of their territorial implications. The natives the Portuguese captured, they argued, belonged to "nations friendly with Spaniards" *(afectas a España)*, were already conquered by Spain *(conquistadas por España)*, were vassals of the crown, or were outright Spaniards. If they allowed the Portuguese to remove them, the Portuguese would soon be proprietors of all the land *(dueños de todas aquellas tierras)*.[89] That the struggle over people had territorial effects was particularly clear in complaints that a Portuguese official voiced in 1765, according to which, using "good politics," Spaniards had contracted friendship with local natives. Their success, he explained, was prejudicial to Portugal because it threatened its "dominions and conquests."[90]

Historical records thus clarify that not only territory but also people were up for grabs and that both could be possessed and become the property of one power or the other. Because territory could be acquired by integrating people, thereafter both powers competed over which would incorporate more Indians more quickly.

As a result, although in their discussions with one another Spaniards and Portuguese focused on bilateral agreements and European legal doctrines (see Chapter 1), the dynamics that took shape in the American interior suggested that equally, and perhaps even more important, to determining their rights was the presence of Indians, both allied and enemy. Natives could of course be possessed by conversion, yet, as the eighteenth century unfolded and as European presence in the interior intensified, natives often became civic rather than religious targets who were to be occupied by making them allies first, Christians second. Coinciding with disappointment at the perceived failure of the conversion effort and with a conviction that natives hindered rather than facilitated European presence, and that they played the Portuguese and Spaniards against each other, contemporaries suggested that if Spaniards refused to accept native trading conditions, natives would then threaten to deal with the inhabitants of the other power. And, if their demands were not met, they swore they would ally with the enemies.[91] The move to attempt direct understanding with natives was also frequently accompanied by complaints about Indians attacking European settlements, forts, and farms, killing their inhabitants and stealing livestock.[92] Led by the perception that natives carried out their own deliberate and unjustified guerilla warfare against both Europeans and the acculturated or converted Indians who had allied with them, both Spaniards and Portuguese concluded that unless the Indians were properly controlled, the land would never be. Because some Indians were hostile while others not, it became vital for Europeans to distinguish not only the already converted from the still pagan but also—perhaps even mainly—friends from foes.[93] And, because most believed that some native groups were "redeemable" while others were not, they proceeded to offer peace to the former while waging war against the latter. The way these two strategies operated and the choice between them, read together with conversion and missionary activities, explain how relations with natives could and often did influence the Spanish–Portuguese conflict in the Americas.

Most Europeans imagined peace with natives as a fairly simple transaction. They assumed that gift giving formed friendships, and that friendships guaranteed good relations. Sometimes portrayed as an exchange, but mostly imagined as a one-way grant from Europeans to Indians, gift giving, Europeans believed, created "alliances" that guaranteed native support or at least promised native nonbelligerence. Often spontaneous and involving very few people and a rather minimal material exchange or divided into several episodes over a long period, gift giving became so frequent (and so expensive) that, at least on the Spanish side, regulations were enacted in the late eighteenth century regarding who should be giving those gifts to whom and how expensive they should be.[94] Yet attempts to control these processes—which contemporaries believed were essential to their security and well-being—were rarely efficacious and seldom did signs of failure discourage those who participated in them. Considered a long-term investment, no one expected gift giving to perform immediate miracles because it was believed that alliance making required time and that only repetition would ensure that natives would learn to "love the Christians."[95] Yet while patience was called for, the presence of rival Europeans enhanced the sense of urgency because at stake was not only which Indians would ally with you but also which would contract with your enemies. In the words of a contemporary observer, "the felicity of this enterprise is not only looking at the heavens [i.e., the ability to convert them] but also to Earth, because with this alliance [with the Indians] the conquest of the state of Maranhão has been completed. With the Ingaybas Indians as enemies, Pará could be of any foreign nation that would ally with them, and with the Ingaybas Indians as allies, Pará becomes safe and impenetrable to all foreign powers."[96] As a result of these considerations, the stronger the competition among Europeans was, the greater the desire to befriend natives.

Whether formally authorized to engage in alliance making or not, local authorities constantly reported to their superiors on their attempts to win over Indians. These reports, abundant in both Spanish and Portuguese archives, demonstrate that alliance making could be informal and oral or extremely well spelled out and documented, even notarized. Portuguese records are most generous on these issues, describing some of these agreements in great detail.[97] Though accords differed depending on place, period, and parties, they pro-

duced extremely repetitive narratives. These stories usually began
with an affirmation that Indians had requested to meet with Europeans and offered to ally with them (part 1: native initiative). They
continued describing how in the following days, weeks, and even
months and years and over several encounters, the two parties got
acquainted (part 2: the conversations). Mediated by converted or domesticated Indians or by friars, they involved Indian chiefs on the
one hand and European missionaries, military commanders, or experienced settlers on the other (part 3: the parties). During these conversations, gifts were exchanged, and natives were informed of the
need to establish peace, settle permanently near Europeans, and convert and were told that, if they agreed, they would become vassals and
win royal protection (part 4: the conditions). In Portuguese America,
they could receive either passports (*passaporte*) certifying they were
vassals or "certificates of services" (*certidão do serviço*), which would
protect them from harm.[98] Native consent was given either verbally,
by signing the papers, or by using gestures, for example, hugging and
kissing, which Europeans interpreted as communicating acquiescence
(part 5: native consent).

How this common narrative developed is hard to establish. Nonetheless, the transformation of individual events into a standardized
plot is clear. Consider, for example, what happened in 1771 near the
Portuguese post of Iguatemi in the Amazon region. As reported by
the military commander to the governor of São Paulo, early one
morning some thirty Indians led by three *caziques* or captains, each
holding a cross, came to the fort and requested to meet with the
commander (a *bandeirante* from São Paolo).[99] They responded cheer-
fully to his questions—which he asked "in their language"—offering
him the cross as a symbol of peace. Retiring to converse with the
three native captains, the commander accepted the crosses, placed
them on the ground, and assured his interlocutors that they needed
no weapons other than these religious symbols to win over him and
his soldiers. He conditioned the continuation of the talks (*praticas*)
on the chiefs disarming their Indians. The individual, whom he
identified as the principal leader, gave the order, and all bows and
arrows were placed on the ground. The Portuguese commander
then asked the rest of the Indians to join them. After he hugged

them, he offered them peace, and they promised in the name of "their nation" not to offend the Portuguese, receiving assurances that the Portuguese would do the same. Both also agreed that if they met in an open field, they would inform each other that peace had already been established and that, as a result, they must treat one another in a friendly manner. The commander also promised the Indians "all that they lacked" and immediately supplied them with clothes and tools. He assured the natives that after the governor and the king were informed of what had transpired, they would give them additional presents.

Before the Indians departed "very happy," they nevertheless asked a few questions, which the commander classified as "impertinent" *(algumas impertinentes perguntas)*. The first was why the Portuguese had come to take the lands that God had given them for their livelihood *(qual era razão por que lhes vinham tomar as suas terras que deus ilhes tinha repartidos para suas vivendas)*. The commander responded that the Portuguese did not want their lands because they had sufficient territory. Their sole aim, he said, was to acquire their friendship *(respondi-lhe que eu lhe não vinha tomar as terras e que delas não carecia antes vinha buscar a sua amizade que hera só o que queria)*. To this, natives responded that "this was good and that they wanted the same, that is, to avoid deaths that God did not want" *(respondeu-me que estava bem e que isso mesmo queriam eles, para que entre nós não houvesse mortandades que deus não queria)*. For his part, the commander asked whether they knew God, to which they responded that "he had bled on the cross for men" *(tinha derramado na cruz seu sangue pelos homens)*. The second and third questions natives posed were whether the governor of São Paulo and the king were married and had children. Having answered these queries, the commander asked the Indians whether they and their families wanted to come and live under the protection of the king and among the Portuguese. If they did, he asserted, he would immediately communicate the good news to his superiors and ensure that they received all the things—cloths and tools—they needed. The Indians answered that for the moment they could not come to settle in the fort.

Soon after they left, the house of one of the Portuguese settlers was attacked, but it was unclear whether this assault was carried out by the group that had visited the Portuguese. One could not tell, the commander asserted, and anything was possible. After all, these natives were barbarians who could not be trusted. A week later, some additional sixty Indians arrived at the fort with crosses in hand requesting to speak to the commander. When invited to enter the settlement, they refused. It was thus necessary to receive them outside. The commander reported that he had established "the same peace" with this group and gave its members tools as well as marmalade, which they liked a great deal. Yet, despite his efforts, the members of this second group did not leave the fort as content as those of the first group because they were more ambitious and "wanted to receive everything they saw." The commander concluded his report by estimating that if the right effort were invested, these natives would convert to Christianity and become friends of the Portuguese.

The events that the local commander described took on a much more fantastic dimension on the one hand and ordinary standardization on the other in the report the governor of São Paulo sent to Lisbon.[100] Insisting on the importance of what had transpired, the governor omitted to mention that the natives had crosses with them and thus already had had previous contact with Europeans, that they realized the Portuguese were after their land, that peace was possible but had not yet been established, and that, at any rate, conversations may have not produced tangible results because the Indians might have attacked the Portuguese the following day and they refused to settle. Instead, the governor told the king a powerful tale about four indigenous chiefs who had come to see the Portuguese to request help. In order to "win them over" (ir ganhando as vontades) and obey royal instructions, the Portuguese gave them "a collection of all of the things they considered most attractive and appetizing" (um sortimento de todas as coisas mais atrativas e apetecíveis para eles). The Indians surrendered their arms to the Portuguese. What had transpired, the governor insisted, was of great importance. Referring to this meeting as a true diplomatic exchange, he compared it to what the ambassador of Morocco had once said at the court of Paris regarding the exchange of presents: that the quantity or quality of gifts was not important; what was essential was the homage and respect they communicated.[101]

If this was typical, then it is possible that "conversations" with nonsubjected Indians were more convoluted, complex, and ambiguous than the standardized reports we currently consult allow us to imagine. While the Portuguese suggested peace, settlement, and conversion, the Indians responded that peace was possible but that they wanted to remain where their forefathers had lived and where they could support themselves.[102] While the Portuguese suggested that the Indians become dependent on them, the Indians preferred to remain outside in their own villages. And whereas the Portuguese reported that peace had been reached, it was perhaps in the making but was not truly finalized. Clearly, by the 1770s, natives were afraid of Portuguese encroachment on their lands and might have sought out the Portuguese in order to halt, not advance, their penetration. They might have wanted to check what the Portuguese were doing and might have desired gifts. Evidently, they were not looking to convert or become vassals. Yet, however natives responded, as long as they were not overtly hostile, the Portuguese concluded that they had "good faith" (boa fé). They also suggested that by giving Indians additional gifts, things were well on their way to an enduring alliance.

On rare occasions, archival documentation does suggest that negotiations were particularly long and complicated. For example, the Portuguese held dozens of "conversations" in the 1780s with the so-called Mura Indians.[103] Initially, they disbelieved the natives' promise to be loyal and commit no crimes because they suspected that the true intention of the Muras, "well-known barbarians," was to spy on them. Yet, because they were unsure that this was the case, they did give the Indians a few gifts and reported to the authorities on what they regarded as a "good beginning" (bom princípio). When the Muras returned a few months later with translators and some minor gifts, the Portuguese considered these insignificant because of their small value (coisa pouca). Both dismissing what the Muras could give them and giving the Muras additional and more substantial presents, the Portuguese instructed natives to bring their wives along on their next visit. Several other meetings took place, the Portuguese asserting, as with other indigenous groups, that they would be willing to forgive the Muras their crimes and insults if they, the

Muras, were willing to become Christians and vassals. If they refused, the Muras would be led to their "ultimate destruction" (a sua
última ruína). Several months went by with exchanges continuing.
During this period, the Portuguese were particularly obsessed with
identifying the native leader whose promise would bind the entire
group. As various leaders came and went, some leaving their children, mothers, or wives behind, others bringing additional members with them, the Muras gradually began to trust the Portuguese,
or so the Portuguese believed. Yet confidence was not reciprocal:
while they negotiated with the Muras, the Portuguese continued to
consider their interlocutors "barbarians" and judged their leaders to
be "monsters" (monstro). They also suspected that the Muras might
be negotiating with Spaniards or collaborating with dangerous individuals. And, although a few Muras were baptized and others collaborated with the Portuguese, the Muras' request for new praticas
was denied because the Portuguese commander conditioned all further negotiations on their settling first. The local commander concluded that peace could not be achieved in one day. Instead, it had to
be gradual and would become possible only through a combination
of mildness and rigor.[104] During the negotiations, he asserted, natives should not feel that they were mistrusted (as indeed they were),
but neither should they feel they were trusted, as this might lead
them to commit treachery.

In Spanish territories, too, agreement making could be a simple
or highly ritualized affair, spontaneous or planned, oral or written.[105] It usually began with gift giving, the offer of missionaries,
and the exchange of prisoners, and it depended on the mediation of
native allies and missionaries. Part of this very early accumulated
know-how was already gathered and reproduced in the Ordenanzas
de Nueva Población (1573) and other works explaining the need to approach natives by exchanging gifts, nurturing conversion, and detail-
ing to them the powers of the king and the obligation to obey him.[106]
These texts also recommended that while conversations took place,
Spaniards hold the sons of natives hostage under the excuse (so color)
of instructing them in the mysteries of the faith. Military commanders, they asserted, must inform natives of the obligations and privileges of peace, which consisted of the duty to cease all belligerence

against Spain and its allies and to be obedient vassals. Spaniards would do the same and, to demonstrate their good intentions, would embrace native lords and fire a salvo as a sign of their joy, give Indians gifts, and share food with them. Pacts were also sealed by sounding drums and invoking, repeatedly, the name of the king. Like Portuguese *praticas*, in some places conversations with natives were titled "parliaments," while in others they had no particular name. Unlike the Portuguese, however, Spaniards were particularly keen on celebrating these alliances in their capital cities, which were often located dozens of miles away. Making a public display of what they considered their success, in 1771, for example, "two principal caciques" of the "Moscovi nation" who presented themselves to a small Spanish garrison in the hinterland were sent to the provincial capital (Corrientes, present-day Argentina).[107] There they allegedly agreed to cease their war against the Spaniards in exchange for a few gifts. Spaniards also hoped that they would persuade allied Indians to do the same and perhaps even agree to convert. Somewhat similarly, the governor of Asunción (present-day Paraguay), accompanied by the local town council *(cabildo)*, military officials, and other "individuals of distinction" *(varios sujetos de distinción)*, met in 1776 with a group of "infidels" with whom peace negotiations had been completed two months earlier. Using an interpreter, he asked the Indians whether they truly wanted to settle on the site that was assigned to them and whether they truly wished to become Christians and observe a "firm peace" with the province, its inhabitants, and all Christians who lived there.[108] After they answered affirmatively, he enumerated the conditions, including the gifts and animals that natives would receive and the promise to settle them in a convenient place. Next, he spelled out the obligations: admitting priests, baptizing their young children and raising them Christian, each one sending a son as a hostage to be educated by Spaniards, and the duty of Indian soldiers to act only at the request and command of the governor as well as to patrol the territory.

Despite these ceremonial engagements, peace was rarely permanent. Europeans blamed natives. They presented them as free agents who initiated contacts, decided what to do next, and easily changed sides.[109] Coming and going as they pleased, natives born in Spanish territories could migrate to Portuguese domains, return to Spain, and move to Portugal again. They could convert, desert the missions, return to them, and disappear once more. Natives, Spanish and Portuguese interlocutors said, alternated between an indigenous world and a colonial reality, and they could be friendly, turn hostile, and become allies again. Because they acted as friends or foes alternately according to their needs and desires, they could not be trusted. While Europeans were committed to peace, Indians were not; "treacherous behavior" was typical of them. These constant fluctuations forced Europeans to exercise extreme caution.[110] They had to consider that whatever arrangements they might have made with natives, these were unlikely to persist because natives waged barbarian war against civilized peoples. For some, this conclusion implied that natives could never be trusted. Others suggested the need to teach them what peace meant and the duty to preserve it. Yet a third group resisted the idea of alliance making altogether.[111] Peace agreements, they said, were prejudicial. While they limited what Europeans (who observed them) could do, they allowed natives (who did not) to continue their treacherous behavior, assaulting Spaniards and their properties. They led to Spanish submission, transforming those in the interior into "subordinates and tributaries of native control" (habernos subordinado y hechos tributarios a su imperio).

Whereas these complaints classified all Indians as untrustworthy, it is nevertheless clear that many indigenous groups were loyal to the Europeans with whom they reached an understanding. Furthermore, while complaints against indigenous "inconsistency" coincided in blaming natives, there was plenty of evidence that pacts were often enforced on Indians against their will. Indians were told that they could either consent to friendship and protection or suffer war and annihilation.[112] There was no room for discussion: any questioning could lead Europeans to "withdraw as a sign of rupture," promising to punish Indians "with the greatest severity possible to give them a lesson."[113] Most accords took for granted European superiority and the subsequent subjugation of Indians. They spelled out carefully what Indians would do and cede, but they rarely enumerated European commitments. And while Europeans understood what these accords implied and they agreed to enter into them, it is unclear that natives exercised a choice or truly voiced consent. Portuguese officials, for example, sometimes confessed that they guessed rather than knew what the Indians wanted. In the absence of a common language, they trusted native actions (which they interpreted according to their own wishes) rather than native words.[114] Archival documentation also suggests that European commanders were predisposed to believe that natives would collaborate and quickly moved from speaking with them to celebrating what they gathered was their success. In most cases, native acquiescence was assumed rather than attested. It was read into native response and was imagined by Europeans who a priori sought to prove its existence. As a result, if consent had any meaning in this context, it was by way of presumption. Natives were presumed to have assented to certain things, and this conclusion acted on reality. Rather than being a manifestation of free will, consent was (as it often is) a juridical and a political construction. Thus, although Europeans insisted in the Americas, as they did in Europe, that vassalage as well as conversion depended on a personal decision, both in the Old and the New Worlds religious and civic subjection was usually compulsory.[115] Freedom, in short, did not entail the ability to negotiate (as it often does not). As already specified in the (In)famous Requirement *(requerimiento)*, elaborated by Spanish jurists in the sixteenth century to justify the war against natives, it mainly embodied the possibility of choosing between exclusion and inclusion, war and peace, all ultimately leading to the destruction of one order and the emergence of another.[116]

As a result, though historians have tended to portray these encounters as negotiations and their conclusion as "treaties," it is clear that in both Portuguese and Spanish America, accords with Indians rarely included full-fledged negotiations or ended with a clear and detailed, mutually binding understanding.[117] Even when extreme duress was lacking, native choice might have been limited because natives might have needed the supplies Europeans could offer.[118] They might have collaborated with Spain or Portugal because they feared the rival power or were threatened by their native enemies, whose conditions might have altered by the presence of Europeans. Natives might have adhered to such agreements because they included a pledge to stop European penetration into indigenous territories or the promise to allow natives to recover ancestral lands. But even when Indians did agree to enter into these accords, contemporary documentation suggests they might have believed that they could withdraw from them if they were treated incorrectly or if gains did not meet their expectations.[119] Natives might have considered agreements with Europeans conditional because, as far as they were concerned, Europeans who entered their territories were intruders who owed them payment (in the form of gift giving), not superiors to whom they owed allegiance. They might have also believed that both war and peace were forms of social exchange. If any of the above was true, then native alternation between peace and war might have indicated not a change of heart but instead a form of interaction that Indians practiced and that contemporary Europeans might have understood better than they were willing to confess.

Inter-indigenous feuds also played an important part in these dynamics. Existing before Europeans arrived, they were greatly modified by Spanish and Portuguese presence, which destabilized old equilibriums.[120] The gradual extension of colonial power also pitted converted against pagan Indians and allied versus nonallied. Hostility among native groups could be the consequence of the use by Europeans of mission Indians in their struggle against one another and in their relationship with not-yet-domesticated natives. Yet Indians also could use Europeans to gain prominence inside their group and in their relationships with one another. But whatever the case, as the colonial period advanced, Europeans became frequent mediators, arbiters, or even judges of native disputes.[121] On occasions they employed a divide-and-rule policy; on others they attempted to establish peace among different groups with the aim of pacifying the region and ensuring their control.[122] These interactions could take different forms. For example, in 1726 the principal of a "barbarian nation called Arauzes" explained to a Portuguese commander that he had come to seek refuge in the fort against his native enemies who wanted to revenge the death of their kinsmen.[123] When two of his rivals arrived at the camp with a similar story, the commander brought the three before the local governor who, having examined the antecedents, decided that peace must be established among them. In the presence of a royal judge *(ouvidor geral)*, the captain of the fort, the *visitador* of the Jesuits, the prior of the convent of São António, the local municipal judge, and many other Portuguese, the three indigenous leaders agreed to settle their dispute. Somewhat similarly, in the early eighteenth century, the Lules, a native group, were told by Spaniards that before Spaniards would agree to contract peace with them, they must first "sincerely reconcile with the Malbalás, their ancient enemies and . . . forgive all their complaints against them," which the Malbalás would do, too.[124] Because Europeans increasingly were mediators in native disputes, it should therefore not surprise us that in 1790 the cacique Negro, head of the Peguelches, complained to Spaniards about another native leader and group whom he accused of settling in an area he considered his own, or that in 1799 the cacique Guayquilem (Pampas), worried that the "Guineas" might attack him, sent representatives to discuss his defense with Spaniards.[125]

On occasions, natives contended that Europeans, not they, were untrustworthy. For example, responding to the demand that they become Christians and vassals, Indian leaders could claim that they were already thus and that, having been loyal to the king and friends of the Portuguese, peace was breached because the Portuguese did not behave as they promised.[126] As the cacique Lepin argued in 1770, though he and his people perhaps were barbarians, the Spaniards who attacked them despite prior agreements were not precisely civilized.[127] Yet, though Europeans sometimes understood—or at least recorded—the reasons for which natives withdrew from these agreements and though they recognized that "there is nothing that upsets the conquered Indians more than breaking and not fulfilling the conditions and promises by which they have been subjected to dominion and vassalage," only rarely did they confess that they, Europeans, bore the blame.[128] The mere suggestion that Indians were responding to European aggression was unacceptable and the question of whether Europeans kept their word irrelevant.[129] Dictated to natives and requiring their complete capitulation and total subjection, rather than embodying a recognition of indigenous sovereignty or rights, these agreements often led the processes that resulted in the modification, removal, control, and dispossession of the indigenous world. And because contemporary Europeans insisted that ini-

tiative for contact as well as the safeguarding of peace were in Indian hands, they could present themselves as being on the defensive.
According to this narrative, reproduced in both Spanish and Portuguese documentation, Europeans were forced into aggression by
Indians' bellicosity. These reports portrayed Europeans as victims
rather than victimizers and as people under siege; they inverted the
relationship between Europeans and natives and argued that Indians were encroaching on European land and fighting a legitimate
European occupation.[130] Presenting natives as peoples who were
usurping territories that settlers already possessed and which had
been won with great sacrifice, these reports silenced the fact that the
European presence pushed many indigenous groups off their lands,
forcing them into permanent exile.[131]

While Europeans attested that "redeemable" Indians could be approached by offering them alliance, their categorization of others as
enemies and barbarians was usually a prelude to justifying war. Violence was particularly normalized in Portuguese America, where
from as early as 1655 formal procedures existed for authorizing "just
war."[132] Practiced until the late eighteenth century, these required
making a formal complaint to the local authorities, arguing that violence was the only appropriate response to native belligerence. Most
reports contained repetitive narratives that described how Indians
had attacked the Portuguese or their missionaries, obstructed their
movement in the American interior, allied with their enemies, or assaulted their friends.[133] For example, the inhabitants of São Luís suggested in 1679 that the Indians known as Tremeberes, who were once
their friends and whom they treated well, had nevertheless attacked
them, causing the loss of lives and property.[134] In 1726, the Tapuias
Indians, who violently resisted conversion, were identified as members of a "barbarian" and "insolent" group that could be disciplined
and subdued only by war.[135]

Upon receipt of these complaints, the authorities opened a judicial investigation and presented its results to a *Junta das Missões* or a
local committee (some were permanent, some ad hoc) that studied
the material and heard the opinion of different authorities, usually
the governor, the bishop or vicar, the royal judge *(ouvidor)*, and the
provincials of the religious orders in charge of missionary activity.

Because investigations rarely produced conclusive evidence as to what transpired and who was responsible, members were often divided over how to proceed.[136] They sometimes suspected that witnesses were in reality interested parties either because they had suffered hostilities or because they stood to profit from war. Committee members also were unsure whether entire groups should suffer the consequences of what only a few of its members had done and what should happen in cases in which violence was motivated by Portuguese bad behavior. Legally, war was justified only if launched against an enemy that had unjustly attacked or occupied Portuguese territory and was not willing to satisfy the damages inflicted or reverse the situation created. These guidelines were often interpreted in seventeenth- and eighteenth-century Luso-America as also justifying a preventive war against an enemy who was likely to attack in the future. Cannibalism and other "sins against nature" were also invoked as reasons for a just war, as was the attack on missionaries. By the eighteenth century, the breaking of pacts and the assault on friendly or allied indigenous nations was also a pretext for war. To strengthen the argument favoring war, Portuguese Americans could sometimes portray what were in reality separate violent episodes as a single major "bloody war" that the Indians had launched against Europeans and that required, as a result, a comprehensive and severe response.[137]

Although declaring war because of the wish to extend Portuguese territories was illegal, and despite lack of evidence and constant divisions among its members, most juntas did authorize war. Fearing such consequences, on various occasions the Portuguese kings reserved for themselves the final decision, ordering that only wars in self-defense could be sanctioned locally.[138] Yet, because centralizing decision making in Lisbon was impractical, on other occasions this policy was reversed and local committees were authorized to declare all wars, with royal approval required only a posteriori. Hesitation over who could declare war in which case continued throughout the early modern period, as successive Portuguese monarchs favored one policy or the other. Despite these permutations, the one thing that remained constant was the imperative that war declared without following existing procedures was illegal. Illegality meant that captured Indians should be freed, and those who captured them should be censured. This insistence on formalities was motivated by fear that unless structures were put in place, any Portuguese could arm himself at his pleasure and engage in the wars that best suited his interests. The temptation to do so, it was often observed, was too great. A just war not only involved annihilating rivals and freeing their lands and properties, it also justified their captivity and enslavement. In order to limit wars and to distinguish between wars that were necessary and those that were not, it was thus vital to institute formal procedures. Yet, while in the Americas pressure to punish Indians was mounting, so was opposition in Lisbon. By the 1770s, the Portuguese Overseas Council was thus willing to reject claims that Indians engaged in gratuitous violence. How could natives be accused of killing the inhabitants of São Paulo with "dissimulation and treachery" *(com a maior dissimulação e alevozia)* when it was well known that Paulistas had murdered *(assassinado)* many thousands of them?[139] The memory of these atrocities justified native belief that Portugal, a nation that had murdered their ancestors *(uma nação assassina dos seus ascendentes)*, was their mortal enemy. What the Portuguese needed to do was not wage war but rather convince them that their intentions were now different.

No formal mechanisms authorizing war existed in Spanish territories, where violence against indigenous peoples was theoretically banned starting in the mid-sixteenth century, when the monarchy instructed its agents to move from "conquest" to "pacification." In practice, though, campaigns identified as "just wars" and producing, as in Portuguese America, dispossession and enslavement were waged against Indians whom the Spaniards classified either as particularly savage and hostile or as rebellious.[140] These campaigns, called *correrías* (forays), *entradas* (incursions), or *expediciones* (expeditions), were usually organized locally and sometimes followed the recommendation of local juntas. As in Portuguese America, enthusiasm for war was mostly located in the interior and was linked to the wish to force Indians into a de facto, although not a de jure, slavery. But, as in Portuguese America, what was advocated locally did not always find support elsewhere. In 1797, for example, residents of Santa Rosa (present-day Paraguay) requested permission to wage war against a group of Indians who they said constantly attacked their settlement.[141] While they advocated changing the policy that authorized defensive but not offensive war, royal officials responded that violence could be exercised only as a last resort and only if natives attacked first. Somewhat similarly, in 1805 the inhabitants of Sauces (present-day Bolivia) wanted to punish the Indians who had allegedly assaulted them and argued that this was the only possible method to ensure their conversion, preserve the frontier, and "secure and augment the conquests" *(seguridad y aumento de la conquista)*. The honor of king was also at stake: his sovereignty required acting against rebels who had attacked his subjects. "Because the barbarians not only became owners of his dominions but also destroyed his vassals and their properties with a most bloody persecution," it was vital that Spaniards teach them a lesson.[142] A proper reaction was also called for in order to defend native allies, whose preservation was mandated by the law of nations *(derecho de gentes)*, royal laws, and the "honor" of the Spanish flag. These allies had complied in good faith with their "heroic contract" with Spaniards, and therefore Spaniards must comply with it by offering them protection. What was needed, in short, was a "general expedition" *(expedición general)* by professional soldiers, not volunteers. While the local military commander agreed, stressing the vileness of indigenous attacks and the impossibility of reaching an agreement with them, the *audiencia* of La Plata (present-day Sucre, Bolivia) vacillated. The court and the junta it named to examine the issue sought additional information as to why natives rebelled. While preparations for war continued, so did negotiations. Eventually, the situation improved sufficiently so that no "offensive war with firepower and blood" *(guerra ofensiva a fuego y sangre)* was necessary. True, some hostilities continued, but these were "typical of border situations" *(ni una ni otra excede de la clase de ocurrencias comunes de la frontera)*, requiring only an "ordinary response," that is, moderate punishment.

Whether formally or implicitly authorizing war, both Spaniards and Portuguese insisted that violence was a means to produce obedience, not extermination.[143] It was a strategy designed to guarantee complete and total submission and was thus to be used only against Indians who could not be appeased otherwise. Because war was considered a method to obtain peace, in Portugal, at least, the same committees that oversaw the commencement of violence could also be, and in fact often were, charged with negotiating and declaring peace. Their members examined and sanctioned both violence and agreements, both military campaigns and peaceful maneuvers, and were often involved in the ceremonial making of accords. Portuguese committees also could instruct local actors to avoid certain areas in order not to provoke natives or make other recommendations that would ensure the good relations—or at least the nonbelligerence—among colonists, missionaries, and indigenous peoples.

Because war was a means to produce peace and the breaking of peace produced war, in the South American heartland peace and war constantly alternated. Considered two legitimate instruments to achieve and maintain control, Spaniards and Portuguese used them according to the circumstances of case, place, period, and parties. Their conviction that some Indians were particularly barbaric and exceptionally hostile to Europeans justified violent campaigns against them. The assurance that other Indians could accommodate to colonialism permitted them to choose peace. Yet, in order to distinguish those who merited punishment from those who could be pacified, Europeans had to decipher which native groups existed, who were their members, and who led them. This was an extremely arduous task, as governors, missionaries, committee members, settlers, and military commanders engaged in both waging war and offering peace often disagreed on who they were dealing with.[144] Was the cacique identified as "commanding many Indians in Charcas [present-day Sucre], Potosi, and Santa Cruz" (all in present-day Bolivia) indeed in charge of all these groups? Was he likely to influence their inclinations? And what was the relationship between the different groups (tolderías) that roamed the River Plate? Did they form a nation (cuerpo de nación), or were they divided into clans (hordas) that allied in war yet were enemies in peace? Wishing to identify groups and leaders, yet faced with a world they barely understood, both Spaniards the Portuguese introduced into their agreements with natives conditions that spoke to these issues. These stipulated, for example, that the Indian who had made peace would, in the future, be recognized as "the main leader" *(cacique principal)* of the Pampas and head *(cabeza)* of a new republic *(nueva república)*, which he would thereafter govern.[145] They similarly suggested in 1791 that the Indian leader with whom Spaniards reached an agreement would be instituted as "captain general and governor of the tribe," a condition to which the other Indians allegedly agreed. To consecrate their newly endorsed powers, in Spain native leaders could receive title and a staff of command; in Portugal they were promoted as hereditary leaders and received formal letters of nomination and military distinctions.[146] Particularly helpful Indians could thus gradually be transformed from leaders of one settlement to leaders of entire nations or from persons holding minor military posts to "principals" with military decorations. By the end of this process, rather than the authorities of a group reaching an agreement, what often happened was that accords with natives instituted both the group and its authorities. In their aftermath, pacts that recognized the contracting parties as valid in fact made them thus, or so the Europeans believed. This meant that rather than reproducing a preexisting reality, agreements with natives acted on it, making both war and peace performative instances that affected rather than acknowledged social relations.[147] The ensuing processes of internal social change and ethnogenesis meant that it was often unclear whether Spaniards and Portuguese used Indians to consolidate their overseas expansion or whether Indians used them to gain prominence, as well as control, in their relationship with other natives—or perhaps both. What was clear, at any rate, was that rather than various discrete groups clashing or agreeing, as has often been portrayed, the confrontation between natives and Europeans formed and re-formed both parties.

THE STUDY OF CONVERSION and alliance making demonstrates that Indians could be Christian or pagan, vassals or alien, allies or enemies, and that their classification in one way or the other affected European entitlements. But did this imply that natives had possession, or right, to the territories where they lived? Although the affirmation that after Indians became vassals or allies so did their land suggests a positive answer, such was not always the case. In contemporary imagination, the issue of rights vis-à-vis other Europeans could be distinguished from the relationships linking Europeans to natives. As a result, while both Spaniards and the Portuguese could incorporate native right to land in their conflicts with one another, they also could deny it, or at least deny its implications, when coming to deal with natives.

Native right to land was central to sixteenth- and seventeenth-century debates regarding the rights of Europeans in the New World. After a brief period in which the Spanish and the Portuguese argued for title on the basis of papal donation, Iberian scholars, most famous among them Francisco Vitoria, moved the conversation from the arbitrary decision by a universal power (the pope) to a "natural law" that was to be the basis of a new "international" order.[148] According to him, the rights of Indians and how Europeans were to interact with them were to be determined by rules that, presented as universal and permanent, nevertheless originated in European traditions to a large degree inspired in Roman law as it was conserved and used in medieval and early modern Europe.[149] In the aftermath of this development, Europeans sought to identify, select, control, and change this "natural" law so it would fit both their sense of justice and their interests. They drew up a huge array of doctrines that, although justifying European domination of native populations and lands, also limited it in important ways.[150] How these doctrines evolved and what their concrete consequences were is the subject of the following pages, in which I describe their theoretical and practical implications as they played out in the confrontation between Spain and Portugal in the Americas.

Although Vitoria's contribution was vital to modifying the terms of the debate, his main concern remained the distinction between "just" and "unjust war." While the first could produce legal results, such as domination over people and their properties, the second did not. Vitoria encored the justness of war in "natural law" rather than in papal authority, arguing that violations of the freedom to travel, settle, trade, and preach were (the only true) motives that justified war. However revolutionary this might have been, in retrospect, the greatest legal novelty introduced in the transition from the Middle Ages to (early) modernity that was to have an enormous influence on New World debates was found not in the nascent identification of European law as natural and thus universal law but in the question of what this natural law included and how it was to be understood. This law, we now know, slowly evolved during the late Middle Ages, and its biggest mutation happened long before Europeans arrived to the New World. The point of departure was a great difference between private and public law; the point of arrival was their surprising similarity. The story of how this happened is as follows. During the Middle Ages, there was a fairly general agreement among Roman law jurists that while property rights constantly mutated, the rights of communities and kings did not. According to this vision, because property depended on possession, discovery and occupation of things that belonged to no one could give title in the private sphere (property rights). However, such rules did not operate in the public sphere (communal property and jurisdiction), which did not depend on possession. Furthermore, neither did prescription (the acquisition of title by the passage of time) because the public possession of lands as well as jurisdiction could never prescribe.[151] As a result, those who occupied public land or usurped the jurisdiction of another did not win title because of the passage of time. This meant that, contrary to private property, the political space was immutable, fixed, rigid, and unchanging. It expressed a natural order, mandated by God and supported by the church. While this was the consensus in the early medieval period, from the mid-fourteenth century onward, European jurists inspired by the search for new moral principles that would justify the emergence of a modern economic and political order slowly began questioning these assumptions. They proceeded to do so by using Roman notions regarding private property to create doctrines regarding public borders and jurisdiction. Transposing arguments from relations among individuals to relations among princes and states, *Ius Commune* authors gradually began presenting the political space also as an expression of the lived experience and activities of those who resided in it. Centering their attention on how humans modified the territory rather than obeyed preordained divisions, these jurists suggested that, like private property, political divisions also rested on agreement among individuals and groups. By the end of this process, they identified property with jurisdiction and reached the conclusion that both could be acquired in similar ways.

The European expansion that was sometimes contemporaneous, sometimes posterior to these discussions added to them new dimensions by converting these perceptions into general norms and by applying them also to non-European populations and non-European spaces. The genealogy of how this second development came about usually begins in 1516, when Thomas More, taking into account existing debates in Europe, suggested that overpopulated communities engaged in agricultural pursuits could fix a colony in territories where natives "have more soil than they can well cultivate."[152] Not only was this expansion legitimate but resistance to it would be "very just cause of war" because no one had the right to "hinder others to come and possess a part of their soil, of which they made no use, but let it lie idle and uncultivated; since every man has by the Law of Nature a right to such a waste portion of the earth, as is necessary of his subsistence." Allowing communities rather than individuals to occupy unused land and implying that the result would be not only the acquisition of private property but also the constitution of new sovereignties, More's affirmations opened the road to settlers' colonialism. They were taken up and enhanced by Alberico Gentili, who argued in 1588 that God did not create the world to remain empty.[153] The seizure of vacant places, the existence of which he did not doubt and which could be discovered and occupied, was therefore not only a possibility but also a duty. It was mandated by a "natural law" that "abhorred" vacuum and commanded its repair. As if by way of prophecy, Gentili nevertheless admitted that identifying what was occupied and what not was a highly complicated affair. Was Italy unoccupied because of the small number of its inhabitants? Were the Americas under Spain? Intervening in this debate and insisting on presenting the division of the world as the consequence of human activity, not a natural order, was Hugo Grotius. In 1609 he asserted that all property, including land—private and public—arose from occupation.[154] Affirming that what could not be occupied belonged to no one (thus asserting the freedom of the seas, so that the Dutch East Indies Company, which he represented, could trade in Asia), he suggested in 1625 that abandoned land, in which he included uncultivated commons, had no truthful owner. Grotius also opened the way to prescription in public property by agreeing that the need to eradicate war and ensure the peaceful resolution of conflict between sovereigns mandated that both public ownership and jurisdiction in land could prescribe. Samuel Pufendorf added to the equation in 1672 the insistence that civil, not natural, law fixed which occupation would produce title.[155] The only condition that was truly enforced on humans by nature was the need to ensure that the activity that would constitute occupation would communicate sufficiently well both the act of taking possession and the intention of making use of the things possessed. Contrary to Gentili and Grotius, Pufendorf asserted that while individuals could never appropriate more than they could use because their rights were contingent on occupation, communities could possess regions they did not fully occupy. Nonetheless, Pufendorf agreed that prescription existed for both private and public property, both property and jurisdiction. He even suggested that its implementation was more important in the public than in the private domain because if the aim of prescription was to preserve peace, "public possessions cannot be disturbed without far greater confusion and danger than private."

As a result of these discussions, from the seventeenth century onward, the legal question most Europeans asked with regard to the Americas was not what the rights of natives—which they recognized were present there—were but which parts of what land were occupied. In order to do so, they proceeded to define what (valid) occupation meant and, by implication, when it was absent. They examined what natives were doing and suggested that their lack of proper occupation implied that despite their presence, their territories were nonetheless vacant. Rather than respecting past entitlements, European discussants moved to judge whether certain territories were "vacant" according to the standards they set, thereafter concluding that such was the case and that these were therefore open for (their) penetration. This decision delegitimized the possession of many indigenous groups, now portrayed as insufficient. It allowed for the argument that some Europeans, such as Spaniards, were conquerors because they appropriated the territory and jurisdiction of "advanced," settled, Indians, who used the territory "appropriately," while others—for example, the English—were settlers because they penetrated the territories of nomadic tribes that were still "vacant." Eventually, it also sustained claims that while some Europeans appropriately occupied the American land, which as a result became "theirs," others, their competitors, had not.

The need to identify what occupation meant and when it was absent generated long debates, and answers varied by place, time, and author.[156] Writing in mid-seventeenth-century Peru, Juan Solórzano Pereira, for example, argued that unless a territory had never been inhabited or had been completely deserted by those who had resided there, it could never be considered truly empty.[157] Yet, while occupied land could not be possessed, land that was physically abandoned and left uncultivated (inculta) could be ceded to the first person or community who found and occupied it "as a prize for their effort" (premio a la industri). Because by that stage it was clear to Solórzano that Spaniards might have contravened this norm, he appealed to prescription, arguing that the Catholic monarchs had acquired both land rights and sovereignty in the Americas mainly because of their good faith and the passage of time. Other Spanish authors maintained on the contrary that while individual land rights depended on possession and use and ceased when those did, such was never the case with lands belonging to communities, title to which could never prescribe.[158] Explaining that such was the case in Europe, where no foreign nation was allowed to settle in territories that were deserted, these authors—echoing similar concerns as Pufendorf—argued that the same rule must also apply to the Americas. The implications of this reasoning were clear: foreign powers could not settle on Spanish New World territories because of their (relative) nonuse.[159] But the same reasoning could potentially also protect Indians, whose "empty" lands Spaniards could not possess. To make sure this did not happen, other authors asserted that Spain formed a single community, thus making all its territories in both the New and the Old Worlds "internal" spaces that could be possessed independently of use. They nevertheless asserted that indigenous societies, on the contrary, were made of many separate political entities. As a result, while territories mediating between

Spanish enclaves were not open for possession even if barren, empty lands between different Indian republics could and must be occupied.

Tied to specific interests and directed at legitimating certain claims or activities, these debates were often passionate. They involved accusations and cross-accusations, as well as the constant use of sarcasm. The English criticized the Spanish for attempting to possess lands already held by civilized nations such as the Aztecs or the Incas. The Spanish ridiculed the English for arguing that their part of the Americas was empty because it was preposterous to maintain that natives had no notion of property as, in their condition as humans, all individuals knew what was theirs.[160] Spanish authors also pointed out that many in Europe lacked the attachment to property or the type of occupation the English required natives to have, and they rejected the claim that Europeans could conserve their unused lands while natives could not.

Debates on native right to land thus provoked confrontations not only between Europeans and natives but also, perhaps mainly, among Europeans themselves. They involved different colonial powers, but they also had domestic repercussions. The tying of internal developments to external ones was most obvious in Locke's *Treatises on Government*, in which he searched for a method to (1) justify the dispossession of the English poor and the attack on common lands, while conserving the property of landholders (in England); and (2) criticize the activities of Spain and France (in the New World) while legitimizing the dispossession of American Indians by the English.[161] The formula he suggested was ingenious. It involved drawing a distinction between different types of occupations and between Europe and the Americas. According to Locke, while some occupations, mainly agricultural pursuits that "improved" (and thus transformed) the land, instituted possession, other uses, such as gathering and hunting, did not; while in the Americas occupation was instituted by a "natural law" that required the constant use of the territory, in Europe—where civil laws existed—rights could also depend on legal entitlements. Presenting appropriation as an activity confronting man with nature rather than with other men, authors such as Locke concluded that in both the Old and the New Worlds communal lands were in reality territories left in a state of nature and therefore irrationally and insufficiently used.[162] That they were widespread in Europe and indeed formed the most common and traditional form of property holding there became irrelevant. Equally inconsequential was the question of whether Native Americans truly used the land in the way Locke (and others) described or whether their stereotyping as hunters and gatherers was more wishful thinking than a reflection of reality.[163]

If, on the one hand, these developments were revolutionary, on the other, they were the result, perhaps the distillation, of earlier discussions. They were based on a long dated conviction (coming from private law) that land rights depended on use and that labor merited compensation.[164] Already Greek and Roman writers were unanimous in holding that property was a man-made institution that emerged as a consequence of the adoption of agriculture. According to them, while hunters had no property, pastoralists had property in their animals and farmers developed property in land. Most medieval and early modern authors agreed with these suggestions.[165] Many pointed out that God gave man the land so he could satisfy his needs. As a result, all property in land was conditioned by its proper use. Making cultivation a religious duty, these authors insisted that property holding must serve the public good. These visions were dominant in Spain and Portugal during the medieval Reconquest in which, rather than claiming territory by victory in a just war (against the Muslims), the legal construction Iberians used suggested that the lands that were conquered were vacant and thus open for repossession.[166] Thirteenth-century Castilian law codes (*Siete Partidas*) reproduced these beliefs, stating that God's first command to men was to populate the earth and that this included the duty to multiply as well as cultivate the soil. It established that possession could be achieved either by force or by exercising an "art" or an occupation.[167] In Portugal, too, perceptions of crisis—the abundance of vacant land and a general depopulation in the fourteenth and early fifteenth century—led to renewed insistence on the connection between land rights and cultivation. The *Lei das Sesmarias* of 1375 (confirmed in 1446, 1521, and 1603), for example, mandated expropriation in cases of failure to use the land properly, and although its implementation was plagued with difficulties, there is plenty of evidence for attempts (not always successful) at developing mechanisms that would impose the requirement to either work the land or allow its transfer to others who would.[168] Thereafter, relations between use and possession were continuously affirmed. In Spain, many authors insisted on the obligation of kings to reward those who cultivated land by giving them title and, on the contrary, to punish those who abandoned cultivation by forcing them to either use the land or surrender it.[169] Believing that the welfare of the state depended on agriculture, that agriculture depended on human endeavor, and that labor, not land, produced wealth, these authors identified work as property.[170] They also proposed that each community appoint special magistrates to inspect the land to ensure it was not abandoned or insufficiently worked. Making agriculture a metaphor for the transformation of both territory and men and considering it the most important of human activities, by the seventeenth and eighteenth centuries they asserted that agriculture distinguished civilized from savage peoples. In early modern Portugal, too, the belief that agriculture tied individuals to the land more strongly than any other economic pursuit was predominant, and there, too, its existence was considered the element that best distinguished the civilized from the uncivilized.[171] When faced with the prospect of abolishing the duty to cultivate in return for possession, in 1642, some Portuguese authors argued that adopting such a measure would be a grave mistake, as the tying of property to usage was an essential component of the economic well-being of the kingdom.[172] By the eighteenth century, Iberian authors also agreed that the best use of land was agriculture, and they opposed the privileges traditionally granted to herders.[173] Like Locke, they questioned the economic wisdom of allowing communities to maintain large common lands, and they argued for the need to privatize them because they believed that only private property gave sufficient incentive for cultivation. The redistribution of land that had been abandoned or scarcely used was also discussed, although disagreement was frequent as to whether it should be proportioned to the landless or granted to people who knew how to work it best.

These ideas affected both legislation and practice. In Spain, they found ample echo in campaigns in the seventeenth and eighteenth centuries that identified depopulation as one of the major reasons for economic decline and advocated the urgent need to put vacant territories to use.[174] These campaigns triggered heated debates regarding both use and abandonment. As in the Americas, in Spain use was usually equated with agriculture, pasturage being classified as "waste" leading to no improvement. Here too it was suggested that leaving land in its barren state or as common grounds was never an informed or reasonable decision but instead willful, at times even criminal, neglect. Forcing communities or private proprietors to either use the land or cede it to others who would settle it was justified by the claim that owners who did not cultivate their land had absolutely no rights. After all, they received it on condition that they would cultivate: "For centuries, these lands have been fruitless. Their owners did not have, nor do they have at present, nor can they have in them any utility other than what they could have in possessions situated in imaginary spaces."[175] Also helpful was the conviction that the king could intervene in the legal order. This, it was argued, was the meaning of sovereignty: the king's superior power allowed him to redistribute properties and territory according to public need, abolishing existing rights and creating others. Thereafter, the cultivation and population of the land through the creation of new settlements (often titled "colonies") was portrayed as a patriotic activity that was "more glorious, useful, and secure than the conquest of distant lands."[176]

If the association between use and rights was common in the Old World, its transformation into a doctrine that was also powerful in the public domain that began in medieval Europe (where *Ius Commune* jurists gradually adopted private-law notions of property to public-law notions of political territory and preferred prescription to ancient rights) was accelerated by the European expansion. Colonialism encouraged Europeans to amplify their understanding regarding private waste land and property rights by creating a theory concerned with public waste land and jurisdiction. Although timidly appearing in the Old World, this theory was to have a dramatic effect in the Americas. Crossing this conceptual and legal bridge at around the same time were individuals and communities all over the Atlantic world. Thus, although many of these developments were usually identified with the English colonial enterprise, they emerged in a European space not yet divided by national traditions. Their presence was clearly registered, for example, in the colonial courts of Quito (present-day Ecuador) that recognized the rights native communities had to the "land of their ancestors." Yet, rather than reconstructing pre-Columbian entitlements, they reproduced European doctrines that determined that rights depended on occupation.[177] Quito's judges were thus willing to recognize the "ancient titles" only of communities that continuously inhabited and cultivated their territories, and they refused to do so in other cases in which natives had abandoned the land or used it in ways other than for grazing or planting. Asking who was present on the land and what they were doing, not what their original title was according to a precolonial law, these judges also affirmed that native rights were conditional rather than permanent, contingent rather than absolute. They could be maintained only as long as natives continued to cultivate and use the land.

The Spanish kings followed suit, ordering that all Indian communities would receive the land they required for their livelihood but making this concession conditional. The land, the monarchs ordered, would be indigenous only as long as natives needed it. If they no longer did, it would revert to the crown and be redistributed. Periodical campaigns (called *composiciones*) were thereafter instituted to verify which territory was occupied and which not.[178] Echoing the visions expressed by Solórzano and Locke, these developments signaled the coming of a new age, in which land would be the property not of those who had it "first" but instead of those who used it "better."

Similar processes might also have taken place in Portuguese America. Although most historians have assumed that these territories were "conquests" and that their natives as vanquished people were denied all rights to land, or they suggested that Brazilian territory was "virgin" or "unoccupied," contemporary documentation includes plenty of indications that the legal status of indigenous land was much more convoluted.[179] During the union between Spain and Portugal, for example, Philip II recognized indigenous land rights, and in 1680 (after the union had ended), João, the new Portuguese monarch, ordered the end of all land distribution to settlers that might dispossess natives who were "first and natural masters" (*primários e naturais senhores*) of the soil. Orders in 1755 and 1758 also recognized the obligation to acknowledge native land rights, and in 1808 the king ruled that Indians should be restored to lands taken from them in "just war." It is also clear that, regardless of the position the crown might have taken or the orders it might have issued, many Portuguese intellectuals agreed with their Spanish counterparts that even vanquished peoples conserved their rights to their territory. Following the same *Ius Commune* and canon law doctrines, they insisted that this was what natural law determined, therefore identifying it as the right and just thing to do.[180] While natives might have conserved at least some on their entitlements, in practice, from the 1690s or perhaps earlier, Portuguese land grants (*sesmarias*) in the New World were conditioned by use, and its absence could be a motive for repossession and redistribution.[181] Grants were also theoretically restricted in size according to the supposed capacity of their holders to cultivate the soil and could not harm third parties. Although mainly referring to private, not public, landholding, they were also applied to Indian communities. Formulated as donations dependent on royal goodwill, these royal concessions nevertheless allowed Indians to remain in their ancestral lands as long as they continued to cultivate them.

As a result, it is possible that de facto (although perhaps not de jure) differences between those who respected native rights to land (Spaniards) and those who did not (the English and the Portuguese) were not particularly great.[182] Mocking and criticizing one another in the abstract, in the concrete the inhabitants of these powers linked use to rights in ways that dispossessed most natives. They (most particularly the Spanish and the English) also coincided in arguing that Indians should be left at the subsistence level, which meant that they could (in fact must) possess the land necessary for their survival but had no right to accumulate property or live off rents. Invoking fairness, they suggested it would be unjust not to give Indians the land they needed, but it would be equally wrong to give them too much because it would impede the subsistence of other groups who might use the land more appropriately. The road leading from criticism to criminalization was extremely short but meaningful. By the end of this process, not only were native Americans dispossessed, but this outcome was presented as their own doing. It was a punishment for their neglect, which constituted a sin and was meant to force them to improve their ways.

Colonialism was one reason for these developments; the general reorganization of land regimes was another. On both sides of the ocean, contemporaries coincided in seeking to alter existing structures in ways that seemed more "reasonable" to them. Whether "reasonableness" was the motive or the excuse, we will never know—it is probable that both were equally present—but whatever the case, it is clear that, rather than respecting existing entitlements, what early modern intellectuals, judges, litigants, administrators, friars, settlers, and military men on both sides of the Atlantic did was to discuss how to change them, undermine them, or relinquish them altogether. It was as if they were willing to reinvent the social contract and the legal basis for ownership (as eventually they did) by giving new spin to existing theories. The debate on land, possession, and jurisdiction was therefore not only legal but also moral, religious, and political. It confronted individuals and states whose interests were at odds but, most important, it penetrated society to a surprising degree. It was not debated exclusively by intellectuals but was frequently invoked in quotidian interactions in which contemporaries discussed land rights with one another and the authorities sought either to authorize or delegitimize their interpretations.

Given these developments, it is not surprising that in the American interior, seventeenth-, eighteenth-, and early nineteenth-century discussants described their entitlements as if they existed in a vacuum. Claiming rights by virtue of bulls, treaties, or possession, they often pretended to disregard the fact that the territory was indigenous. The presence of Indians was, of course, obvious to them and it greatly preoccupied most of them, yet they did not believe it should bar Europeans from acquiring jurisdiction and territory. On the contrary, the more bellicose Indians were, the greater the tendency was to consider their land as the object of legitimate expansion. The more natives resisted, the more their territories were portrayed as infinite and boundless spaces that embodied all that was disruptive and dangerous because it was unchristian, uncivilized, and hostile—in other words, all that was vacant and required elimination and transformation.[183]

When native rights were discussed in the South American heartland at all, it was usually as a means to support or deny the rights of Europeans.[184] In the 1750s and 1760s, many criticized the Spanish monarch's decision to cede certain territories to Portugal with the Treaty of Madrid. Because this agreement required the abandonment of seven missions, some writers might have claimed—there were more rumors than evidence—that this decision was both unjust and illegal.[185] It was unjust because it placed a huge burden on Indians who had always been loyal and obedient subjects, forcing them to leave prosperous villages and go into an exile that exposed them to both physical and moral (i.e., religious) danger. It was illegal because it was against the royal promise not to alienate territory or, alternatively, because the land ceded was not royal: it either belonged to the Jesuits (who first discovered, conquered, and possessed it), or it was native. Confusing property and jurisdiction, according to the second view, the Indians possessed this land from time immemorial.[186] Because they were never conquered but instead willfully subjected themselves to Spain, the conclusion was that Indians, not the king, were "true, absolute, and legitimate owners" *(verdaderos, absolutos y legítimos dueños)* of the territory. It could thus be ceded only if Indians chiefs agreed.[187]

Although the discussion in the 1750s and 1760s was somewhat exceptional, the instrumentalization of native rights and their subjection to European needs was continuous. To attack the Jesuits, some individuals were willing to affirm that they illegally took indigenous land: Indians were proprietors of their land because "the law of nature" *(il diritto de la natura)* and the "law of nations" *(diritto delle genti)* determined that land belonged to the first inhabitants and occupants regardless of who they were and what they did with it.[188] To back Portuguese claims, others suggested that the lack of opposition by "Indian nations" living on the territory *(sin menor*

contradicción de las naciones de los indios habitadores de ellos) implied
that they consented to their occupation and thus recognized Portugal's claims to the territory.[189] Spaniards equally argued that after
certain native groups had allied with them, their territories were
"integrated into this province by reversion, being that they were
now vassals of our monarch and natural lord and they have given
him his oath of fidelity and subordination."[190] On other occasions,
they pointed out that as long as the natives were infidels, they had
temporal dominion and possession *(dominio y posesión)* of their land
but that once they had converted, their lands became part of the territory of the nation responsible for their evangelization.[191]

The idea that some Indians might have certain rights was also
upheld in several agreements reached with natives. These accords,
mostly concerned with peace, vassalage, crime prevention, commercial rights, and conversion, could include a paragraph recognizing that land occupied by natives since the "time of their ancestors"
would remain "in their possession, which they already had."[192] Alternatively, these pacts could determine that natives would retain
possession of that land, but the king would obtain a "superior dominion" *(dominio alto)* over it.[193] Some agreements said that Indians
who "considered themselves as having rights to the land" now ceded
it to Spain.[194] On rare occasions, accords even demarcated an indigenous space that Europeans promised not to invade.[195] Peace agreements could also allow Indians to settle where they wanted as long
as their choice did not interfere with Spanish activity or penetrate
Spanish "habitual domains" *(usuales territorios).*[196] But, more often
than not, pacts mentioning land rights mainly confirmed, albeit implicitly, indigenous dispossession. They mandated the resettlement
of Indians in new missions or villages, thus producing the de facto
abandonment of their previous habitat that, because it was no longer occupied or used, could potentially be open for European expansion. Not only were native groups relocated, according to most
accords the new territories that were assigned for their resettlement
were not be truly their own. Instead, they were considered lands
bestowed on them by royal grant. Stipulating that Indians would
receive these lands only after they submitted and as a consequence
of their accords with the Spaniards or the Portuguese, these pacts

conditioned the receipt as well as the duration of the grant on their loyalty.[197] The Portuguese were particularly adamant on this point, suggesting that even Indians who remained in their ancestral territories did so by virtue of a royal grant. Rather than being original proprietors and owners of that land, they now possessed it because the king protected them as he would any other vassal.[198] As the procurator of an indigenous group attested in 1735, "by natural and common law . . . dominion was acquired by the first occupant, which is why successive royal decrees and laws mandated that possession by Indians of the land that their ancestors [*mayores*] or the gentiles from whom they descended occupied should be preserved without disturbing their successors, who received instruction in the Catholic and true faith and subjected themselves to the sovereign; but if some lands were not occupied, or barbarians had depopulated them, continuing in their blind idolatry and escaping from conversion and subjection to the kings, these can be occupied by others."[199]

It is therefore fair to say that whatever theories said, whatever Portuguese and Spaniards might have argued, and whatever pacts they might have made, almost no contemporary record indicates that indigenous rights could be a detriment to European expansion. Rejecting claims that the jurisdiction of Portugal in certain areas was unclear because these were still occupied by "barbarian Indian nations," in 1797 a Portuguese commander asserted that it was unthinkable that the presence of Indians would prevent European powers from owning the territory.[200] Not only was it against "public law" and the "law of nations," which required only a "general" and not a "privative" occupation, but if such was the case, no European would ever own anything in the Americas. Spain certainly would not be able to stop the penetration of other Europeans given that "much of its vast terrain was occupied only by ancient and wild inhabitants." Similarly, in 1805, Spanish interlocutors suggested that whatever agreement they might have reached with the natives to whom they promised not to enter certain territories, Spanish advances should not be halted. Any other solution would be preposterous.[201] Old demarcations could certainly be transgressed if new territories were needed and if those who lived on them were savages with no permanent settlement who allowed the land to remain barren. As a natural law professor at the University of Buenos Aires argued in the early nineteenth century, creating borders in order to demarcate the land each community possessed and to reject the penetration of foreigners was a natural thing.[202] But because it was linked to the basic human need for residence and subsistence, the occupation of land had to be just and rational. As a result, no nation could occupy and demarcate a space too big to settle and cultivate because such behavior would constitute an usurpation. People who found their territory too small could ignore "old frontiers" and settle and occupy uncultivated and deserted land beyond their original dominions. This was particularly true if this land was only roamed by savage tribes who did not need it. As if they had read Turner's "Frontier Thesis," contemporary observers thus asserted that existing divisions separating those who were today enemies were destined to disappear as part of a process that would culminate in the conversion and civilization of all mankind.[203] They also explained that frontiers were "all the lands that are unknown and are occupied by barbarians and our belongings continue always to extend with the settlement of new missions and farms that are established further ahead with the interest [of having] good pasture and fertile terrain, as has always been the case since this continent had been pacified."[204] As a Spanish captain is reputed to have remarked in 1599, the final aim was to achieve "more, more, more, and more."[205]

These perceptions downplayed the importance of territorial arrangements with natives. Such arrangements were interpreted as temporary and practical rather than final and enforceable. That is to say, though a territorial conflict existed not only between the Spanish and the Portuguese but also between them and the Indians, this second conflict with the Indians could be ignored by classifying it as "interior" rather than "exterior" (as it still is today). This taxonomy allowed both the Spanish and the Portuguese (and their present-day successors) to incorporate native right to land in their conflicts with one another but to deny it, or at least deny most of its implications, when dealing with natives.[206]

Although native property rights could be dismissed, both the Spaniards and the Portuguese recognized that unless they pacified the local population, contracted with it, converted it, or exterminated it, they would never become masters of the New World. Constantly alternating between war and peace according to their evaluation of which was the best strategy, Spaniards and Portuguese ended up codifying their relationship with the indigenous world to a surprising degree. Because of the conviction that religious conversion also entailed a civic mutation, missionaries became agents of territorial expansion. Their activities, consisting of discovery, conquest, and occupation, as well as taking possession of lands and their inhabitants and defending them against foreign powers, won them both friends and enemies. Divided by orders and into provinces, friars who were often of foreign extraction competed with, criticized, and fought with one another as well as confronted settlers and military commanders in the struggle to confirm the rights of their order and their king. But whether they took one position or the other, the one thing all European discussants agreed on, however, was that nothing could or should bar them from expanding as much as they could.

IT IS THEREFORE FAIR to say that the Europeans that cohabited in the Americas claimed parts of it as their own. As individuals, in groups, or in state-sanctioned expeditions, they penetrated new areas motivated by economic or political ends or inspired by missionary zeal. The arrival of one power usually fostered the arrival of the other, thus leading to a competition over who would expand, where, and how quickly. Although all actors affirmed that their actions were justified and those of their rivals were not, the bulls, treaties, and doctrines they cited contained no clear indication as to who was right and who wrong. Kings might have believed that the situation in the Americas was static—indeed, they constantly insisted on preserving the status quo or appealing to bulls and treaties, which they believed gave clear solutions—but in the interior of the continent no one was able to determine what these things meant and how they could be defended.

Conversion, alliance making, and war were mechanisms that could be simultaneously or separately used in order to control the indigenous inhabitants and their land. Crucial to guaranteeing the welfare of local colonialists and the success of their enterprise, these mechanisms also operated—often silently—to convert natives into foils against which debates among Europeans were argued, lost, or won. The clerics, settlers, and military men who fought over the right, presented as duty, to assimilate natives religiously and politically might have cared for their souls or might have wanted their labor, but they clearly also assumed that indigenous adhesion to one country or the other would guarantee their land rights. Making natives the true *terra nullius*, which they hoped to possess, in the process they both recognized and dismissed native claims. But natives also pursued their own agendas. The records at our disposal—although relatively few—are nonetheless telling. They demonstrate that the indigenous inhabitants could use the Spanish and the Portuguese in their quarrels with one another or to win prominence locally. They could initiate contact with Iberians wishing to find out their plans and perhaps receive the gifts that they often distributed. But however tentative and careful these encounters might have been, they ended up absorbing natives in a man-made hurricane that was to turn their world upside down.

Distinguishing Spanish from Portuguese territories, in short, was an intricate affair that could not be easily resolved, among other reasons because, rather than reflecting a permanent state, it embodied a dynamic, open-ended process that involved many actors, multiple possibilities, and (frequently) numerous (contradictory) justifications. Clear in contemporary documentation was the sense of urgency, even competition. Also clear were constant attempts to order what seemed (and indeed often was) extremely chaotic. The need to know and control what was happening in the interior pushed contemporaries into a desperate effort to collect, systemize, and understand. Yet these efforts mostly failed because knowledge was lacking but also because the ability to process and digest it was scarce. Because territorial divisions were the by-product of many different tensions produced by a plethora of actors for different ends, telling the story of the Spanish and Portuguese confrontation in the Americas as a tale about how courts and diplomats negotiated is extremely misleading. Also misleading is a separation of the struggle between Europeans from the conflict confronting them with natives and dividing natives internally. Assuming that one side was justified while the other not is just as deceptive. It is perhaps a faithful reproduction of what contemporaries argued, but contemporary claims must be read in conjunction not only with their immediate interests but also with what political and juridical norms dictated. Understanding how contemporaries imagined their right to land is thus essential if we wish to analyze how they confronted one another and why they could obtain certain results.

PART II

Defining European Spaces: The Making of Spain and Portugal in Iberia

IBERIAN TERRITORIAL CONFLICTS—which sometimes began in the Middle Ages but mostly developed during the early modern period, thus paralleling debates in the Americas—allow a complementary understanding of how contemporaries viewed their entitlements, argued for their rights, and, in the process, also constructed their communal territories. If these conflicts sometimes acted as precedents that explained how things had developed in the New World, other times they demonstrated how discords mutated over time and where they could end in the nineteenth and early twentieth centuries. Their added value, therefore, is their ability not only to illuminate the background to colonialism but also to demonstrate how notions employed across the ocean acted in the *longue durée*. Iberian confrontations, in short, serve here to add additional dimensions to the questions already asked, serving as an image, truthful but not exact, of what had transpired in the New World.

Conflicts between Spain and Portugal in Iberia began in the ninth and tenth centuries with the creation of Portugal as an administrative unit, and they continued alongside its gradual separation from León and Castile and its affirmation as an independent kingdom in the twelfth and thirteenth centuries.[1] Experiencing multiple confrontations in the fourteenth and fifteenth centuries, in part civil wars, in

part succession crises, in part international conflicts, Portugal's relationship with the other Iberian kingdoms stabilized over time,
was drastically modified between 1580 and 1640 (during the union
of the crowns), and was again altered in 1640 after the Duke of Braganza declared himself king of Portugal. Spain officially recognized
this claim for sovereignty in 1668 after almost three decades at war.
Thereafter, though full of challenges and armed conflicts during
the eighteenth and early nineteenth centuries, the history of both
countries mostly featured attempts to define what Spain and Portugal included, where they began, and where they ended.

Most historians who studied the emergence of Portugal as a separate political unit have described it as a by-product of the process by
which the Christian communities of northern Iberia expanded
southward, the so-called Reconquest. For them, the struggle against
the Muslims led to the formation, crystallization, and territorialization of several kingdoms that, as they were integrating new territories, were also forced to rearrange their relations as well as to fix
their boundaries.[2] According to this narrative, from the ninth to
the fifteenth century, a military frontier against Muslims was followed by a frontier of occupation manned by Christian settlers who
slowly penetrated the areas now open for their use. Initially, these
were scarcely populated and mainly controlled by powerful nobles,
military orders, and the church. Yet, after occupation became sufficiently dense, a political frontier also made its appearance. Set by
war, treaties, or both, and championed by kings who imposed and
then enlarged their jurisdiction, by the early modern period the
various kingdoms of the Iberian Peninsula (Portugal, Castile, Aragon, and so forth) were already identifiable units. The border between Castile and Portugal grew out of these developments. Endlessly discussed in the twelfth and thirteenth centuries, it was finally
concretized in 1297 when both monarchs signed the Treaty of Alcañices, which identified which communities would belong to which
crown. As happened elsewhere on the peninsula, here too a frontier
made of several enclaves (mostly castles and monasteries belonging
to the military orders) was thereafter transformed into a zone of
constant expansion and eventually into a line demarcating a clear
separation between what were now differentiated political entities.[3]

The 1297 arrangement persisted over time, making the border between Spain and Portugal "the oldest surviving border in Europe."[4]

These conclusions, reflecting important political and diplomatic, perhaps even military developments, nevertheless failed to describe the processes by which an extremely imprecise and highly theoretical border set in a treaty materialized on the ground. If, initially, most debate between the Spanish and Portuguese monarchs focused on the question of which communities would become part of which kingdom (a particularly contested issue until Alcañices, although continuing even after it was signed), eventually, the transformation of what Alcañices determined in 1297 into a concrete reality entailed the need to identify communities and their inhabitants as well as territories and their occupation. Contemporaries also had to consider whether change over time (in the territorial projection of different settlements, their distinct modes of using the territory, their dependence on one another, and their subjugation to kings, nobles, or the church) influenced these questions and how. Imagining the territory as a space made of islands of occupation in a sea of land, they had to decide whether abandoned terrain belonged to one community, several, or none. Pitting neighboring municipalities against one another, these discussions also involved the church, the military orders, royal officials, and a plethora of individuals who, as residents of these communities, property owners, office holders, animal raisers, smugglers, or worshipers, had a stake in deciding which territories would belong or could be used by whom. The end result of all these developments was a highly complex multilogue (often a mis-dialogue) among a great variety of actors with an enormous diversity of interests. These involved guaranteeing livelihood but also questions of municipal liberties, seigniorial rights, ecclesiastical privileges, and royal jurisdiction, to name just a few. Honor and shame were also frequently invoked, as were family relations, friendship, alliances, and rivalries. Thus, although over time the separation between Spain and Portugal was indeed gradually reaffirmed (even if, on occasions, still questioned), it was not until the nineteenth century, perhaps even the early twentieth century, that their boundaries consolidated in the way we know them today. The appearance of Portugal as a separate unit was therefore gradual, and its legitimacy and borders were constantly negotiated, questioned, and reaffirmed throughout the Middle Ages, the early modern period, and into modernity.

The need to create, identify, and fix municipal jurisdictions in order to ascertain the existence of a border between states has led some historians to suggest that until the eighteenth, perhaps the nineteenth century, Iberian frontiers were mainly a local, not a royal affair. Juxtaposing a history of border formation from below to a history of border formation from above, these scholars suggest that processes of "local" and "national" territorial construction were separate, perhaps even antagonistic, to one another. The collaboration between a "center" and a "periphery" was guaranteed only when the interests of both coincided, and it usually produced the nationalization of the border, because in order to interest the state in their plight and as a result of its intervention, locals gradually assumed identity also as nationals.[5] Meanwhile, borders established against local wishes were mostly ignored or undermined. Although partly correct, these portrayals nevertheless commonly assumed that local communities and their boundaries were fixed and that kings or states were called on to represent their interests or undermine them vis-à-vis foreign powers. Yet historical records indicate that the territorial dynamics that unfolded were substantially more complex because the extension of communities also constantly mutated in accordance to who their members were and what they sought to achieve. A territory defined for grazing was different than a territory constructed for agricultural purposes or for tax collection. It could expand or contract with the passage of time and the subsequent changes in the community or in the way the right to land was comprehended, constructed, or defended. These constant mutations involved a plethora of agents, interests, and developments, some local, some royal, some even global (as the gradual attack on common land and the move to sanctify private property); in the process of vindicating rights, communities also defined themselves as well as distinguished their inhabitants, territories, and usage rights from neighbors both across and on the same side of the border. Rather than either "from below" or "from above," what transpired was a highly convoluted interaction between different social actors who, while defending their particular interests and influenced by practices and ideas, some traditional, others modern, also defined, sometimes even defended, their communal space.

European debates shared many traits with discussions on the other side of the Atlantic. As happened in the New World, most territorial discussions in the Old focused on possession. They unleashed similar dynamics by implying that certain activities such as using the territory or performing jurisdictional acts on it could be read not only as ensuring livelihood but also as a means for proving or even making territorial claims.[6] Rivals could agree to such acts by remaining silent, but they mostly opposed them by protesting verbally or reacting violently. In both the Old and the New World, dependence on possession also required that contemporaries distinguished between acts that were directed at establishing territorial claims and merited protest and those that did not. Yet, in contrast to the Americas, in Europe there was no presumption that all territorial incursions were aimed at acquiring rights. This difference was evident in 1601, for example, when the authorities of Badajoz in Spain obtained recognition that the entry of their inhabitants with cattle to the jurisdiction of Elvas in Portugal should be tolerated as part of the good relations among neighbors and should not be comprehended as a territorial aggression.[7] Somewhat similarly, in 1691, the desire of a few Galicians to cultivate exclusively a land, which they formerly used jointly with their Portuguese neighbors, was interpreted as an infringement of an accord, not as a behavior that challenged the status quo.[8] In 1696, the penetration of Portuguese authorities to Spanish territory in order to imprison a person accused of contraband was thus dealt with as a diplomatic incident, not as a discussion regarding jurisdiction and territory.[9] In the same manner, in 1716, the entry of the inhabitants of Monsarraz (in Portugal) to Alconchel (in Spain) in order to collect acorn was bitterly rejected by the owners of the estate to whom this crop belonged and by Spanish customs guards.[10] However, the case was treated as theft, not as an attempt at a territorial expansion. All these activities, which in the Americas would have probably provoked confrontations, did not in Europe because what distinguished them from others was not what was done but how it was understood. Precisely for that reason, in Europe but not the Americas, foreigners could cultivate a piece of

land in a territory that was allegedly not their own without suffering opposition unless their activities were understood as indicating
the intention of establishing not their private property rights but
the rights of their community or kingdom.

Dependence on possession also explained the degree of violence
these conflicts sometimes involved on both sides of the ocean. Rather
than being gratuitous or purely emotional and irrational, aggression
was mandated by the legal doctrine that equated silence with consent
and made violence a perfect method to communicate disagreement.
Remembrance and forgetfulness also played a juridical role. The immemorial practice that contemporaries invoked could have been genuinely old, but from a legal point of view it mainly operated to change
the burden of proof because, contrary to "simple" possession, immemorial possession admitted no evidence to the contrary.[11] Considered
a fundamental element ensuring legal stability (when such stability
was required), immemoriality constituted a presumption that jurists
called *juris et de jure*. It was aimed at guaranteeing peace, not distinguishing what was true from what was false.

Although in both Europe and the Americas military conquests
might have played a role in augmenting or reducing territorial control, most territorial changes happened during peace and as a result
of the acts that different community members constantly performed.
Treaties might have framed these dynamics—Alcañices certainly
helped to define the border in Iberia—yet, as happened in the
Americas, because accords had to be implemented, interpreted, and
materialized on the ground, they often posed more questions than
supplied answers. Thus, although contemporaries in Europe lamented
the fact that territorial issues were not sufficiently resolved in the
treaties that recognized the independence of Portugal in 1668 or
finalized the war in 1715, they also agreed that accords did not necessarily solve their differences. As happened with Colonia de Sacramento, Verdoejo, for example, could be retained if its inclusion in
the treaty was mistaken and the secession of the castles of Noudar
and Picoña to the Portuguese could be delayed until the parties
could agree on what these units included and which was their territory. The union and disunion of Spain also played a similar role,
aggravating conflicts on both sides of the ocean. Simply put, while

the union lasted, divisions were not particularly respected and, after it ended, finding out what they previously had been or who acted for which state became an impossible, highly convoluted task.

Eighteenth-century monarchs sought to improve their knowledge of the territory and timidly began intervening in its administration.[12] They sent delegates to conduct censuses of cities, villages, and lords, to describe rivers, mountains, and roads, and to prepare maps. Yet, even in the late eighteenth century, even in Europe, some parts of their territories and huge tracts of their borders were fairly unknown, inaccessible, and badly controlled.[13] It was time, some Spanish interlocutors argued, to discover not only the New World but also the Old.[14] These concerns coincided with calls to reform the economy and improve the general welfare.[15] In response, in the second half of the eighteenth century the Spanish court devised plans to revive the province of Extremadura, bordering with Portugal.[16] Making it a symbol for the struggle of kings to consolidate simultaneously what historians have identified as an internal frontier (of occupation) and an external frontier (vis-à-vis a neighbors), during this period royal ministers asserted that both borders were interconnected. Unless Extremadura stopped being a "desert," the border would never be completely secured. Similar perceptions were also invoked in Portugal with regards to the Alentejo, whose social and economic desolation was explained by the constant wars.[17] Coinciding with a desire for agricultural reform and the struggle against grazing and common lands, in Spain, at least, these calls expressed alarm at the possibility that the border would be abandoned by Spaniards and settled by the Portuguese.[18] Thereafter, contemporaries suggested that repopulation of that area was a goal more glorious, useful, and imporant than the conquest of foreign lands.[19]

Despite these important similarities that both explained and shaped how the Spaniards and the Portuguese conducted their affairs overseas, there were also some crucial differences that depended on the conditions on both sides of the ocean. In the Americas, confrontations between Spaniards and the Portuguese and between them and natives were relatively short-lived because in most cases they had begun only twenty, thirty, or forty years earlier, because occupation was precarious rather than permanent, and because European

presence and alliances with natives constantly changed, concretiz-
ing and disappearing over time. Also evident in the New World was
European effort to erase the longer history of the continent, recom-
mencing it with their arrival as if the conquest was a moment of
foundation, not destruction.[20] While the time span covered in the
Americas was relatively short, in Iberia, conflicts could (and often
were) extremely ancient and could last in some cases even six hundred years. The longevity they acquired allowed many of them to
become particularly complex and convoluted. Historians might have
fossilized these confrontations, assuming that as long as they persisted they pitted the same people over the same tract of land and
for the same reason, but a detailed analysis demonstrates that such
was not the case (see most particularly Chapter 3). As if they were
living organs, territorial conflicts constantly mutated as the parties
evolved or changed, realigned their alliances and rivalries, and as
some left the scene and others made their debut. The objects in
contention also greatly transformed, as did the allegations and the
terms of agreement and disagreement. The Iberian scenario, as a result, demonstrated not only where notions implemented in the Americas came from but also what could happen to them when they
persisted. It exemplified the degree by which territorial confrontations could acquire the features of shifting sands, which, although
constantly moving place and changing shapes, could, from the outside, appear steady.

The Iberian story also helps illuminate the role of different arguments and perceptions in the making and remaking of territorial
divisions. If, on both sides of the ocean, law failed to supply a solution and all parties swore obedience to a status quo they could hardly
ever commonly identify, in Iberia they tended to escape more often
to history (how we got here and what that implies). Faced with a past
they assumed was familiar and trusting their immemorial rights,
they nevertheless discovered that history would fail them, too. Repeating references to distant times, ancient loyalties and dependen-
cies produced a density of rights, traditions, and customs that, rather
than solving their differences, complicated them even further. This
feature required actors to engage constantly with change over time,
distinguishing mutations that would be considered consequential

from those not and debating what their meaning should be. The inability to agree on these issues led contemporaries sometimes to mock one another, but it mainly reinforced their disagreements, making clear that their vision of the past was as contested as was their understanding of the present.

But if the inability to reach an accord regarding what had transpired guaranteed that disputes would linger, during the time span in which European conflicts took place, attitudes toward property and jurisdiction were radically modified. This process (which would eventually culminate in the invention of private property and state jurisdiction as we know them today) also entailed a new vision of the territory.[21] Whereas an older understanding conceived of property and territory as by-products of a universal divine order, in which both animals and things participated, the newer version that emerged during the late medieval and early modern period insisted on human agency. Whereas the earlier law centered mainly on situations rather than rights and its jurists insisted on continuity as well as on a strong pluralism that allowed many to enjoy different types of relations to the same land coetaneously, the emerging order emphasized rights and change over time, and it sought to identify and unite all privileges in a single individual owner or a single sovereign. Conjured by philosophers and moralists mainly in the fourteenth and fifteenth centuries, it transcended into the legal realm in the sixteenth and seventeenth centuries and became dominant in the eighteenth century. These mutations allowed contemporaries to assume gradually that human wishes, as well as human accords, constituted the order rather than passively acknowledged it. Thereafter, late seventeenth- and eighteenth-century discussants no longer asked which was the existing objective situation, but instead they wished to explain how man constituted his dominion over things as a function of his needs and desires. Property and dominion, in short, were now presented as projecting human aspirations and became disposable and changeable rather than given and permanent. In the process, man became master of his acts, and property was portrayed as natural (part of the nature of man), absolute (only subjected to his will, not external limitations), and global (as including all faculties and actions). These mutations allowed individuals and communities to acquire a new understanding of what tied them to the land. On the Spanish and Portuguese border in Iberia, they were noticeable, too, often provoking new confrontations. If in the Middle Ages most interlocutors insisted on immemorial customs that were to freeze the past as well as conceive the space as naturally given, in the sixteenth, seventeenth, and eighteenth centuries they began to employ a more voluntaristic vision of the territory that suggested instead that divisions depended also (or mainly) on agreements. This change might have been slow in the making, and both a naturalistic and a voluntaristic understanding of space might have coincided on many occasions. Yet, over time, a consensus emerged that land entitlements were created by agreement between individuals and communities. This enabled contemporaries to make claims against the existing status quo and provided them with intellectual, political, and juridical means to change it. Even immemoriality changed its nature as seventeenth- and eighteenth-century interlocutors now suggested that persistence over time was the result of their agreements, not the automatic expression of some natural order. Thereafter, customs lost their undefined and atemporal character as habits that began in an unknown past by unknown actors. Instead, they were now identified with certain accords that were said to have constituted them. As a result, customs, even immemorial, now had a firm beginning point and a specific content. Meanwhile, in the Americas, possession—initially a method to prove title—became also a powerful tool that could be used to introduce change. Comprehended as a means to take over rather than maintain control over lands or peoples as was theoretically the case in Europe, it now gave expression to human ability to modify rather than respect what had previously existed.

The Iberian example was also useful as a means to consider the participation of "natives" in territorial conflicts. Natives, often treated as objects, were, of course, an essential component in the discussions taking place in the New World, but their presence in Iberian debates was never registered mainly because in Europe such characterizations were not habitually applied. But what would happen if we considered the individuals who lived near the border in Iberia as a separate group, which was distinguished, classified, and stereotyped? In the eighteenth and early nineteenth centuries, royal officials in both

Lisbon and Madrid and in provincial capitals such as La Coruña, Viana, and Seville certainly portrayed them in this way. They insisted that the border was a chaotic territory that was both badly known and difficult to access and control.[22] It felt so remote that in 1640, Spanish royal officials could compare the territory next to Portugal to the American frontier, which was equally foreign.[23] Distance allowed border conflicts to become the subject of rumors: "the long distance between here and Lisbon," the governor of Galicia argued in 1703, "had confused the news."[24] Not quite a chaotic, uncontrolled, and unknown interior (sertão) as in Portuguese America, the European border was nevertheless a space considered dangerous because, among other things, its inhabitants lacked respect for royal law and because monarchical absence was more pronounced than its presence.[25] Fronterizos—who now acquired a status of their own—were thereafter presented as a subgroup of rural inhabitants whose activities affected not only their own interests but also the interests of their states. Inventing them anew by classifying them as different, fronterizos, officials insisted, were free agents who decided what to do and whose behavior, which could not be regulated, was hazardous because it could easily provoke "real" conflicts that would endanger the relations between courts. They were primitive, wild, and unyielding. Because (as rústicos) they were "simple folk" who acted with passion rather than reason and were unable to comprehend the gravity or implications of their behavior, their proximity to a border that was in the process of definition made them particularly menacing. Their activities were at times so threatening to the state that its officials considered them not as compatriots with whom one could reason but as aliens with a different culture, a distinct rationality, and a differentiated set of aims.[26] It was thus vital to subject them to the higher interests of states by enforcing on them agreements that perhaps benefited them, perhaps not, but that were primarily aimed at promoting the well-being of kingdoms.[27]

Essentializing fronterizos as if they had existed before the border itself was set, contemporaries thus downplayed the importance of territorial conflicts in making them thus. Early nineteenth-century interlocutors were particularly adamant about discriminating against them, arguing that as outsiders they, royal officials, knew and understood the territory and its needs much better than did locals. These officials eventually affirmed that *fronterizos* neglected the territory. Their (common) use of the land did not constitute true possession, nor could it improve the terrain. Because by the end of the process *fronterizos* neither insured territorial jurisdiction nor guaranteed economic progress, officials concluded that they could (and must) be dispossessed. Thus, although in none of these debates were *fronterizos* likened to Indians, much of what was said against them hinted at similar directions. If in the early sixteenth century, European rustics were a means to understand the Indians—in 1517 the governor of Hispaniola asked colonists whether Indians were comparable to European peasants, and in 1537 Francisco de Vitoria made this comparison in order to conclude that, like peasants, Indians were also (partially) rational human beings—by the seventeenth and eighteenth centuries the contrary was also true.[28] By that time, whether openly admitted or silently suggested, the Americas became a metaphor that contemporaries used in order to understand European peasants.[29] In Spain in 1568, it was said that "no Indies . . . have such a need for priests as the kingdom of Asturias." During the same period, Jesuits working in southern Italy, Germany, and France complained that the people they wished to indoctrinate were similar to the Indians: they were just as pagan, savage, and uncultured. Like Indians, or even worse, these Europeans lacked all social and political organization.[30] The Indies, these friars said, were everywhere, Europe included.

The Iberian case also serves as a site to reexamine the distinction most historians have intuitively made between internal frontiers of occupation and external frontiers vis-à-vis neighbors. Extremely powerful in scholarly descriptions of the New World, this bifocal division originated with medieval historians who argued that Christian Europe domesticated its hinterland before it expanded externally to conquer new regions, confronting, converting, acculturating, and integrating new peoples as well as constituting (and defining the boundaries of) new states.[31] Historians of Iberia followed suit, describing how after internal occupation was established, new political borders emerged. Meanwhile, historians of the Americas suggested that in the New World these processes happened on the inverse. But if

The Spanish–Portuguese Border in Europe

Contested localities, rivers, and areas in Iberia. Not all the contested territories are included, only those specifically cited in the text.

possession gave rights also vis-à-vis "external" rivals, how could it be distinguished from the processes defining the community from the "inside?" If territorial acquisition called for clarification of which communities existed and who their members were when it assigned them their living space, how could internal developments be distinguished from external? It is also clear that the question provoking territorial conflicts was not necessarily the presence or not of individuals on the ground. Communities might have existed for a long time, and they might have utilized the areas around them for many years without any contestation from neighbors. What made for territorial disputes was not sheer presence but the question of whether those present wished to roam, graze, or plant, have it exclusively as their own, or share it with others. The answer hinged not only on what was actually done but also on how their intentions were interpreted (see Chapter 1). As the type of use constantly mutated, it habitually produced new conflicts and, as a result, new types of frontiers also vis-à-vis neighbors.

In order to understand developments in Iberia and suggest how they can enrich our understanding of the Americas (and vice versa), in what follows I examine in detail several case studies that together demonstrate that European territorial conflicts were more complex than what met the eye. Presenting their development over time, I am particularly keen to demonstrate how contestations changed and how the parties, constantly in variation, fought for different terrains for a diversity of reasons while constantly adopting and dropping different explanations as to why. Getting as near as possible to the ground, I return here to chronology and observe specific contestations as they unfolded from the Middle Ages through the Early Modern period and into modernity. Meant to be read alongside the American part rather than as an introduction or a conclusion to it, my goal here is not to compare one side of the ocean with the other but instead to ask how bringing these cases together modifies our understanding of both.

3 Fighting a Hydra: 1290–1955

O NE OF THE CLEAREST examples of how European conflicts could mutate over time was the confrontation that for some six and a half centuries pitted the neighboring communities of Aroche, Encinasola, Moura, Noudar, Barrancos, and Serpa (in present-day Andalusia in Spain and Alentejo in Portugal) against each other. Habitually regarded as a by-product of the 1283 and 1297 reorganization of territory and its redistribution between Spain and Portugal, it is during this period that we first hear of a conflict between Aroche (in Castile) and Moura (in Portugal) and between both and Noudar (in Portugal) regarding the usage of certain terrains.[1] Attempts at demarcating these areas, identified in the sources first as a "land in contention" and then as "Campo de Gamos" and distinguishing the territory of Moura from that of Aroche and Noudar, were aborted in 1311 because the representatives of the Castilian king who were to judge the rights of the parties—mainly the entitlements of the orders of Templars (in charge of Serpa), Hospitaller (in charge of Moura), and Aviz (in charge of Noudar)—failed to arrive.[2] Already at that stage, the confrontation was bitter, with residents assaulting properties and attacking and killing one another. Despite Castilian absence, in 1311 the Portuguese commissioners proceeded to examine witnesses, as well as a book allegedly including the "ancient" demarcation (*tombo*) of Moura and its distinction from Aroche. The declarations suggested that Aroche's pretensions to possess Campo de Gamos were a fabrication because it was "well known" that this territory belonged to Moura. Because the proceedings included no recognition of the claims made by Noudar, the order of Aviz charged with manning its castle, proceeded to populate the region, among other things by attracting to it settlers from Castile.[3] It is possible that in 1312, King Jaime II of Aragon was instituted as an arbiter in the dispute that by now included not only the definition of municipal limits but also the question of whether Serpa and Moura indeed belonged to Portugal (as Portugal suggested and Castile contested, a stand that perhaps explained why royal delegates were absent in 1311) and Aroche to Spain (as Spain argued and Portugal disagreed).[4] If this arbitration ever took place, it carried no other results than the insistence that Moura and Aroche should treat one another as "neighbors," not enemies. After new negotiations taking place in 1315 also failed, some suggested reviving previous agreements that allowed all neighboring villages to use the contested territory jointly.[5] In 1332, representatives of the Castilian and the Portuguese kings, local councils, Seville (whose municipal jurisdiction included Aroche and Encinasola), and the order of Aviz (in charge of Noudar) met to identify where their boundaries were according to "ancient men" *(hombres ancianos)* and land grant books *(libros de particiones).*[6] While locals acted as plaintiffs, royal delegates fashioned themselves as judges who were to adjudicate conflicts among rival claims. During the proceedings, witnesses for Moura mainly affirmed having heard from their elders that in a remote past, in which the three communities belonged to Castile, authoritative individuals placed boundary stones delimiting their jurisdiction.[7] Although the territory was now partitioned, these divisions were not respected because the inhabitants of Aroche constantly infringed them, leading to violent confrontations that included the sequester of animals, the burning of houses, and attacks on men, women, and property. After Noudar and its castle were depopulated (circa 1320s), no longer fearing opposition, the residents of Aroche intensified their use of this territory. While Moura argued for clear rights that were violated, witnesses for Aroche defended an opposite theory, which sustained that no well-defined partitions ever existed. Indeed, there had been many attempts at establishing a separation, but they all were aborted because of disagreement, thus enabling all to use the territory jointly. This had been the custom since Aroche was refounded as a Christian enclave (circa 1255). It was only in the 1290s when the knights of Aviz arrived that, accompanied by troops, they expelled the inhabitants of Aroche from their ancient possession. Although they continued to vindicate their rights, from the early 1300s, the citizens of Aroche no longer dared to use that land.

All agreed that the conflict dated back to when the four communities (Aroche, Moura, Noudar, and Serpa) were under Castilian jurisdiction and that it had originally confronted the friars of the Temple (in charge of Serpa) and Hospitaller (in charge of Moura) with Seville (in charge of Aroche), only later involving Noudar (and the order of Aviz). Featuring on occasion extreme violence, it also included a constant search for a negotiable solution. In 1346 and 1353, representatives of all interested parties were to meet again to discuss a partition. After the delegates of the Spanish king, Seville, and Aroche failed to arrive, the representatives of Moura, Noudar, and Serpa asked the Portuguese commissioners to pronounce that they could "have as their uncontested limits all these places that their testimonies declared were theirs" *(houvessem os termos sem contenda por aqueles lugares que as suas testemunhas depuseram que era seu).*[8] The Portuguese magistrates refused, explaining that they were empowered only to decide on a division together with Spanish judges, not alone. As conflict lingered, in the 1420s the Portuguese king recommended that Moura and Noudar adopt a friendly agreement regarding the use of Campo de Gamos (and perhaps also an area identified as La Rossiana). The aim of such a solution was not to divide or demarcate the territory but instead to allow the citizens of both communities its common use, with Moura paying some fees to Noudar.[9]

By the fifteenth century, Serpa (in Portugal) initially involved in these confrontations, disappeared from archival records, while a new contender, Encinasola (in Spain), made its debut. The first signs of a confrontation between it and Noudar (in Portugal) date from the 1450s, when the warden of Noudar's castle sequestered animals that, grazing in Campo de Gamos without license or paying dues, belonged to citizens of Encinasola. Rejecting its neighbors' claims that it had absolutely no right to use this terrain, in 1488 Encinasola appealed to Seville for help, receiving in return a judicial decision recognizing its rights as well as instructing it not to allow anyone to enter the territory without the consent of its proprietors. Contemporaneously, Encinasola also appealed to Seville against Aroche (in Spain), whose authorities, it argued, illegally prohibited its inhabitants from using a territory it identified as "La Contienda" that its citizens had always possessed, drinking its water, cutting its wood, and using its pasture.[10] The judges of Seville again favored Encinasola, yet restricted its rights to grazing and gathering, prohibiting its citizens from enclosing the territory for agricultural purposes. Problems between Noudar and Moura (in Portugal) also reemerged during this period as citizens of both communities constantly moved and removed their border stones, leading to new (failed) attempts at demarcation.[11] Efforts to resolve some of these differences by royal delegates, who met in 1493 at the request of the councils of Moura and Noudar, which complained of "Castilian aggression," again produced no results.[12] In 1503, the inhabitants of Moura entered the jurisdiction of Aroche armed, destroying property and removing boundary stones in their favor. To these challenges, the citizens of Aroche responded by sending a military force that destroyed the new demarcation and reestablished the older one. Because these episodes repeated several times, the following year, both monarchs decided to intervene yet again, naming procurators not only to determine where the border was but also to free those who had been jailed during the hostilities as well as to liberate their sequestered animals.[13] Apparently unsuccessful, in 1510, the inhabitants of Moura protested again to the Portuguese king that citizens of Encinasola infringed on their jurisdiction by planting and laboring in their territory.[14] Sent to gather information, a royal envoy visited the terrain accompanied by a contingent of 150 men. Having collected testimony that Castilians were cultivating a contested territory that earlier was used for pasture by both *(terra da contenda pasto mistiquo)*, he ordered the evacuation of Castilian farmers because their lands were located on Portuguese territory. As narrated by Moura, the penetration of Castilians was recent and was accompanied by claims for exclusivity that would prohibit the Portuguese from using their own land. Sotto voce, residents of Moura acknowledged that they had arrived at a modus operandi with Aroche (which mostly used this territory for grazing) when the inhabitants of Encinasola (who also used it for grain farming) interrupted this understanding and upset the delicate balance, perhaps as recently as twenty or thirty years earlier. Their protests against these developments were accompanied by their rejection of the idea that Encinasola had rights to that territory, because once upon a time it was a hamlet of Aroche and as a dependent could thus benefit from its privileges also vis-à-vis Moura.[15]

In 1517, 1528, and 1538, new hostilities took place.[16] While Moura accused inhabitants of Aroche and Encinasola of modifying the status quo, Seville complained to the Spanish king about the Portuguese and requested his protection. Because royal commissioners appointed in 1537 to resolve the conflict could not agree on a just partition, new negotiations were under way in 1542. This time, considering the antiquity of the conflict, which "has lasted among them for much time without ending or resolving until now" (como ha muy gran tiempo que dura entre ellas sin se poder acabar ni determinar hasta ahora), representatives of both monarchs were adamant about reaching an agreement. In an accord expressing compromise rather than justice (concordia or concordata), they divided the contested territory among neighboring communities, reserving its most disputed part, now identified as "La Contienda" and distinguished at least to a degree from Campo de Gamos, for the common use (insolidum) of Aroche, Encinasola, and Moura.[17] The ruling, extremely long and detailed, also included norms concerning the administration of this common property that were mainly directed at its conservation and prohibited activities that could potentially constitute exclusive possession such as cultivating the land or building on it. The agreement clarified that Encinasola had equal usage right but no jurisdiction and that none of the three communities should consider this terrain as "its own." The judges, who refused to divide the territory between Spain and Portugal or make it joint to both kingdoms, also declared it "Castile for Castilians, Portugal for the Portuguese." In order to allow these two distinct jurisdictions to coexist peacefully, they mandated that Aroche would represent Castilian jurisdiction, punishing Spaniards who contravened the accord, while Moura would do the same with the Portuguese. Elaborated a few years after the Treaty of Zaragoza, which ended the conflict regarding the Moluccas (1529), both kings confirmed the accord soon after. In order to ensure peace, in 1543 they proceeded to pardon those having committed crimes on the border and ordered a monetary arrangement to compensate victims.

In the years, decades, and centuries following its adoption, the 1542 accord became a foundational document that was constantly invoked by all parties as the canon by which La Contienda would be managed, as well as the proof (often the only proof) that it commonly belonged to Encinasola, Aroche, and Moura.[18] Because the accord included specific instructions on the administration of the territory, the three communities constantly appealed to it to justify their activities or censure what their rivals were doing. How it was initially abided by we do not know, but from the 1620s until the late nineteenth century (and perhaps beyond), the authorities of Aroche, Moura, and Encinasola visited the territory regularly and punished individuals whom they found in violation of the accord.[19] Intensifying in the eighteenth century, these inspections were initially concerned with the cutting of young tree branches in order to feed pigs (prohibited by the accord), but from the 1740s they also persecuted those who used the land for agricultural purposes and, from the 1780s, they opposed the erection of different structures and walls.[20] Carried out by armed men including local judges, several councilors, and on occasions as many as one hundred others, these inspections usually took place at night or in early morning, sequestering animals or destroying crops or structures illegally found there. Because only the citizens of Aroche, Encinasola, and Moura could use La Contienda, inspections verified not only that activities were permitted but also the identity of their perpetrators. In order to facilitate this task, from as early as the 1710s, they required those using the terrain to carry proof of their citizenship (vecindad).[21] Generally transpiring without great upheaval, on occasions these visits resulted in violent clashes that justified the intervention of royal officials and ambassadors who, reproducing local grievances, demanded that municipal authorities take action to ensure the status quo.[22]

All three municipalities habitually conducted these inquests either on an annual basis or after they received news of particular abuses.

But the activities of Encinasola from the 1730s aroused considerable opposition. Not only did its authorities act more frequently and perhaps more severely, but Moura and Aroche constantly asserted that the 1542 accord gave Encinasola usage rights, not jurisdiction. As a result, its authorities could not conduct inquests or punish violators. The more Aroche and Moura repeated this accusation, the more prone were Encinasola's officials to contest it by visiting La Contienda with their rod of justice raised.[23] The result were violent and frequent confrontations that pitted the judges of Aroche—theoretically the only Spanish authorities who could legitimately act on La Contienda—against the magistrates of Encinasola. Yet, whereas the exercise of jurisdiction by Encinasola triggered extreme tension, its pretension to punish not only Spanish but also Portuguese offenders went unnoticed. Apparently, by the mid-eighteenth century no one considered La Contienda as either Spanish or Portuguese depending on the identity of actors as the 1542 accord mandated. Instead, all parties seemed to agree it was a mixed territory, where all justices—if they had jurisdiction—could act against all violators.[24] By that time, too, the most common agents on La Contienda were delegates of Encinasola, and the most common offenders were citizens of Barrancos in Portugal who constantly used this land, which was right next to their village but to which they had absolutely no rights.[25]

Initially, Encinasola explained its activities by reference to the need to safeguard the 1542 accord, which guaranteed peace among neighbors. However, by the 1780s its authorities indicated that their actions also ensured the well-being of the state. Because La Contienda was a deserted area *(yermo y despoblado)* surrounded by difficult terrain, it served as a sanctuary *(coto y asilo)* for outlaws, deserters, and smugglers. The presence of Encinasola's judges, now often accompanied by royal guards charged with prosecuting contraband *(guarda mayor del resguardo)*, was thus essential to curbing these illegal activities.[26] Portraying its undertaking as a duty that pitted poor yet loyal vassals against powerful crime lords who were "enemies of human nature" *(enemigos de la naturaleza humana)* and "who turned their back at their creator" and were thus atheists *(cuyos hechos publican el ateísmo de sus conciencias por haber vuelto enteramente la espalda a su creador*), Encinasola asserted that it prosecuted the citizens of Barrancos not only because they habitually infringed the 1542 accord but mainly because Barrancos was a *refugium peccatorum* (a refuge place for sinners).[27] Thereafter, and justifying their extreme militarization, inspections were presented by Encinasola's authorities as a means to both imprison criminals and safeguard La Contienda.[28]

Although hostilities among citizens of Encinasola, Aroche, Moura, and Barrancos (Noudar was by then completely depopulated[29]) continued, so did attempts to reach an agreement that would either guarantee order or consensually enable their residents to infringe the 1542 accord.[30] Explaining in 1760, 1762, 1768, and 1779 that clearing the terrain was mandated by need—vegetation was so thick it was impossible for animals to graze there without risking being devoured by wolves—and that, once cleared, its use for agricultural purposes was both logical and convenient, the inhabitants of Encinasola and Aroche requested royal permit to cultivate the land. Overtly including a petition to infringe the 1542 accord, which prohibited such use, these pleas responded to pressure from below and sought to sanction legally a practice that had already been followed for a long time. They asserted that the changes solicited would improve municipal rents and enable both communities to pay royal dues. Pleas also stated that the regular law, which banned the transformation of pasture into arable land, was not applicable here because La Contienda was not a normal Spanish territory. The 1542 accord instituted on it a particular legal regime that was not subject to what Spanish law otherwise mandated. Insisting on local poverty, the lack of resources, and the absence of fertile ground, Aroche and Encinasola pleaded for an urgent solution. They also mentioned that, because there was practically no border between Spain and Portugal and no permanent cultivation, theft and other "excesses" *(excesos)* were frequent on La Contienda. Attempts to involve Moura in these pleas constantly failed. Aroche and Encinasola reasoned that its silence could be explained only by it having sufficient agricultural land and not needing more. But even as its authorities refused to engage in these formal requests, locals knew that many citizens of Moura habitually planted on La Contienda, thus de facto doing what Aroche and Encinasola now requested to authorize de jure.

·

Suggestions to divide La Contienda between the rival municipalities became common from the 1750s. However, it was not until
the 1800s that they found considerable support at the Spanish court.[31]
This backing was based no longer on the need to remedy public order, as had been the case, but instead on the wish to improve the land,
which according to the standards operating at that time required
privatization. If joint use was a widespread solution in the past, its
continuation was now deemed extremely prejudicial because it caused
fighting among neighbors and allowed the presence of undesirable
elements and fertile grounds to remain barren. Suggesting that grazing (the main activity on La Contienda) was "waste" that restricted
the development of arable land, in the 1800s Spanish royal officials
concluded that there was an urgent need to partition the territory
between Spain and Portugal not because of the need to fix the border but rather because this partition would allow them to divide it
into plots that could be sold or given to individual owners.[32] Having
nominated delegates in 1803 to discuss these issues, as soon as bilateral conversations began, the question of how partition would be
accomplished provoked heated debates.[33] Some Spaniards suggested
a division in thirds, giving Encinasola, Aroche, and Moura an equal
share. Others asserted it was more appropriate to consider not the
extension of land but its worth. They also pointed out that the rights
of Aroche and Moura were different than Encinasola's because
while the first two had both usage and jurisdiction, the last did
not.[34] These ideas led to a Spanish proposal to divide the territory
into sixteen parts, with six to Aroche and Moura but only four to
Encinasola.[35] On the Portuguese side, several suggestions were also
made. Initially, the Portuguese commissioner argued in 1803 for
partition in halves because Moura's population was much larger than
that of Aroche and Encinasola combined and because the number of
its animals pasturing in La Contienda was double. It therefore de
facto had possessed more than half of the usage rights there. When
his offer was rejected, the Portuguese commissioner suggested another solution that advanced the hypothesis that Encinasola had no
rights vis-à-vis Moura (and Portugal) at all because its usage was a
by-product of its dependency on Aroche. Its entitlements, therefore, were an affair that its authorities would have to settle with

Aroche and Spain, not Moura and Portugal. For its part, the Portuguese court proposed to the Spanish ambassador in Lisbon that if disagreement continued, it would perhaps be wiser to abandon the 1542 accord altogether, drawing a new line that would divide the territory according to "natural" frontiers.

While commissioners on the border, ambassadors in the courts, and kings accused one another of willful and intentional procrastination, locals did their best to stop the division altogether because, according to them, partition would harm the three communities. "United, this land produced common utility to all and, divided, each would only have a small portion" *(porque reunido este terreno produce . . . utilidad común a todas y dividido tocaría a cada una muy corta porción de él)*.[36] Pleading in 1805 and 1806 that the 1542 accord be upheld, they also requested approval of a new agreement that rearranged their relations more efficiently. According to the Spanish commissioner, they made sure that Lisbon would give its delegates orders that would made the adoption of an agreement impossible. In 1808, as the Duke of Cadaval sailed with his king to Brazil, abandoning Noudar as well as the struggle with his neighbors regarding territory and rights, Aroche, Encinasola, and Moura exchanged several letters concerning La Contienda.[37] In order to debate these issues as "cultivated nations" *(naciones cultas)* did, Aroche suggested meeting with Moura to decide "what would be best *[lo que se conceptúa más oportuno]* for their citizens." Though several meetings were planned, all were canceled, leading Encinasola to argue with Aroche over who was to blame and whether Encinasola—who lacked jurisdiction—should have been invited. These exchanges were extremely bitter. After the authorities of Encinasola waited for over forty hours in La Contienda only to discover that their counterparts would not arrive, they expressed "horror" *(horror)* and asked whether the other two municipalities were mocking *(burlar)* it. Aroche contested that it certainly was not. Moura maintained its distance, explaining in two short letters that, given the political situation (the Napoleonic invasion and the constitution of local governing juntas), its authorities were far too busy with urgent affairs to bother with how La Contienda should be managed. Indirect testimony suggests, however, that sometime before 1813 the three municipalities did reach an agreement regarding how to divide La Contienda into plots and assign them to individual citizens.[38] In 1816, 1834, 1863, and 1865, the three communities again concurred on how to infringe the 1542 accord, mainly by allowing residents to use La Contienda for agricultural purposes.[39] It is therefore not surprising that a description of La Contienda in a Spanish geographical dictionary dated 1847 stated that it was a fertile territory belonging to Moura, Encinasola, and Aroche but neither to Spain nor to Portugal.[40] The Spanish commissioner named in 1885 to divide the territory partially agreed with this. Mocking his Portuguese interlocutor for arguing that the question involved the jurisdiction of Spain and Portugal, he affirmed that La Contienda was neither.[41] During this period, the three municipalities equally sustained that La Contienda was a "neutral" territory that, rather than subject to Spanish or Portuguese law, had its own particular legal regime. Collaboration between their councils continued into the early twentieth century.[42] And though Spain and Portugal agreed to divide La Contienda in 1893 and 1894 and this partition was included in the 1926 border treaty between both countries, contestation continued thereafter. It was only in 1932, when the territories of Aroche and Encinasola were finally separated and demarcated and, in 1955, when border stones between Spain and Portugal were at last placed, that a conflict that had lasted for 650 years came to its (formal) termination.[43]

While the situation on La Contienda dramatically changed over time, so did relations between Aroche and Encinasola. Particularly tense between 1591 and 1637, conflicts between these two Spanish communities might have begun long before (perhaps as early as 1485) and persisted long after.[44] The most important disagreement between their citizens and authorities centered on whether from "time immemorial" they were "undivided" (indivisos), thus sharing the same territory and jurisdiction (as Encinasola would argue) or not (as Aroche would claim). The answer was of no small consequence, because if the former interpretation was correct, then despite their apparent separation into two distinct settlements they each could use the territory of the other as if it was their own. Repeatedly, municipal and royal judges who reviewed this question ruled that the two communities indeed shared usage rights but not jurisdiction and, obstinately, both Encinasola and Aroche endeavored to obtain recognition that the situation was the inverse. This miscommunication lasted for centuries, on occasions featuring extreme violence, as happened, for example, in 1629, when the judges of Encinasola, accompanied by armed men *(con armas en forma de guerra)*, entered Aroche's territory and carried out different acts of jurisdiction such as imprisoning several individuals, disarming others, and mistreating the rest.[45]

If initially Encinasola insisted only on exercising jurisdiction in Aroche, by the eighteenth century its claims extended to La Contienda. This perhaps explains why Aroche reacted so violently to the inspections it conducted there, believing them not innocent attempts to protect La Contienda but instances with potentially a much larger agenda and projection. The determination that Aroche and Encinasola shared usage rights but not jurisdiction might also have indicated how Encinasola got access to La Contienda in the first place, because it would suggest that, regardless of any other consideration, if Aroche could use it, so could Encinasola. The Portuguese commissioner, as a result, was perhaps correct when he concluded that originally, at least, Encinasola's entitlements were derivative rather than independent. Expanding over time, disagreement between Aroche and Encinasola escalated to such a degree that in 1757 Aroche's authorities attempted to capture the judges of Encinasola, whom they found in La Contienda with their rod of justice *(vara de justicia)* raised.[46] The magistrates managed to escape, yet they returned the following day accompanied by some thirty armed men.

During this period, and paralleling what was happening in La Contienda and between the Spanish villages of Aroche and Encinasola, the confrontation between Encinasola, Aroche, and Noudar (in Portugal) over possession of Campo de Gamos also intensified. In 1642, after he had declared in favor of Philip rather than João, the Count of Linhares was stripped of the *comenda* of Noudar, which remained vacant until 1684, when it was reassigned to the Duke of Cadaval.[47] A posteriori testimonies suggest that during the vacancy and the war (1640–1668), Noudar and Campo de Gamos were used by all but that in 1674, perhaps as a prelude to its reassignment, the order of Aviz moved to demarcate the territory.[48] Mainly aimed at

distinguishing Moura from Noudar (both in Portugal), the proceedings taking place that year also identified and demarcated a *terra
da contenda*, that is, a disputed territory. Judging these as attempts to
"renovate the demarcation" and considering them null and void, the
authorities of Encinasola—who were never invited to join because
Noudar constantly negated the rights of Encinasola in Campo de
Gamos—refused to accept what had been decided and instead moved
to collect testimony regarding "the places and sites where the limits
dividing both kingdoms were found from immemorial time until
the present" *(los parajes y sitios por donde de tiempo inmemorial a aquella
parte iban los linderos que demarcaban la división de uno y otro reino)*. Its
council then voted to place border stones between it and Noudar
where, according to this investigation, they were located before the
Portuguese allegedly removed them to a new place.[49]

In 1675, therefore, two demarcations of Campo de Gamos took
place, one conducted by the Portuguese of Noudar, the other by the
Castilians of Encinasola. Each disregarded the other and each
claimed absolute validity. One divided Noudar from both Moura
and Spain; the other distinguished Encinasola from Noudar, Spain
from Portugal. Given this uncertain result, in early 1676, a Portuguese judge returned to the territory to demarcate where Campo de
Gamos ended and where the "terra da contenda" began.[50] Yet, because Encinasola was again not invited, in 1678 its authorities—who
disagreed with the way the Portuguese distinguished Campo de
Gamos from La Contienda—undertook another demarcation in the
presence of various citizens of Portugal *(vecinos de Portugal)*. Soon
after, representatives of the Duke of Cadaval took possession of the
comenda. They remarked in 1686 that "where in old times *[antigua-
mente]*" various houses and a castle had stood, all that remained were
some fortifications and a church.[51] While Noudar and its castle were
completely depopulated, Barrancos, which began at a small hamlet
that depended on the castle, was now thriving and served as a seat
for authorities that beforehand were situated in Noudar (the judge,
the notary, and so forth). According to the duke's men, between
1642 when it was vacated and 1686 when it was repossessed, the *comenda* had lost much of its value and territory. Encroaching on its
rights were mostly the Portuguese of Moura, who began using

Campo de Gamos as if it was their own.[52] Also penetrating its properties were the inhabitants of Barrancos, who treated the entire jurisdiction as if it were public rather than private domain. Spaniards may have also benefited from this chaos, usurping large parts.

During this period, locals also failed to arrive at an accord regarding the extension of La Rossiana (Ruciana, Rocianas), another piece of land that, belonging to Noudar, bordered with Encinasola. In 1688, having inspected the territory and heard witnesses for both Encinasola and Noudar, a Portuguese judge concluded that the case was unclear *(pouca clareza que havia do sitio verdadeiro por onde a dita defeza partia com as terras do conselho de Anzinasolla).*[53] Because the contested territory was small *(da pouca consideração)*, he divided it in halves. In 1693, however, the Duke of Cadaval contested this partition, arguing that it was "badly done" *(mal feita)* because it ignored the old demarcation (dated 1607) and was prejudicial to his *comenda.* He also asserted that the Portuguese judge proceeded as he did because he received bribes.[54] Invited to join the proceedings by the Portuguese Mesa da Consciência, to which the duke appealed, Encinasola refused. Its authorities explained that after peace was reestablished (1668) a Portuguese judge tried to demarcate the territory unilaterally and, in response, Encinasola proceeded to "renew" the border stones according to where they were in 1640 (before the war).[55] Because the inhabitants of Noudar refused to recognize these divisions as valid, the authorities of Encinasola repeated the same demarcation in their presence. Although the council of Noudar agreed with all that had transpired, its members argued that they had no authorization to proceed to a formal partition and thus refused to sign the papers. They did, however, agree that the "piece" *(pedazo)* in conflict would in the meantime be used by both communities. A third demarcation then took place in La Rossiana, in which Encinasola presented to a Portuguese judge documents regarding its rights. Having visited the territory, the judge then retired without reaching a decision or producing a written report. Such was the situation in 1688, when a new judge, sent by the Portuguese king to bring about the end of discord and *mala vecindad,* suggested (and Encinasola accepted) that, given that there was no clear evidence as to who was right and who wrong and that the differences between the parties were small *(era corto el interés)*, it would be best to adopt a compromise to divide the area equally between the two communities. The inhabitants of Encinasola were unhappy with this result because the entire territory was rightfully theirs, but they were willing to accept this solution in order to ensure peace *(evitar las diferencias y estar en quieta y pacífica paz)*. One citizen of Barrancos and another from Encinasola then took an oath and, alongside the judge, they proceeded to demarcate the territory. The 1688 proceedings, in short, represented a good solution, carried out with "justice" and "Christianity." But a few malicious individuals from Noudar and Barrancos conspired to convince the duke that it was badly done. These men persuaded him that Encinasola had bribed the judge and was thus able to add illegally to its jurisdiction a vast tract of land belonging to Noudar.[56] Encinasola pointed out that the 1688 demarcation was carried out by a Portuguese judge who followed the correct procedures. If one of the parties felt injured, it could appeal to a normal royal court, not the Mesa de Consciência, whose role was to oversee the interests of the military orders (and thus the order of Aviz). At any rate, Encinasola was not party to the discussion because the only legitimate partaker was Seville. The Mesa de Consciência ruled otherwise, in 1700 giving the duke the right to redemarcate the territory, which he did in 1703.[57] A posteriori, Encinasola would argue that this was done at the discretion of the judge *(arbitrio)* and that this deprived it of much of its jurisdiction. While appealing to Seville for help, Encinasola also immediately moved to restore the border stones to where they allegedly were in 1688, which was also their correct location before the 1640 war.[58]

All parties appealed to the same 1607 demarcation, which they considered consensual, but they were completely unable to agree on what it had contained. Contestation continued thereafter, with Encinasola appealing again to Seville and requesting the intervention of the Spanish king in 1716.[59] Its authorities explained that during the War of Spanish Succession (which confronted Spain with Portugal from 1703 to 1715), the Castle of Noudar and Barrancos were occupied by Spanish forces, and their devolution to Portugal in 1715 stirred things up again because no one could agree on what the situation before the war had been. As a result, there was heated disagreement on what should (according to the Treaty of Utrecht, in 1715) be returned to Portugal and what should remain Spanish.

Playing cat and mouse, the citizens of Barrancos (who now clearly stood for depopulated Noudar), accompanied by representatives of the Duke of Cadaval, relocated the border stones *(límites y mojones)* and so did the inhabitants of Encinasola.[60] Violent confrontations took place when, according to Portuguese complaints, the authorities of Encinasola, escorted by some two hundred armed men, tried to get in the way of the demarcation by a Portuguese judge. Although to avoid conflict *(tumulto y pelea que se iba encendiendo)* the Portuguese magistrate and his men retreated, the Portuguese king—who defended their activities as both legal and necessary—demanded that Spaniards allow this demarcation, which was based on a decision "pronounced with knowledge of cause, the parties having been heard" *(una sentencia que se pronunció con conocimiento de causa oídas las partes)* by a competent authority (the Portuguese Mesa de Consciência). In response, in 1716 the Spanish royal authorities asked the Portuguese king to ensure obedience to the 1688 division, which was adopted with the consent of all interested parties. The Portuguese authorities answered with a "paper" *(papel)* authored by the Duke of Cadaval rejecting this interpretation.[61] Because the Spanish Council of State believed that the main obstacle for agreement was the duke, it suggested that the ambassador in Lisbon speak to him privately and assure him that his interests would not be undermined even if the territory would be declared Spanish.[62] The duke countered these attempts by furnishing the Portuguese foreign minister with various documents.[63] Proceedings stopped subsequently, the Portuguese minister confessing to be too busy to read these papers and the Spanish ambassador hoping that his nonresponse would ensure that the matter would die on its own, as apparently it did.

If confrontation between Encinasola and Noudar disappeared from royal records, the violent conflicts pitting Moura and Noudar (both in Portugal) over Campo de Gamos continued to occupy locals and the Portuguese court. From the sixteenth century there were a succession of judicial investigations concluding that the land belonged to Noudar (and Barrancos) but that Moura was allowed to use it by virtue of an accord dated 1516 and reconfirmed in 1605 with the previous owner of the *comenda*, the Count of Linhares.[64] Records indicate this arrangement was itself a compromise *(transacção, concerto e amigável composição)* between rivals who constantly disagreed about their rights and whose relationships since the fourteenth century were plagued by a series of lawsuits. The accord they reached in 1516, which allowed Moura to use the Campo in exchange for payment, was meant to settle the dispute. However, as with the 1542 agreement, the 1516 pact between Moura and Noudar opened the way for renewed discord. In the years following its adoption, what exactly had been transferred to Moura became a contested question. Was the agreement limited in time or permanent? Did it include Campo de Gamos or only parts thereof? Was jurisdiction also transferred? And who had the right to collect tithes there? Could Moura, by virtue of this agreement, acquire rights by way of prescription? New judicial confrontations in 1673, 1688, 1691, 1692, 1694, 1699, 1702, 1705, 1709, 1715–1717, 1730, and 1808 repeatedly concluded with the assertion that Campo de Gamos was Noudar's.[65] Yet, the more the duke insisted that it was his, the more the inhabitants of Moura maintained it was not. Entering into the discussion in the eighteenth century were also the citizens of Noudar and Barrancos, who argued that even if it belonged to Noudar, rather than being the private property of the duke, Campo de Gamos was in the public domain.[66] Such debates might have had precedents, as it is possible that even as early as 1594 locals accused their lord (the Count of Linhares) of abusing his privileges by demarcating the territory in ways that converted common property into his private domain. They might have clashed with him again in 1600, when he invited interested individuals to come and work his barren lands, which the inhabitants of Moura and Noudar asserted were common pasture grounds, not his private property.

The Parties

Whereas historians have tended to portray the confrontation among Aroche, Encinasola, Serpa, Moura, Noudar, and Barrancos as pitting Portuguese against Spanish municipalities or suggested that these border communities wished to ignore a division that was imposed on them by royal will, it is clear that the conflicts that took place from 1290 to 1955 were much more complex. Aroche and Encinasola (in Castile) might have confronted Serpa, Moura, Noudar, and Barrancos (in Portugal), but they also constantly challenged one another, the same thing being true of the Portuguese villages. Their

disagreements dated from the period in which they all belonged to
Castile, and although some discussants suggested that they were aggravated after they were assigned to different kingdoms, such insin-
uations were relatively rare. Rather than giving relevance to subjugation to kings, most local interlocutors described as important the
processes that allowed dependent municipalities (Barrancos as dependent of Noudar, Encinasola as dependent of Aroche, and perhaps
Noudar as dependent of Moura, as well as Aroche and Encinasola as
dependent of Seville) to obtain relative autonomy that, among other
things, forced them to redefine their territories as separate, thus pre-
venting old partners from using their land.[67] Records also suggest
that Aroche and Moura (across the border) might have been more
willing to cooperate than, for example, Aroche and Encinasola (both
in Castile). Their collaboration covered multiple areas and lasted for
a prolonged period. Both Aroche and Moura agreed in the late thirteenth century to jointly use La Contienda against the orders of
Seville. In 1510, they again reached an understanding regarding
common use of certain areas.[68] Moura and Aroche consented to the
1542 accord, with Moura appealing only the decision to grant Encinasola usage rights. Moura also sided with Aroche against Encinasola in the early seventeenth century, when Aroche wished to prove
in Seville that its jurisdiction was distinct and separate.[69] In the eighteenth century, Moura repeatedly used Aroche as a channel to communicate with Encinasola both to set and cancel meetings. Allied
with Aroche against Encinasola, Moura nevertheless confronted the
former over certain issues such as the daily management of La Contienda. And while hostilities between Encinasola and Aroche might
have been continuous and might have covered questions much more
essential to their livelihood than La Contienda, such as whether they
shared usage rights and jurisdiction everywhere, equally permanent
were the attempts by both villages to reach an understanding that
would allow their citizens, for example, to infringe the 1542 accord
by allowing agriculture, a desire that Moura might have not shared.[70]
Moura and Noudar (both in Portugal) also constantly confronted
one another over usage and jurisdiction in Campo de Gamos, yet
records suggest that at the same time they were closely connected, as
most of the military captains of the castle of Noudar and most ecclesiastics working there, as well as the individuals who rented land

from the local lord, were from Moura.[71] And while Moura and Noudar were tightly related, Barrancos, theoretically a dependent of Noudar, was closer to Encinasola than to its alleged center.

Seville, whose municipal jurisdiction extended to this territory, sometimes took part in these discussions. Yet, if it often sided with Aroche and Encinasola against what it perceived as outside threats, it also conflicted with them over many other issues. There is even reason to believe that before the 1542 accord was adopted, the gravest problem both Aroche and Encinasola faced was not their repeated conflicts with neighboring Portuguese communities but their constant confrontations with Seville. These might have begun in the late thirteenth century when Seville prohibited Aroche from allowing the citizens of Moura to use its jurisdiction, also admonishing its authorities that usage rights were not theirs to decide.[72] They might have continued after Seville instituted its jurisdiction as a single territory for the purpose of grazing, gathering, and drinking water. This legal development, which created a *comunidad de montes y pastos*, implied that all communities under Seville had to share their common grounds with all citizens of all Sevillian communities. The imposition of Sevillian common grazing grounds, we know, was extremely contentious. In 1453, for example, the council of Cumbres de San Bartolomé (a nearby community) complained to Seville that while the citizens of Encinasola used its territory, Encinasola prohibited Cumbres de San Bartolomé from doing the same. That very year, the council of Aroche also protested that citizens of Fregenal (another nearby village) seized over two hundred animals that its inhabitants left grazing in their territory. Demographic growth only exacerbated these conflicts, as did the war of Castilian succession (1475–1479).[73] Yet the obligation to exclude Moura from its grazing grounds and instead admit all citizens of all Sevillian municipalities might not have provoked so much contestation in Aroche if it were not for the fact that during the Muslim period Aroche, Moura, and Noudar all belonged to Beja (currently in Portugal) and all shared their pastures.[74] In 1253, Aroche was formally subjected to Seville, while Moura and Noudar remained under Beja. Initially, the three communities continued to use jointly their common properties, but competing for hegemony with Beja and desiring to establish authority over its recently instituted territory, Seville gradually restricted such practices,

insisting, as it did in 1290, that Aroche would exclude its old partners. Subjugation to Seville, in short, both intervened with existing
structures and levied new obligations.[75] The requirement to prevent
Moura but allow all other Sevillians to graze was uncomfortable to
Aroche (where in the sixteenth century about half of its economic
activity was based on husbandry), but it was particularly bothersome
to Encinasola, whose livelihood completely depended on it. Given
these antecedents, the 1542 accord could be read as an agreement
against rather than favoring Seville, the jurisdictional lord. It recognized the rights of Encinasola and Aroche to use important grazing
grounds that they would otherwise have to share with citizens of
other Sevillian municipalities, and it protected them from the intervention of Seville in what they traditionally shared with Moura but
not with Cumbres de San Bartolomé or Frenegal, to mention but
two examples. In some odd way, the 1542 accord thus legitimized the
claims Aroche had already made in the late thirteenth century vis-à-
vis Seville, suggesting it had the ability to contract with its neighbors
and share its grazing grounds with whomever it saw fit. If this hypothesis is correct, then the 1542 agreement was not only a sensible
solution that relied on traditional mechanisms of peace making (the
sharing of contested territories), it was also an accord that enshrined
local understanding and local needs and was adopted mainly despite
and against Seville, not in collaboration with it.

If local alliances and divisions were extremely complex, so was
the configuration of actors. By the mid-fifteenth century, Serpa
completely disappeared, and Encinasola made its debut. Soon after,
so did Barrancos, with Noudar gradually depopulating and thus becoming a phantasm, which de facto although not de jure operated
not as a thriving community but as the private domains of a particular lord.[76] Reflecting economic, social, and political changes such
as the growth of certain communities and the reorientation of their
economies, it was a paradoxical result that by the eighteenth century an intensively violent strand of this conflict pitted Encinasola
against Barrancos. Perhaps the citizens of Barrancos were indeed
those who most often infringed the 1542 accord; perhaps because
Barrancos was not party to it, it was easier for Encinasola to harass
its citizens than to attempt jurisdictional undertakings against

Aroche and Moura, which denied it the right to act; perhaps because Noudar ceased to exist, Barrancos took its place as the main protagonist on the border; perhaps the Duke of Cadaval was behind the struggle, as was often argued; but it was also possible that Barrancos and Encinasola clashed mostly because they were nearest to one another and both experienced continuous demographic and economic growth. Yet, if the constant and violent confrontations between the citizens of these two communities were particularly striking, it was because both ancient and continuing family and friendship ties linked their inhabitants. Their common story dated back to the 1300s, when the masters of Aviz allowed or encouraged Castilians to immigrate to their territory.[77] This policy was so successful that records dated 1493/1494 indicate that by that time most of the inhabitants of Barrancos were Castilians and they mostly came from Encinasola or Cumbres de San Bartolomé, another nearby village.[78] During an investigation that year, most of them testified that their village was located on Portuguese soil. Coming under enormous pressure to change their testimony and ascertain that it was Spanish, they complained to the Portuguese commissioner that they were habitually classified in Encinasola as "criminals who were against Castile" *(malhechores de la tierra contra Castilla)*. They also attested that many of their kinsmen and compatriots tried to convince them to modify their declarations rather than risk punishment by losing the properties they had in Spain. The Castilian commissioner and the notary to the proceeding also pressured them, telling those among them who professed loyalty to the Castilian king, saying they had fought for him in Malaga and Granada, that they now betrayed their monarch and were worthy of death. Rumors also circulated that after royal commissioners left the region, war would break out among neighbors, with Barrancos being attacked by Encinasola and burned to the ground. These produced the defection of many Barranqueños, who, paradoxically, found refuge in Castile.

The records of the 1493/1494 proceedings—the same year the monarchs of Spain and Portugal signed two treaties in the town of Tordesillas, the first dividing the Atlantic into spheres of influence and the second assigning territories along the shores of Africa—indicate that the presence of Castilians in Barrancos transformed the territory and affected rights.[79] While Noudar slowly depopulated, Barrancos gradually took its place and controlled its jurisdiction as well as enjoyed its rights. Thereafter, it came into direct confrontation with Aroche and Encinasola, which before the arrival of Castilian inhabitants to Barrancos could use Noudar's territory almost freely. Barranqueños, in short, not only established the rights of Portugal to the territory as the order of Aviz might have wanted, but they also, perhaps mainly, limited what Spaniards who were often their neighbors, friends, and relatives could or could not do. It is therefore not surprising that these developments were not appreciated by their kinsmen and former compatriots with whom they continued to have tight connections, going to and from their settlement. Yet, while during the 1493 proceedings Castilians accused Barranqueños of treason, the Portuguese suspected them, too, suggesting that despite their declarations favoring Portugal, deep inside they harbored loyalty to Spain.[80]

Formally classified as Portuguese thereafter, until the late eighteenth century the status of Barrancos and its inhabitants would continue to be contested and debated, as well as reaffirmed. Its ambiguous status was again revealed in 1641, after the Duke of Braganza declared himself king of Portugal. Marking the first military confrontation between Spaniards and Portuguese in what came to be known as the War of Portuguese Independence (*Guerra da Restauração*), late that year Barrancos was attacked by Portuguese forces.[81] The attack, which destroyed the village, was justified with the explanation that its inhabitants, because of their close ties to Castile, favored King Philip II and pronounced against João, the Braganza duke. It might have also been motivated by the identity of the *comendador*, Miguel de Noronha, Count of Linhares, whose loyalty to João was questioned and who indeed ended up backing Philip, thus losing, among other things, his control over Noudar.[82] As in 1493, although the military commander issued orders prohibiting locals from finding refuge in Castile under penalty of being banished as traitors, in their desperation many Barranqueños fled to Encinasola, where they were received with open arms. Contemporary sources explained that they had no choice, having been reduced to living in the fields "like Gypsies," their constant appeals for clemency protesting that they were loyal to the new Braganza dynasty going unheard, as did the "tears of their women and innocent children." To their compatriots in Encinasola, Barranqueños, however, told another story about how they had always been loyal to Philip and how, as loyal vassals, they had always notified Spaniards of what the "rebel" forces of the Duke of Braganza were doing.[83]

A minuscule episode in a war that formally lasted twenty-eight years (1640–1668) but which mostly featured looting, the destruction of Barrancos, a Portuguese village under the patronage of the order of Aviz yet in the hands of a Portuguese noble who sided with Philip against the Duke of Braganza by Portuguese forces, might have had political and strategic motivations, but it certainly also had local explanations.[84] At least a third of the forces that destroyed Barrancos were recruited in Moura, its traditional opponent as well as close ally. It is therefore clear that among those who ravaged the village there were many individuals who stood to gain. Besides participating in the pillage, they had reason to believe that, now that Noudar was depopulated, the elimination of Barrancos might allow them to use Campo de Gamos freely.[85] If this reading is correct, then the attack on Barrancos might at least be partially explained not by reference to kings and countries but by considering grazing grounds and property. This possibility is backed by current research that affirms that the Portuguese War of Independence was principally a struggle among neighbors who, taking advantage of the global confrontation, sought to loot one another.[86] Indications that such was the case are not lacking. In 1641, for example, the Portuguese military commander ordered the citizens of Moura to return to Aroche the sheep that they had stolen. Moura also sought to profit from the new political situation in other ways, asking the new Portuguese monarch in 1641 if, despite the war, it was still required to obey the 1542 accord.[87] The king responded that it was not.

Even in the eighteenth century, contemporaries still were amazed that, as in earlier times, most Barranqueños were of Castilian origin and most had tighter connections to Spain than to Portugal. Many were born in Encinasola, while others were related by family ties to its citizens or held properties on both sides of the border.[88] The mutual influence between Encinasola and Barrancos led one Barranqueño to suggest in 1796 that his village was situated "half in Spain, half in Portugal and, as a result, had inhabitants of both nations" (*por*

*ser situada na raia de que é metade neste Reino e a outra no de Hespanha,
composta por tanto de moradores de ambas as Nações).*[89] In the judicial
proceedings that he initiated that year, the presence in Barrancos of
first- and second-generation Spanish immigrants, mostly from Encinasola, was quite clear.

The rivalry between Encinasola and Barrancos that focused on
the illegal use of La Contienda could thus be viewed also as a family
feud or a quarrel among friends and relatives who used territories
on both sides of the border but who often disagreed about how to
arrange and rearrange their relations. Not only does that break down
the dichotomy between "Spaniards" and "Portuguese," one side of
the border and the other, it also suggests that private or group interests might have played a greater role in these dynamics than contemporary records allow us to perceive. These records concentrate
on rival municipalities and their actions. Following Spanish and
Portuguese law, they state that villages were corporations that could
and often did act in defense of their jurisdiction. Insistence on communal action is also justified by the nature of the privileges defended, which were collective rather than individual. Because their
enjoyment depended on the existence of communities, which had
rights from time immemorial, individuals who wanted to use La Contienda needed to engage in communal rather than individual action.
By doing so, they made places rather than people the protagonists
of their quarrels. Nonetheless, a detailed analysis of what transpired
shows that even when municipalities were said to have acted, their
activities were initiated, carried out, and concluded by persons who
were mostly protecting their own interests. These individuals let
their pigs eat acorns and drink water, they collected wood, planted
fields, constructed huts, performed judicial inquests, or resorted to
violence for ends that perhaps could benefit other members but were
not necessarily motivated by such concerns. Contemporary records
also clarify that not everybody equally participated in these activities, and many, when questioned about what had transpired, took to
silence. Those who chose to testify could do so in favor of their
community or in order to support rival claims. Concerns with private property might have also played a major role. In 1488, for example, Encinasola (i.e., the community as a legal body) might have
fought for rights in Campo de Gamos because some of its citizens

(as private individuals) owned land there.[90] How these owners elicited municipal support remained unknown, but it was clear that the ensuing debate defended their rights rather than engaged with the privileges of their community.

Once communal agency is closely interrogated, it thus becomes clear that individual action takes the center stage. This was true in the conflict between Encinasola, Aroche, Barrancos, and Moura, but it was also evident elsewhere. In the 1530s, for example, the inhabitants of Vinhais (Portugal) complained to the royal authorities that the annually elected local judges, led by private interests, refused to inspect communal demarcations or ensure that Galicians would not violate them, as was their duty.[91] It is thus revealing that in 1795, several citizens of Barcia de Mera, in Galicia, protested to the royal judge against the local notary who began a confrontation with a neighboring village without their consent or power.[92] Particularly offensive to them was the fact that he now wanted to force them to pay the cost of the litigation, which had transpired without their accord. Because they refused, not only were their properties sequestered but he and his allies threatened them. If such dynamics were typical both between municipalities on the same side of the political division and across it, then the diverse level of activity in different years, the transition from prosecuting grazing to moving against agriculture, could perhaps be read not only as expressing change over time but also as indicating possible mutations in the identity of agents within each community and what they sought to achieve. It is therefore possible that the insistence on municipal action that historical records contained was mostly a fiction. Authorized by the law and perhaps recommended by political considerations, it was mainly a means for individuals to relate to rights, which were collective rather than particular, communal rather than private. This mode of presentation might have contributed to essentialize these debates, it might have led to insistence on places rather than actors, but behind it was the agency of a multiplicity of individuals who pursued their own interests.

Besides municipalities, other collective actors (probably concealing similar sets of interests), such as the military orders of the Hospitaller (in charge of Moura), Templars (in charge of Serpa), and Aviz (in charge of Moura), were also important to these conflicts.

So were several noblemen (the Count of Linhares and the Duke of Cadaval) who, formally instituted as *comendadores* of the order of Aviz, nevertheless treated the territory of Noudar as their private domain. They defended it against invasions by neighboring communities (both Spanish and Portuguese), but they also clashed with their own subjects, with whom they disagreed as to which parts were in private and which in public domain. Other individuals might have also influenced developments on the contested terrains. In 1785, for example, Encinasola pointed an accusing finger at a friar who lived in the convent of La Tomina, adjacent to La Contienda, arguing that he not only encouraged violations but was personally responsible for confrontations that led to one death, several injuries, and the seizure of Encinasola's rod of justice.[93] On that occasion, La Tomina was portrayed as a disorderly space controlled by ungodly priests who constantly violated the 1542 accord. But it is nevertheless clear that the convent was also the site where Aroche, Encinasola, and Moura habitually met to discuss their relations and agree on common actions. Another protagonist was Francisco Mendes, a citizen of Barrancos who, according to some, illegally used La Contienda.[94] Encinasola identified him as its ferocious enemy, arguing that he was a powerful smuggler and crime lord of low birth who had set up a deliberate war against it. Mendes organized a coalition against the village and took the issue to the royal court in Seville, where he affirmed that Encinasola's authorities had no jurisdiction to act against him at La Contienda, also suggesting that, even if they did, they habitually exceeded their powers. Mendes explained that Encinasola's reaction to his activities could be explained only by the animosity of the local notary, who wanted to see Mendes ruined. Indirect evidence suggests that the rivalry between Mendes and the citizens of Encinasola was incredibly complex. Mendes might have used La Contienda illegally and might have engaged in massive contraband as Encinasola asserted, but he was also a powerful and rich local inhabitant. He was the administrator (*feitor*) of the Duke of Cadaval and, in this capacity, might have accumulated both power and enemies but also served as a notary (*escrivão*), which might have explained the animosity of the office holder in Encinasola, with whom he might have competed for clients and influence. Furthermore, he was married, so it seemed, to a native of Encinasola and was closely tied to many who lived there.[95] The individuals acting for Encinasola were aware of these connections. They argued that their (justified) vindications were rejected because Mendes had so many friends, relatives, and allies in their jurisdiction that it was basically impossible to proceed against him. It is therefore plausible that the confrontation between Mendes and Encinasola (or rather the persons who could speak for Encinasola at that point) was an episode in the struggle against the duke (that otherwise seemed to have subsided) or a feud among neighbors and relatives, or perhaps both.

While the protagonists themselves were undergoing important changes, which assigned them to new jurisdictions and kingdoms, subjected or freed them from lords, and witnessed them evolving demographically, socially, and politically, and while local alignments were extremely complex and in constant flux, so too was royal reaction. Appeals to kings to intervene in these conflicts were constant, yet most of them indicated that the inhabitants of rival municipalities, as well as their lords, instrumentally addressed the monarchs because they believed in their ability to provide remedy. Following these requests, from the fourteenth to the eighteenth centuries, the kings sometimes sent delegates to mediate in these conflicts. Rather than represent the interests of their kingdoms or kings, these agents were instituted as judges who were to adjudicate by hearing witnesses, consulting documents, and delivering a sentence. Facing disagreement among different factions or insufficient evidence, they often abdicated their tasks, leaving the contention unresolved. Because royal involvement was geared mainly toward ensuring peace, not protecting individual or even collective interests, it was only after law failed to supply remedy on several occasions that these delegates sometimes agreed to act as arbiters and adopt a compromise not dictated by justice but instead focused on reconciliation. Asserting that "good neighbors" must find ways to solve their differences, they forced contending parties to divide the contested terrain or partition its use. They mostly took this road when they believed that the conflict endured too long or when they feared it might escalate. But whether they acted as judges or arbiters, the intervention of royal envoys was mainly conceived as the intercession of an outsider whose activities were welcomed precisely because he was both superior to locals and external to the debate.

The role of kings (or royal agents) as mediators and outsiders was also confirmed in other cases. In 1701, for example, the inhabitants of Riomanzanas (Spain) disagreed with their neighbors of Guadramil (Portugal) regarding pasture and gathering in a certain territory situated near both.[96] The Spanish Council of State, which received local complaints, first ordered the magistrate (*corregidor*) of Zamora to visit the territory to investigate the rights of the parties and issue provisions that would ensure peace (*la quietud de los naturales*). After this measure was judged insufficient for "avoiding new incidents that could result from the fact that each side maintained its pretensions and rights" (*no obstante reconociendo no era suficiente para evitar los nuevos accidentes que puede atraer el mantener unos y otros sus pretensions y derechos*), Spanish royal authorities suggested a joint meeting of local ministers on the border (*raya*) to look at old papers and hear the parties in order to reach an accord (*asiento y concordia*) so that good relations between the two communities would be assured. When this also failed (according to Spaniards because the Portuguese refused to "clarify the truth") and violence continued, the Council of State moved toward direct negotiations with the Portuguese court.

If on most occasions monarchs intervened by sending judges, on others royal intermediation could be channeled through ambassadors, who communicated, often literally reproducing, local complaints.[97] Ambassadors sometimes collaborated with efforts at mediation, yet by the eighteenth century their most common advice was to do nothing because, judging these conflicts of absolutely no importance to the king, they hoped the disagreements would die of their own. In the end, the most prominent and constant way by which monarchs interfered on the ground was not by sending delegates or naming ambassadors but through regular law courts that adjudicated conflicts that directly or indirectly involved territorial rights. Because the misuse of a territory by neighbors could also be dealt with as a civil affair confronting individuals or communities (rather than as a diplomatic or political question involving the removal of land from one kingdom to the other), royal courts were willing to hear and adjudicate such complaints.[98] Encinasola, Aroche, Noudar, Barrancos, and their individual citizens often demanded these interventions, appealing to Seville's court for help. So did Mendes, a Portuguese. The Duke of Cadaval preferred to plead before the Portuguese Mesa de Consciência, a decision that Encinasola criticized, arguing that he should have taken the case to another court.[99]

The recourse to royal courts in such "international" conflicts (to use an anachronism) was extremely common in other cases, too. In 1753, for example, the inhabitants of Cambedo in Portugal requested the royal court of Galicia (*audiencia*) to oversee a formal demarcation between them and Bousés and As Casas dos Montes (in Galicia), arguing that none existed.[100] Because the Spanish communities contested that the limits between them and their neighbors were clear and that the request was directed only at gaining land that was not theirs, the magistrates asked both sides to present their evidence. As things lingered, Cambedo and As Casas arrived at a friendly accord (*convenio pacífico*) allowing common use, yet in 1761 disagreement reemerged. Litigation continued until at least 1767. In none of these cases, in which royal courts proceeded to adjudicate conflicts that potentially could affect royal (territorial) rights, were the judges told (nor did they conclude) that the issue was not under their jurisdiction. Neither did anyone advance allegations of extraterritoriality or improper venue. It was as if the question were not whom the judges depended on (which king and which kingdom) but their capacity to render judgment by representing "the law," which was still a-national and still common to the residents of both states. Paradoxically, by the time kings were ready to affirm their sovereignty by demonstrating that they could not only distribute justice but also modify the law and affect rights, locals, who for many centuries insisted on their kings' participation, now argued that they, not kings, were the true and only rulers of their destinies.

The Coveted Object

The multilogues that these interactions produced were extremely complex. Involving a great variety of actors that constantly changed and who also modified their positions and alliances, they indicated that rather than a single conflict, what persisted on the border was a series of conflicts that, shaped like a Hydra, resisted simplistic reduction into a confrontation between locals and kings or among the residents of different kingdoms. But complexity and change over time was evident not only in the construction and reconstruction of rivalries but also in how they defined their object of desire. Initially, disagreement involved a territory generically classified as "land in contention." Extremely ill defined, references were soon made to terrains that locals named "Campo de Gamos," "La Contienda" (literally, "The Disaccord"), and "La Rossiana" (also called "Rocianas" and "Ruciana"). Treating these as identifiable, stable entities, it is nevertheless clear that the municipalities and parties involved in these conflicts constantly disputed what these units meant, what they included, where they began, and where they ended. Otherwise said, their discords covered not only whose animals could graze in Campo de Gamos but what was Campo de Gamos. Because conflicts both questioned and instituted the object of desire, they often degenerated into debates regarding whether certain parts were or were not under contention. Discord was such that in 1493, for example, the judges sent by the Spanish and Portuguese kings to decide on partition could not agree on where they should meet.[101] Habitually, such gatherings were held on the disputed terrain, but how should it be identified? Because the representatives of Moura protested that Val Queimado, where negotiations had begun, was not part of "La Contienda" but instead clearly in their privative jurisdiction, they requested the magistrates to move the hearing to another location. The Portuguese commissioner consented and transferred the sessions to where Moura indicated they should take place. His Castilian counterpart refused, ruling that the question of which territory was contested was precisely what they needed to resolve, not take for granted. Similarly, in 1603 and 1605 the inhabitants of Encinasola, Aroche, and Noudar disagreed regarding the use of certain pieces of land that according to some were shared and according to others were private.[102] Even the 1542 accord was not totally clear as to which was what. The agreement defined "La Contienda" as including several distinct territories such as Pae Joannes, Val Queimado, the lands of Santa Maria, and Campo de Gamos, but it was nevertheless clear that by that stage most contemporaries believed Campo de Gamos was next to rather than inside La Contienda or that perhaps part of it was in La Contienda but another not.[103] Because conflicts were performative, over time Campo de Gamos was

indeed divided into one part that was declared the property of Noudar (regarding which contestation continued between Noudar and
Moura and within Noudar between its citizens and the lord) and
another, called La Contienda (and debated between Moura, Aroche,
and Encinasola, with the occasional appearance of Barrancos as the
remnant of what Noudar once was).[104] By the mid-eighteenth century, conflict over Rossiana disappears from archival records.

As the identity and behavior of discussants slowly mutated, redefining the territory they coveted, their requests changed as well.
Mainly discussing usage rights, some contemporaries also wanted
to demarcate their villages, distinguishing them clearly from
their neighbors'. Usage and demarcation of course influenced one
another—usage could lead to demarcation and demarcation could allow usage—but these connections, although possible, were not necessary, as usage could easily exist without demarcation and demarcation did not necessarily guarantee usage rights. Also concurrent
were questions some individuals and groups raised regarding how
to distinguish common from private grounds. And while grazing
and gathering could be contested on occasions—especially when
they were likely to damage the territory or restrict its use by others—
the cutting of wood and agricultural pursuits provoked most debates. Perhaps because trees cut were irreplaceable, perhaps because
agriculture required a precise definition of the territory and exclusive possession, more than grazing and gathering, these activities
caused most conflicts and motivated most contestations.

Although much was at stake and clarity was utterly missing, the
question that was least treated was whether the contested territories
were Spanish or Portuguese. It is significant, for example, that the
1542 accord that sanctioned common use of La Contienda did not
settle this issue. While dividing the rights of locals, it maintained
untouched those of kings, allowing both the Spanish and the Portuguese monarch to conserve their dominion intact, as if the territory
were never contested nor divided. La Contienda, in short, was to be
Portugal (and Portugal alone) for the Portuguese, Spanish (and Spanish alone) for Spaniards. Locals seem to have initially observed this
rule, but by the mid-eighteenth century the authorities of Encinasola began asserting powers also over Portuguese violators. Thereafter, La Contienda became both Spanish and Portuguese. These

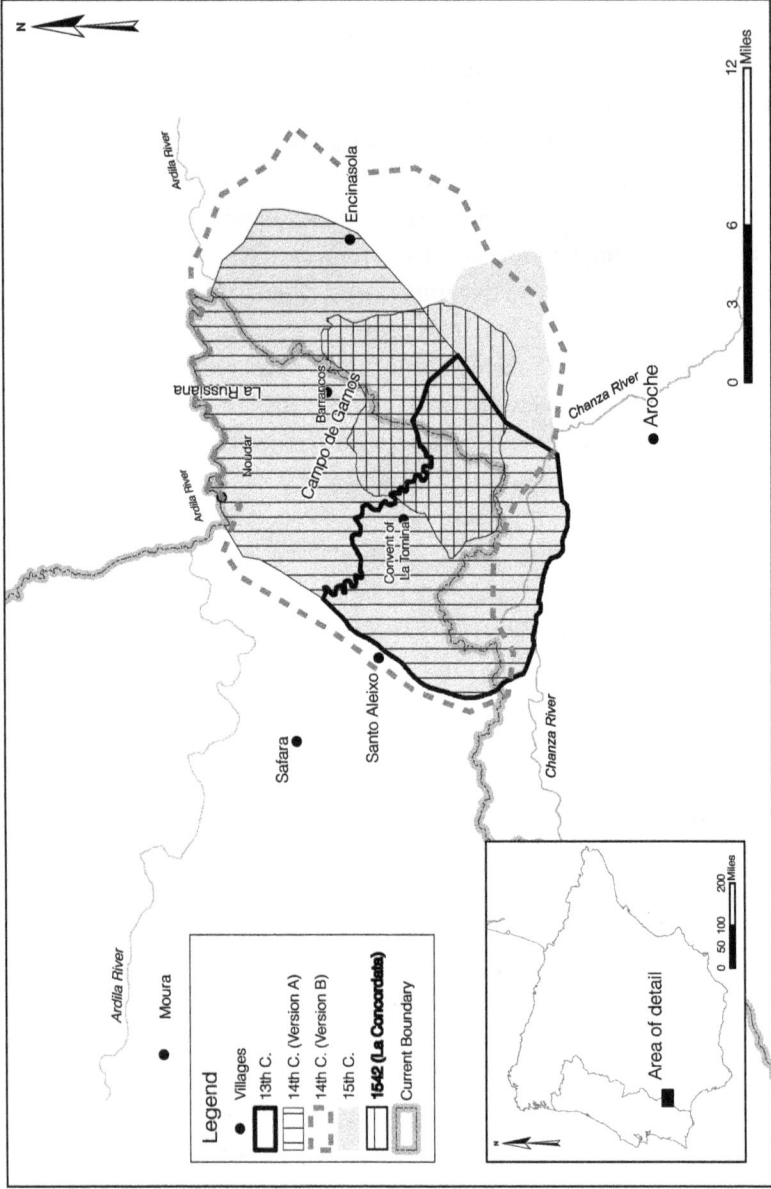

"La Contienda"

Various possible interpretations of the territories in contention between Encinasola, Aroche, Barrancos, Noudar, and Moura as they might have changed over time.

changes, later adopted by other agents, transpired informally, without authorization, perhaps even without notice. However, they greatly affected the rights of kings because by the end of the eighteenth century and more clearly in the following one, even royal delegates asserted that La Contienda was either shared by both countries or belonged to none. It became extraterritorial, or a neutral piece of land between two rival powers.

The Claims

Initially, Aroche, Encinasola, Moura, Noudar, Barrancos, and Serpa argued their case by reference to immemorial customs. They suggested that many years of use and a long succession of attempts to divide the territory produced certain habits that instituted rights and that these had to be safeguarded. Some of these assertions were based on documents located in local and royal archives, but most depended on the declaration of witnesses who recalled certain events or had heard about them from their elders. Taking immemoriality seriously, these witnesses asserted that no one remembered how or why the conflict first emerged or what had transpired thereafter. It was evident, however, that both forgetfulness and recollection were purposeful because they served certain ends and were a means to obtain favorable results. Different members of different communities thus produced diverse, sometimes completely opposed, narratives. On occasions, the story they each told was profoundly contradictory. For usage to be immemorial (as they all claimed), it had to be continuous and consensual. But the constant failure to demarcate and the lasting contestation demonstrated it was not. Both affirming and undermining their entitlements at the same time, what contemporaries best did was to insist on continuity that was more fictitious than real. They all referred to an elusive status quo that had existed (so they argued) until recently, while they also confessed that it was broken on multiple occasions. They pretended that it was consensual (when it never was), and they claimed that what had existed in the past should continue to the present despite dramatic changes in who they were, which territory was debated, and what they pretended to do with it.

Because these allegations led nowhere, already in the sixteenth century the 1542 accord settling the relations between Moura, Aroche, and Encinasola in La Contienda became the basis for all future negotiations. Whether this happened because it sanctioned a compromise rather than "justice," because it represented the only agreement the contending parties ever reached, because all three communities—whose archives were otherwise destroyed[105]—conserved copies of it, or because they vindicated its instructions each time they inspected La Contienda and censured violators is unclear. However, what is evident is that by the seventeenth century, the 1542 accord was no longer questioned. Well kept and constantly copied, it was upheld by both locals and royal authorities, thus forming a foundational myth of sorts. After its adoption, most confrontations between these three communicites evolved around what it meant and how it was to be implemented. The importance of the 1542 accord was such that some referred to it as a treaty *(tratado)*.[106] In its aftermaths, although the rival parties continued to present their possession as "immemorial" and invoked the same set of arguments as they did before 1542, it was nevertheless clear that the accord completely transformed their rights as well as their allegations. Among other things, after it was accomplished all parties pointed to 1542 as a clear foundational moment (which was no longer truly immemorial in the sense of unremembered) and to a deliberate human action that, adopting a mutual accord, instituted rather than recognized reality. Otherwise said, instead of customary use, which naturally and spontaneously emerged, at the center of their legal arguments in the post-1542 period was now an agreement that initially was forced on these communities but eventually was accepted by them.

The looming presence of the 1542 accord was particularly noticeable in the nineteenth century, when though considering themselves envoys of sovereign powers, commissioners appointed by the two crowns nevertheless made repeated appeals to it.[107] Yet, whereas the 1542 agreement could hold water (albeit with difficulties) in the sixteenth and seventeenth centuries, by the mid-eighteenth century its viability was no longer evident. Simply put, the shared use of a territory belonging to two states at the same time was perhaps a good solution when the accord was adopted, but such was not the case by the late eighteenth and early nineteenth centuries. Locals continued to vote in favor of common possession, arguing that if it produced conflicts, they were now willing to solve these by way of an amicable agreement. Yet, while they adhered to this part of the 1542 accord, saying communal property was superior to private, mixed jurisdiction preferable to privative, and belonging to two kingdoms better than belonging to a single one, nineteenth-century authorities disagreed and so did kings and their ministers. By that time, the fate of common versus private land, usage versus property, and grazing versus agriculture was already decided. In debates raging in Spain and Portugal from the seventeenth century and intensifying in the eighteenth century, many argued that economic improvement mandated the division of communal property in plots and their sale to agricultural laborers who would acquire permanent possession.[108] Thereafter, they portrayed common property as belonging to a dark age and made agriculture and private property symbols of a coveted future. Reformers also argued that land had to be assigned not according to who had used it in the past but who would use it better in the future. If very few supported common property, even fewer backed grazing, which most assumed hampered economic progress.[109] Legal traditions that favored grazing throughout the sixteenth, seventeenth, and eighteenth centuries were thus gradually abolished, and instead of an economy based on husbandry and gathering, Portugal and Spain were to become lands of intense cultivation requiring enclosure. Contemporaries argued that these developments would save the poor, revive the economy, and enrich the state. Local petitions to conserve La Contienda in its current state as common grazing grounds were thus rejected in the late eighteenth and early nineteenth centuries not because it was believed that commonness produced disorder or because a border between Spain and Portugal had to be fixed but mainly because commonness and grazing prevented the land from reaching its full potential.[110] The result was a curious inversion that led royal officials to insist on intervening where for many centuries they were absent and led locals, who had constantly appealed for their help, to reject their presence. If in earlier periods the citizens of Aroche, Encinasola, Moura,

Noudar, and Barrancos fought with one another, they now joined hands to halt the involvement of kings, whom they now considered unfriendly interlopers.

These developments could explain why historians often insisted on portraying the border as a royal invention that was constructed, debated, and decided against local wishes.[111] A faithful projection of what perhaps had transpired in the late eighteenth and early nineteenth centuries and of what locals argued as they rallied against the intervention of states, it is nevertheless clear that this interpretation was a modern invention. A longer history of the border demonstrates that the only persons who fought, struggled, and insisted on maintaining divisions were locals, not kings. While kings generally seemed disinterested in fixing borders or knowing where they would pass (as long as quarrels among locals did not result in too much violence), locals, claiming that they were observing the status quo rather than innovating, were truly interested in defining where they could pasture, where they could plant, where they could collect wood, and where they could apprehend criminals. The conflicts they maintained with one another required both constant vigilance and continuing actions. They sometimes produced so much animosity among neighbors that contemporaries believed that *fronterizos* felt a natural aversion to one another and were natural enemies *(naturalmente guerreros contra sus vecinos).*[112] This, however, does not negate the importance of local pacts. As happened in the Americas, in Europe too, violence and peace were alternative mechanisms that complemented rather than contradicted one another. In the midst of the greatest confrontations, locals often searched to reach an agreement, and such accords often sanctioned compromises that allowed rival communities to either partition the territory or use it commonly. On some parts of the border, these local pacts were indeed achieved relatively early and persisted for a long time. A good example for such a case were the bilateral relations between Valencia de Alcántara (in Castile) and Marvão (in Portugal). Covering a similar period (1313–1906) as the confrontations between Aroche, Encinasola, Moura, Noudar, and Barrancos, their story began in 1313, when records indicate that after a prolonged period of disagreement and because they could not decide on how to divide their territories, with the permission of their monarchs, both communities reached an accord *(concordia y compromiso)*.[113] It allowed citizens to use their jurisdiction almost indistinctively for grazing, drinking, and gathering but prohibited activities that required exclusive domain such as cultivation or construction. Because attempts at demarcation failed in 1351, 1455, 1488, and 1519, this accord, initially adopted as a temporary solution, became permanent.[114] There is no record in municipal archives as to how it functioned in the sixteenth and seventeenth centuries, but its survival into the eighteenth century was constantly noted, most particularly by the council of Valencia, whose minutes are more extensive and detailed than Marvão's. According to that information, whenever doubts arose over whether certain territories and activities were included in the agreement, both municipalities negotiated with one another.[115] They also mutually swore to respect the accord by ensuring that their citizens would respect it, too, for example, by not using territory illegitimately in ways that might give raise to claims of exclusive possession, such as planting.[116] In order to ensure obedience, the authorities of Valencia and Marvão proceeded to visit the territory habitually.[117] Both Valencia de Alcántara and Marvão not only made constant appeals to the accord and closely honored its implementation but, above all, they insisted on royal compliance. During the eighteenth century, whenever Spanish royal officials infringed the bilateral accord by sanctioning the citizens of Marvão who used Spanish territory mainly for pasture, the authorities of Valencia came to their neighbors' aid. They defended the latter's activities by arguing that they were legal by both municipal and royal law and that they ensured peace and harmony among neighbors.[118] These local arrangements led the Spanish and the Portuguese commissioners meeting in the 1850s to settle all pending border issues between the two countries to conclude that although once upon a time there were doubts regarding the partition between Valencia and Marvão, none had survived, because they were all "healed" *(sanado)* by local accords.[119] Agreements on joint use continued as late as 1868, the authorities of both villages consistently calling upon each other and the state to respect them. Also persevering was the insistence that unless these accords were observed, peace would be disrupted.[120]

This state of things persisted until 1906, when the jurisdiction of Valencia and Marvão, Spain and Portugal, was finally divided and both communities were given an exclusive territory.

Indications for local arrangements, which trumped all other accords and discords, can be found throughout the archives. In fact, they even existed between Aroche, Encinasola, Moura, Noudar, and Barrancos. It is hard to evaluate how well they functioned or why on occasions they generated better collaboration than in others. Our image of what transpired is determined by the archives, and these clearly privilege conflict over accord. When agreements are mentioned, it is usually because they were infringed, not respected. Record keeping was perhaps a practice that depended on many factors, yet its effects on how we study the past were particularly noticeable in the case of Marvão and Valencia, whose relations were spelled out and described more clearly by the latter than by the former. Local practices might have been different, but the cause might also have been the different importance each of the two municipalities gave to the accord or their varying relations with the royal guards who were said to infringe it. But whatever the case, because documentation from Valencia was more abundant, what we know today focuses only on how Spanish authorities might have contravened the accord. It leaves pending the question of whether the Portuguese did, too, and whether other confrontations, less willfully registered, also transpired. But if relations between Marvão and Valencia were different than what happened among Aroche, Encinasola, Moura, Noudar, and Barrancos, they were also surprisingly similar. In both cases, constant attempts to clarify the legal situation failed because even in the fourteenth century, contemporaries disagreed as to the meaning and extension of a status quo they all pretended to adopt. Disputes over what the past meant, how it was to be restored, and how it affected the present led to violence, and the violence led to accords. Agreement, however, required implementation. It was at that stage that developments took a different path in each one of these conflicts, possibly because the devil was not in the abstract accords but in their detailed and quotidian concretization.

But whether local agreements were respected or not, whether they provoked heated debates or were followed peacefully, whether they were used by municipalities against one another or jointly against the king, after law (in the form of immemorial possession) failed to solve the contention and after compromise (the 1542 accord) could no longer be legitimately maintained, contemporaries turned to reason. In the mid-eighteenth century they stated that the conflicts that pitted Encinasola, Aroche, Moura, Noudar, Serpa, and Barrancos against one another must have originated in an "obscure time" that could no longer be penetrated. Instead of trying to figure out how they had begun or searching for documents or witnesses to testify what the rights of the parties were, eighteenth-century discussants suggested examining the situation on the ground. This led Antonio de Gaber to conclude in 1750 that La Contienda was originally Spanish.[121] Explaining that it was a frequent, albeit vulgar, mistake to consider common pastureland as territories that belonged either to all those having usage rights or to no one, he argued that because for over two hundred years locals used it indistinctively they might have forgotten to whom it truly belonged, they might have given the territory a new name ("La Contienda"), and they might even have thought that the agreement to share it implied that Spanish kings abdicated their rights to its possession. These suppositions might have been justified by the local authorities' reluctance to exercise their jurisdiction because they feared conflicts. Yet, however reasonable these conclusions were, they were nonetheless incorrect. La Contienda was not a common terrain, nor was it a no-man's-land. Clearly belonging to Spain because located on its territory, its authorities allowed foreigners (Portuguese peasants) to use it by way of "hospitality" (hospitalidad). The 1542 accord supported this interpretation because it distinguished usage (grazing and gathering), which were allowed, from possession, which was not, by prohibiting activities such as planting or construction. Ensuring that no one could claim rights to La Contienda, what the accord did was to settle usage, not property rights. This was the proper interpretation according to the law of nations (derecho de las gentes) and according to natural and divine law. It was also the correct solution according to the laws of both the Spanish and the Portuguese monarchies and the most reasonable conclusion. As far as Gaber was concerned, La Contienda was but one example, indeed a prototype, among many.

The border with Portugal, he asserted, often featured territories commonly used by several municipalities. In each one of these cases locals could not explain how this situation had come about or when it had originated, but Gaber was certain that it was always due to Spanish toleration of Portuguese abuse. He therefore concluded that it was vital not to record what locals thought—all they did was to repeat what their elders had told them—but to discover what nature and common sense indicated. As the Spanish commissioner to divide the territory in 1803 said, "geography" demonstrated that La Contienda was Spanish because, situated outside the current border *(raya)* and inside Spanish territory *(territorio de España)*, it was contiguous to the jurisdiction of Aroche and Encinasola, not Moura. These indisputable facts, as well as "the traditions of the elders of the land" *(tradiciones de los mayores del país)* and other "strong presumptions" *(fuertes presunciones)*, implied, he concluded, that only violent usurpation by the Portuguese living on the border *(fronterizos)*, which must have begun in a "period lost in the obscurity of time" *(cuya época se pierde en la obscuridad de los tiempos)*, could have produced the current situation.[122] The commissioner hypothesized that this irregularity might have begun during the reign of Isabella of Castile or her ancestors (in the fifteenth century or earlier). Though he gave no explanation as to why he chose this period over others except for indicating that monarchs must have been preoccupied in the wars against the Moors to the degree that they did not care about their rights vis-à-vis Portugal, it is nevertheless clear that by the time the commissioner was writing (1803), the reconquest and the reigns prior to those of the Catholic monarchs were already stereotyped as featuring not only important territorial rearrangements but also political strife and a generalized social and economic chaos.

If some discussants appealed to common sense, others drew on history. Following this route, the Portuguese commissioner to the 1804 division suggested that because until 1399 Encinasola was dependent on Aroche, its rights in La Contienda were derivative, not independent. If partition took place, it should be compensated by Aroche and Spain, not Moura and Portugal. To this contention a first Spanish commissioner contested that this alleged dependency, even had it existed, was irrelevant because it had expired long before the 1542 accord was adopted. A second Spanish commissioner, however, inverted the argument. According to his version, Moura rather than Encinasola had no rights.[123] Moura was founded in the Middle Ages by citizens of Aroche, and its cession to Portugal in the late thirteenth century transferred to that country only its urban site, not its hinterland. This interpretation, he argued, found support in a book titled *Historia eclesiástica de la ciudad y obispado de Badajoz*, published in 1670. Written by Juan Solano de Figueroa Altamirano, it vindicated Mora (Moura) as a Spanish enclave and as a dependent of the bishopric of Badajoz (in Spain).[124] The book explained that Moura was founded by the Greeks in 1221 BC, that in Roman times it was rebuilt by the inhabitants of Aroche, who called it Aroche la Nueva, and that, during the Roman civil wars, both communities fought together under the common name of "Aroche." Conquered by the Moors, it was freed by King Afonso Henriques, who, in order to thank the knights who helped him, changed its name to Moura. Conquered and reconquered on several occasions, it was won definitively by King Alfonso el Sabio of Castile, who passed it to his daughter Beatriz, the Portuguese consort queen. Other evidence also affirmed, the commissioner argued, that in 1257 and 1294 Moura was either Castilian or in a contested territory. Because Moura depended on Aroche, its rights were derivative, not independent. This situation continued after its subsequent surrender to Portugal, and indeed the struggle between Aroche and Moura over usage rights in La Contienda begun when Aroche refused to allow Moura to pasture there because of its inclusion in that kingdom. Not only did Moura have no rights in La Contienda, even its own territory was obtained by way of usurpation and in reality belonged to Aroche. The judges who elaborated the 1542 accord erred by not taking into account this longer history. Their failure, however, need not affect the present discussion, he said, unless the king decided of his own volition to grant this land to Portugal by way of grace.

This was the most audacious attempt to imagine the beginning of a conflict whose initial episodes, even in the fourteenth century, resisted reconstruction. Dismissed by the king, who did not consider this historical narration relevant, nevertheless, it was not until the

1880s that contemporaries were willing to mock such narratives. During this period, responding to Portuguese recollection that Portugal had ceded Aroche to Castile (in 1306), the Spanish commissioner affirmed that he remembered even an earlier time, in which Portugal did not exist.[125] Closing the circle, the failure of the past to supply solutions left contemporaries with the present as their only recourse. Their rights, they thus asserted, existed because they had and because they did. Given the passage of time and the political and economic upheavals they had experienced, no one should expect them to demonstrate their entitlements other than by observing their possession. That they did not know when it began, that they treated it ahistorically by assuming it had never changed, that they had no proof of its existence, and that their rivals constantly challenged them—all this no longer mattered.[126]

4 Moving Islands in a Sea of Land: 1518–1864

THE MULTIPLICITY OF PARTIES, constantly on the move, the continuous mutation of the contested territory and what was demanded, as well as the frequent changes in claim making were also present in other conflicts. In some of them—as the first one narrated here dealing with the island of Verdoejo—at stake were problems that partially arose from changes in the landscape, namely, the appearance and disappearance of islands. Yet, however natural these changes might have been, the way they were detected, comprehended, and given meaning involved complex thinking about territory and rights, as well as membership and belonging. These questions—how individuals and communities related to their surroundings and how they attempted to make sense of what was natural and what was historical; what traditional and conventional and what scientific—were also evident in the second case under scrutiny, dealing with how the Mountains of Magdalena (to the Spanish) or Lindoso (to the Portuguese) would be divided among rival communities. In the third and last case, contemporaries were mainly engaged in understanding what they came to regard as an extreme irregularity, namely, the existence of settlements that were "mixed" and "promiscuous," with residents belonging to both countries and with no clear territorial ascription. How they reimagined their past in order to modify their present is, I would argue, one of the most important legacies of territorial conflicts today.

Verdoejo (1683–1863)

According to surviving records, the conflict that pitted communities along the Miño *(Minho)* River separating southern Galicia (in Spain) from northern Portugal began in 1683, when ecclesiastical authorities disagreed over to whom fishermen who casted their nets from Verdoejo, a small sandy island in the middle of the river, owed tithes.[1] The friars of the Jesuit monastery of San Fins in Portugal said that because the island was "in Portuguese lands" *(terras de Portugal)* and because there was a "very old custom" in this regard, tributes were due to them. The abbot of Caldelas (in Spain) replied that the territory was never Portuguese and that at the present time it was clearly Spanish because the river that once upon a time ran between Spain and the island now separated it from Portugal.[2] After several violent episodes with delegates of both sides attempting to force fishermen into paying and quarreling with one another, the monastery requested the assistance of the Portuguese monarch, who instructed the authorities of nearby Viana to investigate the case. Ordering the abbot to appear before them, he came accompanied by a Portuguese lawyer. He refused to discuss "property rights" *(matéria de propriedade)* because these were not in his competence, but he did argue that as far as taxing the fishing activities the answer was evident. The island was contiguous to his parish and thus part of its territory. As a result, independently of the question of who the fishermen were, all those casting their nets should pay him. Though archival records contain no indication as to how the proceeding ended, in 1684, the abbot boasted that he had won the case because the royal judge *(corregedor)* of Viana declared in his favor.[3] Whether these affirmations were correct or not, we do know that soon after, the monastery again requested royal intervention, which materialized when the Portuguese ambassador in Madrid complained to the Spanish Council of State that the abbot of Caldelas sought to alter the existing arrangements without right or reason.[4] In order to ensure his success, the abbot used violence and threatened that "this fishing, which belonged to Portugal," would become Castilian. Because small disputes among neighbors could prompt war between crowns, it was essential to respect the "immemorial possession" en-

joyed by the monastery and the crown of Portugal, and the abbot
should cease all disruption.

Initially agreeing with this analysis, Spanish officials changed
their opinion after they received a lengthy report from the governor
of Galicia, who said the problem was more complicated than it appeared.[5] Sixteen witnesses of high quality (*mayor excepción*) had informed him that before the war (1640) both the Galicians and the
Portuguese had fished along the shores of the island, each paying
tithes in his parish. During the war (1640–1668), Spanish troops
stationed on the island prohibited the Portuguese from using it, but
after peace was reestablished (1668), the previous custom prevailed.
It was only a few years earlier that this situation had changed, with
the monastery attempting to collect tithes also from Spaniards. This
led to violent confrontations, including various deaths. While the
governor of Valença do Minho, the nearest Portuguese settlement,
insisted with his Spanish counterpart of Tuy (on the other side of
the river) that because the territory was Portuguese tithes were due
to the monastery, the Spaniard answered that they should resolve
the matter amicably by adopting the ruling of the Portuguese judge
of Viana that favored the abbot. The governor of Galicia also asserted
that, regardless of the payment of tithes, the island was Spanish because the river had changed its course, making it almost contiguous
to Galicia and distant from Portugal. Thus, even if once upon a time
the monastery had rights, nature, not Spaniards, had taken them away
by reassigning them to Spain. This was the correct reading according
to the law, but this conclusion also made sense because any other
solution would allow the Portuguese to have a stronghold on the
Spanish side of the river, which would be unacceptable. To bring the
matter to a close, he suggested, it would be sufficient to visit the area
and look at the flow of the river.

Noting that Verdoejo was extremely small (about an eighth of a
league long and one musket shot [*tiro de mosquete*] wide) and of very
little importance (*de poca estimación*), in 1684 and 1685 most members
of the Spanish Council of State recommended letting the matter
drop. The legal solution might be evident—according to the law,
changes in rivers affected both property rights and jurisdiction—
but there was no reason to insist with the Portuguese if they did not

persevere either. Only one dissenting councilor doubted that this was a viable solution because he believed that the Portuguese were unlikely to accept it. He proposed a formal settlement that would recognize Spanish rights. His opinion rejected, the king ordered the abbot to avoid further confrontations with the Portuguese.[6] Yet if he was ordered to maintain peaceful relations, he also explicitly was charged with defending his rights, that is, with collecting tithes.

In February 1691, the Portuguese ambassador to Madrid raised the issue of Verdoejo again.[7] This time, less interested in tithes than in jurisdiction, he accused the authorities of Tuy (in Spain) of trespassing on the island that, according to him, was Portuguese. Having arrested the person charged with collecting tithes for the monastery, in the following days, the justices of Tuy roamed the territory with their rod of justice raised. If the Portuguese king did not covet territories that were not his, neither was he willing to cede what rightfully belonged to him. The ambassador requested that the Spanish monarch ensure that these territorial penetrations immediately cease and that the ministers of Tuy be punished. Verdoejo, he explained, was once part of the Portuguese mainland. Made into an island by alterations in the flow of the Minho, it was nevertheless Portuguese according to registries (tombos) dated 1538 and 1548. Until 1640, only Portuguese fishermen could use it; between 1640 and 1668 (during the War of Portuguese Independence), both Spanish and Portuguese did; and after hostilities ended (1668), this second custom persisted. Tithes were always paid to the monastery, and custom dues (alfândega) were always collected by Portuguese officials, with the justices of San Fins visiting the island with their rods raised. The abbot of Caldelas was encouraged to challenge this status quo by his patron (amo), Rodrigo Antonio, resident of Tuy and administrator (feitor) of the Countess of Regalados, who lived in Madrid and whose grandparents had once owned the island. Whether it was located nearer to Galicia than to Portugal was of no consequence to the ambassador because rivers often changed their course, but no one had ever suggested before that these natural mutations would affect ownership or jurisdiction.

In 1691, therefore, a debate over tithes evolved into a conflict concerning jurisdiction. This development was authenticated by Spaniards, too, who complained in 1691 that Portuguese judges now imagined they had jurisdiction on the island (which they did not). This belief was evident in their activities: they attempted to imprison the tax collector of Rodrigo Antonio Falcón, Marquis of Bendaña, who was the legitimate owner of this litigated territory and who lived in Spain.[8] Requesting information as to what exactly was at stake, the Spanish Council of State was particularly alarmed by Portuguese threats to use violence. The Portuguese king instructed his military that under no circumstance were they to allow the presence of Spanish authorities on the island, and Spaniards responded by advising the governor of Galicia to prepare for war.[9] Writing from Tuy, the bishop insisted that the true name of the island was Caldelas, not Verdoejo.[10] Because the Miño River, which divided the two kingdoms, now passed between the island and Portugal, Verdoejo (or Caldelas) was clearly Spanish. Anyone visiting the territory, as he had recently done, would confirm this obvious fact, but confirmations also existed in writing. Local archives contained at least two letters dated 1321 that attested as much. Verdoejo was also included in a description of the bishopric of Tuy dated 1528, when it was given by the diocese in rent to a citizen of that city. From time immemorial, the justices of Tuy, not Portugal, exercised jurisdiction there. In 1640, the island belonged to Pedro Gómez de Abreu, who passed it to his relative Antonio Falcón de Sotomayor, and upon his death it became the property of his son Rodrigo Antonio Falcón, Marquis of Bendaña. According to local witnesses, the recent Portuguese involvement on the island was provoked by their anger against the marquis's collector, who had refused to sell them a salmon.

None of those declaring in 1691 remembered when the conflict began, but they all agreed that the year following the signature of the 1668 peace treaty (ending the War of Portuguese Independence), Portuguese and Spanish fishermen were already quarreling over who could fish what and where. These rivalries were settled amicably, allowing the Marquis of Bendaña to enjoy quiet and peaceful possession, yet sometime in the 1680s (during the term in office of Juan Francisco Pacheco Téllez-Girón, fourth Duke of Uceda, as governor of Galicia) the Portuguese began challenging this status quo. While the city of Tuy, its judges, and bishop characterized the conflict as severe and demanded immediate royal attention, the governor of Galicia disagreed. Because the incidents reported by the authorities of Tuy were not important and the Portuguese authorities had promised to ensure they would not happen again, he believed his personal mediation would be sufficient to appease the situation.[11] In 1693, however, the Spanish Council of State ruled otherwise, recommending that the king tackle the controversy by directly negotiating with the Portuguese crown.[12] The council openly confessed that the island was not important and that the trouble there was probably motivated by greed, but it nevertheless expressed its concern that the controversy would, as it almost did, bring the two kingdoms to the verge of war. Because by that time the Portuguese were requesting not only to restrain the abbot from collecting tithes and the authorities of Tuy from exercising jurisdiction but also to instruct the Marquis of Bendaña not to collect seigniorial fees on the island, the Spanish Council of State determined that the only people who would be affected by a settlement would be those who had interests on the island, namely, the abbot, the owner, and the judges of Tuy. As a result, how the affair would conclude was of no concern to the council or the king. The only thing that mattered was to ensure its termination.

Frustrated by procrastination, in 1694, the monastery of San Fins again took matters into its own hands, suing the abbot of Caldelas in the royal court (*audiencia*) of Galicia, where it accused him of attacking its immemorial possession of tithes.[13] If the convent stuck to its position, so did the abbot, who responded that the island was used from time immemorial by the citizens of Tuy and that it belonged to a Spaniard (Don Rodrigo Antonio Falcón, Marquis of Bendaña). Testimony from local witnesses confirmed both these (very) contradictory claims, with some Galicians supporting the monastery and some Portuguese helping the abbot. The monastery also presented documents that indicated that in the sixteenth century the island was part of its properties because either its authorities so declared in a testament or they so attested in proceedings that led to the elaboration of a registry (*tombo* or *apeo*). A copy of formal possession taking, dated 1691, also accompanied the proceedings. Yet, as the Spanish negotiators would eventually claim in the nineteenth century, the

documents presented by the monastery proved claims, not entitlements. All they attested was that from as early as 1520s the monastery
had argued that the island was his and that neighboring jurisdictions in Portugal as well as the Portuguese king consented. What
Spaniards thought about it remained unknown.

While the monastery appealed to a long succession of precedents
and accused its rivals of "great violence and disrespect," the abbot
said that regardless of ancient rights, the island was Spanish because
it was geographically contingent to Spain. When the river changed
course he did not know, but he and his witnesses attested that from
as early as 1580, perhaps earlier, they had treated the island thus,
also referring to it as Caldelas, not Verdoejo. As litigation went on,
the Portuguese secretary of state gave the Spanish ambassador in
Lisbon allegations as well as various documents demonstrating the
rights of Portugal.[14] These, centered on issues of royal sovereignty,
not tithes or jurisdiction, repeated what the Portuguese had already
claimed, mainly the insistence that natural changes did not affect
the boundaries of states. The ambassador attributed the "confusion" regarding the status of the island to the union and disunion of
Spain and Portugal and argued that the Portuguese might have allowed Spaniards to fish on the island but that they did so as friends
and with no intention to grant them title. He also asserted that Spaniards were deliberately obscuring the debate by conflating Caldelas,
an island that was truly theirs, with Verdoejo, which was not. Considering the matter sub judice, Spanish officials responded that they
could not act until the *audiencia* of Galicia had rendered its decision.
However, when the royal court finally ruled in the case, granting in
1695 the monastery temporary relief in the form of provisional possession of all tithes, the city of Tuy and royal councilors reacted
furiously. The court, they suggested, had no jurisdiction over the
question of whether the island was Portuguese or Spanish, and its
decision, they asserted, effectively transferred title to the monastery and Portugal.[15] Because it had territorial implications, the audiencia of Galicia should have never reviewed the case but instead
should have asked the king how he wanted to proceed. Paradoxically, as if all this had not transpired because of the monastery but
against it, the Portuguese secretary of state agreed, protesting the

intervention of a Spanish court in matters beyond its jurisdiction.[16] Threatening to treat all Spaniards entering the island as enemies who sought to dispossess the Portuguese, the Portuguese king concluded that there was no room for negotiation because the case was crystal clear. The only thing he would admit would be Spain's recognition that the island was his.

The audiencia of Galicia defended its decision by pointing out that it gave temporary relief that did not juridically affect either possession or property rights, let alone the jurisdiction of states.[17] The entitlements of the parties, its judges explained, were far from obvious, among other things because even at that stage it was unclear how to identify the island, whether it was identical to the one the documents and the witnesses described, and whether the river had indeed changed its course. Because this uncertainty produced confrontations, it would be best, the magistrates believed, if both kings sent commissioners to resolve these questions amicably in the "usual way." Back to the drawing table, in late 1696 the Portuguese ambassador to Madrid and the Spanish Council of State tried to reach a solution. Yet while they all expressed their firm commitment to peace, they each insisted on maintaining their original propositions, which clearly contradicted one another. These differed not only over legitimate proof and its consequences but also over the proper method and criteria to employ. The Portuguese were adamant on reconstructing the legal situation and preserving ancient rights; the Spaniards responded that it would be sufficient to send engineers to verify where the river passed.[18] The question, Spaniards asserted, was not what might have happened in a remote past but what "justice and reason" (justicia y razón) dictated at the present. As far as they were concerned, in the case under review law intervened not in order to confirm what had already existed (ancient rights) but in order to mandate how it should change (recognizing the mutations in the flow of the river). These deliberations were accompanied by news that the situation on the border continued to deteriorate and that locals insisted on their demands being met.[19]

Almost twenty years passed before the island of Verdoejo was again discussed, this time as a by-product of negotiations concerning the implementation of the Treaty of Utrecht. According to the treaty,

signed in 1715, both monarchies were to regain the "fortresses, castles, cities, places, territories, and fields, which they had before the
war" (i.e., the War of Spanish Succession, 1701–1713, which Portugal entered in 1703). Among the very few locations specifically mentioned in the treaty as examples for the required restitution was the
"island of Verdejo [sic]," which Spain, having stationed military
forces there during the war, promised to return to Portugal.[20] It is
not quite clear how the island made its way into the treaty alongside,
for example, Colonia de Sacramento, but according to local interlocutors, after the treaty was signed, the Portuguese living in the
vicinity, arguing that Verdoejo was theirs, began using it while also
prohibiting Spaniards from doing so.[21] Asked by the local authorities how to respond to these challenges, initially the Spanish Council of State replied that the treaty was clear and its instructions must
be followed. However, after it was informed by the governor of Galicia of what had transpired in the 1680s and 1690s, the council asserted that inclusion of the island among Portuguese territories to be
returned by Spain might have been a mistake because the island was
not truly Portuguese before the war had begun. If such was the case,
then despite Spain's obligations according to the treaty, the island
should not be ceded to the Portuguese because the treaty mandated
"restitution," not the seizure of new lands.

What happened next remains unknown. It is possible that the
expulsion of the Jesuits from Portugal in 1759 and the subsequent
transfer of the monastery of San Fins to private hands as well as its
consequent abandonment and destruction allowed the Spanish abbot to renew his claims. We do know that the fate of Verdoejo was
discussed again in 1859, when the authorities of both countries appointed a joint commission to settle all pending border issues.[22]
Clarifying that entitlements should be determined according to private possession and considering the Treaty of Utrecht as evidence
for Portuguese title (as happened in the Americas, where treaties
were interpreted as proofs), the Portuguese commissioner explained
that by the time the 1859 negotiations began, rather than one island, Verdoejo consisted of several, making it unclear whether the
rights that corresponded to Portugal should be transposed on one,
various, or all of them. Confusion also grew because many of these

changes were not truly natural but instead man-made, caused by what riverine communities had constructed on the margins. Adopting a Solomonic decision, in 1864 the treaty fixing the boundaries between Spain and Portugal declared that of the "island group called Verdoejo" three islands would become Spanish and two Portuguese.[23]

Verdoejo: The Parties

The conflict over Verdoejo initially involved the monastery of San Fins (in Portugal) and the abbot of Caldelas (in Spain). Joining it later were the Council of State and bishop of Tuy (in Spain), as well as the governor of Valença do Minho (in Portugal). Although on occasions these diverse authorities coordinated their activities and supported one another, on others they acted independently and pursued distinct goals. The ecclesiastical jurisdiction of the convent and abbot were not dependent on secular divisions, which during this period often dramatically differed, allowing religious authorities on one side of the border to have jurisdiction on the other side. Similarly, there was no reason why local authorities would care about tithes. Yet soon after the confrontation began, these two issues, as well as the question of political subjection to Spain or Portugal (again, not necessarily related), became entangled, local authorities apparently supporting ecclesiastical claims and vice versa, and kings, most particularly, the king of Portugal, intervening in the debate to defend their sovereignty. Why these individuals and bodies tied the collection of tithes to the exercise of municipal jurisdiction and why they considered them related to political subjection to a kingdom was never explained. But regardless of what the law dictated (namely, that these issues were distinct), with regards to Verdoejo, at least, the different parties, caring for different results, found allies in one another. Fishermen also took a position; though mainly portrayed in the records as being forced to pay dues, they, in fact, decided whether to consent, thus recognizing the authority to which they paid as legitimate or not. Their decision to follow one strategy or the other might have not always been completely free, yet its results were performative because payment could acknowledge, even constitute, title to the land, and its absence could be considered an act of disposses-

sion. Fishermen also took sides by agreeing to sell fish or by defending collectors against the attack of their rivals. The governors of
Galicia consistently presented themselves as external observers who
reported to the royal authorities on what had transpired and attempted to appease the local population by imposing their personal
authority. Yet, in their reports to Madrid they, too, took sides, offered solutions, and performed different administrative, military,
and judicial activities that modified the situation on the ground.
Rather than being neutral observers, as the conflict progressed they
became actors. So did monarchs, who suggested that their sovereignty was at stake and who were willing, more on the Portuguese
side, to risk military confrontation in order to affirm that this minuscule island was either Spanish or Portuguese, as if this decision
could settle (which it could not) who could collect tithes and who
could roam the island with their rods of justice raised.

One party whose absence loomed large in the proceedings were
the owners of the island. Spanish and Portuguese documents constantly mentioned their existence and continually asserted that private
property could be affected by these discussions, because decisions
on belonging could sometimes indicate whether proprietors could
collect fees, rent parts of the island, and so forth. Yet the documentation reveals that property rights were contested, too. According to
the Portuguese foreign minister, in 1520 the monastery of San Fins
sold the island of Verdoejo to Leonel de Abreu, lord of the House of
Regalado.[24] This transaction was confirmed when the monastery
was transferred in the 1540s to the Jesuit order. Contemporary records also indicate that after the original owner died, the property
passed to several of his successors, the island remaining in the family until Pedro Gómez de Abreu, a Portuguese who lived in Salvaterra (Galicia) voted with his feet against the Portuguese uprising,
moving to Madrid in 1640 and declaring loyalty to King Philip of
Spain.[25] Classified in Portugal as a rebel, the administration of the
House of Regalado, as well as its estates, rights, and properties, re-
verted to the crown, which appointed the governor of Minho as the
new lord, granting him, among other things, possession of Verdoejo.
The Portuguese asserted that these circumstances proved that the
Abreu lost all their rights to the island. Spaniards, however, affirmed

that such was not the case. They asserted that Pedro continued to own the island and that he transmitted his rights to his relative Antonio Falcón de Sotomayor, citizen and lord of Parderrubias, who then transferred them to his son Rodrigo Antonio Falcón de Ulloa, since 1692, Marquis of Bendaña.[26] Given these opposing narratives, it is probable that in the 1680s and 1690s (when the discussion on Verdoejo first took place), one of the points of disagreement between the Spaniards and the Portuguese was precisely who was the legitimate owner of the island. The Regalados (supported by Tuy and Spain) continued to vindicate their rights, yet the Portuguese suggested they had none. These discussions might explain what transpired on the island in the 1680s, not very long after peace with Portugal was reestablished (1668). According to contemporaries, the Regalados might have used the abbot of Caldelas to assert their claims because, if the island were Spanish then their version that it was still part of their patrimony would win the day and they would be able to recover its property. Yet, if the Portuguese obtained recognition that it belonged to their kingdoms, this would be impossible because the Portuguese denied they had any rights. Indications that this reading was perhaps justified could be found also in sources that asserted, for example, that among those promoting the Spanish cause locally was a certain Rodrigo Antonio, a "powerful citizen of Tuy" and administrator (*factor*) of a lady identified in the documentation as "the countess of Regalado," who at that time lived in Madrid and who, according to the Portuguese, wished to "recover the property of the island that had belonged to her grandparents." If "Rodrigo Antonio" mentioned in Portuguese sources was the same as "Rodrigo Antonio Falcón de Sotomayor" in Spanish documentation, then he was perhaps not the proprietor of the island (as some Spaniards had suggested) but instead administered it for the Spanish House of Regalado, which sought recognition that the island was still part of its patrimony. Or he might have succeeded the Regalados as owner and was defended by a countess who otherwise feared a confrontation with him over family properties that were allegedly his.

The question of who owned Verdoejo and how the union and disunion of the crowns might have affected private entitlements thus added another layer of complexity to the conflict that already involved tithes, jurisdiction, and subjugation. Because ownership was important, contemporaries who suggested this reading were disconcerted by the silence of Rodrigo Antonio Falcón de Ulloa and the Countess of Regalado. They insinuated that they might have preferred to act indirectly by employing agents, but, whatever the case, their silence was criticized in 1716 by Spanish officials who could not understand why they failed to defend their cause. After all, it was clear that as early as the 1690s, if not earlier, the Portuguese deprived them of the land, as well as its fruits, wood, and fish, which were rented out to a Portuguese who thereafter used it as if it were his own.[27]

During the years in which this confrontation lasted, the minute size of the territory and its utter insignificance did not seem to be of great concern. Whether the island won prominence because Jesuits were involved, because the authorities of Tuy were able to recruit the governor of Galicia to their cause, because the long hand of the owners of the island was operating, or because, although inconsequential from Lisbon's and Madrid's point of view it was vital to the local economy remains unclear. What was evident was that while the Portuguese caucus managed to interest the crown early on, it took a long while before locals could recruit the attention of the Spanish royal authorities. Initially, these authorities hoped that no action would be the best strategy to follow. But even after Spanish royal officials took matters into their hands, they acted not as interested parties but as external observers, perhaps judges. Suggesting that unless they acted war might begin, they nevertheless insisted that the contestation was absolutely of no interest to the king, who was not truly a party to it. How it ended was indifferent to them, as long as it did.

Verdoejo: The Coveted Object

Between 1683 (when the conflict was first documented) and 1863 (when it was resolved), the object in contention, that is, the island of Verdoejo, was both difficult to identify and constantly suffered substantial mutations. Contemporaries believed that it was originally part of the Portuguese mainland, had become an island, and, having been located on the Portuguese bank, it was washed by the waters and transferred to Spain. Initially, there was one island. By the mid-nineteenth century, there were several, perhaps as many as five. Verdoejo might have had two distinct names, as Spaniards attested, or Caldelas might have been a different island, as the Portuguese argued. Although plenty of records existed and many testimonies were collected, most supplied no clear answer to these questions. The solution to these inquiries, as a result, remained contentious even among locals who, while they affirmed their certainty, could not date the transformations they reported nor were they willing to concede that on occasions even they were unsure as to how to identify the territory they coveted in the documentation they possessed. Confusion was such that the audiencia of Galicia remarked in the 1690s that the main problem its judges faced was not to uncover past entitlements but to decide which territory they referred to. Was the island of Verdoejo mentioned in sixteenth-century documentation the same as the one the Portuguese now identified? Had it mutated since? In which ways? The situation was so convoluted that when royal officials in 1691 received complaints that the Portuguese claimed jurisdiction over a small island in the Miño River where inhabitants of both countries collected herbs and planted wheat, they immediately concluded that Verdoejo was again stirring trouble.[28] Many factors indicated this might be the case: at stake was an island that according to locals was Spanish, among other things, because it was now contiguous to Galicia; the Portuguese began using it after peace was reestablished in 1668, impeding Spaniards from doing so by capturing their animals, placing fines on their owners, and destroying their crops; natural changes in the course of the river, which transported the island closer to Galicia than to Portugal, were perhaps to blame. Yet, despite these similarities, the territory at fault was another island (Canosa), not Verdoejo.

If the object of desire changed, so did what was expected of it. Initially, the Council of State suggested that the question involved "fishing rights."[29] Yet, as events unfolded, it became clear that a conflict regarding ecclesiastical tithes had become another, concerning municipal jurisdiction and political subjection, perhaps even private property. Conceptually differentiated and not necessarily interdependent (tithes depended on ecclesiastical, not political, subjection and could be paid to a parish in a foreign country), de facto, even if not de jure, these aspects closely influenced one another. This was particularly true in areas such as here, where both political and ecclesiastical ascriptions had changed over the years, as dioceses and their extension were rearranged and so was the border.[30] Challenges by ecclesiastical authorities led to massive local involvement, justifying the intervention of secular powers and eventually the state. Both locals and kings sought to implicate the owners of the land, who were mostly absent. Ecclesiastics, local authorities, and other individuals involved in these confrontations each pursued their own interests, yet on occasions they found in one another excellent allies. These coincidences allowed them to connect tithes with the exercise of local jurisdiction and with property and property with political subjection. Thus, whatever the law might have mandated, protection of ecclesiastical jurisdiction also entailed territorial defense and vice versa. The same happened with regards to usage rights and private ownership, even seigniorial rights. Not only did private interests manage to mobilize agents on the border as well as authorities in capital cities, not only were these interests able to convert a conflict over a small and insignificant territory into a major international affair (sufficient to be included in the Treaty of Utrecht), discussants suggested that if the territory was owned by a Spaniard, if tithes were collected by Caldelas, than these were good indications it was also Spanish. But the contrary was also true: if this was Spain, then the abbot could collect tithes and the Marquis of Bendaña and the Regalados conserved their rights. Whether a question of chicken or egg, contemporaries were compelled into action by these convictions that depended on their daily experience rather than legal doctrines (that mandated otherwise). The overlapping of property rights, tax collection, jurisdiction, and submission perhaps also explained why both the Spaniards and the Portuguese involved local tribunals in their quarrels. The monastery of San Fins first addressed the Portuguese judge of Viana and then the Spanish *audiencia* of Galicia. The abbot of Caldelas and the city of Tuy conceded to the jurisdiction of both, never suggesting (until it was too late) that they were incompetent to rule on these issues. Royal councils and the Spanish monarch seemed to agree, refusing to consider judicial involvement as a nuisance until it became clear that it was. It was as if as long as property and taxes, even local jurisdiction, were debated, royal courts could intervene. Only when the jurisdiction of kings was at stake could they not. Yet, as demonstrated here, this artificial division of one affair into distinct parts and different jurisdictions was unsustainable. At the end of the day, because of the coexistence of these different aspects, which contemporaries considered were closely related, a temporary relief granted by the court of Galicia could (and indeed probably had) produced the effective transfer of the territory to Portugal.

The story of Verdoejo also clarifies that struggle for land could be comprehended as and confused with struggle over people. After all, tithes were to be collected from individuals either because of where they performed their activities or according to whom they were. One way or the other, at stake was not necessarily which land belonged to whom but who would pay taxes to which authority. Answering this question required that individuals using the territory recognized certain authorities as legitimate, but it also demanded that these authorities would be able to classify these people subject to its jurisdiction.

Verdoejo: The Claims

During the centuries in which these debates lasted, the parties could not agree on what exactly had transpired in the past, yet they coincided in suggesting that the union of the crowns of Spain and Portugal, as well as the 1640 rupture, were transformative because they affected the ascription of the territory. The War of the Spanish Succession and the stationing of Spanish military forces on the island in the early 1700s might have brought about a similar alteration. In both cases, rather than allowing the acquisition of new territories (which they did not), these changes augmented existing confusion, allowing both Spaniards and Portuguese to acquire rights that were sometimes complementary, sometimes oppositional. Archival documentation also indicates that fishing, which did not require occupation, was better tolerated than grazing (which did) and grazing was better tolerated than agriculture, which excluded other users. There were constant calls to return to the situation prior to the union or the war, but there was absolutely no agreement as to what that situation was. Appeals to immemoriality were repetitive, too, but all that existing records could prove were claims, not entitlements. Witnesses gave their opinion, but their declarations mostly clarified that residents on both sides of the river used the island jointly, none having privative rights and none prohibiting the other from enjoying it. It was only when one side began claiming exclusivity that the other responded with violence. And though we will never know who initiated these challenges, contemporary documentation shows that after confrontation commenced, it was very difficult, perhaps impossible, to stop it. Claims produced responses that conjured further reclamations. This dynamic guaranteed the continuation of hostilities, which were at times symbolic—like roaming the territory with rods of justice raised—at times not. Peace thus alternated with conflict not because the parties occasionally agreed but because action was sometimes required, though often not. Performative and juridically significant, at stake was perhaps not who would actually collect tithes but who would be allowed to do so peacefully.

While the Portuguese based their allegations on acquired rights, Spaniards mostly insisted that the decision hinged on observing nature, because even if Verdoejo was once upon a time Portuguese, changes in the course of the river might have made it Spanish. At stake was not adherence to natural boundaries but to the legal consequences that would be ascribed to how they altered over time. Already in the thirteenth century, *Ius Commune* jurists discussed these questions. Bartolus de Saxoferrato examined them most eloquently, arguing in the fourteenth century that though rivers were useful dividers, natural changes in their course could affect legal entitlements by adding or subtracting land to riverine owners.[31] Mainly concerned with property rights, he, like other *Ius Commune* jurists, nevertheless suggested that that if the alterations were sufficiently slow as to produce the creation of new customs and new ways to understand the modified landscape, jurisdiction could be affected,

too. This doctrine, widely accepted among experts, was partially reproduced in Castilian legislation that determined, for example, that
land that gradually accumulated on one side of the river became the
property of and was subject to the jurisdiction of those who had rights
there.[32] Similarly, new islands that materialized in the river were to be
jointly owned unless they were closer to one bank than to the other,
in which case they would belong to the nearest neighbor. By the late
eighteenth century, these assertions were included in Emmer de
Vatttle's *Law of Nations* and thus formed part of the growing body of
a nascent international law. By that time, however, Vattel expressed
no doubt that these changes (always) affected jurisdiction. He also
concluded that, rather than fixed or clear, natural borders were mostly
"indeterminate" *(territoria arcifinia)*.[33]

The parties to the discussion on Verdoejo might have adopted
one position or the other according to their convenience, but their
disagreement revealed not only their diverse interpretations of the
existing legal order but also other concerns present at the time in
which this debate took place. In the eighteenth century, preference
to rights and ancient entitlements that were permanent was viewed
as legitimate, as was the acceptance of (inevitable) natural changes.
Yet increasingly the former lost ground to the latter. As the early
modern age drew to a close, the tendency of many was to suggest
that rather than respecting existing rights, contemporaries were to
examine them and, if needed, modify them. This happened in the
Americas with regard to native rights, but it also transpired on the
Iberian Peninsula, where "justice and reason" in the present became
more powerful than what had transpired in the past. Thus, if natural changes in the course of rivers could, according to *Ius Commune*
jurists, call into question ancient rights, the willingness to implement this reading was particularly strong in a century that concen-
trated its attention on change rather than continuity. Yet, while
Verdoejo became an international incident of sorts and required
constant royal attention, debates regarding similar cases, for example, Canosa, did not. Why was hard to tell. Both islands were small
and insignificant and both were commonly used by the inhabitants
of both sides of the Minho/Miño River. The decision regarding usage was, in both cases, considered by extension also a determination

about jurisdiction and sovereignty. Yet, while in Canosa the conflict mostly centered on grazing versus agriculture, suggesting that
fracture lines perhaps ran between animal raisers and cultivators,
not Spaniards and Portuguese, the debate in Verdoejo was much
more complex and involved many more actors and interests. It was
thus likely to continue for a longer time and present a greater challenge for peace. It is also possible, however, that the greatest distinction between both conflicts was not what had transpired on the
ground but the identity of the parties: in Canosa anonymous farmers; in Verdoejo a Jesuit monastery, a Spanish abbot, and a noble
family.

Verdoejo and Canosa were not the only cases in which nature
imposed, perhaps furnished, an excuse, to reimagine existing divisions. Similar problems emerged in the mid-eighteenth century
along the Spanish–Portuguese border on the mouth of the Guadiana River, whose bed was made of "moveable sands" *(arena moved-
iza)*, thus allowing its shape to constantly alter.[34] During a relatively
short time span, islands appeared and disappeared, new access path-
ways opened or closed, and some channels became so narrow or
shallow that they no longer allowed the passage of certain vessels.
How these mutations that were constantly shaped and reshaped
changed the rights of the parties was heatedly debated. At stake were
fishing and navigation rights, as well as taxation and jurisdiction
(who would collect taxes on the activities taking place there but also
who would stop pirates from entering the river and would control
trade on it). In an effort to establish his jurisdiction, in 1764 the
Portuguese customs officer in Castro Marim arrived at one of the
islands that Spaniards claimed as their own on board a ship flying a
Portuguese flag, and he ordered fishermen and their customers to
obey his orders. Locals explained that Portuguese actions were based
on the fact that the island at stake used to belong to Portugal, but
natural changes in the course of the river that placed it nearer to
Spain clearly now made it Spanish *(con la mutación de la misma canal,
se han mudado también naturalmente los límites)*. Making local fishermen into representatives of Spanish interests, royal officials instructed them to insist on Spanish rights and disobey the Portuguese
official. This would be a sufficient response to his challenges, they

asserted, and there was no reason to involve Lisbon. Yet, while Spaniards argued in 1764 and again in 1840 that natural alterations produced new divisions, the Portuguese denied these claims, suggesting
that the "violence of the river" could never undo their "rights of
dominion."[35]

The Magdalena/Lindoso Mountains (1773–1864)

The study of confrontations involving the neighboring communities of Lindoso, Compostela, Trasportela, and Manín in southern
Galicia and northern Portugal illustrate yet another facet of territorial debates, namely, the belief that in the absence of clear evidence
or juridical determination, reason should serve as an antidote. Records set the beginning of this conflict in 1773, when inhabitants of
Lindoso complained to their king that a large group of armed Galicians entered their vineyards in the Magdalena Mountains, chasing
and wounding individuals who were toiling in them.[36] Attempts to
reach an understanding through the mediation of the local Portuguese and Spanish governors "so it would be unnecessary to occupy
the courts with something that can be provided for so easily" nonetheless failed. The Portuguese military commander informed his
monarch of what had transpired and expressed his frustration as
well as his fear that the citizens of Lindoso would resort to violence.
This reaction, he asserted, would be justified because they would be
defending their properties and land coveted by their opponents, but
it would nevertheless be regrettable if such incidents occurred. In
response, the Portuguese royal authorities, who suspected that aggression would lead to the intensification of violence, insisted that
only self-defense was authorized and instructed locals to reach an
agreement that would ensure harmony among neighbors.[37] Because
Madrid was also informed of what had transpired, Spanish royal officials ordered an investigation as to why the confrontations first
took place, only to receive the expected answer that the Portuguese
were to blame.[38] According to the governor of Galicia, the territory
was not demarcated, but it was generally acknowledged that the
border between the two countries ran by the Cabril River, where
Spanish authorities collected taxes and imprisoned smugglers and

where the Portuguese placed their military men during wars. Recently, however, the Portuguese of Lindoso began cultivating a territory called La Magdalena east of the river, on the Spanish side. They acted as if they owned this land (which they did not), they privately used what was common (agricultural use was read as an attempt to privatize common lands), and they tried to annex it to their community and kingdom (to which it did not belong). This led to skirmishes that included confiscations, the destruction of property, fines, and even one death. It also produced a Portuguese prohibition against the Spanish municipal authorities reaching the riverside, to which Spaniards responded by denying the Portuguese the right to work the lands they considered their property. Both parties were certain about their entitlements, and both made appeals to a previous status quo, yet evidence collected in 1774 demonstrated that already in 1538 neighboring communities struggled over which territory was theirs. That year, as a result of these confrontations, the Portuguese unilaterally demarcated the land without Spanish knowledge or consent.[39] This might have been indeed the point of departure because testimonies dated only ten years earlier (1527) suggested that at that time Lindoso was almost completely depopulated (only some forty-one individuals inhabited it) and its castle abandoned and in ruin.[40] Yet, if records indicated the conflict was ancient and might have began alongside the repopulation of Lindoso, locals insisted that it was not. Dating the first hostilities to the mid-eighteenth century, they asserted that their rivals innovated and thus terminated a long period that mainly featured accords.[41] Using physical assaults leading to deaths, confiscations, destruction of harvests, and fines, the Portuguese (according to Spaniards) or the Spanish (according to the Portuguese) managed to expand their territory. New confrontations, as well as new attempts at negotiation, took place in 1777, 1778, and 1779. Their failure led the Portuguese ambassador to Madrid in 1779 to issue a formal complaint that basically reproduced local versions according to which the territory was and had always been Portuguese because possessed and worked by the inhabitants of Lindoso who grew grapes on it and used its pasture. Desperate for peace of mind, they were willing to finance the cost of demarcation, but they needed the consent of Spaniards, which they were unable to secure locally.[42] What was needed, in short, was a Spanish royal declaration that by asserting where the frontier *(fronteira)* passed according to old versions *(vestígios antigos)* would necessarily favor Portugal.

In response, the governor of Galicia appointed a military judge *(auditor de guerra)* and an engineer to inspect the territory, examine witnesses and documents, and draw maps.[43] He then suggested to the Spanish king that he consider three distinct areas of questioning: (1) Was the territory really necessary for the state? Did its extension and utility justify the confrontation? (2) Was the territory important for military concerns, that is, strategic reasons? (3) Could existing demarcation, practices, and documentation clarify the rights of the parties? To evaluate the first, the governor observed the map that demonstrated that the terrain was so mountainous it could barely serve any useful purpose. From the state's point of view, he concluded, it was of very little interest, indeed almost none. As for military concerns, the Cabril River could serve as a good defense line against invasions. It was thus sensible to adopt it as the border between the two countries. Regarding the rights of the parties, there was absolutely no proof in local archives as to where the border passed. There were, however, many indications that the contested territory belonged to Spain: division along rivers were both natural and customary, and Portuguese defenses, located on the other side, also indicated that previously even the Portuguese considered the river the true line of separation.

But if locals were unable to agree on their entitlements, neither were they capable of deciding what had transpired between them. Attempts to verify in December 1779 what had happened, for example, in October of that year, led to distinct outcomes. The Portuguese suggested that Galicians had attacked and imprisoned a laborer as well as destroyed many beehives and vineyards owned by the Portuguese.[44] Spaniards responded that the only thing that had transpired was that a single Portuguese man was arrested in revenge for the requisitioning of six to eight head of cattle belonging to the citizens of Compostela in Spain. These discussions, which repeated themselves each time new hostilities broke out, allowed representatives of both countries to accuse one another of misinformation, perhaps even deceit. Each insisted that the other was to blame and asserted that a new demarcation that would reflect their rights and authenticate their claims was required.[45] If a permanent settlement *(legítimos y perpetuos límites)* was too difficult to reach, then at least a provisional line *(línea provisional)* should be drawn that, by way of compromise, would divide the territory.

New episodes took place in 1798, when the governor of Galicia reported that after a period of peace, in January of that year the local judge *(alcalde ordinario)* of Trasportela in Spain, accompanied by many men, arrived at the bridge over the Cabril River, which marked the division observed from immemorial time *(la división que se observa desde tiempo inmemorial)* between its community and Lindoso (in Portugal).[46] Wishing to replace the crosses and stones that demarcated the border according to the "very old custom" *(costumbre antiquísima)* that mandated doing so annually, the judges and citizens of Lindoso interfered in the ceremony, setting fire to the Spanish side of the river and mistreating the members of the group. Problems along the border, the inhabitants of Trasportela argued, had begun only in 1775, when the Portuguese of Lindoso began exceeding their limits, killing a citizen of Trasportela and constantly harassing its inhabitants. According to these complaints, Galicians wished only to continue using their lands *(propias tierras)*, which the Portuguese now wanted to occupy by planting different crops *(plantío)*. While Madrid corresponded with authorities in Galicia, the Portuguese suggested taking two parallel measures: calling a joint meeting to discuss the border and publishing edicts that would prohibit locals *(fronterizos)* from invading the domains of their neighbors.[47] Yet a Portuguese judge thereafter appointed to investigate the complaints of Spaniards concluded that the residents of Lindoso (not Galicians) were the true proprietors of the land east of the river, which they were forced to abandon because of Galician violence.[48] Because Spanish insults were "grave, frequent, and intolerable" to the point of not allowing inhabitants of Lindoso to work the most fertile land they possessed, a new demarcation was required. It would have to confirm what the Portuguese demanded because it would be unjust for the kingdom to lose territory that had always been its own *(não ser justo que este reino perda um terreno que sempre foi seu próprio)*.

Confrontations continued in 1789, 1790, 1791, and 1803, mainly featuring either the Portuguese or the Spaniards (depending on who was speaking) invading the terrains of the other party. While the Portuguese suggested that the land was theirs and accused several citizens of Trasportela (in Spain) of cutting down trees and bushes belonging to the Portuguese, Spaniards responded that the territory in contention was part of Spanish royal lands *(realengos)*, reserved for the use of Spanish vassals and Spanish vassals alone.[49] They also asserted that by using force, the Portuguese wished to become owners of what could not belong to them by law *(a fuerza de brazo hacerse dueños de lo que no puede pertenecerles)*. Because they were facing the option of either losing these mountains that were vital for their survival or risking their lives in battle in order to protect them, the inhabitants of Compostela requested that their king intervene. Thus, while the Portuguese pointed to Spaniards as the responsible party, Spaniards answered that Portuguese complaints sought to hide the fact that they were the true villains. By 1803, the level of violence was such that armed groups constantly patrolled the territory, deliberately collecting wood, setting fire, destroying property, and imprisoning those they found laboring there in order to manifest publically their possession and usage rights.

Although contenders on both sides of the border argued that violence was a means to achieve additional gains and was exercised mainly as a method for illegitimate expansion, it was nevertheless clear that on most accounts it sought either to voice concern over what opponents were doing or to communicate claims. In this dispute, roaming and planting were not neutral, accidental activities performed only when and to the degree that they were required. They might have had tangible results such as providing livelihood, but contemporaries believed that they were telling of territorial intentions. The same was true of violence, which might have been motivated by frustration, fear, or animosity but was also a means to protest, and thus deauthorize, what rivals attempted to accomplish. All parties were aware of the significance of their acts, and all presumed that their rivals were, too.[50] In La Magdalena, at least, they often suggested that many activities carried out by their opponents were not truly necessary but instead were perfomative because aimed at making a certain stand publicly known. Contemporaries had no other explanation why, for example, their rivals insisted on planting small vines where they could not grow or roamed the territory when they did not need to. The accusation that opponents "innovated" was performative, too. While all continuously asserted that they respected a consensual status quo, contemporary records indicate that nothing that happened on the territory in the 1770s to the 1800s was genuinely new and that before confrontations began, agreement between the rivals was an idea, perhaps an aspiration or a horizon, but it did not accurately reflect local experiences. The insistence on innovation was thus an important juridical tool because immemorial rights required not only prolonged exercise but also consensus. To argue otherwise, that is, to sustain that the parties had always disagreed, would undermine the very same entitlements that litigants sought to establish. As evidence accumulated in La Magdalena, however, much of it indicated that most confrontations were provoked by the passage from grazing—which could be accomplished simultaneously by members of different communities—to cultivation, which required a dedicated territory, privatively used. Incitation by particular individuals might also have played a role: Spaniards might have been moved to action by the Portuguese priest of their parish; the Portuguese, by the governor of the nearby castle of Lindoso.[51]

Spanish and Portuguese royal authorities, whose intervention was requested by locals to guarantee both their livelihood and peace, hesitated as to what they should do.[52] Only after they were informed at the end of 1791 that confrontations were motivated by "old hatred" (un odio tan antiguo) and that they often escalated into "true war" (estado de verdadera guerra) or "bloody quarrels and disagreements" (contiendas sangrientas y discordias) did Spanish officials agree that the matter demanded serious consideration.[53] Because there was no conclusive evidence as to which were the entitlements of the parties, the Spanish minister of state resorted to analyzing various indications. He dismissed the Portuguese claim that the owning of land and the construction of a chapel by the Portuguese was telling because, according to the law, owning real estate *(bienes raíces)* in a foreign country did not affect jurisdiction or vassalage. As for the chapel, the territory might well be under Portugal spiritually, but it was under Spain in temporal matters. The behavior of Portuguese justices, he reasoned, demonstrated that they did not consider this territory Portuguese because they refused to investigate crimes there. While Portuguese claims could be easily refuted, Spanish titles were solid. Division by rivers was customary, and the Cabril delimited the territory naturally *(límites naturales)*. Spanish ministers collected taxes and apprehended smugglers east of the river, Portuguese cattle owners paid dues there, and, when in war, the Portuguese staged their defenses on the western side. Convinced that the conflict might have had its origin in the incorrect recollection of where limits passed before the two kingdoms separated (1640), Spanish officials concluded that La Magdalena was but one example among many.[54] Several other Galician villages suffered the same fate, because in many places along the border there was no demarcation or records of one ever having been conducted. Local memory was just as unreliable, because citizens of these villages habitually declared either that they had no recollection of where their jurisdiction ended or that they did not know how it had mutated over time. All that "elderly citizens" *(personas ancianas vecinas)* could testify was that the demarcation between the two kingdoms was uncertain *(incierta)*. Documents were faulty, too. Dating mostly from the fourteenth and fifteenth centuries, they reproduced local arrangements among nobles that delimited their seigniorial domains, not agreements between municipal entities or states.[55]

As complaints regarding the lack of proper demarcation between Galicia and Portugal accumulated, Spanish officials began urging the king to clarify the status of these contested territories *(se determinen y fijen los límites de los terrenos contenciosos)*.[56] Adhering to this advice, the Spanish monarch agreed with his Portuguese counterpart to send commissioners to resolve these issues. Yet, as soon as bilateral conversations began in 1806, disagreement emerged regarding what were these delegates to achieve.[57] The Spaniard wished to demarcate "all the places and lands" *(parajes y terrenos)* that were "doubtful" along the border. The Portuguese contested that his powers were limited to an area he identified as "Monte de Lindoso" and which the Spaniards called "La Magdalena." The Spaniard then suggested that because no authentic documents existed that would clarify the legal situation they should adopt a demarcation that would follow the natural border set by the Cabril River. The Portuguese responded by presenting a 1538 Portuguese demarcation *(tombo)* and insisting that geographers always preferred divisions along mountain tops, not rivers. The Spaniard disputed these conclusions, arguing that rivers were more fixed than mountain tops that were practically unreachable and often caused contention. He also asserted that "scientific and convincing reasons" *(razones científicas y convincentes)* as well as geography indicated that La Magdalena was Spanish because it was nearer to Spanish communities and easier to reach than from Lindoso, which had barely any roads leading to that territory and was located at a considerable distance. These criteria, he argued, were solid. They were certainly more trustworthy than common use or the contrasting allegations of locals who could not agree on who utilized the territory and since when. After all, because villagers were simple folk *(el carácter sencillo de estos fronterizos gallegos)*, they were barely aware of the implications of allowing their neighbors to labor on their land. As a result, even if they had consented to such use, this would prove nothing, most particularly because it was well known that the inhabitants of these Spanish hamlets depended on Portugal for their most basic needs, even food supplies. The Portuguese demarcation of 1538 was useless because it was conducted by the Portuguese alone, without the presence of all interested parties. To these allegations, the Portuguese commissioner answered by affirming that the Cabril River was far too small to form a solid border, that mountain tops were preferable, that the distance between the litigated territory and its rightful owners was irrelevant, that there was no need for a road from Lindoso to La Magdalena because the use the Portuguese made of that terrain required none, and that the 1538 demarcation did not legally require the presence of Spaniards because, rather than innovating, it recognized what was already in existence.

Because no agreement was reached and confrontations continued, new commissioners were appointed in 1821. Yet they, too, failed to arrive at an accord.[58] In 1856, a mixed Spanish–Portuguese delegation dealt with these issues again. Initially, its members repeated what the 1804–1807 interlocutors had already asserted. Yet, while they utterly disagreed about who was right and who wrong, they nevertheless coincided in identifying locals as simple folk who from time immemorial were confronted by hateful rivalry and discord, which not only harmed their particular interests but also constituted an affront to "European civilization," afflicted "honorable" Spaniards and Portuguese, and discredited the "superior authority" of both governments.[59] This "insignificant and uninhabited wasteland" (*insignificante e deshabitado monte*), they asserted, was not a valuable terrain, as locals argued, and it did not merit the attention it had been thus granted. Searching not only to recognize but to re-form the border, and feeling free to act as they pleased, midcentury commissioners thus assumed that they knew and understood what was needed. Proceeding to observe the territory, they debated which were the best natural borders and which division would better serve the interests of both states. The solution they sought to adopt was natural and convenient rather than legal or just.[60] Yet, agreeing in the abstract about the method to employ, they constantly quarreled about its subsequent concrete results. Because reason gave no clear consensual answer, eventually, they turned to compromise. In 1864, they suggested dividing the terrain equally between Spain and Portugal.[61]

Magdalena/Lindoso: The Parties

Identifying and tracing who the parties to the conflict at La Magdalena (or Lindoso) Mountains were was particularly difficult. Royal documentation constantly mentioned a few villages and hamlets identified as Lindoso (in Portugal), Compostela, Trasportela, and Manín (in Galicia), yet, among these, only Lindoso constantly appeared as an actor that alternately confronted residents of the other hamlets who were either identified as such or were simply classified as *gallegos*. Confrontations with Compostela tended to focus on activities that the citizens of Lindoso were said to perform on the territory. Incidents with Trasportela were mostly motivated by the defense of local jurisdiction and took place when the judges of Trasportela visited the territory and placed crosses on it as "a very old custom" (*costumbre antiquísima*) mandated or when they performed other jurisdictional acts there.[62] Manín appeared only once, in 1803, and its mention was similar to that of Compostela. Whether these differences were real and pointed at distinct conflicts we do not know. But, though the three Galician hamlets might indeed have been extremely small and poor, as the Spanish commissioner asserted in the early nineteenth century, and their residents simple folk who depended on Portugal, their rivals nevertheless insisted that they knew exactly what they were doing when they roamed the territory or destroyed vines. Records also indicate that many confrontations, especially with Compostela and perhaps Manín, might have involved grazing and collecting versus cultivation, not Spaniards versus Portuguese. It is also possible that during this period Manín and perhaps also the other nearby settlements, although classified as Galician, were in reality mixed villages, with both Spanish and Portuguese residents and with their jurisdiction also shared de facto between both countries.[63] There were also repeated allegations that the military commander of Lindoso Castle incentivized the Portuguese to act, armed and trained them, wrote some of their complaints, and channeled them to the higher authorities. In 1803, he was also accused of taking an active part in the debate by placing guards on the litigated territory in order to manifest publically that it was Portuguese.[64] Whether he did so in order to defend the interests of the inhabitants of Lindoso or Portuguese territory we do not know, but his protagonism was obvious, though perplexing to his contemporaries.

Because most of the information on conflicts in La Magdalena originated in royal correspondence, it portrayed royal officials as important actors who collected information and negotiated at court. Their involvement tended to color the events as pitting the "Galicians" against the "Portuguese." However, the tendency to so do might have also been encouraged by locals who asserted that the contested territory was not municipal but royal (*realengo*) and thus

open to all vassals but not to foreigners. In other words, to qualify
for its use, contrary to what happened elsewhere, locals did not have
to be *vecinos* (members of local communities) but *naturales* (members
of the kingdom, hence, Spaniards).[65] As a result, contrary to what
had happened in La Contienda, Campo de Gamos, and Rossiana,
where citizenship mattered and so did municipal action, in La Magdalena what was essential was the classification of individuals as
Spanish or Portuguese. Concern with royal property might have
not only presented the conflict as involving kingdoms, not municipalities, but also incentivized the king to intervene. Perhaps the insistence of distinguishing Spaniards from Portuguese was paradoxically due to the high degree of mixing that lead to a real difficulty to
decide clearly who was who, who lived where, and which interests
they defended as in the possibility that Manín was a mixed population. Nonetheless, what was perhaps most determinant in shaping
royal response here was the astounding accumulation of complaints
regarding disorder along the Galician–Portuguese border. There
were frequent incidents in the 1780s, 1790s, and 1800s among the
Portuguese of Monforte and Lama and the Spaniards of El Ríos.[66]
From the point of view of royal officials, these, often degenerating
into violent incidents, were minor discussions that sometimes covered disagreements regarding where the authorities should exchange
criminals, with one party arguing that the correct location was a
quarter of a league, perhaps 138 *varas* or even a *tiro de piedra* or *de fusil*
away from where its opponents suggested.[67] However small, such discussions were alarming because of fears that they might degenerate
into larger hostilities. Similar incidents took place in the 1740s, 1750s,
and the 1780s between Puebla de Sanabria (in Spain) and different
hamlets belonging to the jurisdiction of Chaves (in Portugal).[68]
Here, too, the litigious area was extremely small and what might
have been to blame was the passage from grazing to agriculture.[69]
Conflict among neighbors was perhaps also explained by the fact
that the territory was Castilian, but its private ownership belonged
to several Portuguese who had held it from immemorial times and
who inherited it from their elders. This accumulation of complaints
regarding conflicts on the border between Galicia and Portugal was
accompanied by constant rumors about yet additional confronta-

tions and disagreements. Together they conspired to present border
conflicts as episodes that, rather than occasional and local, were frequent and global.[70] This appreciation might have encouraged the
Spanish monarch to take a stand aimed not at solving one conflict
but all. It also elevated (while vulgarizing) the debate regarding La
Magdalena, which in the process was transformed into a "typical
case" that required a standardized answer.

Magdalena/Lindoso: The Coveted Object

Records indicate that the area in contention was half a league long
and, as the governor of Galicia ascertained, of absolutely no worth
to the state and perhaps even of limited value to locals, who consistently argued that they could perhaps place their beehives there but
that it was otherwise too poor to allow for good vines and was best
used for grazing. Identified by name, La Magdalena, however, also
could have been called Monte de Lindoso in Portugal, or so at least
the Portuguese commissioner argued in the early nineteenth century. What it consisted of and what its contours were was not consensual either. It was, after all, a mountainous region, difficult to
reach, hard to control, and barely used. Although discussions were
mainly centered on whether La Magdalena was Spanish or Portuguese and thus which vassals could use it freely, sotto voce they also
involved the intentions of a few to use what others considered
common land for agricultural purposes. This move was considered
transformative because it required another type of possession, which
implied the privatization of common lands. The conflict at La Magdalena also included a debate regarding secular versus ecclesiastical
jurisdiction (whether the chapel indicated local or royal jurisdiction)
and military questions (which border would be easiest to defend).
Whereas some interlocutors (mainly Portuguese) were willing to tie
these questions together and assume that the answer to one implied
a solution to the other, others (mainly Spanish) rejected these connections by indicating that municipal, royal, and ecclesiastical jurisdiction were diverse and that private property was not the same as
common grounds. It was therefore telling that the conflict in La Magdalena was mostly structured as a dialogue on jurisdiction, subjection,

and usage rights with interlocutors perhaps purposely downplaying the important and evident fact that what locals actually mainly accused one another of doing was illegally privatizing common or royal grounds.

Magdalena/Lindoso: The Claims

All parties to the discussion alluded to the usual criteria that involved immemorial use, as well as challenges and responses to them. Because the versions of the parties were radically opposed, it was hard to tell what triggered specific confrontations, how they began, and when they ended. There were plenty of indications that agricultural use might have been more conflictual than grazing and collection and thus that growing pressure on the land might have played a role in these dynamics and so did the agency of certain individuals, such as ecclesiastics or military men who convinced their fellow citizens to challenge the status quo. In order to back their claims, locals as well as royal authorities searched for documentation that would indicate where divisions were located in the past, but they mostly concluded that these no longer existed or that they reflected old divides based on seigniorial rights and jurisdiction. Memory was faulty, too, with locals specifically attesting that they knew, heard, or saw nothing of where formal divisions once passed. Evidence regarding possession was not particularly helpful either because it mostly affirmed that possession was common rather than privative and could therefore not serve to vindicate rights. Whether joint use was introduced by toleration (as Spaniards argued) or because the Portuguese could not resist it (as the Portuguese claimed) did not matter because as far as the law was concerned it was either consensual or contested, and most evidence indicated it was both depending on the parties, the time, and the interests at stake.

What this case uncovered was perhaps an accurate reflection of a reality of mixing in territories considered remote and of relatively infrequent use, but "confusion" and "forgetfulness" could also be intentional because they allowed changes in the status quo or could support further claims. They also allowed witnesses who often depended on their rivals for their livelihood to take no clear stand.

Faced by what they considered total chaos and an absolute lack of indication as to how they should proceed, Spanish royal officials transformed a particular case into an example of more frequent phenomena and insisted on solving them all. Yet reaching (and sustaining) such a degree of abstraction required that they flee from the specifics of place and time to general principles. Among other things, it mandated abandoning the discussion on rights based on legal evidence and favoring instead common sense. Yet, while royal commissioners on both sides expected reason to produce similar conclusions on both ends, such was not the case. Sharing the conviction that they knew and understood better than locals and agreeing to ignore what they were told and instead observe the territory, Spanish and Portuguese officials nevertheless reached an impasse that resulted in endless debates not so much centered on which criteria to apply but on their concrete implications. And while using reason to supplement or even replace what documents and witnesses could not give them, early nineteenth-century interlocutors also appealed to the ability to change rather than safeguard the existing situation. They thus discussed which would be the best natural borders and which lines would best serve the military interests of states. In their minds, rather than legal or just, demarcation had to be natural and convenient. Yet, when reason also failed to supply a consensual solution, commissioners ended up adopting a compromise, dividing the territory in halves. At the end of the day, regardless of its relationship with the past or the present, tradition or common sense, they concluded that what a border had to do was give certainty and ensure peace.

Mixed and Promiscuous (1518–1864)

The documented history of the three villages of Santiago, Rubiás, and Meaus on the border between Galicia in Spain and Trás-os-Montes in Portugal begins in 1518, when the procurator of the Count of Monterrey filed a criminal suit against the governors of the castle of Piconha (Picoña) and Montalegre, belonging to the Duke of Braganza.[71] His accusation that the two men committed a series of offenses against the jurisdiction of his lord and Spain led to a trial, in which a Spanish and a Portuguese judge acting together heard evidence regarding "differences between Portugal and Galicia" that provoked disorder on the border. According to the procurator of the Count of Monterrey, the two governors constantly invaded Galicia accompanied by armed men, with banners flying in "a style of a declared war" (*con bandera tendida según estilo de guerra pregonada*) and crying out "Portugal, Portugal." They harassed the count's administrator (*merino*), burned his house, stole his properties, and, on several occasions, even threatened to murder him. They also deliberately set fire to his archives, which held documents crucial to his defense of the counts' jurisdiction as well as to managing his accounts. Because the count's vassals in Galicia supported the administrator, these activities provoked public confrontations. As the list of complaints against the two Portuguese governors accumulated, including accusations of repeated violations of the count's jurisdiction and other crimes, such as capturing locals for ransom, robberies, and so forth, other Spanish individuals joined in, narrating how they were imprisoned, insulted, and mistreated by these officials and their collaborators. They all asked the judges to punish these offenders and demand compensation for the losses inflicted. While plaintiffs insisted on obtaining an exemplary reprimand, the procurator of the Duke of Braganza refuted all these accusations. He explained that the governors reacted only to excesses already committed by the count and his officers who imprisoned several Portuguese on Portuguese territory without cause. They particularly resented the allegation that the village of Santiago was not in their jurisdiction. After all, it belonged to the duke and was "almost totally in Portugal."

Both the accusation and the response clarified that under contention were a series of incidents caused by a confrontation between the count and the duke regarding the extension of their respective domains. In order to "punish past offenses and remedy the future" (*para castigar o passado e remediar o porvir*), the judges decided to take extreme measures. Instead of attempting to rule who was right and who wrong, who initiated and who responded, they delivered a "sentence of accord and peace" (*sentencia de concordia y paz*). This verdict ordered the count and the duke to relieve the men involved in these confrontations from all their responsibilities and deprive them of office for life, as well as exile them from the jurisdiction. Because evidence suggested that both parties were to blame and that aggressors and victims constantly changed roles, and because they were all neighbors and relatives "who could not live ones without the others" (*y mirando que son vecinos y parientes y que no puedan vivir los unos sin los otros ni los otros sin los unos*), the judges also proceeded to pardon all other individuals involved in these confrontations. They then determined that Santiago, Rubiás, and Meaus would belong to both lords, and they instructed local authorities to collaborate with one another. The judges also prohibited them from recruiting local inhabitants to their struggle and ruled that territories dedicated to grazing and gathering would be common and would equally belong to all three villages and to the jurisdiction of both the count and the duke "as they had been before." Last but not least, although declaring that those under the jurisdiction of the duke were "Portuguese" and those under the count were "Spaniards," because locals were "of the jurisdiction of both seigniorial domains and kingdoms" (*ambos senhorios e reinos*), they allowed them to import goods from one realm to the other without paying duties and exempted them from military service so that they would not have to fight their neighbors.

This judicial decision created a hybrid compromise. It subjected the three villages to two lords and two countries yet divided their residents into Spaniards and Portuguese, vassals of the count and subjects of the duke. Perhaps justified by the judge's inability to determine the rights of the parties or to find another acceptable solution, the 1518 ruling created an extraordinary situation which even in the sixteenth century contemporaries found surprising. They affirmed, for example, in the 1520s and 1530s, that it was utterly impossible to distinguish who was Spanish and who Portuguese as members of both communities lived and "mixed" together, and "one was taken for the other."[72] They also asserted that, while rearranging local relations, the 1518 accord failed to clarify its territorial implications, determining nothing with regard to where the border between these communities and other enclaves of Spain and Portugal might pass. Sixteenth-century observers also confirmed that inside each village, jurisdiction depended on the identity of the head of the household, not geography. Therefore, rather than divided into a Spanish and a Portuguese part, each one of the three villages was a space dotted with houses that were either Spanish or Portuguese and which were rearranged accidently without a clear pattern. As if islands of jurisdiction in a sea of unclear land, Portuguese houses were under obedience to Portuguese law and authorities and so were Spanish residences. How individuals were ascribed to houses and houses to countries was not documented, but it was frequently implied that after this identification took place, it was both consensual and permanent. What was the status of the streets that linked the houses to one another and the fields surrounding the settlements was also unclear.

The odd situation that resulted from the 1518 decision was not easily tolerated. In 1540, 1563, 1564, and 1570, locals complained that Spanish authorities ignored these "customary" divisions (*uso y costumbre*) and attempted illegally to implement ordinary Spanish jurisdiction in their villages, for example, by imprisoning a Portuguese.[73] They asserted that unless these accords were respected, the Portuguese would violate them, too, as the judge of Montalegre had already begun doing. Obedience to the 1518 ruling, they insisted, allowed them to live quietly and peacefully (*quietos y sosegados*), also ensuring good relations between their kingdoms. Thereafter endlessly repeating, similar allegations were made by locals during the sixteenth, seventeenth, and eighteenth centuries. Mostly echoing their wish to protect a particular legal regime, as in La Contienda, over time the 1518 ruling became a foundational document of sorts. It was constantly copied, read, and cited as demonstrating both the cause and the justification for why this particularity was required and what it entailed. By the seventeenth century, its most coveted part, which was most often vindicated by locals, was the declaration that, according to them, made them "both Spanish and Portuguese" and their communities "mixed," perhaps even "mystic" (the terms *mistos, mixtos,* and *místicos* all appeared). Locals were also keen on conserving additional privileges that depended on this blending, mainly exemption from tax payments and military service.

Mostly viewed as a minor affair involving extraordinary legal privileges, the condition of Santiago, Rubiás, and Meaus was brought to the attention of kings in 1717 when, following the War of Spanish Succession, in which the castle of Picoña/Piconha was occupied by Spanish troops, the Portuguese foreign secretary asked the Spanish ambassador in Lisbon to ensure its return to Portugal along with Santiago, Rubiás, and Meaus.[74] The ambassador explained that, fearing hostilities, during the war the inhabitants of the three villages "made themselves part of Galicia" *(se hicieron a la parte de Galicia)* but that now that peace was reestablished, they should rejoin Portugal. This was, he wrote, what the inhabitants of Montalegre, to whose jurisdiction they belonged, and the House of Braganza, which had lordship *(señorío)* over them, demanded. They had attempted to guarantee their return by appealing to the governor of Galicia, but after he had refused to grant their petition they were forced to request royal intervention. To back his claim, the ambassador presented "authenticated documents" that according to him proved that the castle and the villages had always been Portuguese. Yet, among them was the 1518 ruling that stated otherwise. Because the peace treaties of 1668 (ending the War of Portuguese Independence) and 1715 (after the War of Spanish Succession) did not mention the castle of Picoña/Piconha or the villages of Santiago, Rubiás, and Meaus, the Spanish Council of State ordered the captain general and the *audiencia* of Galicia to investigate.

Although we do not know what happened next, complaints dated 1723 suggest that "the limits" between Rubiás and Montalegre (in Portugal) were "confused," causing local disturbances. Attempts to clarify them apparently failed, and as late as 1793 doubts persisted as to where they should be located.[75] In 1730, the notarial office *(escrivão das honras)* of Montalegre (in Portugal) included jurisdiction over the three villages which, according to contemporary records, were "in the kingdom of Galicia in a mixed form" *(que estão dentro no reino de Galiza místicamente).*[76] In 1756, the House of Braganza took possession of the "mixed places" *(couto misto)* and, in 1788, it did the same with regards to the castle of Picoña/Piconha—now completely in ruins—which its representatives declared was in Galicia, not

Portugal.[77] When asked, for example, in 1753, how this confusion came about, locals confessed their ignorance.[78] The only thing they could report was what the situation was at the present. They described how the three communities had, on their own, elected a local judge to oversee civil disputes and how criminal jurisdiction was partitioned between the judges of Galicia and Portugal, who either had to act together or ask those whom they charged whether they wanted to be punished in one kingdom or the other. Witnesses also pointed out that when the residents of the three villages constructed new houses they were formally required to declare whether they wanted their domicile to be subject to Spain or Portugal. These narratives were again confirmed in 1786, when the census of local citizens failed because officials found it completely impossible to distinguish among the 150 inhabitants who was Portuguese and who Spanish. The district, officials then explained, was common to both crowns, and criminal judges of both countries had to act together against offenders unless they were caught in a house classified as wholly Portuguese or completely Spanish. In 1786, there was still a local elected judge who oversaw civil litigation but, according to some complaints, residents could take on the condition of either Spanish or Portuguese at their pleasure. All they needed to do was give a toast, usually during their marriage ceremony, to the health of one monarch or the other.[79] And, though political subjugation depended on houses (there were Portuguese houses and Spanish houses, and it is possible that they were marked with "P" for Portugal and "G" for Galicia), most constructions included two distinct sides, one catalogued as Spanish, the other as Portuguese. This allowed locals to find refuge in the part that best suited their interests according to the circumstances of each case. Furthermore, local inhabitants could alternately claim to be Galician or Portuguese according to their convenience. In 1786, the citizens of Santiago, Rubiás, and Meaus also enjoyed other privileges. For example, they could import and export their animals and goods from one kingdom to the other without paying fees, and they were exempt from military service. Whereas according to the 1518 ruling, subjection to two lords and two kingdoms might have been presented as doubling obligations, in 1786 and 1791 contemporaries suggested that it released locals from all duties because de facto (even if not de jure) they lived independently of both crowns (*no pertenecen ni a uno ni a otro reino*), they were "neutral" (*neutros*) in regard to both, and their territory was a refuge for criminals and smugglers, even rebels.[80]

This personal freedom had direct bearing on territorial questions. Not only was the partition between the three municipalities and surrounding territories unclear, but even before the 1518 ruling was adopted questions persisted regarding the extent of land each lord ruled.[81] These intensified thereafter. By the eighteenth century, most interlocutors affirmed that because residents lived "in confusion" in communities that were "half Galician, half Portuguese," the terrain was mixed, too. As a result, there was no point, a Portuguese judge concluded in 1796, to prepare a map of the border in this area "because of the confusion [regarding] the settlers of this kingdom and Galicia."[82] The inability to fix divisions on the ground was also evident in 1819, when the authorities of Spain and Portugal disagreed regarding the exercise of jurisdiction, taxation, and military service in the territory.[83] That locals constantly shifted their personal subjection from one country to the other only made these territorial debates more convoluted.

Disconcerted by this strange situation, delegates of the Spanish and Portuguese monarchs met in 1819 to remedy what they considered a grave disorder. In order to introduce some measure of legibility, instead of allowing locals to choose their status freely, they planned to draw up lists that would determine who was who once and for all.[84] They also prohibited Spaniards and Portuguese from residing at the same house and insisted that in the future Spaniards would be judged in both civil and criminal matters according to Spanish laws by Spanish judges, the same applying to the Portuguese. Similarly, crimes committed in Spanish houses would be under Spanish jurisdiction, and those committed outside would be examined by the first magistrate who attended to them. All individuals who were not permanent citizens of Santiago, Rubiás, and Meaus would have no right to reside there and, though locals would continue to enjoy exemption from tax payments, customs dues, and military service, they would reimburse a small tribute to both sovereigns in recognition of their common lordship. Making no direct reference to territorial questions, this ruling suggested the theoretical continuation of the previous situation that, according to some, identified the territory of states according to the subjection of houses, thus making it discontinuous with islands of jurisdiction in a sea of mixed land, or that took the entire jurisdiction to be mixed, therefore, both Spanish and Portuguese.

Despite efforts at clarity, mid-nineteenth-century documentation indicates that confusion continued thereafter. Local residents were still allowed to choose their political adhesion at leisure, but they now did so formally by declaring their intentions before the local authority in the presence of a notary, with copies of this act left in the archives. Although as a result it was theoretically possible to prepare lists that would indicate who was who, in reality it is unclear whether such lists were ever elaborated, and it was well known that many houses included individuals of different subjections.[85] Furthermore, while some residents identified themselves as Portuguese and others as Spaniards, contemporaries observed that on most accounts they considered themselves neither, and that regardless of formal declarations their special privileges made them neither truly Spanish nor wholly Portuguese. Nor were they willing to concede that some parts of their communities (houses) were Portuguese territory while others Spanish. Instead, they asserted that the entire jurisdiction was "mixed." If locals accepted this reality as normal and believed it even profitable, by the mid-nineteenth century, officials in Madrid and Lisbon disagreed.[86] They rejected the idea that some individuals and villages were "independent" or mixed, and they said that this condition transformed their territory into a safe haven for outlaws. These officials did not understand how such a strange situation ever came into being, but they were certain it must immediately cease. Implementing this decision, the commissioners working for both countries in 1864 thus agreed to make the three villages Spanish in exchange for other enclaves that were thereafter declared Portuguese.[87] In what was to be their last act of grace, the authorities of both states allowed locals to declare whether they wanted to belong to one nation or the other. While most of the inhabitants of Santiago and Rubiás declared themselves Portuguese, those of Meaus pronounced themselves Spanish.

Mixed and Promiscuous: The Parties, the Coveted Object, the Claims

If initially the inhabitants of Santiago, Rubiás, and Meaus disagreed about who they were, who ruled them, and what their territory was, existing records indicate that by the sixteenth century they found an answer that satisfied their interests and settled their affairs. It did not, however, pacify their neighbors or necessarily agree with municipal and royal authorities. "Disorder" was the term these outsiders used, but during the sixteenth, seventeenth, and even eighteenth centuries, their complaints that it led to gross mischief were not powerful enough to justify altering local privileges, considered sacrosanct. It was only in the middle of the nineteenth century that royal officials on both sides of the border suggested for the first time that they had both the power and the will to intervene in the status quo and regularize what in their eyes was profoundly extraordinary. For this to happen, they had to affirm the sovereignty of states and their capacity to modify the legal order by eliminating privileges. But, if the authority to act was indispensable, so was the inclination. The latter was justified by the perception that the situation of Santiago, Rubiás, and Meaus was irregular and needed remedy, but it was also encoded in who contemporaries were and how they sought to reconstruct, perhaps even reimagine, their past. Searching to explain the origins of the confusion they "discovered" and finding no documentary trail that would help them achieve this goal or local testimony that would illuminate their path, nineteenth-century experts looked for indications in their understanding of both past and present.[88] In 1819 (to reconstruct local institutions after the Napoleonic invasions) and in the 1850s (to decide on the border between Spain and Portugal), they appealed to a distant time, which they partly knew, partly guessed at, partly imagined. They reasoned that according to "old traditions" the three communities of Santiago, Rubiás, and Meaus must have originally belonged to the House of Lemos and Monterrey (in Spain). They suggested that in the fourteenth, perhaps fifteenth, century, after the House of Braganza acquired jurisdiction over the castles of Picoña/Piconha and Portello, its officials must have tried to expand their powers to this terrain, too.[89] They consented that, if this was the case, then the result was repeating conflicts between the two feudal lords and their officers. When the two crowns separated in 1640, they hypothesized, the three villages remained in Spanish territory, and when feudal domains were abolished in Spain (in 1811 and again in 1823), they were subjected to the Spanish crown. Nineteenth-century observers thus concluded that a quarrel between lords each belonging to a different political allegiance naturally produced confusion among kingdoms. Their understanding that this was the case held strong despite clear indications to the contrary in the 1518 ruling, which instituted a juxtaposition of two jurisdictions but instructed that they coexisted without mixing because it identified the subjects of one lord as Spaniards (and their territory or houses as Spanish) and those of the other as Portuguese. In other words, if blending occurred, it was not because of what the 1518 ruling mandated but because of what had transpired thereafter. As had happened in La Contienda, if initially Portuguese and Spaniards lived together side by side without necessarily losing their individuality, it was during the late sixteenth and the seventeenth and eighteenth centuries that contemporaries began considering the three villages either mixed or completely independent. Rather than Spain for Spaniards, Portugal to Portuguese, as was the case initially, according to contemporary perceptions by the early modern period the entire territory was subject to both powers or to none. As with La Contienda, this transformation transpired quietly and informally. It was sanctioned not by a judicial or political decision but by the way locals interpreted and reinterpreted their privileges and neighboring powers and kings allowed them to. Subversive yet performative, by the end of this process, observers indeed remarked with amazement that personal status also affected allegiance to a king as well as a territorial subjection. Coming to explain how this was possible, nineteenth-century interlocutors linked this result (which they abhorred) to feudalism (which they also loathed). They suggested that "under the shadow," of feudal times (tempos feudais), the residents of the three villages "obeyed absolutely no law, alternatively claiming to be Portuguese or Spaniards depending on the circumstances and origin, on occasions even claiming they were neither."[90]

The classification of what they observed (and disliked) as feudal was more revealing of the nineteenth century than of the past. By the time this discussion took place, most disorder and chaos were habitually classified as remnants of ancient practices that, because arbitrary and unreasonable (and thus, according to contemporary notions, feudal), had to be destroyed or at least discarded in the name of progress. Making Santiago, Rubiás, and Meaus relics of a past that hindered development was therefore part of a moderniz-ing, not a historically oriented, discourse.[91] That what existed on the territory was the result of a sixteenth-century design and that it had transformed its meaning in the seventeenth and eighteenth centuries no longer mattered. Nor was it relevant that this arrange-ment was propelled, adopted, and then closely safeguarded by hum-ble peasants, not powerful feudal lords. Yet, while nineteenth-century Spanish and Portuguese officials found the situation of the three villages intolerable, locals continued to vindicate its normality. In April 1855, for example, the residents of Santiago, Rubiás, and Meaus, now formally identified as "mixed places of the two crowns" *(couto misto das duas coroas)*, requested the intervention of the Portu-guese monarch in his capacity as head of the House of Braganza against the authorities of Montalegre, who required them to pay customs as if they were foreigners when in reality they were subjects of both Portugal and Spain *(sujeitos à coroa de Portugal estando o tam-bém à de Hespanha).*[92] In 1862, when locals understood that negotia-tions between the two crowns were leading to a solution that would "extinguish" *(extinguir)* their particular regime, they protested.[93] The conclusion that the *couto misto* was "inappropriate for the current po-litical system of both nations" *(pela sua inconveniência com o sistema político que hoje rege as duas nações)* was not enough, they argued, to justify eliminating immemorial local privileges. If the situation did not suit contemporary conditions, this dissonance could be reme-died by slightly modifying the existing structure, not destroying it altogether. The best remedy would be to give locals more indepen-dence and prerogatives rather than less. In fact, it would be advis-able to grant them the very same status that the small state of An-dorra had recently received. The prospects that the *couto misto* might be adjudicated to Spain also brought about a 1857 protest by its neighbors in Portugal, who asserted that they needed the land that was to become Spanish for their survival, mostly for grazing and gathering.[94] Separating the territory of Santiago, Rubiás, and Meaus from Portugal, they argued, would constitute a division where none had existed before. Why would Portugal renounce a territory to which it had equal dominion rights as Spain? Why couldn't they continue to use their grazing grounds as they always had?

Making Santiago, Rubiás, and Meaus relics of a feudal past was helpful for explaining and justifying why their ambiguous state should be eliminated, but presenting their situation as exceptional was also an important tool. As happened with common pastureland which, having been the most frequent and legitimate form of land use, was in the eighteenth and nineteenth centuries reimagined as an illegitimate anomaly, Santiago, Rubiás, and Meaus underwent a similar transformation. Famous because different, eliminated because extraordinary, it was nevertheless clear that their status might have been much more normal than what nineteenth- century interlocutors were willing to admit. According to some, mixed in the same form as Santiago, Rubiás, and Meaus were also in 1764 the villages of Manín, Villameá, and Vilariño.[95] But other types of mixing also existed. In the 1530s, for example, the inhabitants of Vilar de Perdizes (in Portugal) were formally exempt from subjection to Portuguese law and Portuguese taxation because they had originated in Spain. This particular privilege was read by them as confirming their independence from both countries and their duty to obey only their local authorities. Many "promiscuous villages," with both Spanish and Portuguese inhabitants and belonging half to Spain, half to Portugal, also existed. Most famous among them were the three enclaves of Soutelinho, Cambedo, and Lamadarcos; on the border near Chaves, in Portugal, they were partially in one country, partially in the other, the frontier sometimes crossing inside houses or even dividing rooms, therefore allowing some buildings to have one door in Spain and another in Portugal.[96] Of unknown origin, they were already mentioned in 1526 and 1530, among other things, as places where contraband was extremely frequent. Contrary to the *couto misto*, the promiscuous villages were extraordinary because of their geographical location, not their legal regime, as they had no special privileges and both states had full jurisdiction in the part and over the people that belonged to them. In 1764, Almeida was divided into two sections, one Portuguese, the other Spanish.[97] So was Rihonor (Rio de Onor), which already in the thirteenth century was partly in Portugal and partly in León but possibly was populated on both sides by Castilians.[98] Attempts to demarcate its territory in 1347 apparently failed, and it is probable that in a certain moment, its Spanish citizens abandoned "their" part, moving to Portugal. This development enraged the local lord who demanded their return, as well as the reimbursement of dues that they had paid the House of Braganza, the Portuguese local lord, instead of to him.[99] In 1385, ruling nobles and friars might have reached an accord according to which the village would indeed be half Spanish, half Portuguese. This agreement was challenged thereafter by the Count of Benavente, a Portuguese noble who, by moving to Spain, obtained this title as well as many properties along the border but in return lost his possessions and titles as the Portuguese *senhor de Bragança*. Attempting to expand his control to the Portuguese side of the border, which was previously his, he came into direct confrontation with the House of Braganza, which now owned it. After constant confrontations between lords and their vassals, in 1451 both sides agreed to adhere to the status quo but frequently disputed what it included. Confrontations continued into the sixteenth and perhaps the seventeenth centuries. It is nevertheless possible that the situation was resolved thereafter, with residents of both sides collaborating despite their subjection to different lords and monarchies. This extraordinary situation led the Portuguese commissioners in the mid-nineteenth century to conclude that the inhabitants of the Portuguese part, at least, lived in relative liberty and autonomy that subjected them to neither state. Judging them as hardly civilized and living an exceptional existence without satisfying any of the obligations that as citizens they had to their country, the commissioners concluded that their situation was intolerable.[100] They explained that the Portuguese part had some thirty-three houses and the Spanish only eight but that residents moved from one side to the other according to their desire (*mas quando convém a uns ou a outros mudam de bairro e de nação)*, thus pretending to be alternately Spanish or Portuguese. They were "uncivilized" and lived in an "exceptional way" without fulfilling any duty to their nation, for example, military service or taxation, and they did not obey the authorities. It was thus vital, the Portuguese commissioners concluded, that the village be divided between both powers so that "these social aberrations not continue because they violate the good customs and the obligations of both villages to their authorities" *(pois interessa a ambos os Estados, que não continuem estas aberrações sociais com as quais sofrem os bons costumes, e as obrigações dos povos para com as suas autoridades.)* If for no other reason—the territory of Rihonor (Rio de Onor) was barren and of little economic value—the division of the village in two clear parts would produce the important gain of ending the present promiscuity *(promiscuidade)*, which was inexcusable. On that occasion called *couto misto*, and implicitly compared to Santiago, Rubiás, and Meaus, Rihonor nevertheless survived the 1850s border commission and continues in its mixed existence today.

THE DIVISION BETWEEN Spain and Portugal in Europe emerged gradually through a series of developments that involved the activities of a multiplicity of agents who, defending their own interests, also constructed a border. The examples I chose to study demonstrate the complexity of these procedures that depended on rivalry or collaboration between neighbors on the same side or across the border and that were influenced by economic, social, legal, and political processes. Sometimes struggle was focused on usage rights—indeed, this was the most typical case—but also questioned were issues of jurisdiction, tax collection, ecclesiastical subjection, and the like. The accumulation of claims, often concurrent or even contradictory to one another, was so dramatic that the search for clear answers, although constant, mostly failed. All parties made references to a past, which they suggested was evident, yet none could reproduce this certainty juridically, either because documents no longer existed or because memory was lacking, because the various sides to a conflict remembered differently, or because they all made plausible albeit contradictory claims. As a contemporary observer remarked in 1745, at the end of the day they could present no other evidence than the allegations they themselves made *(sem mais prova ou documento que a sua asserção).*[101]

Worried about what their opponents might be doing and what they might wish to achieve, locals often reacted to what they perceived as challenges with violence or the threat of violence. In their complaints to higher authorities they suggested that they were weaker and less prepared to defend their rights and that their enemies took advantage of their benevolence. They alluded to a status quo that was infringed and argued that contestation was new because until recently their immemorial rights had been respected. Yet their allegations and the response of their rivals clarified that the past was as contentious as the present. The passage of time could perhaps introduce forgetfulness, but in most cases it allowed change. Under the guise of continuity, time was not only a historical factor but also a juridical and political fiction that was carefully used to remember certain things while forgetting others.

Because challenge led to response that led to further questioning, after Pandora's box was open, it could not be easily closed. These endless chains of provocation and reaction were perhaps mandated by social and political reasoning, but they were also enforced on the parties by a juridical doctrine that equated silence with consent, protest with disagreement. This doctrine explained why conflicts could persist over time but also how different episodes could be tied together despite radical changes in the parties, their alignments, the desired object, the goals to obtain, and the justifications to employ. It also elucidated why a solution was (often) so difficult to reach. As confrontations unfolded, the situation frequently became so entangled that the only viable solution was either to use the land jointly or to divide what was contentious among rivals.

Called *dúvidas, refertas,* or *contendas,* the way these conflicts developed could be tied to certain uses, people, places, or periods. They could be affected by the general political climate or by specific local conditions, mainly economic and social mutations and by changes in the way individuals, groups, and communities evaluated and perceived certain terrains and by how they imagined their entitlements. Conflicts could be initiated on one side, by a single individual, or involve numerous actors on multiple sides. Officially, they confronted municipalities who were engaged in defending their communal rights. Yet, in reality, they usually called for the intervention of particular individuals or groups who stood to profit (or lose) from what would transpire. These individuals and groups could ask their villages to act on their behalf, but on occasions they performed their activities without searching for local consensus or despite its absence. In other cases, municipal authorities intervened a posteriori, authorizing what had already been achieved (or lost).

Constant rivalry and confrontation did not stop litigating individuals, groups, and communities from collaborating with one another. Many were relatives and friends; others shared grazing grounds, festivities, shrines, and markets.[102] These relations did not necessarily hinder their competition; on the contrary, they often intensified it. On occasions, it seemed that the closer they were, the more likely they were to fight. The best example was Encinasola and Barrancos, whose citizens and authorities bitterly struggled despite the fact that most Barranqueños either came from Encinasola or had married there or had property in its jurisdiction. But other examples were not wanting. In 1500, Pedro Rodrigues testified that the inhabitants of Villarinho (in Portugal) had initially allowed the Spaniards of La Tejera to plant in their territory because they were relatives.[103] Yet he also knew that for over two hundred years they fought, often violently, with one another, attacking both properties and persons. In the island of Canosa, the same authorities who complained in 1691 that the Portuguese prohibited Spaniards from using the terrain also testified that the Portuguese, appealing to Spanish charity, behaved as if "they belonged to the same bishopric and kingdom and as if both were of the same owner [dueño]." Many were married and settled in Spain, where they were considered citizens, although, according to their detractors, more with their bodies than with their souls.[104]

It is therefore wrong to affirm, as some historians have done, that the border between Spain and Portugal was imposed by kings on locals.[105] Not only were locals keenly interested in where divisions passed while kings were (relatively) not, for hundreds of years they persisted in their demands while also constantly elaborating and reelaborating what they wanted to achieve. Because of this logic, even as late as 1760 and 1780, territorial incursions could still be defined as a civil matter confronting individuals who could be appeased if damages were paid.[106] That they married or traded with one another, that they were friends and associates, that they participated in the same religious processions (as some historians have rightly remarked), did not necessarily mean they could not be ferocious rivals. On the contrary, it was often proximity that made them compete most bitterly, initiating multiple conflicts that might have been essential to their livelihood but which, from the point of view of the capital cities and the court, were vulgar events of little consequence.

If the making of the border between Spain and Portugal should not be told as a narrative of a growing state protagonism against local wishes, neither should it be told as the history of a fortified alliance between a state and local communities that led to the nationalization of the frontier. Some conflicts might have pitted "Spaniards" against "Portuguese," some might have led contemporaries to adopt such denominations strategically or honestly, but more often than not divisions ran in other directions, for example, separating those who wished to use the territory in different ways or confronting the members of communities that were in the process of accepting their dependence on another locality or achieving their autonomy.

The concretization and negotiation of the border, in short, took hundreds of years to complete. The Portuguese notary Mendo Afonso de Resende, who described parts of it in the 1530s, discovered that of the seventy villages he visited, at least twenty-two were involved in serious conflicts with their neighbors in Spain and many others reported on the continuing loss of territory.[107] Uncertainty might have continued thereafter; contemporaries reported, for example, in the mid- and late eighteenth century on frequent *contiendas* along the border and on areas where the location of the frontier was either unknown or utterly irrelevant.[108] And although the presence of both conflicts and accords was continuous thereafter, even as late as 1854 Spanish officials could argue that there was absolutely no understanding between Spain and Portugal regarding their frontiers. All that existed were "private demarcations" between villages that served to limit their "particular property" and by extension the state.[109]

Like Hydras, territorial conflicts allowed rivals to move from seeking to affirm legal rights to adopting a compromise, from imagining what was just to wondering what would be efficient to asking how history had both grounded and affected their rights. These changes sometimes reflected social, economic, political, and legal mutations, but they were also related to the way contemporaries remembered (or forgot) what had transpired and imagined (or reimagined) their entitlements. As they compared themselves with their forefathers and as they distinguished themselves from others, they also refashioned themselves anew. They continue to do so today. As I was concluding the research for this book, the inhabitants of Valença do Minho (in Portugal), protesting the decision to close their local emergency room, hung a thousand Spanish flags in their municipality, chanted "viva España," and placed signs reading "Valença is Spain." This demonstration, aimed at attracting media attention and provoking governmental reaction, was also a means to express gratitude to the mayor of neighboring Tuy (in Spain), who invited them to use his town's emergency room. An anecdotal incident of little consequence between municipalities that for almost two hundred years were bitterly opposed over a small island (Verdoejo) in the Miño/Minho River that both separated and connected them, the discussion it unleashed was nevertheless revealing.[110] Most of the Portuguese readers who commented on these developments reacted with amazement.[111] They explained in a blog in one of the Portuguese newspapers that they sympathized with the plight of their compatriots but felt offended by the reference to Spain. Calling the behavior of Valença treason that merited punishment, they concluded that it violated the sovereignty of Portugal. Images of the past, mainly the union and disunion between Spain and Portugal, loomed large in these comments. One reader mentioned the battle of Aljubarrota, won by the armies of the king of Portugal in 1385. Others suggested that traitors also existed in 1640, when Portugal declared its independence of Spain, and asked whether it was possible that their forefathers fought to free themselves of foreign occupation when they now wanted to resubject themselves to the same power. Another reader mentioned Olivença (Olivenza), conquered by Spanish forces in 1801 and never returned. While Portuguese readers reacted to these developments mainly by affirming Portuguese independence vis-à-vis Spain, Spaniards mostly focused on the question of whether Spain and Portugal should unite again.[112] Many advocated such a solution, either through a union of equals, by transforming Portugal into one of several autonomous regions within Spain, or by constituting a new federation that perhaps, as in Roman times, should be called "Hispania." Reunion, the overwhelming majority of Spanish commentators suggested, would be in the interests of both states, but it would also reestablish a historical reality that had existed in the past and was even evident *(se impone)* in the present. Citing Luis de Camões, one reader asked, were not both Castilians and Portuguese Spaniards *(castellanos y portugueses, que españoles somos todos)*? As happened in the past, for Spaniards, union and disunion with Portugal was also an occasion to discuss the existence of a single or a plural, a united or a divided Spain. Relations between Madrid and Barcelona, Santiago de Compostela and Vitoria, some asserted, were not substantially different than those linking Madrid to Lisbon. Others affirmed that historical ties joined Portugal with Galicia but not with Spain. After all, was not Portugal "Galicia del sur" or Galicia "Portugal del norte"? Forgetting that the border also unified and separated the residents of Alentejo and Extremadura, to mention just one other example, they thus suggested that proper integration would feature the union of Portugal and Galicia, not Portugal and Spain. They even argued that the residents of Valença should have used Galician, not Spanish flags because their admission into Tuy's emergency room depended on the Xunta de Galicia, not the authorities of Madrid.

In these discussions, the existence of the border also mattered, and Portuguese interlocutors constantly alluded to the particular status of *fronterizos*. Were they closer to their neighbors across the border than to their states? Or, because of their geographical position and historical experience, did they tend to be more patriotic? Among Spaniards, suggestions were made that frontiers were "artificial walls" that expressed the interests of states, not local inhabitants. Yet, while some readers reminded their compatriots that "the Iberian peoples were more frequently united than separated" *(los pueblos ibéricos hemos estado unidos más tiempo de lo que hemos estado separados)*, others affirmed that Spain and Portugal were different and that what history parted, political and economic interests could never unite. The phantasm of Alcañices also made its appearance. According to some, Portugal was "the oldest state in Europe because it maintained its borders the longest" *(el país más antiguo de Europa . . . es Portugal, que se mantiene sus fronteras desde hace siglos).* Whereas "Spain" was created only in the eighteenth century (a probable reference to the Nueva Planta decrees that, after the War of Spanish Succession, abolished local political privileges by unifying the public law of Spain, and which present-day Catalan nationalists identify as the moment when "Spain" was imposed on them), Portugal had already existed six hundred years earlier. A union between these two countries could perhaps be attempted, but history, they argued, had already taught us that it would never last.

Conclusion

In both Iberia and the Americas, territorial divisions came into being through complex processes that involved a plethora of agents and a diversity of interests. Searching to define the spaces where they could perform certain activities by sometimes excluding others, sometimes joining them, individuals, communities, and groups invented and reinvented their entitlements according to their needs and abilities, as well as the needs and abilities of their neighbors. Their acts were guided by their understanding of what was right, what was just, what was possible, and what was effective. Reacting spontaneously or planning their activities with great care, they engaged in multidialogues that involved what they did as well as how they did it and what they said. Informed by categories that might have proceeded from erudite legal theories but that according to them represented the way things were or ought to be, those struggling to affirm their rights over certain territories were also guided by the stories they had heard and the loyalties or disloyalties they harbored as they imagined themselves as participants in families, groups, and communities. These processes that transpired daily as a result of the need to know where one could pasture, where one could roam, and which indigenous group and territory were dangerous ended up consolidating rights as well as defining communities. They eventually brought about, also, the creation of borders that thereafter could be presented as ancient and natural or political and artificial. Kings were sometimes party to these discussions. But even in their absence their presence loomed large because contemporaries appealed to their courts or requested the intervention of their ambassadors. Monarchs were also implicitly involved when actors identified themselves as their vassals and claimed rights as a result. Thus, if treaties were faulty and negotiations between courts rarely effective, royal image, if not royal long hand, was nevertheless noticeable in these conflicts, which were far more chaotic and individualized than existing narratives of state formation, border development, or national affirmation allow us to perceive.

In Iberia, conflicts could persist for hundreds of years, thus allowing the parties, claims, and object of contention to mutate considerably. History played a major role because contemporaries often made allusions to a remote past and to ancient entitlements that theoretically justified their current claims. Although barely ever capable of connecting present to past or proving that their recollection was legitimate, memory and forgetfulness were nevertheless important, though not in order to guarantee persistence but instead as a means to allow change. In the Americas, conflicts tended to be shorter than in Iberia, and the immemoriality they addressed was much closer in time—indeed it might have transpired only a few decades earlier—yet the territory that was coveted was much larger and potentially harbored a much greater promise. Because such was the case, whereas on most occasions monarchs hoped that European conflicts would die on their own, or they acted not as interested parties but instead as judges who adjudicated rights, in the Americas they often took up local complaints and made them their own. At stake was probably the perception that while discussions in Europe were of little consequence, what would happen in the New World was not. Yet the result was that while in Iberia monarchs often seemed impatient with local conflicts over what they considered were meager lands in which they had absolutely no stake, they tended to be more involved in American disputes. Perhaps this explains why in Europe municipal bodies were the main actors in such conflicts while in the Americas most activity was taken up by individuals who pretended to act for king or country. This flattening of what in Iberia were multiple levels of jurisdiction into a modern design of subjecthood and the prospects of a greater royal involvement gave rise to a tendency—more pronounced in the Americas than in Europe—to present territorial conflicts as involving "Spaniards" versus "Portuguese." Forgetting the omnipresence of frairs (usually of foreign origin) and paired with the existence of a native population against which both groups defined themselves, American conflicts often seemed more "national." They mostly involved *naturales* (members of the kingdom community) or vassals, not *vecinos* (members of municipal communities). Yet, in the process of discussing rights, the category of Spanish and Portuguese often metamorphosed. Not only were individuals coerced into being classified into one or the other group—a process much more convoluted than contemporary notions allow us to imagine—not only foreign friars were "nationalized," but for expansion to happen, Spanishness and Portugueseness had to be redefined in ways to allow also the incorporation of natives. Pacified and cataloged as members of either the Spanish or the Portuguese commonwealth or eliminated altogether, in the Americas natives were the true *terra nullius*, the real object that was to be occupied. Yet the placement of indigenous peoples under a European framework, rather than defending them, paradoxically accelerated their dispossession. At the end of this process, they were portrayed as indolent individuals who by both justice and reason should have no right to the land of their ancestors. This narrative, which we now identify with colonialism and which indeed had a major influence on developments in the New World, nevertheless found echoes on the Iberian Peninsula, where contemporaries, accusing their compatriots living on the border of savagery, eventually concluded that they, too, had no right to their land because common use and grazing, which they pursued, did not lead to improvement.

On both sides of the ocean, local agreements and disagreements played a major role in fixing also the extension of states. In the Americas, attempts by kings to institute bilateral accords that would frame the debate (or terminate it) were more frequent than in Europe, but here too they mostly failed because, negotiated at a distance and consisting of abstractions, treaties required interpretation, and interpretation required consent (rarely ever present). Possession was also omnipresent on both sides of the Atlantic. Making it the basis for entitlement forced individuals, communities, and authorities to discuss their rights as they sought to pasture, collect, or settle. It required that they defend what they believed was theirs or wanted to make thus, mainly by protesting, even violently, against the activities of their rivals. These discussions that took place on a continuous basis were more common than war, and peace was more dangerous than a bellicose confrontation because from both a practical and a legal point of view, the slow penetration enabled by amicable relations was more substantial and more continuous than anything a military confrontation could ever achieve. Yet, whereas in Europe all interlocutors pretended to adhere to the status quo by defending what was allegedly already theirs (even when it was not), in the Americas possession was also invoked as a means to acquire new territories.

On both sides of the ocean, the "simple folk" involved in these debates were well versed in the language of territorial rights and jurisdiction. This familiarity with what were in reality complex legal doctrines affected their behavior and gave it meaning. If the influence of law on the way conflicts developed was enormous, it was mainly because contemporaries considered its basic tenets (action and reaction, consent and protest, the need to interpret not only what was done but with what intention, and the obligation to catalog actors as members of specific communities) well-known and generally acknowledged principles that needed no justification or proof. As if forming part of the social pact or as perhaps "an economy of conventions," these ideas included cultural tools that actors could use to pursue their goals, as well as interpret what their rivals were doing even as they constantly fought over what these principles implied and how they were to be implemented.[1] Because law mattered a great deal, all those involved in territorial debates constantly produced and reproduced evidence that was meant to legitimize their behavior. Yet the paper trail that resulted recorded mostly claims rather than entitlements. In the end, legal doctrines might have explained, even justified, what transpired, but law itself was unable to solve their differences. Otherwise said, the constant invocation of rights framed the debate but did not necessarily disentangle it. Neither did history, which also failed to act as an antidote to chaos.

Although there was no substantial difference between Spanish and Portuguese understanding of these issues—both referred to the same *Ius Commune* doctrines and in none of the conflicts was a distinction between a Spanish and a Portuguese tradition ever invoked, among other reasons because discussants considered their system universally true and universally binding[2]—one Portuguese specificity most clearly pronounced in Europe was the abundance of *tombos*, that is, descriptions (also understood as lists or enumerations) of the territory. During the early modern period and most particularly in the sixteenth century and with renovated vigor in the late eighteenth century, Portuguese monarchs sent delegates far and wide to recollect and put on paper what they owned.[3] This interest in enumerating royal properties resulted in the production of hundreds of *tombos* and explained how the Portuguese royal archives came to be known as *Torre do Tombo* (literally, the tower where these lists were conserved). Yet, as they listed properties, goods, and vassals, Portuguese royal delegates who visited different communities also demarcated their territory and, as a by-product, the border with Spain. The same thing happened on the local levels where municipalities, obeying royal orders, also proceded to prepare lists of their properties, as well as jurisdiction.[4] This effort was not directed at bilateral relations with the neighboring power, but in the seventeenth, eighteenth, and nineteenth centuries these *tombos* helped Portuguese communities and the crown advance in Europe claims that were otherwise undocumented. They repeatedly presented *tombos* as an authentic and trustworthy reflection of the past and thus as an unquestionable proof of their titles. However, despite this important and repetitive political use, Portuguese jurists pointed to the legal fragility of *tombos*. They explained that under normal circumstances, *tombos* were produced mostly where conflicts existed or were expected, not where consensus and peace reigned. They asserted that what these documents did was to record local declarations as to what the legal situation was according to the interested party. They were thus lists containing "memory of what was done, with the aim that it remain authenticated in the future."[5] As guardians of certain recollections, there was no reason to trust *tombos* more than the original knowledge memorialized in them. After all, if one was incorrect or false, so would be the other. Otherwise said, rather than proving entitlement, all *tombos* did was to testify that the claims currently made had already been invoked in the past.

But whatever the value of *tombos* might have been, and however they were used, archival documents suggest that contemporaries on both sides of the ocean asserted that the land they coveted was scarcely populated or used, which is why they could take hold of it. For most of them, an "internal" frontier of colonization—which they desired to eliminate—coincided with the so-called exterior boundary vis-à-vis foreign communities because it was their wish to occupy their "vacant" surroundings that brought them into conflict in the first place. Because the stakes in the Americas were larger and the sea of (theoretically) empty land greater, competition among actors was much clearer, as was the rush to occupy and control peoples and territories. Yet, as also happened on the Iberian Peninsula, rather than a clear genealogy distinguishing those who arrived first from those who came second, in most cases the presence of one encouraged the presence of the other, often making their incursions contemporaneous, or almost so. And while these occupational dynamics framed what would transpire on the territory, they also constituted and consolidated the opposing parties. They not only demanded the identification of Spaniards and their distinction from the Portuguese (a particular arduous task during the union between both crowns and in its aftermath), they also classified individuals as members of municipal communities and as vassals of certain crowns. They distinguished which communities depended on whom and to whose jurisdiction they belonged. In the Americas, they brought about important processes of ethnogenesis among American natives, and in Europe they created a hybrid group of peasants that would be classified in the eighteenth and nineteenth centuries as including a particular prototype, identified (and discriminated against) because of its condition as *fronterizo*.

This accumulation of actors, interests, activities, and justifications resulted in a highly dynamic, open-ended process that involved individuals and groups that did not necessarily represent a state but that nevertheless ended up constructing and defining one. Whether as farmers, judges, settlers, merchants, ecclesiastics, military men, scientists, or indigenous peoples, a great variety of contemporaries were deeply involved in these conflicts, which affected their lives as well as defined their territory. For most of them, knowing what their legitimate space was was not a political or diplomatic affair. It was information they needed in order to ascertain what they could or could not do. Far from mechanical, artificial, or imposed from above or below, the border that resulted was a living organism.[6] It could unite individuals and communities across the frontier or on the same side as much as it could lead them to disagree. But, above all, it constantly and persistently changed as their activities and aspirations mutated. As a result, the border in Iberia might have not been the oldest in Europe, as some have asserted, but neither was the American frontier as new as others sustained.

Reconstructing Iberia: The Histories of Spain and Portugal

Spanish and Portuguese histories are often written in ignorance of or against one another.[7] The general assumption is that despite their common origins, after Portugal was created in the low Middle Ages the two countries took different paths, which allows us, perhaps even forces us, to treat them separately. The period of their union (1580–1640) is portrayed as an exceptional moment, cherished by some, abhorred by others. For most Portuguese, these assumptions are crucial because they assert that the separation between the two countries was natural and necessary. To delineate this, many of them adopt the convention that the borders between Spain and Portugal were "the most ancient in Europe," and they reject any suggestion that there was an important Iberian trajectory that both countries experienced together.[8] For most Spaniards, ignoring Portugal is a habit that echoes deeply enshrined prejudices that began in the Early Modern period and matured into Modernity, suggesting that although Portugal was a neighbor with whom Spain shared a past, it was nonetheless irrelevant to explaining how Spain had emerged, consolidated, and expanded.[9] Foreign scholars working on these countries tend to imitate these visions. They identify Hispanism mainly with Spain and Spanish America, excluding Portugal, and when they designate

themselves as Iberianists, like some of their colleagues working in
the Iberian Peninsula, they do so mainly in order to disassemble the
historical existence of Spain, not to study it alongside Portugal.[10]

In recent decades, however, a younger generation of historians,
more frequently in Portugal than in Spain, began questioning these
metanarratives. Gradually undoing the existing portrait, these
scholars asserted that Spain and Portugal consolidated side by side
and were tightly connected to one another. Highlighting forgotten
symmetries in their common ancient and medieval past (the Roman
conquest, the Muslim invasion, the Reconquest, and the slow formation of the Christian kingdoms), they also stressed their striking
similarities after their separation during the age of expansion, the
formation of the modern state, the Napoleonic invasions, the liberal
revolutions, and twentieth-century dictatorships and democratization,
to name just a few. Reversing the narrative that presented the union
of the crowns as a foreign occupation and the uprising of 1640 as a
national liberation, they concluded that many Portuguese supported
the union and that the independence Portugal obtained in the mid-
seventeenth century was the result of a rebellion by a group of nobles
who, caring for their own welfare, were able to recruit, elicit, or force
the collaboration of others. On the Spanish side, similar revisions are
still in the making, but—although not much has yet been achieved—it
is clear that some historians, at least, have come to suspect that the
two countries had much more in common than was traditionally assumed and that Portugal had influenced Spain in ways we had not yet
imagined.

Coming to terms with how intertwined Spanish and Portuguese
histories are has therefore been a slow process. If in the beginning,
some scholars attempted a comparative history, it was only in a second stage that they ventured into writing an integrated story that
presented both countries as protagonists of the same events and developments. Influential among those who studied the union of the
crowns and who were indeed willing to consider Iberia as their unit
of analysis, this historical reading is still extremely marginal among
scholars studying other periods.[11] Nonetheless, when Spanish and
Portuguese sources are interrogated together, it becomes evident that
even in the late seventeenth, eighteenth, nineteenth, and twentieth

centuries the development of these two powers was to a degree interdependent. As I crossed the border from Spanish to Portuguese, Spanish American to Portuguese American archives, I found the same allegations, the same visions, and the same concerns that I had already identified on the other side. The conflicts I studied suggest that individuals, communities, and kingdoms could be violently opposed over certain issues but that they discussed them by reference to what they believed was a common understanding regarding justice, rights, order, and disorder. Their interpretation of what these meant depended on who was speaking and from where, not necessarily on their identity as Spaniards or Portuguese. Instead of highlighting differences, all interlocutors assumed that they belonged to a single commonwealth, in which norms, customs, and understanding were shared. They remembered a past in which they were united, even mixed, and were conscious of the accidental nature of their separation. These convictions were perhaps tied to a historical memory that persisted in some communities or among certain groups; they were perhaps motivated by the belief that Christianity was an important normative source that both countries equally shared; they could be explained by the dependence of both countries on a legal system inspired in Roman law or even by the suggestion that they might have shared an older "Hispanic customary law" (consuetudo hispaniae) that predated their separation in the thirteenth and fourteenth centuries. But whatever the reason for this commonness might have been, the records I studied never suggested that the division into Spaniards or Portuguese was necessarily meaningful.[12] If, on occasions, separation into kingdoms mattered, it was not because each had its own history, independent trajectory, separate culture, distinct existence, or differentiated norms but because the interests of their king or inhabitants were diverse, even oppositional. But such divisions also existed within both countries, and while these acquired prominence in certain situations, they were completely overlooked in others. There were, of course, some variations between the ways the members of both communities proceeded to implement their common heritage. As mentioned in Chapter 2, while the Portuguese carefully delineated war, Spaniards were more occupied with outlining peace. Yet, as far as I can tell, residents of the two countries exercised both methods in similar ways and to similar ends. Land-related documentation was much more frequently produced in peninsular Portugal than in Spain. Yet *tombos* nevertheless registered behavior that was meaningful also in Spain.

The stories I found in the archives also suggested that during the medieval and early modern period neither Spain nor Portugal was a predefined entity. Not only did they unite and separate, but the prospects of both unity and separation were constantly in the recollection as well as on the horizon of their inhabitants (as apparently is still true today). Where each of these powers began and ended and who their natives were was also a frequently debated question, as individuals, communities, and territories changed hands and as identities and alliances were extremely fluid. Rather than thinking of these two countries as objects already in existence that conflicted with one another, I slowly began to see them as entities that were in the process of making and that were influenced, among other things, by the dynamic relationship tying them together. Was there no way, I asked myself, to reconstruct Iberia as it used to be? To ask how a frontier between Spain and Portugal was carved over time and justified rather than assuming that it was natural or inevitable?

The telling of a common Iberian, rather than a separate Spanish and Portuguese history, would restore a narrative that in the early modern period, before the triumph of the nation-state, contemporaries adopted as their own. During the union of the crowns and even in its aftermath, many contemporaries believed in the existence of a "Spain" (*Hispania*) made of a triple alliance among Portugal, Aragon, and Castile. They argued that Spaniards and Portuguese shared a culture and, to some degree, a language, a geography, and a history, and they continuously harbored or feared plans that would reunite them. In the aftermath of their separation, Spain and Portugal, Spaniards and Portuguese, continued to be closely associated.[13] Visions of a united Spain also persisted, as did the possibility that Spaniards would turn Portuguese or Portuguese would become Spaniards.[14] Indifference to the identity of agents also continued, as local governors could use the services and aid of Portuguese in Spain, Spaniards in Portugal.[15] The residents of both powers also looked to one another for inspiration and frequently wondered why their neighbors succeeded where they had failed.[16] It is therefore not surprising that in the second half of the eighteenth century an anonymous author could conclude that "the Portuguese are generically understood to be Spanish because they are compatriots of the same Peninsula, religion and customs and because of this . . . they are all reputed and held to be of the same nation, without any difference, especially if compared with other nations, which are held to be greatly different and absolutely diverse."[17] As a result, it is possible to argue that the greatest challenge faced by the Braganza dynasty, which came to power in 1640, was to legitimize the break with Spain. And though its success might have been somewhat spectacular, rather than affirming that it was natural, perhaps it is time we asked—as some historians have begun doing—how this process of alienation took place and why, when, and to what a degree it had succeeded.[18]

Reconstructing Early Modern Spaces: Europe and the Americas

If Spanish and Portuguese histories are usually told apart, so are the histories of Europe and the Americas. Usually allocated into distinct academic fields, until fairly recently most historians of Europe tended to ignore the early modern colonial experience altogether or they treated it as marginal and thus inconsequential to European history. On their part, colonial historians usually made some tribute to European history, which they argued was a necessary antecedent to explain empire, but they tended to limit their examination to specific issues or periods that were said to be of particular importance. Only a few among them kept up with the most current historiography of the "homeland" and even fewer seriously considered that Europeans, too, underwent important processes of change.[19] In the Spanish and Portuguese case, comparisons were thus made between European medieval practices and Early Modern American ones. As a result of this unbalanced contrast, the conclusion many reached was that the Old and the New Worlds were radically different. Here, too, a relatively recent questioning suggested these two worlds were connected by an Atlantic that had a history of its own, which a new imperial historiography has sought to describe. Yet proponents of

Atlantic history often understood their task as an exercise in comparative history that contrasted colonies to a motherland.[20] By doing so, they failed to write an integrated story that would consider both sides of the ocean as participants in a connected world.[21]

But what would happen if we attempted to write such a story? If we reconstructed the polycentric entities that existed in the past by imagining them as networks, in which there was no clear center nor evident peripheries but instead many focal points tied to one another in different ways and degrees?[22] If we went this way, we would discover that the Old and the New Worlds could be compared and contrasted as they often are but that they could also serve to elucidate what we sometimes take (too hastily) for granted.[23] The effects of change over time and the uses of memory, as well as the invocation of an ancient past, offer one example of what Europe could teach us about the New World; but the briefness of recollection, the short time span of occupation, and the enormity of the conflict would allow us to perceive why American debates were particular. Together, both sides of the ocean would assert the precariousness of immemoriality and the degree by which the status quo was contemporaneously both invoked and invented. The status of natives as it functioned on both shores is also likely to help us understand how contemporaries reacted to the presence of elements they considered internal yet foreign. In other words, by observing the Americas from Europe, and Europe from the America, one could obtain a better perspective about both.

If we followed this understanding, here too we would be adopting contemporary visions as our own. During the early modern period, tensions on one side of the ocean produced tensions on the other.[24] The suspicion that Spaniards coveted peninsular Portugal or that the Portuguese were not to be trusted influenced how their overseas activities were viewed and comprehended. As individuals circulated between one realm and the other, several became experts of both. The Treaty of Utrecht (1715) tied both sides of the Atlantic together by ordering, for example, Spain to return to Portugal, on the one hand, Verdoejo and Noudar (in Iberia) and, on the other, Colonia de Sacramento (in the New World).[25] The need to defend their land sometimes led individuals in both Iberia and the Americas to search for a global solution that would settle all their disputes.[26] Some even adopted a transatlantic rather than a European or an American vision, affirming that this was a unified world, in which—to borrow the terms used by António Manuel Hespanha—an Old Regime also existed in the tropics.[27]

South and North: Writing Imperial Histories in a Prenational Age

In recent years, scholars have drawn our attention to the need to transform the study of early modern empires also into a global, perhaps even a connected, history.[28] Nonetheless, and following more established routes, most colonial historians still tend to concentrate either on the relationship with a motherland, or they proceed to compare one Atlantic with the other. They thus juxtaposed a British Empire with a British Atlantic, with a French, a Dutch, a Spanish, or a Portuguese one.[29] Implicitly affirming the existence of national spheres, national law, and national culture in a period, they would refute the presence of the same in Europe, a few among them have even asserted that European national identities were to a large degree formed during the European expansion and as a result of it. The conversion of the English, Scottish, and Irish into Britons or the unification of the natives of the different Spanish kingdoms into Spaniards thus first happened in the colonies, where national (or protonational) political identities flourished and gained concretization.[30]

One result of this positioning is that many imperial histories are still written with their back to one another. Important efforts at comparison do take place, but very few scholars analyze the various early modern colonial domains together by linking not only their histories (as a comparison would do) but also their historiographies, pondering how their slicing into national expertise influenced the way we have reconstructed the past.[31] But what would happen if we considered that early modern Europeans shared much more than we currently give them credit for and that their states were much more polyvalent and composed than the nineteenth- and twentieth-century national narratives allow us to perceive?[32] If we highlighted the importance of their common intellectual, religious, and cultural heritage that, without wishing to flatten out differences, had them often speak not necessarily in the same language but certainly about the same things?[33] If, when studying Spain and Portugal, we would be aware of what scholars of Anglo-America have achieved or, on the contrary, we took Spanish and Portuguese historiography into account when we described developments elsewhere?

As I was writing this book, the habitual comparison between a Spanish and a British model of empire was constantly on my mind. In its most stereotyped, caricatural form, this comparison holds that British colonialism was a peaceful enterprise in which farmers took possession of vacant land and in which they treated Indians as foreign nations and mostly cared about commerce.[34] Such an approach claims that Spanish practices, on the contrary, had violently integrated Indians into the commonwealth while also marginalizing them and dispossessing them of their religion and the fruits of their labor. These differences, we are told, were not rooted in the conditions that each power found on the ground but instead depended on local (national?) customs and practices that trumped commonalities across Europe. Although over the years a much more nuanced and interesting version of this comparison has been proposed, it is still the case that according to most historians Spain and England as well as their empires were substantially different.[35] Was this distance, I wondered, as vast as historians had affirmed, or was it equally due to the development of separate historiographies that asked different questions and looked for the answers in different ways? What would happen, I asked, if we distanced ourselves from how contemporaries accused and mocked one another and if we avoided overrelying on national historiographical traditions? Could we dissipate some of these distinctions?[36]

To answer some of these questions, in this work, I conversed silently with the literature on Anglo (and to a lesser degree French) North America. Rather than comparing north with south, as I did with Spain and Portugal, Europe and the Americas, I attempted instead to pose to my sources interrogations that originated in my familiarity with that other bibliography, hoping that it might provide me with important insights. Adopting a foreign historiographical tradition to my research, I concluded that if we asked the same questions and used the same source material, we would more often than not ascertain that what the Spanish and Portuguese were thinking and doing was not that radically different than what their rivals of the north did. The Spanish experience, which was earlier in time if one considers its point of departure, might have set a precedent for colonialism, as many historians have rightly argued, but the historiography on Anglo- and French America could teach us to observe Latin America in new ways.[37]

To allude to just one example, it is a well-known fact that in 1690 John Locke argued that property and industry were tied together.[38] Those who cultivated a land that had been abandoned or was insufficiently worked by mixing their labor with the earth created a new object to which they had now acquired rights. Applying this understanding to the American colonies, Locke concluded that, because Native Americans did not improve the land, they had no title to it, nor could they prohibit its occupation and use by others. While this story is widely remembered, a much less celebrated fact is that some forty years earlier, in 1648, Juan de Solórzano Pereira, analyzing the rights of Spain in the New World, suggested that they, too, depended on Spaniards having "searched, found, and occupied" the territory first. The Indians might have inhabited it, he asserted, but their entitlements expired because they had "abandoned it, leaving it uncultivated." It was part of natural law and the law of nations, he concluded, to give such a land to the first true occupier in reward for his "industry," that is, his diligence or ability to perform better.[39]

By invoking Locke and Solórzano together I am not interested in the questions of who was first and who second or how original was Locke's analysis. Instead, what I want to suggest is that both authors linked (correct) use to rights, both asserted that knowledge and application were a method to acquire title, and both assumed that insufficient or improper use could be generically applied to certain people, such as the American natives, who could be stereotyped as wasteful or at least as inadequate candidates to transform "deserts" into fertile gardens.[40] Furthermore, although both writers, deeply engaged in legitimizing the colonial enterprise, cared most about what would happen overseas, they both knew that the questions they were asking had their origins and ramifications in Europe. Like their other contemporaries, rather than searching to uncover existing titles or affirm the validity of "historical rights," they too were mostly interested in how they could be modified.

A transatlantic conversation that involved many other important discussants and that raged across Europe (as seen in Chapter 2), it suggested to me that what we now identify as British, Spanish, or Portuguese (as well as French or Dutch, to name just two additional examples) might have been more cosmopolitan than we had imagined in the past. Legal and intellectual history certainly bound different parts of Europe together, as did their "republic of letters," but it is clear that intellectuals, jurists, administrators, settlers, soldiers, and merchants were also engaged in such similar conversations.[41] Rather than the English mostly caring about land and the Spanish and the Portuguese mainly searching to control labor, individuals and communities belonging to all three powers tied labor to land, also suggesting that their ability to dominate the New World depended on both their agreements with one another as well as their relationship with the indigenous peoples. This relationship was managed by alternating between war and peace according to the conditions of place and time, as well as by controlling the image of natives and their "dangerosity." But whatever strategy Europeans chose to adopt, their final aim was to extend and legitimize their presence.[42] And although it resulted in the demise and destruction of the indigenous world, during the colonial period these concerns guaranteed that both Europeans and natives constantly redefined themselves and that they underwent important processes of change and mutation.[43]

As a result of such questioning, as I was writing this book, I constantly wondered whether in Spain and Portugal, too, a discourse of *imperium* and *dominium* coincided with a demand for improvement. Against the habitual affirmation that treaties with natives were fairly rare, I proceeded to examine and explain how they operated.[44] Familiarity with the literature on Anglo-America also led me to see more clearly how European agents, preoccupied with controlling the land, tied conversion and treaty making to territorial claims by arguing that evangelization and alliances not only transformed the indigenous peoples into Christians and subjects but also were instrumental in appropriating their land.[45] This linkage explained the fierce competition over Indians that might have supplied the desired labor but whose subjection also justified possession.[46] As happened in other parts of the Americas, the Spaniards and the Portuguese thus proceeded to classify Indians as peoples under the dominion of one power or the other, or they at least argued that natives were neutral or independent and thus "belonged" to no one. Under these circumstances, the division of Indians into pagans or Christians, uncivilized or domesticated, foes or friends became a justifying and foundational tool vis-à-vis natives as well as vis-à-vis other Europeans.[47] Thus, although the Anglos, the Spanish, and the Portuguese might have accused the Indians of being "fickle" and untrustworthy, they also suggested, on occasions, that arrangements with them had no formal effect until they, Europeans, acknowledged and formalized them in their bilateral agreements with one another. And although common-sense assumptions would lead us to believe that alliance making implicitly recognized native right to land, perhaps even sovereignty, such was not necessarily the case. Caught by a fundamental dichotomy distinguishing civilized from barbarians, those who properly occupied the land from those who did not, the British, the Spanish, and the Portuguese coincided in concluding that European domination was inevitable because Europeans were more worthy, better governed, or more likely to observe the divine mandate, now also part of natural law and the law of nation, to occupy what was "empty."[48]

The literature on Anglo-America was also helpful in discovering the role of local frontier diplomacy in colonial Latin America. Here, too, I found that the accords locals adopted were in theory only practical, transitory solutions but that they often were converted into permanent and enforceable agreements that substantially transformed the legal landscape, sometimes to the displeasure of the higher authorities. Multiple agents were involved in such dynamics that depended on religious, economic, political, and social issues. Also apparent was the way all interlocutors alluded to a status quo, which they all agreed to respect, yet they could rarely concord on what it contained. Treaties might have structured these conversations, but discussants mostly argued about occupation, which sent them to the complicated dynamics earlier described.

Thus, although it is true that the English and their apologetics accused Spaniards of having abandoned the land or insufficiently improved it, or they portrayed their own colonization as an enterprise based on trade and industry in order to distinguish it from a Spanish colonialism allegedly based on violence and conquest,[49] and although Spaniards responded by mocking the English for pretending that their part of the Americas was vacant and its inhabitants lacked notions of property,[50] this discussion did not necessarily reflect either their convictions or the reality of what they were doing. And if once upon a time, a distinct British legal system was said to have separated the English from other Europeans, we now know that the English common law had deep roots in European traditions, that canon law was also important in the British Isles, and that, when discussing empire, the British appealed to Roman law, which they, too, claimed reflected a law of nations, perhaps even a natural law.[51]

Deconstructing Borders

If the historiography of Spain and Portugal, Europe and the Americas, Anglo-, Spanish, and Portuguese America were on my mind while I was writing this book, so was the literature on border formation. This literature has long suggested a series of opposites according to which borders were either linear or zonal, internal or external, natural or artificial, or imposed by the state with local acquiescence or opposition. But none of these distinctions were useful to analyze the cases I studied. The conflicts I examined sometimes involved a line that one could not pass, but on most occasions they included contestation over very large areas, indeed—as in the American case—over the interior of a continent, which was only sparsely dominated on both sides by small islands of occupation. Each confrontation and each place, time, and parties had a shape of their own. Sometimes the focus was on identifying routes; on others divisions followed the whereabouts of human groups (natives) as they moved in space. Rather than asking where borders passed or which shape they had, contemporaries mostly sought to establish which part they could use in what way and the possession they took changed accordingly. Gathering usually produced a different territorial pattern than grazing, which in turn was distinct from cultivation. The same was true if at stake was an alliance with an indigenous group, missionary activities, occupation by settlers, or the establishment of a military fort.

As I witnessed this complexity, I came to think of my object of study not as a border or a frontier but instead as a "territory." This, I hoped, described what the parties cared about more accurately than terms that placed on center stage divisions that could be completely nonexistent at times, unimportant at others. I found the distinction between "internal" and "external" borders just as problematic. In the cases I reviewed, the struggle to occupy the land and control its inhabitants (the so-called internal frontier) coincided with and was simultaneous to fixing the border vis-à-vis neighbors (the so-called external frontier). The inverse was also true, as the struggle against neighbors motivated or justified occupation. Rather than expanding internally and then externally (as European historians have described) or proceeding on the inverse (as historians of Latin America have asserted), both processes were contemporaneous, because whatever the pretensions of the parties might have been, no external frontier could be claimed de jure or exist de facto without a hinterland of occupation, and no occupation could peacefully endure if neighbors did not acquiesce to it. But external and internal also coincided in other ways. Because territorial expansion required classifying actors as members or aliens, rather than existing a priori, the identification of individuals and groups as both internal and external was simultaneous to the construction of territorial distinctions. It was as if, rather than communities slowly territorializing (as the literature had described), communities and territories were constructed concurrently and interdependently.

The division between natural and artificial borders was equally unhelpful. On the one hand, historians have already demonstrated that natural borders were an artificial construction that involved an arbitrary decision that nature itself never mandated.[52] On the other, historians who insisted on "natural" frontiers in Europe and "artificial" in the colonies, imagined a dichotomy between territorial divisions that slowly emerged through indigenous processes (in Europe) and boundaries that were imposed from the outside, unilaterally and swiftly (in the colonies).[53] To justify this juxtaposition, many of them constructed a straw man, because neither the Europe they described nor the colonies they imagined ever existed. In early modern Iberia, territorial formation involved the intervention of outsiders and the imposition of norms; in the colonies, it allowed for the agency of a plethora of actors and interests. Colonial powers might have pretended to resolve these questions by signing treaties, but it was clear that these did not necessarily explain or determine how things took shape on the ground.[54] At the end of the day, the extension and form territories took depended on human interaction rather than on stable or formal divisions. Its history still waits to be rewritten or at least retold.[55]

These interpretative problems originated partially in the frequent framing of boundary formation as the end result of political, diplomatic, or military processes. But as I have tried to demonstrate, territorial conflicts implicated a much larger set of actors and interests, and they involved considerations of economic, social, political, legal, and religious dimensions. They were affected by constant changes in the identities of parties, their alliances, the lands they coveted, and the justifications they invoked. If it was time that the history of border formation became also a social and a legal history, it might also be time for diplomatic, political, and military history to undergo the same transformation. On the border between Spain and Portugal in both Iberia and overseas, politics and diplomacy (and often war) were not necessarily state-sanctioned activities. They, too, implicated a huge array of actors who negotiated as well as formed the physical contours of what they called their own.

Reconnecting History and Law

In all these dynamics, law mattered to an enormous degree. Most contemporaries whose allegations I studied were not jurists. Many of them were illiterate, living in small hamlets in territories that some of their contemporaries suggested were remote and dangerous. They were often characterized as not quite civilized and were frequently accused of spontaneous and irrational behavior. Nevertheless, to those familiar with Roman law doctrines, what they said and did was surprisingly recognizable.[56] How they familiarized themselves with these highly complex and nuanced legal concepts is unclear. A few might have studied them in university, but most had probably socialized into them through living in the community, observing the behavior of others, or listening to tales about what was right and what was wrong, what could succeed and what stood to fail. These narratives might have vulgarized what jurists asserted, but contemporaries believed that they embodied a divine, perhaps even a natural law that had been inherited from ancient times and was common to the entire humanity.[57] Because they conducted their lives in accordance to these norms, their activities must be comprehended by referencing this particular framework, which gave their acts and their allegations specific meanings.[58]

Understanding these rules, which structured contemporary interactions, would allow us to perceive why actors did certain things in certain ways, and why they avoided others. It would help us distinguish between what they argued because the law mandated they would, from what might have expressed their particular vision. Following this road would, for example, also permit us to appreciate that although reactions to territorial invasions could express an emotional, instinctive response, they were also required by a doctrine that asserted that silence was consent. It would demonstrate that memory might have faded on occasions, but immemoriality was constantly invoked because it was a powerful juridical tool. Certain acts such as tax collection, we could thereafter observe, embodied claims for possession, not necessarily evidence for it. The same happened with Portuguese *tombos*, which, rather than proving title, were written pretensions for entitlements. Viewed from this perspective, the story of the formation of Spain and Portugal in Europe and the Americas could therefore be regarded not only as a tale about who was right and who was wrong—as it was usually studied— but also as an opportunity to understand how contemporaries imagined their relationship to land and how they sought to communicate it to others.[59]

If on the one hand it is time that we took law seriously, on the other it is also time that we put to rest the constant appeals to an alleged gap between "law" and "practice."[60] More often than not, these appeals are based on a very limited understanding of the law, one that equates it with legislation and assumes that legislation can exist independently of other legal sources and requires no interpretation. But law in general, and early modern law in particular, was a completely different affair. Until the eighteenth century, legislation was a very secondary legal source, and it mainly reflected the duty of the king to adjudicate conflicts, not his ability to direct or innovate.[61] More important than royal orders were the commands of God as expressed in canon law and as taught by the clergy. Also essential was a customary law that depended on social norms that often reflected to a surprising degree what medieval Roman jurists described. Judicial practice, justice, and equity were guiding principles, not legality. If we took these factors into consideration, if we looked at what kings ordered alongside what the church ruled and the doctrine and customs instructed, we would be astonished at the degree by which most contemporaries sought to obey the law. They did so in both Europe and the Americas, the colonies never consisting of that space of freedom from law and treaties that Carl Schmitt once described.[62] This does not preclude the obvious fact that contemporaries chose the interpretation that suited them best or preferred one source over the other. But their legal system allowed for that, and, in fact, it still does today. Despite our hopes or illusions, even today the law rarely supplies firm answers. It guides and structures debates and is meant to enable human interaction, not define it. Like a soccer match, it supplies an arena, a referee, players, and rules to which one must adhere, but none of these elements guarantees how the game will play out, who will win, and who will lose.

Deconstructing Historical Rights to Land

If law was one way by which people imagined their entitlements, history was another. Coming to discuss their frontiers today, many communities make reference to their historical rights to territory.[63] Enumerating certain facts that allegedly point to their entitlements, they uphold the importance of occupation that had expired and argue for the need to recover it. They compare the chaotic present to a past, which they depict as a period in which the rights of claimants were evident and consensual. But the conflicts I studied in the Old and New Worlds demonstrate that the past was as contentious as the present. Contemporaries might have argued that their entitlements were clear, but neither the law nor their rivals acknowledged these pretensions. All actors constantly referred back to a status quo, but all were completely unable to agree on what it had contained. This happened in part because the law allowed legitimate yet contradictory interpretations. Disagreement was common also because more than a single community could use the land, albeit in different ways, and because community membership itself was in flux. But more often than not, the allegations of the parties demonstrated that the legal situation itself continually mutated. Dependent on occupation, possession, and usage rather than on treaties or wars, rights to land were fluid rather than permanent, conditional rather than absolute. Remembrance and forgetfulness also colored these experiences, revealing in different moments different shades of what had transpired. At stake was how the circumstances had changed but also the diverse meaning and normative value society chose to give them. Historians of Europe have described to us in great detail how private property, on the one hand, and territorial jurisdiction of states, on the other, were invented in the seventeenth century, matured in the eighteenth century, and became sacrosanct in the nineteenth century. In the process, property and territoriality were redefined. Rather than contingent and dependent on use, by the nineteenth century they became permanent and, rather than tied to a series of requirements that limited their utilization by considerations of common good, they also became unconditional.[64] Gone were arguments, extremely powerful during the early modern period, that sustained rights by referencing just wars, conversion, civilization, or even improvement.

The difficulty of tying present to past was perhaps most noticeable in Latin America, where the new states created in the early nineteenth century adopted the principle of *uti possidetis*, by which they would each conserve the territory that was theirs during the colonial period.[65] In the aftermath of this agreement, the new political entities—which refashioned themselves as heirs to a colonial past—strove to defend their territorial claims by making references to what had transpired in the early modern period. Justifying archival missions abroad and the organization of local and national archives, the basic assumption their elites made was that the past was clear.[66] Reality, however, proved them wrong. Disagreements, emerging as soon as they set out to clarify their borders, included many of the same questions early modern discussants raised, namely, whether treaties and royal decrees were preferable to occupation, as well as how each would be implemented and what its specific, concrete results would be. They also covered other fundamental questions, such as which colonial units existed in the past, how they would be reconstructed in the present, who belonged to them, and what to do with territories and peoples that were altogether external to the imperial system.[67]

If rights are entitlements, history is the study of change over time. Making the former static when the latter continuously mutates necessarily involves classifying all changes as irrelevant or inconsequential. It also implies accepting as historically valid the theoretical dichotomy between communities that were fixed and original and whose lands are currently held by the legitimate heirs of the first occupiers and those whose members immigrated, transgressing into alien territories and occupying them by violence. Although such distinctions may be the appropriate, perhaps even the long overdue response, to the modernizing discourse that in the late seventeenth, eighteenth, and early nineteenth centuries allowed the reorganization of rights by invoking civilization and "improvement," they nonetheless confuse a philosophical and ideological debate with a historical reality. Historical rights may be part of what some have titled corrective justice, but they are also an oxymoron. They might play an important political role, but they cannot be part of history.

In the long run, what the study of early modern Spanish and Portuguese conflicts suggest was that neither history nor law could give definite answers. History as it is practiced today may be a humble pursuit. While economists and political scientists wish to predict the future (even when they fail), medical doctors pretend to cure it (even when they do not), and anthropologists invite us to understand the "other," all historians usually do is to argue that

things were more complicated than they appear. Unpacking historical narratives, they seek to demonstrate how they were constructed, by whom, and to which purpose. Witnessing the constant
instrumentalization of the past to discredit or support certain claims,
they hope their work might illuminate alternative ways to think
about what transpired. Departing from the study of genealogies
that argue that the present was inevitable, they suggest that there
were roads not taken, possibilities not explored. Their principal task
today is to explain not how we got here but what we have missed in
the process.

Abbreviations

AC	Actas Capitulares
ACDC	Arquivo da Casa do Exmo. Sr. Duque de Cadaval, Lisbon
ACEDAL	Archivo de la Casa y Estados de los Excelentísimos Duques de Abrantes y Linares, Jerez de la Frontera
ACL	Arquivos da Administração Central
ADC/L	Academia das Ciências, Lisbon
ADD	Additional
AGI	Archivo General de Indias, Seville
AGMM	Archivo General Militar, Madrid
AGN/BA	Archivo General de La Nación, Buenos Aires
AGN/M	Archivo General de La Nación, Montevideo
AGOC	Archivum Generale Orden Carmelitarum, Rome
AGS	Archivo General de Simancas, Simancas
AHCB	Arquivo Histórico da Casa de Bragança, Vila Viçosa
AHM	Arquivo Histórico Militar, Lisbon
AHME	Arquivo Histórico Municipal de Elvas
AHMLC	Archivo Histórico Municipal de La Coruña
AHMO	Archivo Histórico Municipal de Olivenza
AHMS	Arquivo Histórico Municipal de Serpa
AHN	Archivo Histórico Nacional, Madrid
AHPM	Archivo Histórico de Protocolos, Madrid
AHPP	Archivo Histórico Provincial de Pontevedra

AHPS	Archivo Histórico Provincial de Sevilla, Seville
AHU	Arquivo Histórico Ultramarino, Lisbon
AMA	Archivo Municipal de Aroche
AMAE/M	Archivo del Ministerio de Asuntos Exteriores, Madrid
AME	Archivo Municipal de Encinasola
AMM	Arquivo Municipal de Moura
AMN	Archivo del Museo Naval, Madrid
AMQ	Archivo Municipal, Quito
AMRE	Archivo del Ministerio de Relaciones Exteriores, Quito
AMS	Archivo Municipal de Sevilla, Seville
AMT	Archivo Municipal de Tui
AMVA	Archivo Municipal de Valencia de Alcántara
ANC/S	Archivo Nacional, Santiago de Chile
ANQ	Archivo Nacional, Quito
ANTT	Arquivo Nacional do Torre do Tombo, Lisbon
APB	Arquivo Público da Bahia
APEP	Arquivo Provincial Estado do Pará, Belém do Pará
APMG	Arquivo Público do Estado de Mato Grosso, Cuiabá
ARG	Archivo del Reino de Galicia, La Coruña
ARSEMAP	Archivo de la Real Sociedad Económica Matritense de Amigos del País, Madrid
ARSI	Archivum Romanum Societatis Jesu, Rome
art.	article
Asign.	Asignatura
ASPF/R	Archivio Storico della Sacra Congregazione per l'Evangelizzazione dei Popoli, Rome
ASV	Archivio Segreto Vaticano, Rome
BA	Biblioteca de Ajuda, Lisbon
BL	British Library, London
BN	Biblioteca Nacional (section of the AGN/BA)
BNC	Biblioteca Nacional de Chile, Santiago de Chile
BNE	Biblioteca Nacional, Madrid
BNL	biblioteca Nacional, Lima
BNP	Biblioteca Nacional, Lisbon
BPE	Biblioteca Pública de Évora, Évora

BPR	Biblioteca del Palacio Real, Madrid
BRAH/M	Biblioteca de la Real Academia de la Historia, Madrid
Bras.	Provincia Brasiliensis e Maragnonensis
CC	Corpo Cronológico
CCA	Cámara de Castilla
CE	Catastro de Ensenada
CMG	Capitania de Mato Grosso
CMM	Arquivo Histórico da Câmara Municipal de Marvão
Cod.	códice
CRC	Consejo Real de Castilla
CU	Conselho Ultramarino
Cx.	Caixa
DIV	Divisão
doc.	document
Exp.	Expediente
Fasic.	Fascículo
FDE	Fundo Direitos Extintos
FE	Fondo Especial
GJ	Gracia y Justicia
GTT	Gavetas da Torre do Tombo
IG	Indiferente General
LA	Libro de Acuerdos
LC	Libro de Cabildo
leg.	legajo
LH	Limites com Hespanha
Liv.	Livro
Mç.	Maço
MNE	Arquivo do Ministério dos Negócios Estrangeiros, Lisbon
MRE	Fondo Ministerio, Sección Reservada
Ms.	manuscript
MT	Mato Grosso
Nav.	Colección Fernández de Navarrete
no.	number
OLV	Olvidados

PC	Pleitos civiles
RA	Real Audiencia
RCV	Archivo de la Real Chancillería de Valladolid, Valladolid
Res.	Reservados
RG	Respuestas Generales
SC	Scritture Riferite nei Congressi
SG	Secretaria de Governo
SGU	Secretaría de Guerra
SMA	Secretaría de Marina
SOCG	Scritti Originali Riferiti nelle Congregazioni Generali
STM	Sala Toribio Medina
TP	Tombo de Provisões, Cartas Régias, Alvarás e Ordens
Tr	Tratados y Negociaciones, siglo XIX, Portugal
VM/CV	Vicaria Maragonensis, Commune Vicariae

Notes

Introduction

1. Lucien Febvre, "Frontières. Le mot et la notion," in Lucien Febvre, *Pour une histoire à part entière* (Paris: SEVPEN, 1962), 11–24; Malcolm Anderson, *Frontiers: Territory and State Formation in the Modern World* (Cambridge: Polity Press, 1996); Daniel Nordman, *Frontières de France. De l'espace au territoire XVIe–XIXe siècle* (Paris: Gallimard, 1998); Daniel Power and Naomi Standen, eds., *Frontiers in Question: Eurasian Borderlands, 700–1700* (New York: St. Martin's Press, 1998); and Daniel-Erasmus Khan, "Territory and Boundaries," in Bardo Fassbender and Anne Peters, eds., *The Oxford Handbook of the History of International Law* (Oxford: Oxford University Press, 2012), 225–249. For the case of Spain and Portugal, see, for example, Amélia Aguiar Andrade, "A estrátégia dionisina na fronteira noroeste," *Revista da faculdade de letras: História* serie II, 15(1) (1998): 163–176; and Leontina Ventura, "A fronteira luso-castelhana na Idade Média," *Revista da faculdade de letras: História* serie II, 15(1) (1998): 25–52.

2. Peter Sahlins, *Boundaries: The Making of France and Spain in the Pyrenees* (Berkeley: University of California Press, 1989), 164 and 276. Sahlins discusses some of these issues also on 63–102. He juxtaposes state boundaries to jurisdiction and private property on 95. On the territorialization of local communities, see 156–157. Somewhat similarly, Iria Gonçalves, "Entre a Peneda e o Barroso. Uma fronteira galaico-minhota em meados de duzentos," *Revista da faculdade de letras: História* serie II, 15(1) (1998): 63–76, argues that the border was ignored by locals as long as kings were not at war. When monarchs were confronted, locals—who were tied to one another by family, friendship, and economic relations—went "national" and fought against one another.

3. Robert Cornevin, "Les questions nationales en Afrique et les frontières nationales," *Revue française d'histoire d'Outre-Mer* 68(1–4) (1981): 251–262; and

Alastair Lamb, "Studying the Frontiers of the British Indian Empire," *Journal of the Royal Central Asian Society* 53(3) (1966): 245–254.

4. José María Cordero Torres, *Fronteras hispánicas. Geografía e historia, diplomacia y administración* (Madrid: Instituto de Estudios Políticos, 1960), 97–112; José Antonio Maravall, *Estado moderno y mentalidad social (siglos XV a XVII)* (Madrid: Revista de Occidente, 1972), 87–160; Ana Rodríguez López, *La consolidación territorial de la monarquía feudal castellana. Expansión y fronteras durante el reinado de Fernando III* (Madrid: CSIC, 1994); Miguel-Ángel Ladero Quesada, "Reconquista y definiciones de frontera," *Revista da faculdade de letras. História* 15(10) (1998): 655–691, 655–657; and Amélia Aguiar Andrade, *A construção medieval do território* (Lisbon: Livros Horizonte, 2001).

5. Miguel Ángel Ladero Quesada, "La formación de la frontera de Portugal y el tratado de Alcañices (siglos XII–XIII)," *Boletín de la Real Academia de la Historia* 194(3) (1997): 425–458; Manuel González Jiménez, "Las relaciones entre Portugal y Castilla durante el siglo XIII," *Revista da faculdade de letras. História* 15(1) (1998): 1–24, on 2 and 14; Joaquim Veríssimo Serrão, "Conferencia de Clausura: España y Portugal ante el siglo XXI," *Sexto Congreso de Economía Regional de Castilla y León. Actas (Zamora, 1998)* (Valladolid: Junta de Castilla y León, 1998), 132–140, on 136; Leontina Ventura, "A fronteira luso-castelhana na idade média," *Revista da faculdade de letras. História* 15(1) (1998): 25–52, 51; and Vicente Ángel Álvarez Palenzuela, "Relations between Portugal and Castile in the Late Middle Ages (13–16 Centuries)," *E-Journal of Portuguese History* 1(1) (2003).

6. The explanation of these processes pitted historians who suggested that the separation of Portugal was natural against those who concluded that it combined social, political, and historical factors and was voluntary rather than inevitable. See, for example, Alexandre Herculano de Carvalho e Araújo, *História de Portugal desde o começo da monarchia até ao fim do reinado de Affonso III* (Paris: Aillaud and Bertrand, 1875 [1846–1853]); and José Mattoso, *Identificação de um País. Ensaio sobre as origens de Portugal (1096–1325)* (Lisbon: Estampa, 1985).

7. Lamenting this neglect is Amândio Jorge Morais Barros, "Problemas de fronteira na zona de Olivença em meados do século XV," *Revista de História* 13 (1995): 59–68, 59, who argues it is vital that we study the "more or less profound fluctuations that the border experienced *after* Alcañices." Suggesting the need to study precisely that is also José Luís Martín Martín, "Conflictos luso-castellanos por la raya," *Revista da faculdade de letras: História* serie II, 15(1) (1998): 259–274. Martín Martín also insists on the multiplicity of individuals and interests that played part in such dynamics.

8. María Rosa de Muñoz, "La Guerra de Sucesión en el Río de la Plata y las consecuencias del Tratado de Utrecht," *Revista Lotería* 338–339 (1984): 114–129; Luís Ferrand de Almeida, *Alexandre de Gusmão, o Brasil e o Tratado de Madrid (1735–1750)* (Coimbra: Universidade de Coimbra, 1990); and *El Tratado de Tordesillas y su época. Congreso internacional de historia*, 3 vols. (Madrid: Sociedad "V Centenario del Tratado de Tordesillas," 1995). See also María Eugenia Petit-Breuilh Sepúlveda, "Comportamientos hispanoportugueses en los territorios limítrofes de América durante los conflictos bélicos," in David González Cruz, ed., *Propaganda y mentalidad bélica en España y América durante el siglo XVIII* (Madrid: Ministerio de Defensa, 2007), 95–119.

9. One exception is Rafael Chambouleyron, " Plantações, sesmarias e vilas. Uma reflexão sobre a ocupação da Amazônia seiscentista," Nuevo Mundo Mundos Nuevos, http://nuevomundo.revues.org/2260; doi:10.4000/nuevomundo.2260. Rafael Straforini, "A formação territorial brasileira nos dois primeiros séculos de colonização," *Geo UERJ* 18(1) (2008): 63–90, examines the various ways Brazilian geographers explained the territorial formation of their country.

10. Lía Quarleri, *Rebelión y guerra en las fronteras del Plata. Guaraníes, jesuitas e imperios coloniales* (Mexico-City: Fondo de Cultura Económica, 2009), 70–71; Alberto José Gullón Abao, *La frontera del Chacó en la gobernación del Tucumán (1750–1810)* (Cádiz: Universidad de Cádiz, 1993), 70 and 76; and Guy Martinière, "Les stratégies frontalières du Brésil colonial et l'Amérique espagnole: Notes introductives," *Cahiers des Amériques Latines* 18 (1978): 45–68.

11. Antonio Stopani, *La production des frontières. État et communautés en Toscane (XVIe–XVIIIe siècles)* (Rome: École Française de Rome, 2008). Although mainly centered on "internal" frontiers, Stopani's work is an essential tool in reconstructing how territorial appropriation took place on a local level.

12. Tamar Herzog, "The Meaning of Territory: Colonial Standards and Modern Questions in Ecuador," in Luis Roniger and Carlos H. Waisman, eds., *Globality and Multiple Modernities: Comparative North American and Latin American Perspectives* (Brighton: Sussex Academic Press, 2002), 162–182. See also Lauren Benton, *A Search for Sovereignty: Law and Geography in European Empires, 1400–1900* (New York: Cambridge University Press, 2010).

13. Benton, *A Search for Sovereignty*, 284 and 298–299.

14. Jean Gottman, *The Significance of Territory* (Charlottesville: University Press of Virginia, 1973), 123; and Michael R. Redclift, *Frontiers: Histories of Civil Society and Nature* (Cambridge, MA: MIT Press, 2006), 23.

15. "Copia do auto das demarcações de Villarinho e Teixeira que por inquirições de Portugal e Castela se determinarão," 24.4.1500, in "Documentos sobre a demarcação de limites entre a Hespanha e Portugal 1803," AHM/DIV/4/1/10/10.

16. I owe some of this formulation to Anthony Pagden.

17. "Il panorama europeo, se viene contemplato nello specchio della cultura giuridica indiana, si presenta con i suoi elementi centrali e fondamentali, mentre sfumano o scompaiono del tutto le asprezze di contrasti veri o presunto che appartengono solo ad aspetti marginali della storia europea, e più ancora alla storiografia europea dell'Ottocento e del Novecento. Ecco dunque perché, a mio parere, fra altre ragioni altrettanto valide, lo storico del diritto europeo deve impegnarsi a indagare le opere dei giuristi indiani: per contemplare in esse, come in uno specchio, e per comprendere meglio, le linee fisionomiche essenziali del diritto europeo." Manlio Bellomo, "Perché lo storico del diritto europeo deve occuparsi dei giuristi indiani?" *Rivista internazionale di diritto comune* 11 (2000): 21–32, 32.

18. Gustavo de Matos Sequeira e Rocha Júnior, *Olivença* (Lisbon: Portugália Editora, 1924); Ricardo Rosa y Alberty, *A Questão de Olivença—por quê Olivença não pertence à Espanha* (Lisbon: Grupo Amigos de Olivença, 1960); and Carlos Eduardo da Cruz Luna, *Nos caminhos de Olivença* (Estremoz: El Autor, 2000).

What the territory of Olivenza might have consisted of in the early modern period, before its seizure by Spain, was discussed, for example, in "Dudas sobre términos y mojones que separan Olivenza de varias aldeas de Castilla," 20.11.1466; "Llamamiento del concejo a todos los vecinos para defender la villa ante temor de incursión de los de Alconchel," 18.2.1514; and "Autoridades de Alconchel y Olivenza dirimen amistosamente los pleitos entre sus vecinos y anulan acciones judiciales por ello," 13.3.1514, demarcation dated 5.4.1532; all in AHMO, leg. 1, carpetas 40, 50, 51, and 61.

PART I   *Defining Imperial Spaces*

1. The Treaty of Tordesillas generated endless bibliography. See, for example, *El tratado de Tordesillas y su proyección. Segundas jornadas americanistas. Primer coloquio luso-español de historia ultramarina*, 2 vols. (Valladolid: Universidad de Valladolid, 1973); and Antonio Rumeu de Armas, *El Tratado de Tordesillas. Rivalidad hispano-lusa por el dominio de océanos y continentes* (Madrid: Mapfre, 1992).

2. António Dias Farinha, "A fixação da linha de Tordesilhas a oriente e a expansão portuguesa," and Mariano Cuesta Domingo, "La fijación de la línea de Tordesillas en el extremo oriente," both in *El Tratado de Tordesillas y su época*, vol. 3, 1477–1482 and 1483–1517; and Consuelo Varela, "Los problemas de frontera en el Maluco," in *A união ibérica e o mundo atlântico. Segundas jornadas de história ibero-americana* (Lisbon: Edições Colibrí, 1997), 341–351.

3. Eventually, the debate concerning Asia involved not only the Moluccas but also Macao and the Philippines: Juan Bautista Gesio, "Discurso sobre la isla y ciudad de Macao," AMN, Nav. XVIII, fols. 408r–410r, doc. 80; and Juan de Zúñiga, "Carta del comendador mayor de Castilla ... con fecha de 27.12.1578 sobre la erección del obispado de Macao," AMN, Nav. XVIII, fols. 63r–v, doc. 15.

4. Copies of the Zaragoza Agreement dated 22.4.1529 are included in AHN, Estado 4626 and 2842. Its enduring importance is clear, for example, in "Voto dos comissários do sereníssimo príncipe de Portugal," dated 1681, AHN, Estado, libro 677, fols. 180r–v; and Francisco Inocêncio de Souza Coutinho to Marqués de Grimaldi, Madrid, 16.1.1776, AHN, Estado leg. 2842, apartado 1. AGS, Estado 367, 368, and 371, contain ample documentation regarding the 1524 discussion.

5. Consulta of 15.11.1530, AGI, IG, libro 137, cédulas dated 17.2.1531, 18.3.1531, and 31.8.1531, AGI, IG, 422, libro 15, and undated letter of ambassador Hurtado de Mendoza to the Portuguese monarch and the response of the king (undated), AGI, Patronato 28 and 41, respectively. See also "copia de ciertos capítulos de la carta que don Luis Sarmiento escribió a Su Majestad el 11.7.1535," and cédula real of 13.6.1554, both reproduced in *Campaña del Brasil. Antecedentes coloniales* (Buenos Aires: Archivo General de la Nación, 1931), vol. 1, 5–6 and 6–8. AGS, Estado 369 and 377, contain ample documentation regarding Portuguese plans to discover, perhaps conquer and occupy, the River Plate in 1531 and 1554. These questions are described in Analola Borges, "El tratado de

Tordesillas y la conquista del Río de la Plata," in *El Tratado de Tordesillas y su proyección*, vol. 1, 345–356.

6. "Como desde esta época fueron ya vasallos de un mismo soberano los españoles y portugueses habitantes de la América meridional, no se cuidó ni hubo necesidad de celar la observancia del tratado de Tordesillas e indistintamente hacían unos y otros los descubrimientos, conquistas y poblaciones en aquella parte." Vicente Aguilar y Jurado and Francisco Requena, "Historia de las demarcaciones en la América entre los dominios de España y Portugal," Madrid, 1797, AHN, Estado 3410-2, punto 311.

7. Marqués de Valdelirios to the Marqués de Grimaldi, Madrid, 11.3.1776, AHN, Estado 4371, pp. 8–9. Also see Marqués de Valdelirios to Pedro Cevallos, Buenos Aires, 12.5.1761, AGN/M, Archivos particulares, Caja 333, Colección Mario Falcao Espalter, Carpeta 4.

8. "No tempo da união das duas coroas em que poderá cessar a controvérsia de elas foi tão forçoso o direito da divisão dos domínios que cada uma se conteve nos seus limites sem que se permitisse fraude ou usurpação de uma ou de outra parte o que se observam tão abertamente que contendendo neste mesmo tempo castelhanos e portugueses sobre as ilhas dela linhas não obstante que todos obedeciam a um mesmo governo, foi tão poderosa a razão de conservar distinto o direito de cada reino, quepor que não cedesse um a outro, se deixaram contender ambos sobre ação dos seus estados." "Papel que fés o marquês de Fronteira," in "Pareceres do Exmo. Marquês de Fronteira conselheiro de estado sobre . . . a fundação da Nova Colónia," probably dated 1680, BPE, Cod. CXVI (2-12), no. 1, fols. 4r–8r, on fols. 6v–7r. See also "Discurso em que se mostra as varias opiniões que se acham nos aa. sobre a linha da demarcação entre as conquistas de Portugal e Castela," anonymous, Elvas, 24.11.1681, BPE, Cod. CXVI (2-12), no. 2, fols. 3v and 19v–20r; and Marquês de Lavradio to Martinho de Mello e Castro, Lisbon, 12.2.1781, AHU_ACL_CU_059, cx. 3, d. 220.

9. The struggle regarding Colonia de Sacramento has generated a huge bibliography. I found the following most useful: Antonio Bermejo de la Rica, *La Colonia del Sacramento, su origen, desenvolvimiento, y vicisitudes de su historia* (Toledo: Editorial Católica, 1920); Luís Ferrand de Almeida, *A diplomacia portuguesa e os limites meridionais do Brasil* (1493–1700) (Coimbra: Universidade de Coimbra, 1957), vol. 1, 111–285; and Jaime Cortesão, *Tratado de Madri: Antecedentes; Colónia do Sacramento, 1669–1749* (Rio de Janeiro: Biblioteca Nacional, 1954). Echoes of these debates can be found in "Notícia e justificação do título e boa fé com que se obrou na Nova Colónia do Sacramento," anonymous, undated (c. 1681), BA, Cod. Ms. 51-VI-48, fols. 117r–146r; and "Parecer de grandes letrados sobre a fundação da Nova Colónia de Buenos Aires," Lisbon, 7.9.1680, BA, Cod. Ms. 50-V-39, fols. 587r–89v.

10. The 1681 treaty as well as the opinion of both the Spanish and the Portuguese teams are reproduced in *Campaña del Brasil*, vol. 1, 311–315 and 320–343.

11. Some of these treaties are reproduced in Alejandro del Cantillo, *Tratados, convenios y declaraciones de Paz y de comercio* (Madrid: Imprenta Alegría y Charlain, 1843); and Carlos Calvo, *Colección completa de los tratados, convenciones,*

capitulaciones, armisticios y otros actos diplomáticos (Paris: Durand, 1869). The Portuguese version was published in José Carlos de Macedo Soares, *Fronteiras do Brasil no regime colonial* (Rio de Janeiro: Livraria José Olímpio, 1939).

12. Joseph Dibuja to Jose de Gálvez, Quito, 18.7.1776, ANQ, FE 37, vol. 102, n. 3754-16, fols. 29r–32v, on 31r; the opinión of Joseph de Molina, Río Grande de San Pedro, 18.2.1772, AGN/BA, IX.15.7.15, for example, point 45, fol. 271r; point 46, fols. 271v–273r; and point 55, fol. 273r; and "Usurpaciones hechas por los portugueses en dominios de España en América meridional desde que se concluyó el tratado de límites de 1750 hasta hoy día," draft, undated, and unsigned in AHN, Estado 3410.

13. Unsigned letter, dated Seville, 20.2.1691, ANC/S, Jesuitas, vol. 197, pieza 2, fols. 12r–14v; "Representación del cabildo de Tucumán al marqués de Valdelirios," Tucumán, 6.4.1752, reproduced in *Campaña del Brasil*, vol. 2, 45–51, 48–49; and Lázaro de Ribero to viceroy Antonio Olaguer Feliz, Santa Rosa del Paraguay 24.3.1798, AHN, Estado 3410, no. 13.

14. Vicente Aguilar y Jurado and Francisco Requena, "Historia de las demarcaciones de límites en la América entre los dominios de España y Portugal," Madrid, 1797, AHN, Estado 3410-2, points 301, 304, and 307.

15. "Minuta para el bando que el Excmo. señor Marqués de Lavradio debe mandar publicar," AGN/BA, IX.4.3.7; "Déduction dans laquelle on démontre les notoires objets des pernicieuses transgressions du dernier traité faites par la cour de Madrid," anonymous, 1768, BA, 54-XIII-16 no. 154; "Compêndio histórico dos fatos políticos... como que os castelhanos manifestaram o seu caráter nas negociações e nas guerras com Portugal (1750–1773)," undated anonymous manuscript, AGN/BA, IX.4.3.7, no. 25, IV; Joseph Marcelino de Figueiredo, "Compêndio substancial dos últimos atentados e irrupções que os comandantes espanhóis tem acumulado nos domínios de Portugal," Rio Grande de São Pedro, 30.1.1774, AGN/BA, IX.4.3.7, no. 37, VI; José César de Meneses to Martinho de Melo e Castro, Recife, 29.11.1776, AHU_ACL_CU_015, cx. 125, d. 9500; and Marquês de Lavradio to Martinho de Mello e Castro, Lisbon, 12.2.1781, AHU_ACL_CU_059, cx. 3, d. 220.

16. "Mas contentasse de as andar arranhando ao longo do mar como caranguejos." Fray Vicente de Salvador, "Livro primeiro do descobrimento do Brasil," Bahia, 20.12.1627, ANTT, Manuscritos do Brasil, no. 49, fols. 5v–8r, on fol. 6v.

17. "Esta máxima tan reprobaba en tiempo de paz entre todos los príncipes cristianos sólo reaprende en el pleno del machiavalismo y en las zahúrdas o mezquitas del otomano consistorio en dónde los muftíes inculcan a los renegados de nuestra religión la insana resolución de revolverse contra su origen." Carlos Morphy to Luis Antonio de Souza, Asunción, 18.9.1770, AGN/BA, IX.4.3.6. See also Juan Guardia, "Relación de las horrendas maldades que hicieron los portugueses judíos de Brasil a los indios del Paraguay," Córdoba de Tucumán, 6.10.1629, BRAH/M, Jesuitas, vol. CIX, no. 6. In 1775, Spaniards accused the Portuguese of behaving "contra la buena fe de que hacen alarde las naciones cultas." Miguel de Tejada a Joseph de Alvisuri, Río Grande de San Pedro, 23.11.1775, AGN/BA, IX.15.7.15, no. 27, fols. 306r–v.

18. Jose Marcelino de Figueiredo to the Marquês do Lavradio, AHN, Estado 4553, nos. 1 and 2; and José Miralles, "História militar do Brasil desde o ano 1549 em que teve princípio a fundação da Cidade do Salvador da Bahia de Todos os Santos até o de 1762," 1762, APB, Colonial, 626–7, fols. 8ov, 82v, 83v–84v, and 11v–112r. This text was published in *Anais da Biblioteca Nacional do Rio de Janeiro* 22 (1900): 4–213.

19. Cayetano Pinto de Miranda Montenegro to Lázaro de Ribera, Vila Bela, 30.6.1797, AGI, Estado, no. 15 (1d), and the response of Ribera, following.

20. Letter of Abad de Maserati to the king, dated 30.12.1680, AGI, Charcas 260, fols. 35r–v.

CHAPTER 1 *European Traditions*

1. On the role of Roman law in the European expansion, see Bernardino Bravo Lira, *Derecho común y derecho propio en el Nuevo Mundo* (Santiago de Chile: Editorial Jurídica de Chile, 1989); and Aldo Andrea Cassi, *Ius commune tra vecchio e nuovo mondo. Mari, terre, oro nel diritto della conquista (1492–1680)* (Milano: Giufrrè Editore, 2004).

2. Juan Baltasar Maziel, *De la justicia del tratado de límites de 1750* (Buenos Aires: Academia Nacional de la Historia, 1988 [1760]), 71–98.

3. Juan Nuix, *Reflexiones imparciales sobre la humanidad de los españoles en las Indias* (Madrid: Joachin Ibarra, 1782), 159–183. See also Julio Valdeón Baruque, "Las particiones medievales en los tratados de los reinos hispánicos. Un posible precedente de Tordesillas," in *El Tratado de Tordesillas y su proyección*, vol. 1, 21–32; and Anthony Pagden, "The Struggle for Legitimacy and the Image of Empire in the Atlantic to c.1700," in Nicholas Canny, ed., *The Origins of Empire: British Overseas Enterprise to the Close of the Seventeenth Century* (Oxford: Oxford University Press, 1998), 34–54, on 49.

4. Jorge Juan and Antonio Ulloa, *Disertación histórica y geográfica sobre el meridiano de demarcación* (Madrid: Instituto Histórico de la Marina, 1972 [1749]), 9, 22, 27, 54, 96–97, and 167.

5. *Recopilación de Indias* (promulgated 1680), libro 3, title 1, law 1 (citing sixteenth-century cédulas); and Juan de Solórzano y Pereira, *Política Indiana* (Madrid: Compañía Ibero-Americana de Publicaciones, 1972 [1648]), book 1, chapter 11, points 3–6, on 1008–1109. See also Alfonso García Gallo, "El título jurídico de los reyes de España sobre las Indias en los pleitos colombinos," in "Memoria del IV Congreso Internacional de Historia del Derecho Indiano," special issue, *Revista de la Facultad de Derecho de México* 26(101–102) (1976): 130–156, on 142–145 and 147–152.

6. Maziel, *De la justicia*, 93 and 135–136; and Solórzano y Pereira, *Política Indiana*, book 1, chapter 1, points 9–15 and 20–23 on 109–110 and 112.

7. "Voto dos comissários do serreníssimo príncipe de Portugal," AHN, Estado, Libro 677, fols. 174r–v; Sebastião de Veiga Cabral, "Representação estudiosa e útil para as majestades grandeza de vassalos de Portugal," Abrantes, 20.9.1711, BRAH/M, Ms. 9-5556; and "Noticia e justificação do titulo e boa fé com que se obrou na Nova Colônia do Sacramento," anonymous undated (c. 1681), BA, Cod. Ms. 51-VI-48, fols. 117r–146r, on fol. 39. See also André Ferrand

de Almeida, *A formação do espaço brasileiro e o projeto do novo atlas da América portuguesa (1713–1748)* (Lisbon: Comissão Nacional para as Comemorações dos Descobrimentos Portugueses, 2001).

8. The importance of the bulls to Portuguese imperial theories most particularly in the late fifteenth and early sixteenth centuries was described in Giuseppe Marcocci, *A consciência de um império. Portugal e o seu mundo (sécs. XV–XVII)* (Coimbra: Universidade de Coimbra, 2012).

9. "Aprobación del padre Juan de Andosilla al discurso que formó el capitán Joseph Gómez Jurado cerca de la línea de la demarcación," Madrid, 10.11.1680, BPR, Ms. II/2821, fols. 58v–60r, on fol. 60r.

10. Informe de Alonso de Vaca, Seville, 9.8.1680, AGI, Charcas 260, fols. 74r–75r, fols. 74r–v. See also W.G.L. Randles, "Portuguese and Spanish Attempts to Measure Longitude in the Sixteenth Century," *The Mariner's Mirror* 81(4) (1995): 402–408.

11. "Papeles tocantes a las conferencias que hubo entre los ministros de su majestad y los del rey de Portugal, 1681," AHN, Estado, libro 677, fols. 127r–137v.

12. "Resposta sobre os papéis dos geógrafos em ordem a defenderem o direito da Nova Colónia do Sacramento," Lisbon, 11.11.1680, in "Pareceres do Exmo. Marquês de Fronteira conselheiro de estado," probably dated 1680, BPE, Cod. CXVI (2-12), no. 1, 15v–16v; "Discurso em que se mostra as varias opiniões que se acham sobre a linha da demarcação entre as conquistas de Portugal e Castela," anonymous, Elvas, 24.11.1681, BPE, Cod. CXVI (2-12), no. 2; and "Sentença dos comissários portugueses sobre a Nova Colónia do Sacramento," Elvas, 21.1.1682, BPE, Cod. CIII (2-16), fols. 64r–65v.

13. "Parecer de Tomás Durán, Sebastian Caboto y Juan Vespucci," Badajoz 15.4.1524, AGI, Patronato 48, r. 14.

14. "Discurso em que se mostra as varias opiniões que se acham sobre a linha da demarcação entre as conquistas de Portugal e Castela," anonymous, Elvas, 24.11.1681, BPE, Cod. CXVI (2-12), no. 2.

15. "Dictamen de la junta formada a consecuencia del real orden de 3.6.1776 . . . para examinar varios puntos relativos a . . . ajustar y determinar los límites de los dominios de España y Portugal en la América . . ." (1777), BPR, Ms. II/2855, fols. 53r–77v; Consulta of 16.12.1776, AHN, Estado, 4443/1, no. 2; and Vicente Aguilar y Jurado and Francisco Requena, "Historia de las demarcaciones en la América entre los dominios de España y Portugal," Madrid, 1797, AHN, Estado, 3410-2, prologue.

16. "Informe del virrey Nicolás de Arredondo a su sucesor don Pedro Melo de Portugal y Villena sobre el estado de la cuestión de límites entre las cortes de España y Portugal," 1795, AGN/M, Museo Histórico, Caja 206, Carpeta 30, p. 2.

17. "Instrução que ao General João d'Albuquerque de Mello Pereira e Cáceres deixou a seu antecessor e Irmão Luiz d'Albuquerque de Mello Pereira e Cáceres" (post 1788), APMG, Livro C-03, doc. 03, fols. 53v–57v, on fol. 54v.

18. João de Abreu de Castelo Branco to the king, Belém, 18.9.1739, AHU_ACL_CU_013, cx. 22, d. 2082; and Luís de Albuquerque de Melo Pereira e Cáceres to Martinho de Melo e Castro, Vila Bela, 10.8.1780, AHU_ACL_

CU_010, cx. 21, d. 1285. See also Iris Kantor, "Cartografia e diplomacia: Usos geopolíticos da informação toponímica (1750–1850)," *Anais do museu paulista* N. Sér. V. 17(2) (2009): 39–61, on 39–41 and 49–50; and Nuria Valverde and Antonio Lafuente, "Space Production and Spanish Imperial Geopolitics," in Daniela Bleichmar, Paula de Vox, Kristin Huffine, and Kevin Sheehan, eds., *Science in the Spanish and Portuguese Empires, 1500–1800* (Stanford: Stanford University Press, 2009), 189–215, on 189 and 210.

19. "Toda esta grande obra depende de las operaciones astronómicas y sería indecoroso que en el siglo de las ciencias dudasen todavía dos naciones cultas del modo infalible de señalar los parajes por donde debe pasar el meridiano de demarcación convenido en el tratado de Tordesillas." "Memoria del Marqués de Grimaldi sobre límites con el Brasil 1776," AGN/M, catálogo de libros del Fondo Documental ex Archivo y Museo Histórico Nacional, libro 72, fol. 1R, and points 16, 26, 79–81; point 80. Additional copies of this manuscript can be found in AGN/BA, BN 180, Exp. 785, fols. 1r–31v, AGN/BA, BN 354, Exp. 6169; and BN 384, Exp. 6598; and in BRAH/M, 9-1663, Colección Mata Linares, vol. 8, fols. 59r–129r. The degree by which the parties believed that the issue was scientific rather than political is also described in Almeida, *A formação*, 66–68.

20. "Estableciéndose una línea divisoria de los terrenos que en este nuevo orbe debían poseer ambos monarcas, se fabricaban una valla y muro que hacían incontrastable la misma garantía de nuestro soberano y por la cual no sólo quedaban manifiestos los límites de una u otra dominación asunto que hasta entonces se había conceptuado inverificable sino que dirimidas todas las discordias que por más de 250 años habían agitado ambas cortes se cortaba al mismo tiempo la raíz de que habían brotado las funestas ramas de tantas disensiones y ponía sus vasallos a cubierto de que experimentasen en adelante los fatales efectos de la discordia." "Breve y exacto diseño de la justicia del tratado de límites celebrado entre las majestades Católica y Fidelísima en 13.1.1750," anonymous, 20.6.1760, AMN, 0115, Ms. 0124/004, fol. 152v. Maziel, *De la justicia*, 123–124, hoped that the Treaty of Madrid would end the conflict: "con esta soberana mira formaron acordes una línea divisoria que, dirigida por los más firmes y seguros linderos, manifestaba sin equívoco los territorios de una y otra jurisdicción." Others suggested that good treaties could provoke no disagreement regarding their implementation: "Realização e execução do tratado de outubro de 1777 entre Portugal e Espanha," undated and unsigned, AHM/DIV/2/1/1/27. See also Marquês de Lavradio to Martinho de Mello e Castro, Lisbon, 12.2.1781, AHU_ACL_CU_059, cx.3, d. 220; and Marqués de Valdelirios Pedro Cevallos, Buenos Aires, 12.5.1761, AGN/M, Archivos Particulares, Caja 333, Colección de documentos de Mario Falcao Espalter, Carpeta 4.

21. "Parecer a rainha de Castela sobre a Guerra dos limites da América," anonymous and undated, BPE, Cod. CXVI (2-12), no. 17, fol. 2v.

22. Natural borders would "sirvan perpetuamente de términos naturales fijos y permanentes pues los mojones, linderos y marcas y otras señales que se erijan serían siempre poco subsistentes y muy fáciles de destruir, derribar y mudar de los sitios donde se coloquen." "Dictamen de la junta formada ... para ... determinar los límites de los dominios de España y Portugal en la

América," BPR, Ms. II/2855, fols. 53r–77v, on fol. 75r. See also Luís António de Sousa to Martinho de Melo e Castro, Rio de Janeiro, 15.8.1775, AHU_ACL_CU_023-01, cx. 30, d. 2713; João Pereira Caldas to Martinho de Melo y Castro, Pará, 19.2.1776, AHU_ACL_CU_013, cx. 75, d. 6279; and Demetrio Ramos Pérez, "'Línea' y 'frontera': De Tordesillas a la borbonización delimitadora," *Boletín de la Real Academia de la Historia* 191(2) (1994): 197–214, on 208–210.

23. The treaty of 1750 was the only to refer directly to this question in the following terms: "El presente tratado será el único fundamento y regla que en adelante se deberá seguir para la división y límites de los dominios en toda la América y en Asia; y en su virtud quedará abolido cualquier derecho y acción que puedan alegar las dos Coronas, con motivo de la bula del Papa Alejandro VI, de feliz memoria, y de los tratados de Tordesillas, de Lisboa y Utrecht, de la escritura de venta otorgada en Zaragoza, y de otros cualesquiera tratados, convenciones y promesas; que todo ello, en cuanto trata de la línea de demarcación, será de ningún valor y efecto, como si no hubiera sido determinado en todo lo demás en su fuerza y vigor. Y en lo futuro no se tratará más de la citada línea, ni se podrá usar de este medio para la decisión de cualquiera dificultad que ocurra sobre los límites, sino únicamente de la frontera que se prescribe en los presentes artículos, como regla invariable y mucho menos sujeta a controversias." It further affirmed (art. 3) the primacy of actual occupation over Tordesillas: *Tratado firmado en Madrid, 13.1.1750* (Buenos Aires: Imprenta del Estado, 1836), art. 1, on 3–4.

24. "Su majestad católica no solamente volverá a su majestad portuguesa el territorio y Colonia del Sacramento . . . sino también cederá en su nombre y en el de todos sus descendientes, sucesores y herederos toda acción y derecho que su majestad católica pretendía tener sobre el dicho territorio y colonia . . . a fin que el dicho territorio y colonia queden comprendidos en los dominios de la corona de Portugal . . . como haciendo parte de sus estados, con todos los derechos de soberanía, de absoluto poder y de entero dominio, sin que su majestad católica, sus descendientes, sucesores y herederos puedan jamás turbar a su majestad portuguesa . . . en la dicha posesión." "Tratado de Paz y amistad ajustada entre España y el Portugal en Utrecht a 6.2.1715," reproduced in Cantillo, *Tratados*, 164–169, art. 6, on 166.

25. *Tratado preliminar sobre los límites de los estados pertenecientes a la corona de España y Portugal . . . San Lorenzo, 11.10.1777* (Buenos Aires: Imprenta del Estado, 1836), art. 21, on 13.

26. Consulta of the conselho ultramarino, 13.8.1717, reproduced in *Documentos históricos. Consultas do Conselho Ultramarino, Rio de Janeiro-Bahia, 1716–1721* (Rio de Janeiro: Biblioteca Nacional, 1952), vol. 97, 58–64, on 62; the protector of royal interests in the consejo de Indias on 21.7.1742, AGI, Quito 15, and Francisco Inocêncio de Souza Coutinho to the Marqués de Grimaldi, Madrid, 16.1.1776, AHN, Estado legajo 2842, apartado 1. These issues are also treated in "Memoria sobre la línea divisoria de los dominios de SM y del rey de Portugal en la América meridional," 30.5.1805, anonymous, BRAH/M, 9-1723, Colección Mata Linares, vol. LXVIII, fols. 697–714, on fols. 703r–v.

27. Fernán Núñez to Conde de Floridablanca, 19.11.1779, AHN, Estado 4443, no. 2; and Feliz Azara, "Memoria sobre el último tratado de límites con Portugal, celebrado en 1777," Madrid, 15.5.1805, AHN, Estado 3410-2.

28. Manuel Ferreira to Diogo de Mendonça Corte Real, Pará, 22.11.1753, AHU_ACL_CU_013, cx. 34, d. 3206 and 3292; Juan Francisco de Aguirre, "Narración histórica de la línea divisoria y juicio imparcial . . . ," Asunción del Paraguay, 17.5.1792, AHN, Estado 3385-1, especially on 5–23; and "Instrução que ao General João d'Albuquerque de Mello Pereira e Cáceres deixou a seu antecessor e Irmão Luiz d'Albuquerque de Mello Pereira e Cáceres (post 1788)," APMG, Livro C-03, doc. 03, fols. 53v–57v. See also Manuel Lucena Giraldo, "Ciencia para la frontera: Las expediciones de límites españolas, 1751–1804," *Cuadernos hispanoamericanos. Los complementarios* 2 (1988): 157–173; and Lucena Giraldo, *Laboratorio Tropical. La expedición de límites al Orinoco, 1750–1767* (Caracas: Monte Ávila, 1993).

29. Consulta of the Conselho Ultramarino, 13.8.1717, reproduced in *Documentos históricos*, vol. 97, 58–64, on 64; and "Memoria sobre la línea divisoria de los dominios de SM y del rey de Portugal en la América meridional," 30.5.1805, BRAH/M, 9-723, Colección Mata Linares, vol. LXVIII, fols. 697–714, on fol. 703. See also Demetrio Ramos Pérez, "Los criterios contrarios al tratado de Tordesillas en el siglo XVIII, determinantes de la necesidad de su anulación," in *El tratado de Tordesillas y su proyección*, vol. 2, 163–193.

30. Count of Bobadella to Pedro Cevallos, Rio de Janeiro, 29.2.1762, AGN/BA, IX.4.3.5; Marqués de Valdelirios to the Marqués de Grimaldi, Madrid, 11.3.1776, AHN, Estado 4371, p. 33; Luís de Vasconcelos e Sousa to Martinho de Melo e Castro, Rio de Janeiro, 21.7.1785, AHU_ACL_CU_059, cx.4, d. 239; Juan Carlos Bazán, "Examen jurídico y discurso historial sobre . . . los confines de los reinos de Castilla y Portugal . . . en el Río de la Plata," undated, BNE, Ms. 3042, fols. 42r–101v, on fol. 91r; the king to Andrés de Robles, Madrid, 25.7.1779, AMRE/MRE/R/G.1.2.1,G-46, Doc. 19, fols. 161–162v; and Carlos Morphy to Luis Antonio de Souza, Asunción, 18.9.1770, and his response, São Paolo, 17.7.1771, both in AGN/BA, IX.4.3.6. See also Eva Botella Ordinas, "¿Era inevitable 1808? Una revisión de la tradición de la decadencia española," *Revista de Occidente* 326–327 (2008): 47–68; and Iris Kantor, "Soberania e territorialidade colonial: Academia Real de História portuguesa e a América portuguesa (1720)," in Andréa Doré and Antonio Cesar de Almeida Santos, eds., *Temas setecentistas. Governos e populações no império português* (Curitiba: UFPR/SCHLA, 2009), 233–249, on 236–237.

31. On occasions the question of whose property these animals were could become highly contested. Such was the case, for example, in the River Plate, where the Portuguese, Spaniards, missionaries, and indigenous people often fought over the right to capture and use cattle that allegedly descended from their animals or had escaped their rightful owners: Helen Osório, "Guerra y comercio en la frontera hispano-portuguesa meridional— capitanía del Rio Grande—1790–1822," in Raúl O. Fradkin, ed., *Conflictos, negociaciones y comercio durante las guerras de independencia latinoamericanas* (Piscataway, NJ: Gorgias Press, 2010), 167–195, on 169 and 178–179. The importance of this "savage" cattle to the local economy was studied in Helen

Osório, *O império português no sul da América. Estancieiros, lavradores e comerciantes* (Porto Alegre: Universidade Federal do Rio Grande do Sul, 2007), 130–141. See also José María Ots Capdequí, *El régimen de la tierra en la América española durante el período colonial* (Ciudad Trujillo: Universidad de Santo Domingo, 1946), 25.

32. What contemporaries barely mentioned was the role of formal acts of possession. Though we know that such acts, greatly discussed and debated in the literature on the New World, were at times performed, they were mostly absent in the Spanish–Portuguese heartland. On formal possession taking, see Francisco Morales Padrón, "Descubrimiento y toma de posesión," *Anuario de estudios americanos* 12 (1955): 321–380; Arthur S. Keller, Oliver J. Lissitzyn, and Frederick J. Mann, *Creation of Rights of Sovereignty through Symbolic Acts, 1400–1800* (New York: Ams Press, 1967); and Patricia Seed, *Ceremonies of Possession in Europe's Conquest of the New World, 1492–1640* (Cambridge: Cambridge University Press, 1995).

33. Letter of Dionisio Martínez de la Vega, Madrid, 12.12.1736, AGI, Quito 374.

34. Consulta of the consejo de Indias, Madrid, 13.6.1715, AGI, Quito 103, doc. 4, fols. 15r–26v; and Solórzano y Pereira, *Política Indiana*, book 1, chapter 9, points 115 and 116, on 91.

35. Samuel von Pufendorf, *Of the Law of Nature and Nations*, trans. J. Spavan (London: L. Lichfield, 1710 [1672]), book 4, chapter 4, points 1, 2, and 4; and Karl Olivecrona, "Appropriation in the State of Nature: Locke on the Origins of Property," *Journal of the History of Ideas* 35(2) (1974): 211–230, on 216–217.

36. Hugo Grotius, *On the Law of War and Peace*, trans. A.C. Campbell (London: Boothroyd, 1814 [1625]), book 2, chapter 4, nos. 3 and 5. According to Carol M. Rose, "property" is not a "thing" but instead a relationship that is defined by what one can do and what others cannot. Not only does it involve communication, as Grotius and Pufendorf had already suggested, but it also implies a shared understanding of what certain things mean. It requires imagining a situation that cannot be seen or asserted otherwise and that is cultivated through storytelling, allegories, and metaphors that justify what property owners do as well as persuade others to accept it. As a result, at the heart of property is the need for constant persuasion of both self and others. Persuasion and imagination are culturally and communally bound and, as a result, so is property: Carol M. Rose, *Property and Persuasion: Essays on the History, Theory and Rhetoric of Ownership* (Boulder, CO: Westview Press, 1994), 5–6 and 269–270.

37. Francisco Bruno de Zavala to Jose Custodio de Sá y Jaria, Estancia de San Borja, 10.11.1768, AGN/BA, IX.4.3.6; "Memoria sobre la línea divisoria de los dominios de SM y del rey de Portugal en la América meridional," 30.5.1805, anonymous, BRAH/M, 9-1723, Colección Mata Linares, vol. LXVIII, fols. 697–714; and Juan Carlos Bazán, "Examen jurídico y discurso historial sobre . . . los confines de los reinos de Castilla y Portugal . . . en el Río de la Plata," undated, BNE, Ms. 3042, fols. 42r–101v, on fol. 93r.

38. "Reflexiones hechas a los artículos de la carta escrita por el gobernador de Chiquitos al Excmo. señor virrey," undated and unsigned, AGN/BA, BN 297, Exp. 4704.

39. Hernán Rodríguez Castelo, ed., *Diario del padre Fritz* (Quito: Studio 21, 1997), 86; "Noticias recibidas en Cádiz por el navío de registro nombrado Nuestra Señora de Begoña . . . el 12.8.1755," Biblioteca Universitaria de Valencia, Tomo de Varios, Var. 348 (10 bis), fol. 1v; Carlos Morphy to Francisco Bucareli y Ursua, Asunción 19.1.1768, and declaration of Gonzalo Gómez, Asunción de Paraguay, 10.4.1768, AGN/BA, IX.4.3.5, fols. 5r and 21r–22r; Lourenço Pereira da Costa to Fernando da Costa de Ataide Teive, Barcelos, 19.7.1765, APEP, Cod. 156, doc. 37; declaration of Antonio Franza, Iguatemi, 30.12.1767, in "Real orden para que los gobernadores del Tucumán y Paraguay estén a las de este gobierno," AGN/BA, IX.4.3.5, fol. 13r; interrogatory elaborated by Juan Francisco Gómez de Villajufre y de Arce on 26.5.1775, ANQ, FE 30, vol. 83, no. 3226, fols. 80r–275v; and Manuel Antonio Flores to Josef de Gálvez, Santa Fé, 28.2.1779, AHN, Estado 4554, no. 1. See also Ângela Domingues, *When the Amerindians Were Vassals: Power Equations in Northern Brazil (1750–1800)* (New Delhi: TransBooks, 2007), 197.

40. "A penas bastaría un tomo tan grande como el sobre dicho para escribir las ridiculeces de los títulos y pretextos cuando llegaban a ser descubiertos . . . unos de estos decían que la causa de su arribo a las tierras y partes del rey de Castilla era el haber a sus mujeres en no sé qué malos latines para ellos indeclinables que el uno le había quitado la vida a él y el otro a ella; y que por eso habían puesto tierra por medio y se pasaban a tierras y ciudades de castellanos. Otros con la misma falta de verdad decía que habiendo salido de su casa al monte, sin advertirlo se había internado en el tanto que queriendo después volver a salir no había sabido y que desatinado de andar de aquí para allá al cabo había ido a parar en los dominios de España cuando menos lo pensaba ni mucho menos lo deseaba o pretendía . . . otro explicaba que en el Brasil era monedero falso que tuvo que huir, o por envidia y mal querencia del gobernador . . . innumerables mentiras": "Papel del señor regente de Buenos Aires sobre la línea divisoria de los reinos de España y Portugal," BRAH, 9-1663, fols. 42–57, no. 1, fols. 47r–v. Somewhat similar is Martinho de Mello e Castro to Luis de Albuquerque de Mello Pereira e Cáceres, Lisbon, 13.8.1771, APMG, CMG-SG, Livro C-18, Estante-01, point 7.

41. Castelo, *Diario del padre Fritz*, 95; Francisco Barreto to Antonio Cattami, Rio Pardo 6.11.1764, and Lourenço Pereira da Costa to Fernando da Costa de Ataíde Teive, Barcelos, 19.7.1765, APEP, Cod. 156, doc. 37.

42. Carlos Morphy to Francisco Bucareli y Ursua, Asunción 19.1.1768, and declaration of Gonzalo Gómez, Asunción de Paraguay, 10.4.1768, AGN/BA, IX.4.3.5, fols. 5r and 21r–22r.

43. These claims appeared as early as the 1720s: "Requerimento dos oficiais do senado da câmara de São Paulo, ant. 26.10.1725," AHU_ACL-CU_023-01, cx. 7, d. 750. By the 1760s, the image of Paulistas as conquerors was already firmly established: copy of "Instruções dadas pelo secretário de Estado dos Negócios do Reino Conde de Oeiras ao governador e capitão—geral da capitania de São

Paulo no ofício de 26 de Janeiro de 1761," AHU_ACL_CU_023-01, cx. 23, d. 2221. Spanish local commanders were aware of these interpretations: letter of the governor of São Paulo to the governor of Paraguay (1769), AHU_ACL_ CU_023-01, cx. 26, d. 2458.

44. John Hemming, *Red Gold. The Conquest of the Brazilian Indians* (Southhampton: Camelot Press, 1978), 238–282; Richard M. Morse, ed., *The Bandeirantes: The Historical Role of the Brazilian Pathfinders* (New York: Alfred A. Knopf, 1965): John Manuel Monteiro, *Negros da terra. Índios e bandeirantes nas origens de São Paulo* (São Paulo: Companhia das Letras, 1994); and Alfredo Ellis (Júnior), *O bandeirismo paulista e o recúo do meridiano. Pesquizas nos documentos quinhentistas e setecentistas publicados pelos governos estadual e municipal* (São Paulo: Companhia Editora Nacional, 1934).

45. Cédula real of 12.9.1628, "relación de los agravios que hicieron algunos vecinos y moradores de la villa de San Pablo . . . saqueando las aldeas de los padres de la compañía de Jesús, Bahia, 10.10.1629," and consulta of the Consejo de Indias, 23.3.1638, all reproduced in *Campaña del Brasil*, vol. 1, 8–30. The argument that Paulistas were interested in slaves, not territory, was almost contemporary: "Memoria sobre la línea divisoria de los dominios de SM y del rey de Portugal en la América meridional, Mayo 30, 1805," BRAH/M, 9-1723, Colección Mata Linares vol. LXVIII, fols. 697–714. See also Synésio Sampaio Gomes, *Navegantes, Bandeirantes, Diplomatas* (Brasília: Fundação Alexandre de Gusmão, 1991), 58–59.

46. Spanish interlocutors argued this transformation, for example, in Vicente Aguilar y Jurado and Francisco Requena, "Historia de las demarcaciones de límites en la América entre los dominios de España y Portugal," 1777, AMN, Ms. 283, points 341–342 (also available in AHN, Estado 3410-2). See also Richard M. Morse, *From Community to Metropolis: A Biography of São Paulo, Brazil* (New York: Octagon Books, 1974), 15–17.

47. Carlos Morphy to Luis Antonio de Souza, Asunción, 18.9.1770, AGN/ BA, IX.4.3.6; Jose Monteiro de Noronha to Manoel Bernardo de Mello e Castro, Barcelos, 14.1.1762, APEP, Cod. 122, Doc. 1, fol. 1r; and "Instrução que ao General Luiz Albuquerque de Mello Pereira e Cáceres deixou seu Antecessor Luiz Pinto de Souza Coutinho," Vila Bela, 24.12.1772, APMG, Livro C-03, doc. 03, fols. 34v–53, on fol. 48v.

48. Two reports by Philippe Sturm, Boca del rio Tucutú, 18.9.1775 and 19.11.1775, APEP, Cod. 294, doc. 6, pp. 20–22, and APEP, Cod. 294, doc. 7, on 25–27; "Instrucción a que deben arreglarse los gobernadores de Mainas, Quijos y Macas para franquear los informes que se necesitan," Joseph Dibuja, 22.2.1770, ANQ, FE 30, vol. 83, no. 3226, fols. 80r–275v; Joachin Alos to Nicolás Arrendondo, Asunción, 13.6.1790, and the "Expediente sobre los medios de verificar el reconocimiento en el río Paraguay . . . 1790," both in AGN/BA, IX.4.4.1. See also Manoel Fernandes Thomaz, *Observações sobre o discurso que escreveu Manoel D'Almeida e Sousa em favor dos direitos dominicais da coroa, donatários e particulares* (Coimbra: Rek Imprensa da Universidade, 1814), 95–114.

49. Letter of Sebastián Félix de Mendiola, Asunción del Paraguay, 13.6.1682, AGI, Charcas 262, and the governor of Pará to the secretary of Navy and Overseas, Pará, 14.1.1777, AHU_ACL_CU_013, cx. 76, d. 6370.

50. Heather Flynn Roller, "River Guides, Geographical Informants, and Colonial Field Agents in the Portuguese Amazon," *Colonial Latin American Review* 21(1) (2012): 101–126.

51. Manuel Bernardo de Melo de Castro to Francisco Xavier de Mendonça Furtado, Pará, 5.5.1761, AHU_ACL_CU_013, cx. 49, d. 4445; Luís Pinto de Sousa Coutinho to Martinho de Melo e Castro, Vila Bela., 29.11.1771, AHU_ACL_CU_101, cx. 16, d. 957; Pedro de Cevallos to Juan de Pestana and Juan Manuel Campero, Buenos Aires, 15.6.1765 and 12.6.1765, AGN/BA, IX.4.3.5; the governor of Paraguay to Nicolás Arrendondo, Asunción, 8.2.1792, AHN, Estado 4555, no. 16; and the interim governor of Maranhão e Pará to Diogo de Mendonça Corte Real, Pará, 16.8.1755, AHU_ACL_CU_013, cx. 39, d. 3618.

52. Francisco José da Rocha to Marquês de Pombal, Colónia, 9.4.1776, AHU_ACL_CU_012, cx. 7, d. 618.

53. Francisco de Tejada, Seville, 16.8.1626, AGI, Charcas 260, fols. 47r–v, on fol. 47v.

54. Luís António de Sousa to Martinho de Melo e Castro, São Paulo, 28.8.1773, AHU_ACL_CU_023-01, cx. 29, d. 2636; José Custódio de Sá to Agustín Fernando de Pinedo, Iguatemi, 16.7.1775, included in the letter of José Custódio de Sá e Faria to Martinho Lopes de Saldanha, Iguatemi, 20.7.1775, AHU_ACL_CU_023-01, cx. 30, d. 2707.

55. Francisco Antonio de Argumosa Cevallos to the King, San Lorenzo de la Barra, 9.1.1739, in "Copia de la respuesta dada por el padre Agustín de Castañares . . . a Francisco Antonio de Argumosa," 12.12.1738, ANC/S, Jesuitas 197, pieza 9, fol. 60r, fol. 62r; and Luís Antônio de Sousa to Martinho de Melo e Castro, São Paulo, 28.8.1773, AHU_ACL_CU_023-01, cx. 29, d. 2636.

56. Letter of Carlos Morphy to Jose Custódio de Sá e Faria, Guacacainimi, 14.12.1765, AGN/BA, IX.4.3.5 (also published in *Campaña del Brasil*, vol. 3).

57. Luís António de Sousa to Carlos Morphy, AHU_ACL_CU_023-01, cx. 26, d. 2458; and João Henrique Bohn to Juan José de Vertiz, Rio Grande, 23.11.1775, AHU_ACL_CU_059, cx. 3, d. 192.

58. Dionisio Alcedo y Herrera, Quito, 28.5.1731, AGI, Quito 374.

59. "Auto de inquirição de testemunhas para justificação da posse e domínio do rio Branco pela coroa de Portugal," 1775," AHU_ACL_CU_013, cx. 74, d. 6261.

60. José Custódio de Sá e Faria to Martinho de Melo e Castro, São Paulo, 20.9.1774, AHU_ACL_CU_023-01, cx. 30, d. 2677.

61. The governor of Mato Grosso to the governor of Santa Cruz, Vila Bela, 22.10.1761, AGN/BA, IX.4.3.5; Lazaro de Ribera de Cayetano Pinto de Miranda Montenegro to the governor of Paraguay, Vila Bela, 30.6.1797, and the response of his Spanish counterpart, Asunción, 7.9.1797, AGN/BA, IX.4.4.1.

62. Already in 1672 the duque de Cadaval was arguing that by law each party could take possession of what it perhaps doubted was its own but which it also doubted belonged to the other: "Voto, parecer e consulta do duque de Cadaval sobre a nova povoação que se devia fazer no Brasil," Lisbon, 5.5.1672, cited in Virgínia Rau and Maria Fernanda Gomes da Silva, *Os manuscritos do arquivo da Casa de Cadaval respeitantes ao Brasil* (Coimbra: Universidade da

Coimbra, 1955), vol. 1, no. 304, on 233–234. To my great regret, I could not consult the original document as this archive, located in Muge, Portugal, is currently under the control of a colleague who refuses to share it with others. See also letter of the viceroy of Brazil to the Navy and Overseas secretary, Rio de Janeiro, 21.7.1785, AHU_ACL_CU_059, cx. 4, d. 239.

63. Tamar Herzog, "Conquista o integración: Los debates en torno a la inserción territorial (Madrid-México, siglo XVIII)," in Michel Bertrand and Natividad Planas, eds., *Les sociétés de frontière. De la Méditerranée à l'Atlantique* (xvie–xviiie siècle) (Madrid: Casa de Velázquez, 2011), 149–164.

64. Joseph Marcelino de Figueiredo to Joseph de Molina, Rio Grande de San Pedro, 26.7.1770, AGN/BA, IX.4.3.6; and Joseph de Molina to Juan Joseph de Vertiz, San Pedro, 24.2.1774, AGN/BA, IX.4.3.7.

65. The governor of São Paulo to the secretary of state, São Paulo, 13.2.1769, AHU_ACL_CU_023-01, cx. 26, d. 2458. See also "Noticias recibidas en Cádiz por el navío de registro nombrado Nuestra Señora de Begoña que retornó del Callao de Lima . . . el 12.8.1755," which reproduces an anonymous information signed Lima, 5.3.1753, Biblioteca Universitaria de Valencia, Tomo de Varios, Var. 348 (10 bis), fol. 2r.

66. Instructions given to governor João Pedro da Câmara by his predecessor Conde de Azambuja, Vila Bela, 8.1.1765, APMG, Livro C-03, doc. 03, fols. 28–34v, fols. 30–31, points 13 and 15–16.

67. Antônio de Sousa to Martinho de Melo e Castro, São Paulo, 21.4.1771, AHU_ACL_CU_023-01, cx. 27, d. 2551.

68. "Relatório do ex. governador da Nova Colónia António Pedro de Vasconcelos sobre as questões dos limites no Rio da Prata," Lisbon, post-1750, AHU_ACL_CU_012, cx. 5, d. 454. See also Joseph de Molina, Río Grande de San Pedro, 30.10.1773, AGN/BA, IX.15.7.15, fols. 277v–282v.

69. Herzog, "The Meaning of Territory"; and Juan Carlos Garavaglia, "Frontières des Amériques ibériques," *Annales HSS* 58(5) (2003): 1041–1048. See also Benton, *A Search for Sovereignty*. Missions also were "islands" in the middle of a "sea" of undominated land: Quarleri, *Rebelión y guerra*, 114.

70. Paulo César Possamai, *A vida Quotidiana na Colónia do Sacramento. Um bastião Português em terras do futuro Uruguai* (Lisbon: Livros do Brasil, 2006), 67–93; and Paulo César Possamai, "De núcleo de povoamento à praça de guerra: a Colônia do Sacramento de 1735 a 1777," *Topoi* 11(21) (2010): 23–36.

71. Memo summarizing the letter of the governor of Buenos Aires, studied at the Consejo de Indias in 1722, AGI, Charcas 264.

72. "Apuntamiento de secretaría," Madrid, 4.7.1716, AGI, Charcas 263; Bruno de Zavala, Buenos Aires, 30.3.1731, AGI, Charcas 265; "Parecer do Marquês de Fronteira sobre a paz com Castela," Lisbon, 31.7.1713, cited in Rau and Gomes da Silva, *Os manuscritos*, vol. 2, no. 177, 120; "carta dando parecer sobre a expedição do governador do Rio de Janeiro a Montevidéu e acerca dos direitos de Portugal sobre aquela região," 2.6.1724, AHU_ACL_CU_059, cx. 1, d. 2; and "Cuatro informes hechos al Excmo. señor don Pedro Cevallos virrey de las provincias del Río de la Plata," anónimo, undated, BPR, Ms. II/2844, fols. 1r–64r, fols. 46v–47r.

73. "Vivir con una constante vigilancia a eludir cualquiera intención que formen para dañar los dominios del rey sin confiar por la paz que subsiste entre las cortes de Madrid y Lisboa respecto a la experiencia que se tiene de que sin embargo de ella y en transgresión de los tratados han intentado apoderarse de estos dominios no tan sólo sin haber hecho declaración alguna, sino antes asegurando por escrito y de palabra observar la constante paz." Joseph de Molina, Río Grande de San Pedro, 30.10.1776, AGN/BA, IX.15.7.15, fol. 277v.

74. The correspondence between Jose Custódio de Sá e Jaria (Portuguese) and Carlos Morphy (Spanish) dated December 1765 and January 1766 is one such example: AGN/BA, IX.4.3.5. Others are the exchanges between the commanders of La Plata and Mato Grosso in 1768, AGI, Lima, 1054; and the commanders at the border of Colonia de Sacramento, for example, in AGN/BA, IX.4.3.7, no. 37.

75. Convention celebrated in the village of Río Grande de San Pedro on 6.8.1763 between Joseph de Molina and Antonio Pinto Carneiro, AGN/BA, IX.4.3.5. Agreement among military commanders could also refer to specific issues such as the return of slaves: "Convenio de 22.1.1770 entre el gobernador de Colonia de Sacramento y San Carlos sobre la restitución de esclavos," AGN/BA, IX.4.3.6. See also Renaud Morieux, "Diplomacy from Below and Belonging: Fishermen and Cross-Channel Relations in the Eighteenth Century," *Past and Present* 202 (2009): 125–183; and Morieux, *Une mer pour deux royaumes. La Manche, frontière franco-anglaise XVIIe–XVIIIe siècles* (Rennes: Presses Universitaires de Rennes, 2008).

76. Archival records include a notebook reproducing the correspondence between the military commanders in the years following one such agreement: "Libro de ordenes que se dieron en el cuartel de Río Grande a diferentes soldados," AGN/BA, IX.4.3.5. See also "Libro de correspondencia con los comandantes portugueses desde 9.1.1771 hasta 2.3.1774," AGN/BA, IX.4.3.6.

77. Joseph Marcelino de Figueiredo a Joseph de Molina, Río Grande de San Pedro, 26.7.1770, AGN/BA, IX.4.3.6. In other cases, too, Spanish and Portuguese commanders referred to these mutual agreements as true pacts that could not be ignored: Joseph de Molina, Río Grande de San Pedro, 18.2.1772, AGN/BA, IX.15.7.15.

78. Carlos Morphy to Custódio de Sá e Faria, Guacacainimi 14.12.1765, 23.12.1765, and 5.1.1766; and Jose Custódio de Sá e Faria to Carlos Morphy, 18.2.1765 and 30.12.1765; all in AGN/BA, IX.4.3.5.

79. José Custódio de Sá e Faria to Martim Lopes Lobo de Saldanha, Igatemi, 20.7.1775, AHU_ACL_CU_023-01, cx. 30, d. 2706. Difference in interpretation was evident in the way each side called what had transpired. The Spanish suggested that at stake were "puntos que deberá tratar el capitán don Manuel García Barazaval . . . con el brigadier Joseph Custódio de Sa y Faria." The Portuguese called it "convénio feito entre Agustín Fernando de Pinedo capitam geral da província do Paraguai e José Custódio de Sá e Faria."

80. On these categories, see Tamar Herzog, *Defining Nations: Immigrants and Citizens in Early Modern Spain and Spanish America* (New Haven, CT: Yale University Press, 2003). Although by the sixteenth and seventeenth centuries

vassalage was clearly distinguished from nativenness, de facto, at least in the Americas, they tended to be confused and conflated. More on this issue follows in the text.

81. Vicente Aguilar y Jurado and Francisco Requena, "Historia de las demarcaciones de límites en la América entre los dominios de España y Portugal," 1777, AMN, Ms. 283, points 310–311.

82. J.H. Elliott, "The Spanish Monarchy and the Kingdom of Portugal, 1580–1640," in Mark Greengrass, ed., *Conquest and Coalescence: The Shaping of the State in Early Modern Europe* (London: Edward Arnold, 1991), 48–67, on 48–52 and 63–65; Antonio Manuel Hespanha, "As Cortes e o reino. Da união à restauração," *Cuadernos de historia moderna* 11 (1991): 21–56; Rafael Valladares, *Portugal y la monarquía hispánica, 1580–1668* (Madrid: Arco Libros, 2002), 15; and Pedro Cardim, "La jornada de Portugal y las cortes de 1619," in José Martínez Millán and María Antonietta Visceglia, eds., *La monarquía de Felipe III. Los Reinos* (Madrid: Fundación Mapfre, 2008), vol. 4, 900–946, on 903, 911, and 917–918.

83. "Cierto no es fácil de saber cuál fue el pretexto (el fin bien lo conoció el mundo) de las armas que el rey don Felipe el prudente introdujo en este reino, porque sus historiadores o confusos o simulados no nos lo dan a entender. Y digo así; ¿si lo heredaba para que lo conquistó? ¿Si lo conquistó por qué afirma que lo heredaba? ¿Por qué quiere llamar conquista lo que no se defendió por armas? ¿Y por qué llamara derecho lo que no obedeció a las leyes? De esta misma ambigüedad nace sin falta la duda del autor, esa que le mueve a escribir que este reino fue conquistado solo en nombre y no el efecto." Francisco Manuel de Melo, *Ecco polytico responde en Portugal a la voz de Castilla y satisface a un papel anonymo ofrecido al rey don Felipe Quarto sobre los intereces de la corona lusitana* (Lisbon: Paulo Craesbeck,1645), BNC/STM, A-36-7 (22), fols. 6r–v.

84. "Las conquistas pertenecientes a estos reinos no ceden sino a portugueses y que cuando se tome algo con ayuda de otras . . . naciones se entregue luego a portugueses." "Papeles históricos portugueses y españoles," BL, ADD. Ms. 20846, fols. 65v–66r.

85. Arthur Cezar Ferreira Reis, *Limites e demarcações na Amazônia brasileira. A fronteira com as colônias Espanholas* (Belém: Secretaria de Estado da Cultura, 1993 [1948]), vol. 2, 14–15; Sebastião Pagano, "O Brasil e suas relações com a coroa de Espanha," *Revista do Instituto Histórico e Geográfico de São Paulo* 59 (1961): 215–232; Stuart B. Schwartz, "Luso-Spanish Relations in Habsburg Brazil, 1580–1640," *The Americas* 25(1) (1968): 33–48; Luiz Felipe de Seixas Corrêa, "O governo dos reis espanhóis em Portugal (1580–1640): Um período singular na formação do Brasil," *Revista do Instituto Histórico e Geográfico Brasileiro* 155(385) (1994): 732–748, on 741–742; and Nicholas Bomba, "The Hibernian Amazon: A Struggle for Sovereignty in the Portuguese Court, 1643–1648," *Journal of Early Modern History* 11(6) (2007): 447–474.

86. King Philip II to Conde de Estêvão de Faro, 5.3.1619, and to the governor of Pará Francisco Coelho de Carvalho, 26.9.1623, AHU_ACL_CU_ 009, cx. 1, d. 28, and AHU_ACL_CU-009, cx. 1, d. 60; and letter of the said governor to Antonio Moniz Barreiros, 27.11.1623, AHU_ACL_CU_ 009, cx. 1, d. 65.

87. "Memorial presentado en el real consejo de las Indias acerca del descubrimiento del rio de las Amazonas que se hizo en el año de 1636 por el padre Cristóbal de Acuña de la compañía de Jesús," AGI, Quito, 158, reproduced in Francisco de Figueroa and Cristóbal Acuña, *Informes de jesuitas en el Amazonas, 1600–1684* (Iquitos: Monumento Amazónica, 1986), 102–107; Alonso Pérez de Salazar to the king, Quito, 18.11.1638, conde de Chinchón to the king, Lima, 20.1.1639, and "Información del licenciado don Alonso Pérez de Salazar, presidente de Quito," Quito, 19.5.1639, all in BA, Cod. Ms.. 51-V-41, fols. 1r–4r, 13r–14v, and 21r–24v, respectively. The involvement of Portuguese authorities in the expedition is described in Jácome Raimundo de Noronha to Pedro Teixeira (post-1636), AHU_ACL_CU_009, cx. 1, d. 110; and consulta of 29.8.1637, AHU_ACL_CU_009, cx. 1, d. 114, fol. 3r. See also M. Jiménez de la Espada, "Viaje del capitán Pedro Teixeira aguas arriba del río de las Amazonas (1638–1639)," *Boletín de la Sociedad Geográfica de Madrid* 9 (1880): 209–231; Bernardo Pereira de Berredo, *Annaes históricos do estado do Maranhão* (Iquitos: Monumenta Amazónica, 1989), 288–293 and 296–323; Tamar Herzog, "La política espacial y las tácticas de conquista: Las 'Ordenanzas de descubrimiento, nueva población y pacificación de las Indias' y su legado (siglos XVI–XVII)," in José Román Gutiérrez, Enrique Martínez Ruiz, and Jaime González Rodríguez, eds., *Felipe II y el oficio de rey: La fragua de un imperio* (Madrid: Sociedad Estatal para la Conmemoración de los Centenarios de Felipe II y de Carlos V, 2001), 293–303; and Herzog, "La Política espacial y su aplicación: Las 'Ordenanzas de descubrimiento, nueva población y pacificación de las Indias' y las tácticas de conquista (siglos XVI–XVII)," in *Actas del XI congreso internacional de Ahila (Liverpool 17–22 de septiembre de 1996)* (Liverpool: Ahila—University of Liverpool, 1998), vol. 1, 30–47.

88. "Auto da posse do Rio do Ouro, no Estado de Maranhão, pelo capitão-mor Pedro Teixeira no ano de 1639," Pará, 26.8.1639, GTT, II, 11–17, vol. 1, no. 606, on 935–938. Its Spanish translation can be found in AGI, Quito 158. It was reproduced in Figueroa and Acuña, *Informes de jesuitas*, 137–141. An English translation is available in George Edmundson, "Introduction," in *Journal of the Travels and Labours of Father Samuel Fritz in the River of the Amazon between 1686 and 1724* (London: Hakluyt Society, 1922), series II, vol. 51, 30–43, on 34–35. In popular imagination, Teixeira remains one of the most important conquerors of the Amazon: see, for example, Anete Costa Ferreira, *A expedição de Pedro Teixeira. A sua importância para Portugal e o futuro da Amazônia* (Lisbon: Ésquilo, 2000), 19–20; and Reis, *A limites e demarcações*, vol. 2, 12.

89. "Ofício respondendo a pretensão dos padres castelhanos em ampliar os seus domínios na fronteira do Grão Pará," Belém, 28.11.1737, AHU_ACL_CU_013, cx. 20, d. 1920.

90. Juan and Ulloa, *Disertación histórica*, 128–131 and 145–147; letter of Juan Bautista Julián to the governor of Pará, Laguna, 8.9.1732; information supplied by Pablo Maroni to the president of the *audiencia of* Quito on 13.6.1733; by Nieto Polo, procurator of the Jesuits in Madrid, on 30.8.1741; and by Joseph María Maugeri, Jesuit, Madrid, 30.8.1741, all in AGI, Quito 158.

91. The realization was contemporary: "Dissertation qui détermine tant géographiquement que par les traites faits entre la couronne de Portugal et

celle d'Espagne quels sont les limites de leurs domination en Amérique, c'est à dire du côté de la rivière de la Plata," undated (c. 1740?) and unsigned (Luis de Cunha?), ADC/L, Serie Azul, Ms. 19, fols. 162r–179r, on 164v–165r.

92. Cristóbal de Acuña, "Memorial que dió el padre Cristóbal de Acuña...," in "Expediente del Gran Pará 1615/1740–1754," AGI, Quito 158, fols. 43r–47r, also reproduced in Figueroa and Acuña, *Informes de jesuitas*, 43–44; and Pereira de Berredo, *Annaes históricos*, 299–302. In 1648 the viceroy of Peru referred to this route as "a new very harmful road" *(nuevo perniciosísimo camino)*: "Relación del estado en que dejó el reyno del Perú el Excmo. Sr. Marqués de Mancera (Lima, 8.10.1648)," reproduced in *Memorias de los virreyes del Perú*, ed. José Toribio Polo (Lima: Imprenta del estado, 1899), 1–66, on 61–63.

93. Consulta of 31.1.1617, AGI, Charcas 260, fols. 830r–v, on fol. 830r. Also compare to "Testimonio de autos sobre la arribada de franceses en Cartagena de Indias, procedentes del río Marañón 1615–1616," in "Expediente del Gran Pará 1615/1740–1754," AGI, Quito 158, on 1–34.

94. Alonso Pérez de Salazar to the king, Quito, 18.11.1638, BA, Cód. 51-V-41, fols. 1r–4r, fols. 2r–v, also reproduced in Lucinda Saragoça, *Da "feliz Lusitânia" aos confins da Amazónia (1615–62)* (Lisbon: Edições Cosmos, 2000), 302–306; and "Relación del estado en que dejó el reyno del Perú el Excmo. Sr. Marqués de Mancera (Lima, 8.10.1648)," reproduced in *Memorias de los virreyes del Perú*, 1–66, on 63.

95. "Relación del estado en que el conde de Chinchón deja del gobierno del Perú al señor virrey Conde de Mancera (Lima 26.1.1640)," in *Relaciones de los virreyes y audiencias que han gobernado el Perú* (Madrid: Imprenta y Estereotipía de M. Rivadeneyra, 1871), vol. 2, 65–128, on 113–114. Linking concern over Portuguese presence with preoccupation for the predominance of individuals who were "poco seguros en las cosas de la fe católica y judaizantes" was also cédula dated 17.10.1602, reproduced in Manuel Josef de Ayala, *Diccionario de gobierno y legislación de Indias*, ed. Marta Milagros del Vas Mingo (Madrid: Ediciones de Cultura Hispánica, 1988), no. 4, on 114; and "Relación de Luis de Velasco, virrey del Perú dada a su sucesor el Conde de Monterrey sobre el estado del mismo," Lima, 28.11.1604, in *Relaciones de los virreyes y audiencias*, vol. 2, 3–28, on 19. The activities of Teixeira against the Dutch were described in Mathias C. Kiemen, *The Indian Policy of Portugal in the Amazon Region, 1614–1693* (New York: Octagon Books, 1973), 24; and Pereira de Berredo, *Annaes históricos*, 292.

96. Consulta del consejo de Indias, Madrid, 28.1.1640, BA, Cod. 51-V-41, fols. 25r–26v, also reproduced in Saragoça, *Da "feliz Lusitânia,"* 320–322.

97. "Memorial que dio el padre Cristóbal de Acuña," AGI, Quito 158, fols. 43r–47r; and "Os padres Cristóvão d'Acuña e André d'Artieda requerem aos oficiais da armada . . . que não alonguem mais a sua permanência no Rio Negro," 1639," reproduced in Saragoça, *Da "feliz Lusitânia,"* 349–351.

98. The expedition (also) unleashed a struggle over which order would gain jurisdiction over the territory, the Jesuits claiming exclusivity by virtue of discovery and occupation: "Capítulo tercero: Misión de los Omaguas, Jurimaguas, Aysuares . . . y otras naciones desde Napo hasta el Rio Negro," undated and unsigned document, BPE, Cod. CXV (2-15), no. 10.

99. "Regimento do governador do Maranhão Jácome Raimundo de Noronha para o capitão-mor do Pará Pedro Teixeira" (post-1636), "Pedro Teixeira to the king, Maranhão, 29.5.1637, and consulta of the conselho ultramarino, before 29.8.1637, AHU_ACL_CU_009, cx. 1, d. 110, 112, and 114; and "O geral Pedro Teixeira faz uma descrição detalhada sobre o que encontrou no decurso de sua expedição, Quito, 2.1.1639," BA, Ms. 51-IX-28, fols. 5r–8, also reproduced in Saragoça, Da "feliz Lusitânia," 309–312. See also Maurício de Heriarte, "Descrição do Estado do Maranhão, Pará, Corupá e rio das Amazonas 1662–1667," reproduced in Francisco Adolfo de Varnhagen, História Geral do Brasil, antes da sua separação e independência de Portugal (São Paulo: Melhoramentos, 1975 [1854–1857]), vol. 3, 171–190; Sérgio Buarque de Holanda, Visão do Paraíso. Os motivos edênicos no descobrimento e colonização do Brasil (São Paulo: Companhia das Letras, 2010 [1959]), 160; and Heidi V. Scott, Contested Territory: Mapping Peru in the Sixteenth and Seventeenth Century (Notre Dame, IN: University of Notre Dame Press, 2009), 122–124.

100. Report of Phelipe de Mattos Cotrim, member of the expedition, Lisbon, 24.10.1645, cited in Rau and Gomes da Silva, Os manuscritos, vol. 1, no. 80, 40–41; and consulta of the conselho ultramarino, Lisbon, 27.8.1645, AHU_ACL_CU_013, cx. 1, d. 58.

101. Petition of Pedro de la Rua, Lisbon, 23.9.1645, annexed to the consulta of the conselho ultramarino, Lisbon, 24.6.1646, AHU_ACL_CU_013, cx. 1, d. 61.

102. "Relación del estado en que dejó el reyno del Perú el Excmo. Sr. Marqués de Mancera (Lima, 8.10.1648)," in Memorias de los virreyes del Perú, 1–66, on 63.

103. João Felipe Bettendorff, Crônica da missão dos padres da Companhia de Jesus no estado do Maranhão (Belém: Fundação Cultural do Pará Tancredo Neves, 1990 [c. 1698]), 50–51 and 59–60.

104. Manuel-Maria Wermers, "O estabelecimento das missões carmelitanas no Rio Negro e nos Solimões (1695–1711)," V Colóquio Internacional de Estudos Luso-Brasileiros (Actas) (Coimbra: Comissão Organizadora do Colóquio 1965), vol.2, 527–572, 540.

105. José Monteiro de Noronha, Roteiro da viagem da cidade do Pará até as últimas colônias do sertão da província (1768), ed. Antonio Porro (São Paulo: USP, 2006), points 104–110, on 50–51.

106. Tamar Herzog, "Una Monarquía, dos territorios: La frontera entre españoles y portugueses, España y Portugal durante (y después) de la Unión," in Carlos Martínez Shaw and José Antonio Martínez Torres, eds., España y Portugal en el mundo (1580–1668) (Madrid: Polifemo, forthcoming).

107. Herzog, Defining Nations, 64–118.

108. Initially, it was unclear whether natives of the crown of Aragon were included among natives of Spain: Demetrio Ramos Pérez, "La aparente exclusión de los aragoneses de las Indias: Una medida de alta política de don Fernando el Católico," Estudios (1976): 7–40; Juan María Morales Álvarez, Los extranjeros con carta de naturaleza de las Indias durante la segunda mitad del siglo XVIII (Caracas: Academia Nacional de la Historia, 1980), 22–24; and Joseph de Veitia Linaje, Norte de la contratación de las Indias occidentales (Buenos Aires: Comisión Argen-

tina de Fomento Interamericano, 1945 [1672]), 328–329. The Portuguese, who also attempted a similar inclusion, were nevertheless rejected: *Recopilación de Indias*, law 28, title 27, book 9, defined natives of Spain as including "natives of our kingdoms of Castile, León, Aragon, Valencia, Catalonia, Navarra, Mallorca and Menorca" but not Portugal. See also Tamar Herzog, "Can You Tell a Spaniard When You See One? 'Us' and 'Them' in the Early Modern Iberian Atlantic," in Pedro Cardim, Tamar Herzog, José Javier Ruiz Ibáñez, and Gaetano Sabatini, eds., *Polycentric Monarchies: How Did Early Modern Spain and Portugal Achieve and Maintain a Global Hegemony?* (Brighton: Sussex Academic Press, 2012), 147–161.

109. "Siendo Portugal parte de España, y los Portugueses tan naturales y tan verdaderos españoles y tan naturales y leales vasallos de su majestad, no los deben en el Perú y más partes de las Indias occidentales los jueces ejecutores interpretar ni incluir en la cédula real de los extranjeros" and "¿no son, señor, los portugueses tan españoles como los navarros, provincianos de Guipúzcoa, vizcaínos, aragoneses, valencianos y catalanes? Que aunque estos dichos son españoles, como nosotros los portugueses, también como nosotros no son castellanos. ¿Son por ventura los dichos más españoles y más leales vasallos de vuestra majestad que los portugueses?" Lourenço de Mendonça, "Suplicación a su Majestad Católica . . . en defensa de los portugueses," Madrid, 1630, fols. 1, 8v–11r, 12v, 16v–18v, and 57v. This text was studied in Pedro Cardim, "'Todos los que no son de Castilla son yguales.' El estatuto de Portugal en la monarquía española en el tiempo de Olivares," *Pedrables* 28 (2008): 521–552; and in Pedro Cardim, "De la nación a la lealtad al rey. Lourenço de Mendonça y el estatuto de los portugueses en la Monarquía Española de la década de 1630," in David González Cruz, ed., *Extranjeros y enemigos en Iberoamérica. La visión del otro. Del imperio español a la Guerra de Independencia* (Madrid: Sílex, 2010), 57–88. I would like to thank Pedro Cardim for facilitating access to a copy of this document. See also Maria da Graça A. Mateus Ventura, *Portugueses no Peru ao tempo da união ibérica. Mobilidade, cumplicidades e vivências* (Lisbon: Imprensa Nacional-Casa da Moeda, 2005), vol. 1, 72–73, 76–77, and 242–269.

110. "Españoles portugueses," "españoles castellanos," and "españoles aragoneses": Lourenço de Mendonça, "Suplicación a su Majestad Católica del Rey Nuestro Señor, que Dios guarde, ante sus reales consejos de Portugal y de las Indias en defensa de los portugueses," Madrid, 1630, fols. 16v–17r and 21v. On fol. 57v, Lourenço de Mendonça suggested that "la unión de los reinos y monarquía de vuestra majestad, que principalmente depende de estas tres coronas de Castilla, Portugal y Aragón unidas y hermandades, que son la cuerda de tres hijos, que dice el espíritu santo que teniéndolos juntos y bien unidos, es dificultosa de romper." Together he calls these three crowns "España."

111. Diego Marques on 17.5.1629 and Juan de Sosa Brito on 14.10.1676, according to AGI, IG, leg. 1536. See also Yvone Dias Avelino, "A naturalização de mercaderes-banqueiros portugueses para o exercício do comércio na América dos Áustrias," *Revista de História* (São Paolo) 42(86) (1971): 389–415; Ventura, *Portugueses no Peru*, vol. 1, 72–73, 76–77, and 242–269; Jean-Frédéric Schaub, *Portugal na Monarquia Hispânica (1580–1640)* (Lisbon: Livros Horizonte,

2001), 46–48; and Tamar Herzog, "Nosotros y ellos: Españoles, americanos y extranjeros en Buenos Aires a finales de la época colonial," in José I. Fortea and Juan E. Gelabert, eds., *Ciudades en conflicto* (Valladolid: Junta de Castilla y León, 2008), 241–257.

112. Parecer del Obispo gobernador del Consejo de Estado, Madrid, 3.3.1683, BPR, Ms. II/2760, fols. 250r–251v.

113. "Instrucción que han de observar los virreyes, presidentes, gobernadores . . . con los naturales del reino de Portugal formada por el licenciado don Manuel de Gamboa y Alsedo fiscal del Consejo de Indias con el motivo de la presente guerra . . . publicada en 30.4.1704," AGI, Charcas 263.

114. "Tan unos en el trato, en la lengua y comercio que si no es la malicia nadie puede hallar vanidad de nación, bando ni parcialidad." Letter of the bishop of Coria to "Portuguese governors," Coria, 13.4.1580, ADC/L, Serie Azul, Ms. 474, pp. 11–32, 13–14.

115. "Cristianos contra cristianos, católicos contra católicos, españoles contra españoles." Letter of Pedro de Rivadeneira to Gaspar de Quiroga, Toledo, 16.2.1580, reproduced in Vicente de la Fuente, ed., *Obras escogidas del padre Pedro de Rivadeneira* (Madrid: M. Rivadeneyra, 1868), 589.

116. Pedro Barbosa de Luna, *Memorial de la preferencia que hace el reino de Portugal y su consejo al de Aragón y de las dos Sicilias* (Lisbon: Geraldo de Vinha, 1627), fol. 14v; and Manuel Faria e Sousa, *Epítome de las historias portuguesas* (Madrid: Francisco Martínez, 1628).

117. This source is cited by Pedro Cardim, *Portugal Unido y separado. Felipe II, la unión de territorios y el debate sobre la condición política del reino de Portugal* (Valladolid: Instituto Simancas, 2014), 204.

118. "Pues no se ha visto en ningún tiempo desde el principio del mundo [a España] tan poblada, tan rica, tan adornada de suntuosos edificios, ricos templos e ilustrada de hombres doctos, en todo género de letras, artes y oficios mecánicos que son los que ennoblecen una provincia y reino y así con razón se pueden llamar los reyes philippos, los más dichosos y bien afortunados de cuantos ha habido en España." Martin Carrillo, *Annales y memorias cronológicas. Contienen las cosas más notables así eclesiásticas como seculares sucedidas en el mundo señaladamente en España desde su principio y población hasta el año 1620* (Huesca: Viuda de Juan Pérez Valdivieso, 1622), fol. 415r. See also fol. 414v.

119. According to this plan, Portugal would also be submitted to Spain in matters of foreign policy, mainly war and peace, and specific provisions were made to subject Brazil to Spain, not to Portugal. Natives of Spain could traffic in Asia as if they were Portuguese, ecclesiastical benefices in Portugal would be presented alternatively by the Portuguese and Spanish king, the Inquisition in Madrid could study appeals against the decisions of inquisitorial courts in Portugal, and the last appeal of all sentences involving natives of the two kingdoms would be adjudicated by the Spanish king, thereafter instituted as emperor of Hispania: "Proposiciones de ajustes entre Castilla y Portugal en favor del duque de Braganza," undated and unsigned document, BRAH, Ms. 9-1070, fols. 209r–210v. The Spanish king as emperor is mentioned on fol. 210v.

120. Consulta of the consejo de estado, 23.12.1665, BNE, Ms. 12020, fols. 8r–16v.

121. "Um dos mais notáveis reinos de Espanha": Antonio Carvalho da Costa, *Corografia portuguesa e desripçam topografica do famoso reyno de Portugal* (Lisbon: Valentim da Costa Deslandes. 1706), vol.1, 1; and Pedro Cermeño to the Conde de Aranda, 13.7.1768, AHN, Estado leg. 4389, no. 6.

122. "Razões contra a união que se pretende fazer do reino de Portugal ao de Castela e suas responsas em junho de 1638," BPE, Cod. CIX (1-13), no. 3; Ana Isabel López-Salazar Codes, "La cuestión de la naturaleza de los ministros del santo oficio portugués. De las disposiciones legislativas a la práctica cotidiana," *Hispania. Revista española de historia* 71(239) (2011): 691–714, cites on 695 an opinion favoring such unification and on 696–698 the contrary view that argues for a separation.

123. Cardim, *Portugal Unido y separado*.

124. "Parecer do bispo capelão-mor sobre a mercês a fazer . . . a o Marquês de Montalvão," Lisbon, 1.11.1649, cited in Rau and Gomes da Silva, *Os manuscritos*, vol. 1, no. 144, 86. See also Charles R. Boxer, *Salvador de Sá and the Struggle for Brazil and Angola, 1602–1686* (London: University of London, 1952), 144–152; Rafael Valladares Ramírez, "El Brasil y las Indias españolas durante la sublevación de Portugal (1640–1668)," *Cuadernos de historia moderna* 14 (1993): 151–172, on 155–161 and 171; Rodrigo Bentes Monteiro, *O rei no espelho. A monarquia portuguesa e a colonização da América, 1640–1720* (São Paulo: Editora Hucitec, 2002), 33–72; Edval de Souza Barros, *Negócios de tanta importância. O conselho ultramarino e a disputa pela condução da guerra no Atlântico e no Índico (1643–1661)* (Lisbon: Universidade Nova de Lisboa, 2008), 96–103; Stuart B. Schwartz, "The Voyage of the Vassals: Royal Power, Noble Obligations, and Merchant Capital before the Portuguese Restoration of Independence," *American Historical Review* 96(3) (1991): 735–762; and Antonio Terasa Lozano, "De la raya de Portugal a la frontera de guerra: Los Mascarenhas y las prácticas nobiliarias de supervivencia política durante la guerra de la Restauração," in Bartolomé Yun Casalilla, ed., *Las redes del imperio. Élites sociales en la articulación de la Monarquía Hispánica, 1492–1714* (Madrid: Marcial Pons, 2009), 227–253.

125. "Manifiesto en que se justifica no haber faltado a su obligación don Fernando Tellez de Faro aunque estuvo en Portugal desde que se levantó aquel reino hacia el año de 1659," BNE, Ms. 8686, fols. 23r–31v.

126. David Birmingham, *A Concise History of Portugal* (Cambridge: Cambridge University Press, 1993), 47–48; Valladares, *Portugal y la monarquía hispánica*, 42; and Leonor Freire Costa and Mafalda Soares da Cunha, *D. João IV* (Lisbon: Círculo de leitores, 2006), 105.

127. Consulta of the Consejo de Indias, 8.5.1680, in "Expediente sobre el desalojo de los portugueses . . . y demarcación de las dos coronas por lo tocante a la Colonia del Sacramento años de 1687 a 1680," AGI, Charcas 260.

128. "Aquel tiempo era muy bueno para no perder los parientes de Portugal y para asegurar nuestros estados y excusarnos de las vejaciones y tributos que pagaríamos." This episode generated much correspondence as well as interest. See, for example, "Copia del papel que dio el Duque de Medina Sidonia en 21.9.1641 y lo que Su Majestad le respondió," AHN, Estado 3028, Exp. 18.

129. "Deseando evitar el derramiento de sangre cristiana, muertes, robos, destrucciones de lugares y haciendas y los más daños y pérdidas que la guerra trae consigo y liberar y aliviar las dichas ciudades, villas y lugares y sus moradores de ellos de los grandes arruinaciones, tiranías, tributos, pechos e imposiciones . . . con que son apremiados y destruidos tratan los más como esclavos que como vasallos." King João to the inhabitants of Castile, Lisbon, 9.7.1641, BNE, Ms 721, fols. 67r–68r. João promised that "queriendo ellos gozar de la paz que hasta ahora hubo debajo de mi dominio y amparo los recibiré por naturales portugueses . . . y no se darán oficios, beneficios y jurisdicciones, encomiendas o rentas alguna en las dichas ciudades, villas y lugares de Castilla y León sino a los naturales de ellos sin que se pueda dar por título alguno a portugueses sino los castellanos y con estos admitidos a todos las honras, dignidades, oficios, beneficios, encomiendas de estos reinos de Portugal promiscuamente con los portugueses naturales de ellos y cesarán las aduanas y derechos de los puestos secos y mojados de reino a reino de los lugares que tomaren mi voz y estuviesen a mi obediencia."

130. Rafael Valladares, "De ignorancia y lealtad. Portugueses en Madrid, 1640–1670," *Torre de los Lujanes* 37 (1998): 133–150; and Fernando Bouza Álvarez, "Entre dos reinos, una patria rebelde. *Fidalgos* portugueses en la monarquía hispánica después de 1640," *Estudis* 20 (1994): 83–103, on 85–86 and 88–90.

131. Costa and Cunha, *D. João IV*, 110 and 113–114; Mafalda de Noronha Wagner, *A casa de Vila Real e a conspiração de 1641 contra D. João IV* (Lisbon: Edições Colibrí, 2003); and Maria Paula Marçal Lourenço, *A casa e o estado do Infantado, 1654–1706* (Lisbon: Universidade de Lisboa, 1995), 30–32.

132. "Discurso que hizo el Conde-Duque de Olivares a portugueses que se hallaron en la corte al tiempo de la sublevación de Portugal 12.12.1640," BRAH/M, Ms. 9-1070, fols. 213r–214r.

133. Valladares, *Portugal y la monarquía hispánica*, 53–54.

134. Ibid., 42.

135. Aureliano Leite, "Amador Bueno, sua vida e, em especial, o seu papel dentro da capitania de S. Vicente do estado do Brasil, nos acontecimentos da restauração da monarquia portuguesa"; and Afonso de E. Taunay, "A reintegração de S. Paulo no império colonial português, em 1641 e o episódio de Amador Bueno da Ribeira"; both in *Congresso do mundo português* (Lisbon: Comissão Executiva dos Centenários, 1940), vol. 7, part 2, 549–567, and vol. 9, part 1, 265–288; and José Carlos Vilardaga, "São Paulo na órbita do império dos Filipes: Conexões castelhanas de uma vila da América portuguesa durante a união Ibérica (1580–1640)" (Ph.D. diss., Universidade de São Paulo, 2010), 352–363.

136. Guida Marques, "L'invention du Brésil entre deux monarchies. Gouvernement et pratiques politiques de l'Amérique portugaise dans l'union ibérique (1580–1640)" (Ph.D. diss., École des Hautes Études en Sciences Sociales, 2009), 470–471.

137. "Aquí todo es estar suspensos, entre el recelo y la esperanza." The Marqués de Mancera to the king, Lima, 22.7.1641, cited in Fernando Serrano Mangas, *La encrucijada portuguesa. Esplendor y quiebra de la unión ibérica en las*

Indias de Castilla (1600–1668) (Badajoz: Diputación Provincial de Badajoz, 1994), 95.

138. Consulta of 27.12.1640, AGI, IG 761. Somewhat similar were two royal cédulas dated 7.1.1641, AMQ, "Colección de Cédulas Reales, 1601–1660," 316–318. Popular sentiment, however, may have ruled otherwise: Stuart Schwartz, "Panic in the Indies: The Portuguese Threat to the Spanish Empire, 1640–1650," *Colonial Latin American Review* 2(1–2) (1993): 165–187.

139. "Relación del estado en que dejó el reyno del Perú el Excmo. Sr. Marqués de Mancera (Lima, 8.10.1648)," in *Memorias de los virreyes del Perú*, 1–66, on 18 and 60; and "Relación del estado en que deja el gobierno destos reynos del Pirú el Conde de Salvatierra, Marqués de Sobroso, al Excmo. señor virrey, Conde de Alva de Aliste y Villaflor," in *Memorias de los virreyes del Perú*, 1–75, on 45; "Autos contra don Domingo Veiga y Vaca, Portugués. . . . Año de 1652–año de 1658," letter of viceroy Conde de Alva Aliste to the king, dated Lima 26.8.1658, both in AGI, Lima 60, no. 40, and royal cédula to the audiencia de Quito, 5.10.1648, AGI, Quito 209, lib. 3. The disunion with Portugal also explained and justified the persecution of many Portuguese who were accused of crypto-Judaism by the Inquisition: Harry E. Cross, "Commerce and Orthodoxy: A Spanish Response to Portuguese Commercial Penetration in the Viceroyalty of Peru, 1580–1640," *The Americas* 35(2) (1978): 151–167; Stanley M. Hordes, "The Inquisition as Economic and Political Agent: The Campaign of the Mexican Holy Office against the Crypto-Jews in the Mid-Seventeenth Century," *The Americas* 39(1) (1982): 23–38; and Alonso W. Quiroz, "The Expropriation of Portuguese New Christians in Spanish America, 1635–1649," *Ibero-Amerikanisches Archiv*, new series, 11(4) (1985): 407–465.

140. "Los portugueses que hoy se hallan en la isla los más naturalizados por vuestra majestad son tan afectos a su real servicio, y aún los de menos raíces que aquí se hallan de paraje, que no ha parecido convenir proceder con ellos con desconfianza, siendo bien no hacerle a vuestra majestad de vasallos enemigos." The governor to the king, San Juan de Puerto Rico, 22.6.1641, AGI, Santo Domingo, 156, cited in Serrano Mangas, *La encrucijada portuguesa*, 138. See also 139.

141. "Relación del estado en que dejó el reyno del Perú el Excmo. Sr. Marqués de Mancera (Lima, 8.10.1648)," in *Memorias de los virreyes del Perú*, 1–66, on 18 and 60. See also Serrano Mangas, *La encrucijada portuguesa*, 95.

142. "No se aborrece la nación, sino la culpa y que sólo se trata de prevenir y preservar el riesgo que puede haber estando junta tanta gente"; cited in Serrano Mangas, *La encrucijada portuguesa*, 142. See also 144.

143. "Son dichos portugueses afectos a su nación y no a vuestra majestad ni a los castellanos." They were "enemies inside home" *(enemigos dentro de casa)*: Pedro Fernández de Castro y Velasco to the Consejo de Indias, Buenos Aires, 18.2.1683, AGI, Charcas 261, fols. 283r–4v, on fols. 283r–v.

144. Town council meeting of 24.11.1631, in *Acuerdos del extinguido cabildo de Buenos Aires* (Buenos Aires: Archivo General de la Nación, 1909), vol. 7, books 4–5, 283–287. See also R. de Lafuente Machain, *Los portugueses en Buenos Aires (siglo XVII)* (Madrid: Tipología de Archivos, 1931), 106–107; Jorge Daniel Gelman, "Cabildo y élite local: El caso de Buenos Aires en el siglo XVII," *Re-*

vista latinoamericana de historia económica y social 6(2) (1985): 3–20, 4; and Herzog, "Nosotros y ellos." Social and family networks linking individuals in Portuguese and Spanish America were also described in Vilardaga, "São Paulo," 347–349.

145. "Manifiesto en que se justifica no haber faltado a su obligación don Fernando Tellez de Faro aunque estuvo en Portugal desde que se levantó aquel reino hacia el año de 1659," 6.6.1659, BNE, Ms. 8686, fols. 23r–31v. See also Costa and Cunha, *D. João IV*, 105.

146. Terasa Lozano, "De la raya de Portugal."

147. This citation appears in his undated "Relación de servicios," currently found in ACEDAL. I would like to thank the Duque de Abrantes for sending me a copy. The hope that the rebellion would be short-lived was clear in the count's petition to pay the *media-anata* on the nobility title bestowed on his first-born "when he will recuperate these properties" found in Portugal: "Grandeza y títulos, Linares, condado de," 13.4.1643, and "Carta de privilegio del rey Felipe IV," Madrid, 28.9.1666, both in ACEDAL.

148. Prince Pedro to Dinis de Melo de Castro, Lisbon, 2.3.1668, BA, 51-VI-12, fol. 173; and Jorge Penim de Freitas, *O combatente durante a guerra da restauração. Vivência e comportamentos dos militares ao serviço da coroa portuguesa, 1640–1668* (Lisbon: Prefácio, 2007), 104–106.

149. Serrano Mangas, *La encrucijada portuguesa*, 38–39 and 154; Teresa Fonseca, "The Municipal Administration in Elvas during the Portuguese Restoration War (1640–1668)," *E-Journal of Portuguese History* 6(2) (2008): 1–15, 13; and letter of the inquisition of Évora to King Felipe IV, 24.5.1663, BNE, Ms. 2390, fol. 291.

150. Fernando Cortés Cortés, *Militares y Guerra en una tierra de frontera. Extremadura a mediados del siglo XVIII* (Mérida: Editora Regional de Extremadura, 1991), 28; and Fernando Cortés Cortés, "Estremadura Espanhola, 1640–1688: Conselhos e cargos concelhios face aos alojamentos militares," *Penélope* 9/10 (1993): 99–111, 99, 104–105, and 110–111.

151. The literature on this subject is extremely abundant. See, for example, Luís Oliveira Andrade, *História e memória. A restauração de 1640: Do liberalismo às comemorações centenárias de 1940* (Coimbra: Minerva, 2001); and Fernando Dores Costa, "Interpreting the Portuguese War of Restoration (1641–1668) in a European Context," *E-Journal of Portuguese History* 3(1) (2005).

152. Sebastião de Veiga Cabral, "Representação estudiosa e útil para as majestades grandeza de vassalos de Portugal," Abrantes, 20.9.1711, BRAH/M, Ms. 9-5556, for example, chapter 1, part 1.

153. Some of the difficulties in admitting Spanish defeat and recognizing Portuguese independence are described in BPR, Ms. II/2825, and BRAH/M, Ms. 9-1070. Even as late as 1665 the Spanish consejo de estado still suggested that there was nothing natural about Spain and Portugal being separated: Consulta of the consejo de estado, 23.12.1665, BNE, Ms. 12020, fols. 8r–16v.

154. "Memoria del Marqués de Grimaldi sobre límites con el Brasil 1776," AGN/M, catálogo de libros del ex Archivo y Museo Histórico Nacional, Libro

72, point 5. Additional copies of this manuscript can be found in AGN/BA, BN 180, Exp. 785, fols. 1r–31v, in AGN/BA, BN 354, Exp. 6169 and BN 384, Exp. 6598, and in BRAH/M, 9-1663: Colección Mata Linares, Tomo 8, fols. 59r–129r.

155. "Por muchos años estuvieron sustraídos del dominio de Portugal, viviendo como republicanos en su país libre." Marqués de Valdelirios to the Marqués de Grimaldi, Madrid, 11.3.1776, AHN, Estado 4371, 59–64, on 59. Arguing that Paolistas lived *sustraídos de toda autoridad, sin ley ni religión* until they subjected themselves to the sovereign of Brazil in the early eighteenth century was the "Memoria sobre la línea divisoria de los dominios de SM y del rey de Portugal, 30.5.1805," BRAH/M, 9-1723, Colección Mata Linares, vol. LXVIII, fols. 697–714, fols. 706r–v. See also "Informe do bispo de Buenos Aires dirigido ao papa sobre as tropelías practicadas pelos portugueses de São Paolo," Buenos Aires, 30.9.1637, reproduced in Jaime Cortesão, ed., *Jesuítas e Bandeirantes no Tape (1615–1641). Manuscritos da Coleção Angelis* (Rio de Janeiro: Biblioteca Nacional, 1969), 281–282; Vincente Aguilar y Jurado and Fracisco Requena, "Historia de la demarcaciones en la América entre los dominios de España y Portugal," Madrid 1797, AHN, Estado 3410-2, points 340–341; and Rafael Ruiz, "The Spanish-Dutch War and the Policy of the Spanish Crown toward the Town of São Paulo," *Itinerario* 26(1) (2002): 107–125, on 118–119.

156. "Brindar a saúde de Philippe V e a darem publicas vivas por el rei de Espanha." Manoel Rodrigues Torres to Luís Mascarenhas, Cuiabá 20.8.1740, AHU_MT_ cx..2, d. 136, cited in Francismar Alex Lopes de Carvalho, "Lealdades negociadas: Povos indígenas e a expansão dos impérios ibéricos nas regiões centrais da América do Sul (segunda metade do século XVIII)" (Ph.D. diss., Universidade de São Paulo, 2012), 517 and 529–530.

157. "A vila de São Paulo há muitos anos que é república de per si, sem observância de lei nenhuma, assim divina, como humana . . . assim que me parece inútil persuadi-los a que façam serviço a vossa majestade, porque são incapazes, e vassalos que vossa majestade tem rebeldes, assim em São Paulo, donde são moradores, como no sertão, donde vivem o mais do tempo e nenhuma ordem do governo geral guardam, nem as leis de vossa majestade": Governor Antônio Luís Gonçalves da Câmara Coutinho in 1692 according to Laura de Mello e Souza, "Vícios, virtudes e sentimento regional: São Paulo, da lenda negra à lenda áurea," *Revista de História* 142–143 (2000): 261–276, 263. See also Luiz dos Santos Vilhena, *Recopilação de notícias da capitania de S. Paolo* (Bahia: Imprensa Official do Estado, 1935 [1802]), 31–32 and 36–38.

158. Jaime Cortesão, *Rapôso Tavares e a formação territorial do Brasil* (Rio de Janeiro: Ministério da Educação e Cultura, 1958); Affonso d'Escragnolle Taunay, *História geral das bandeiras paulistas* (São Paulo: Imprensa Oficial de São Paulo, 1924–1950); and Sérgio Buarque de Holanda, *Caminhos e fronteiras* (Rio de Janeiro: José Olympio & Prolivro, 1975). See also Janice Theodoro e Rafael Ruiz, "São Paulo, de vila a cidade: A fundação, o poder público e a vida política," in Antonio Arnoni Prado et al., *História da cidade de São Paulo. A cidade colonial* (São Paulo: Editora Paz e Terra, 2004), vol. 1, 69–113, on 86, 99–101, and 108–112; and Vilardaga, "São Paulo," 281–363.

159. "Relación de los agravios que hicieron algunos vecinos y moradores de la villa de San Pablo," Bahia, 10.10.1629, reproduced in *Campaña del Brasil,* vol. 1, 9–24; and "auto das penas de excomunhão e rigoroso procedimento, intimados pelo padre Diogo de Alfaro comissário do santo oficio, contra os portugueses de São Paulo," dated 19.2.1638 and 1.3.1638, and letter of Father Diogo de Boroa, 4.3.1637, all reproduced in Cortesão, *Jesuítas e Bandeirantes,* 143–148 and 169–170.

CHAPTER 2   *Europeans and Indians*

1. ANTT, Manuscritos do Brasil, libro 1116, nos. 55 and 56, fols. 604 and 610. See also "Parecer de António Rodrigues da Costa sobre a conquista do Maranhão," post. 1707, AHU_ACL_CU_009, cx. 11, d. 1098; and Juan and Ulloa, *Disertación histórica,* 147–148.

2. "Los países no conquistados son unas selvas y montañas de difícil tránsito, y los llanos muy húmedos, cenagosos y ardientes, por lo que no pueden mantenerse largo tiempo en ellos los españoles. Las naciones que allí habitan son bárbaros, no cuidan de cubrir su desnudez, y sus casas son tan pobres que nada pierden aunque se las quiten, porque con cuatro palos y unas hojas de árboles en pocas horas fabrican otras en el lugar que les parece. Reducirlos por armas se ha tenido siempre por imposible, respecto de que con mudarse de un lugar a otro e internarse en lo más espeso de la montaña, como lo han hecho en las ocasiones que se les ha buscado, quedan frustradas las diligencias, perdidos los gastos y expuestas muchas vidas por las enfermedades que se contraen. Y es la única esperanza que admitan misioneros, y que éstos, con halagos y otras industrias, los atraigan, que ha sido el modo con que se han logrado las reducciones que van referidas, y será mayor la conquista de un misionero que la que puede hacer un numeroso ejército, pero ésta es obra de Dios y no de los hombres." Conde de Superunda. *Relación de Gobierno, Perú (1745–1761),* ed. Alfredo Moreno (Madrid: CSIC, 1983 [1761]), 214. Somewhat similar was the opinion of Viceroy Vertiz: "Memoria de Vertiz," Buenos Aires, 12.3.1784, reproduced in *Memorias de los virreyes del Rio de la Plata* (Buenos Aires: Editorial Bajel, 1945), 144.

3. Bettendorff, *Crônica da missão,* 140–143.

4. "Eu, fulano, principal de tal nação, em meu nome e de todos os mais súbditos e descendentes, prometo a deus e a el rei de Portugal, á fé de nosso senhor jesus cristo, de ser (como já sou) de hoje por diante, vassalo de sua majestade e de ter perpetua paz com os portugueses, sendo amigo de todos os seus amigos e inimigo de todos os seus inimigos e me obrigo assim a o guardar e cumprir inteiramente para sempre." Ibid., 141.

5. "Petición de respuesta a la que presentó el padre Diego de Urena procurador . . . en el pleito que tenemos con los padres dominicos . . . , 19.5.1684," ARSI, Manuscripta antiquae societatis pars I. assistentiae et provinciae, provincial nr. et Quito no. 18, fols. 14r–v; Rodríguez Castelo, *Diario del padre Fritz,* 101–102; "Votos do padre António Vieira," 12.7.1694, BA, 51-V-45, fol. 3r; Manuel Mariano de Echeverría, Quito, 11.7.1771, ANQ, Gobierno 24, Exp. 9 de 14.7.1771, fol. 3r; and letter of Bernardo Pereira de Berredo, colegio de Santo Antão, 14.6.1749, reproduced in *Annaes Historicos do Estado do Maranhão,*

ci–ciii, on ciii. Already in 1917 Herbert Bolton recognized the importance of missionaries as (1) explorers and diplomatic agents, (2) defenders of the frontier, (3) agents who advocated further expansion of the frontier, and (4) agents who were responsible for integrating the Indians into the Spanish commonwealth: Herbert E. Bolton, "The Mission as a Frontier Institution in the Spanish-American Colonies," *American Historical Review* 23(1) (1917): 42–61.

6. "Estos indios de esta nación deben ser tratados no como otros indios sino como españoles porque su vida, obras, fidelidad y amor que tienen a vuestra majestad y obediencia a sus gobernadores acudiendo a todo cuanto se les encarga del real servicio con grande puntualidad." Pedro Baigorri to the king, Buenos Aires, 15.3.1656, reproduced in Jaime Cortesão, ed., *Jesuitas e bandeirantes no Itatim (1596–1760)* (Rio de Janeiro: Biblioteca Nacional, 1952), 273–275, on 274–275. Somewhat similar was the letter of the viceroy of Lima to the bishop of Misque, Lima, 25.10.1765, AGN/BA, IX.4.3.5; and declaration of Alonso Vaca, in "Razón de lo que parece . . . sobre la población que los portugueses intentan hacer 50 leguas adentro del rio Marañón, 1677," BRAH/M, Jesuitas vol. CLXXXVII, no. 23 antiguo, 29 moderno.

7. "Voto do padre António Vieira sobre as dúvidas dos moradores de São Paulo acerca da administração dos índios," Bahia, 12.7.1694, in Padre António Vieira, *Escritos históricos e políticos*, ed. Alcir Pécora (São Paulo: Martins Fontes, 1995), 429–444, on 429–430, and Vieira, letter no. LXXXVI to king Afonso VI, 11.2.1660, reproduced in Luiz Felipe Baêta Neves, ed., *Transcendência, poder e quotidiano. As cartas de missionário do padre Antônio Vieira* (Rio de Janeiro: Atlântica Editora, 2004), 346–363, on 346.

8. "Habiendo dichos indios de sus libres hechose voluntarios vasallos de España (aun cuando sin duda hubieran sido de dentro la línea de Portugal y pertenecientes a la conquista de los portugueses) España en aceptar su libre y voluntario vasallaje no pasó la línea ni se entremetió en los derechos de Portugal; porque no conquistó a dichos indios, sino que ellos que no estaban obligados a someterse voluntariamente ni a España ni a Portugal ni a seguir los cálculos de la línea de Alejandro VI usando de su libertad se sujetaron al dominio de España . . . Porque el derecho de conquistar dentro de los límites, aunque dudosos, no lo tenían sino a favor de la fe y mientras dentro de aquellos términos controvertidos había infieles que convertir y conquistar; luego habiendo ya llegado los portugueses a los términos de los indios guaranís, chiquitos y moxos después que estos son cristianos y después de que ellos libre y espontáneamente se sujetaron a España, ya aquí debe parar y acabarse el derecho de conquista que habían los portugueses en otro tiempo": "Ruegan los padres misioneros . . . al padre confesor del rey considere algunos cargos de la conciencia de su majestad que resultan de la ejecución del real tratado [de 1750]," anonymous and undated, ANC/S, Jesuitas, vol. 197, fols. 109r–110v, on fols. 109v–110r.

9. These Indians "no han conocido otros conquistadores, que los padres de la compañía de Jesús de la corona de Castilla, y aunque todas las naciones que pueblan aquel vasto espacio se entregaron al yugo del vasallaje de los reyes de Castilla antes que al de algún otro príncipe, y que así no hay razón, ni fun-

damento por dónde pueda introducirse el derecho de conquista, ni de posesión en ellos a favor de los portugueses." Juan and Ulloa, *Disertación histórica*, 147–148. See also 135–136 and 165–166.

10. I owe this formulation to Anthony Pagden.

11. "Ni tienen aquí qué predicar los políticos, que pues aquellas tierras están en poder de católicos y tienen misioneros, cualesquiera que sean poco importa estén sujetas al dominio de Portugal o al dominio de Castilla, ya que no tiene que esperar la real hacienda provecho alguno, antes bien mucho gasto de su recuperación; porque según lo dicho cada cual puede claramente echar de ver que permaneciendo aquella región en poder de los portugueses, aunque católicos, a más de que irán cada día más y más extendiendo sus crueldades pretensiones y dominio hasta introducirse en lo más interior del Perú, de la perdición de tantas almas que acontece estando en poder de los portugueses del Pará, no puede no seguirse un cargo gravísimo a los reyes católicos de Castilla a quienes lo sumos pontífices hicieron donación de estos reinos de América con condición de que promoviesen con todos los medios posibles la conversión de los infieles."Andrés de Zárate, "Relación de la misión apostólica que tiene a su cargo la provincia de Quito de la compañía de Jesús en el gran río de Marañón," 3.10.1735, AGI, Quito 158, fols. 246r–257v, on fols. 256r–v.

12. "¿Por qué ley divina o positiva o por qué título pertenecen a los misioneros castellanos los indios, que habitan estos desiertos? ¿Tienen acaso algún decreto de la santísima trinidad, o alguna bula pontificia, para que ellos solos puedan conquistar? Si los portugueses fueran herejes, justa sería la disputa; pero siendo católicos romanos, si pretenden hacer lo mismo . . . de catequizarlos y reducirlos a la fe, ¿por qué razón han de ser prohibidos? . . . si como España no ha muchos años que abrió los ojos para ese celo de ponerles misioneros, por lo mucho que ganaba por ese modo de señorear tierras y alargar sus dominios; así Portugal ahora entra mano en eso, poniéndolo en ejecución; y no debe ser extraño pues tiene el ejemplo de un buen vecino." Antonio de Silva Guzman to the Jesuit Nicolás Altogradi, Arayal de Mato Grosso, 25.9.1751, ANC/S, Jesuitas, vol. 202, pieza 1, fols. 1r–v. The governor also accused Spanish Jesuits of pretending that "todo el gentilismo sea sólo suyo."

13. "Relazione dello stato delle missioni dei gesuiti nel Paraguay, Chile e Tucuman," 16.5.1661, ASPF/R, SOCG, vol. 257, fols. 184r–185v, "Notizie circa lo stabilimento di pp gesuiti nel Paraguay," undated, anonymous, ASPF/R, SC, vol. 1, fols. 98r–111r; "Relação de algumas coisas tocantes a o Maranhão e Graõ Pará escrita pelo padre Luis Figueiroa," undated, BRAH/M, Jesuitas vol. CIX, no. 73. See also Magnus Mörner, *The Political and Economic Activities of the Jesuits in the La Plata Region: The Habsburg Era* (Stockholm: Library and Institute of Ibero-American Studies, 1953), 72; F. Mateos, "Avances portugueses y misiones españolas en América del Sur," *Missionalia hispánica* 5(14) (1958): 459–504, on 486–487; Basílio de Magalhães, *Expansão geográfica do Brasil colonial* (São Paulo: Companhia Editoria Nacional, 1978), 155–164; Guy Martinière,"Frontières coloniales en Amérique du sud: Entre "Tierra Firme" et "Maranhão" (1500–1800)," *Cahiers des Amériques Latines* 17 (1978): 147–181, on 171 and 174; F.M. Renard Casevitz, Th. Saignes, and A. C. Taylor, *Al este de los Andes. Relaciones entre las sociedades amazónicas y andinas entre los siglos XV y XVII* (Quito: Abya-Yala, 1988), vol. 2, 136–140;

and Jans-Jürgen Prien, "O papel dos jesuítas portugueses no Brasil entre 1549 e 1640," in *A união ibérica e o mundo atlântico*, 217–240.

14. Undated petition by fray Domingo de Brieva and royal decision approving the request dated 30.10.1642, AGI, Quito, 7; "Memorial presentado en el real consejo de las Indias acerca del descubrimiento del río de las Amazonas," AGI, Quito 158; and consulta of the conselho da fazenda, Lisbon 13.3.1618, AHU_ACL_CU_009, cx. 1, d. 19. See also Mariano Cuesta Domingo, "Descubrimientos geográficos durante el siglo XVIII: Acción franciscana en la ampliación de las fronteras," *Archivo Ibero-Americano* 52(205–208) (1992): 293–342; and Maria Adelina Amorim, *Os franciscanos no Maranhão e Grão Pará. Missão e cultura na primeira metade de seiscentos* (Lisbon: CLEPUL and CEHR, 2005), 135 and 146.

15. The correspondence dated 1760–1761 between the governors of Santa Cruz de la Sierra (Spanish) and Mato Grosso (Portuguese) included in AGN/BA, IX.4.3.5, alludes to such issues. See also the governor of Paraguay to Nicolás Arrendondo, Asunción 8.2.1792, AHN, Estado 4555, no. 16; and Juan Carlos Bazán, "Examen jurídico y discurso historial sobre . . . los confines de los reinos de Castilla y Portugal . . . en el Río de la Plata," undated, in BNE, Ms. 3042, fols. 42r–101v, fols. 55r and 91r.

16. The Marqués de Valdelirios to the Marqués de Grimaldi, Madrid, 11.3.1776, AHN, Estado 4371, 39–40.

17. "Aumento da cristandade nos índios, como também para a conservação . . . de meus domínios por aquela parte do sertão": "Instruções régias públicas e secretas para Francisco Xavier de Mendonça, capitão-geral do Estado do Pará e Maranhão (1751)," reproduced in J. Lúcio d'Azevedo, *Os jesuítas no Grão Pará, suas missões e a colonização* (Lisbon: Livraria Editora, 1901), 348–356, note F, art. 21 on 352. Also see "Parecer do procurador da coroa para o príncipe regente Dom Pedro sobre as missões religiosas . . . nas capitanias do Maranhão e Pará," Lisbon, before 9.5.1671, AHU_ACL_CU_ 013, cx. 2, d. 143; and Andrés de Barros, *Vida do apostólico padre Antonio Vieyra da Companhia de Jesus* (Lisbon: Nova oficina Sylviana, 1746), book 1, 93–95.

18. Unsigned letter sent to the Marqués de Valdelirios, San Nicolás, 1.12.1757, AHN, Estado 3706; undated report by Diego Altamirano, reproduced in *Campaña del Brasil*, vol. 1, 361–366; João de Maia da Gama to the king, Belém, 15.8.1723, AHU_ACL_CU_013, cx. 7, d. 650; Matias da Costa e Sousa to António Duarte de Barros, Belém, 11.8.1736, AHU_ACL_CU_013, cx. 19, d. 1736; and André da Piedade to Francisco Xavier de Mendonça Furtado, Maranhão, 4.1.1760, AHU_ACL_CU_009, cx. 39, d. 3842. See also "Informe del padre Francisco Ruiz, Jesuita," and the debate that followed it in 1708, "Relación del estado de las misiones del Marañón o Mainas a cargo de la compañía de Jesús por Andrés de Zárate," Quito, 30.10.1735, and Ángel María Manca to Miguel de Villanueva, Puerto de Santa María, 13.12.1740, all in AGI, Quito 158.

19. "Razón de lo que parece por los informes . . . sobre la población que los portugueses intentan hacer 50 leguas adentro del río Marañón, 1677," BRAH/M, Jesuitas vol. CLXXXVII, no. 23 antiguo, 29 moderno. Jesuits also participated in the scientific debate of the 1680s regarding the correct location of the me-

ridian of Tordesillas: Francisco Potrey to Francisco de Amolaz, Madrid, 27.12.1690, AGI, Charcas 261, fols. 607r–608r.

20. Juan de Andosilla to the consejo de Indias, Madrid, 18.11.1680, AGI, Charcas 260, also reproduced in *Campaña del Brasil*, vol. 1, 301–302.

21. "Extracto de lo que resulta del expediente que se vió en el consejo acerca de la visita que hizo el doctor don Diego de Riofrío y Peralta . . . de las misiones que están en los ríos Napo y Marañón," AGI, Quito 158, fols. 147r–154r, especially 152v–153v. See also Inácio Guerreiro, *Os tratados de delimitação do Brasil e a cartografia da época* (Lisbon: Chaves Ferreira Publicações, 1999), 19–25.

22. Informe of father Samuel Fritz, 23.3.1721, AGI, Quito 158, fols. 14v–17v. Fritz's activities are described in his diary (Rodríguez Castelo, *Diario del padre Fritz*). See also M. Jiménez de la Espada, ed., *Noticias auténticas del famoso río Marañón* (1738), a special number of the *Boletín de la Sociedad Geográfica de Madrid* 26–32 (1889–1892), reedited as Paolo Maroni, *Noticias auténticas del famoso río Marañón*, ed. Jean Pierre Chaumeil (Iquitos: Instituto de Investigación de la Amazonía Peruana, 1988); and "Apuntes acerca de la línea de demarcación entre las conquistas de España y Portugal en el Río Marañón," in "Capítulo tercero: Misión de los Omaguas, Jurimaguas, Aysuares . . . y otras naciones desde Napo hasta el Río Negro," undated and unsigned document, BPE, Cod. CXV (2-15), no. 10, fols. 37r–41r.

23. André Ferrand Almeida, "Samuel Fritz and the Mapping of the Amazon," *Imago Mundi* 55 (2003): 113–119; André Ferrand Almeida, "Samuel Fritz Revisited: The Maps of the Amazon and Their Circulation in Europe," in Diogo Ramada Curto, Angelo Cattaneo, and André Ferrand Almeida, eds., *La cartografia europea tra primo Rinascimento e fine dell'Illuminismo* (Florence: Olschki, 2003), 133–153; and Camilla Loureiro Dias, "Jesuit Maps and Political Discourse: The Amazon River of Father Samuel Fritz," *The Americas* 69(1) (2012): 95–116.

24. Information given by Pablo Maroni to the president of Quito on 13.6.1733; Tomás Nieto Polo, procurator of the order in Madrid on 30.8.1741; as well as his letter to Joseph de la Quintana, 3.7.1743; all in AGI, Quito 158.

25. Nicolás de Millinedo, "Relación instructiva del origen y conclusión del tratado de límites y de todos los accidentes que impidieron su ejecución hasta que se pensó en anularle," AHN, Estado 3386; and "Representación hecha al virrey del Perú sobre los inconvenientes que resultan a la corona del tratado del año de 50," Córdoba del Tucumán, 1751, ANC/S, Jesuitas, vol. 197, pieza 14, fols. 123r–133v. Many of these documents were reproduced in *Documentos relativos a la ejecución del tratado de límites de 1750* (Montevideo: Instituto Geográfico Militar, 1938) and in *Anais da Biblioteca Nacional do Rio de Janeiro* 52 (1958).

26. Jose Monteiro de Noronha to Manoel Bernardo de Mello e Castro, Barcelos, 14.1.1762, APEP, Cod. 122, doc. 1, fol. 2r.

27. Aloysio Conrado Pfeil, "Compêndio das mais substanciais razões e argumentos que evidentemente provam que a capitania chamada do Norte situada na boca do rio das Amazonas legitimamente pertencem a coroa de Portugal," Pará, 1.4.1700, BA, 51-VI-11, fols. 151r–166r; and Aloísio Conrado Pfeil, "Anotação contra incoerentes pontos no tratado da justificação formada pelo

plenipotenciários na corte real de Lisboa e impressa em 1681," undated, BA, 51-VI-11-II, fols. 168r–173r. Another copy is included in BA, 51-V-22. The map authored by Pfeil was mentioned in Jódoco Peres to the general of the order in Rome, Coimbra, 27.8.1685, ARSI, Manuscripta antiquae societatis pars I. assistentiae et provinciae, Bras. 26, fol. 112r. The Portuguese might have used it in negotiations in Utrecht: Nelson Sanjad, "As Fronteiras do ultramar: Engenheiros, matemáticos, naturalistas e artistas na Amazônia, 1750–1820," in *Artistas e artífices e a sua mobilidade no mundo de expressão portuguesa. Actas do VII colóquio Luso-Brasileiro de História da Arte* (Porto: Universidade do Porto, 2007), 431–437, on 431. See also Serafim Leite, "As primeiras cartas dos jesuítas do Brasil para o conhecimento da América (1549–1562)," in *Novas páginas de história do Brasil* (Lisbon: Academia Portuguesa da História, 1962), 184–191; and Max Justo Guedes, "A cartografia da delimitação das fronteiras do Brasil no século XVIII," in *Cartografia e diplomacia no Brasil do século XVIII* (Lisbon: Comissão para as Comemorações dos Descobrimentos Portugueses, 1997), 10–38, on 14.

28. Aloysio Conrado Pfeil to the Jesuit general in Rome, Colégio São Alexander, Pará, 27.2.1691, ARSI, Manuscripta antiquae societatis pars I. assistentiae et provinciae, Bras. 9, fols. 361–368v, point 8 on fols. 365v–366r. See also João Philippe Bettendorf, "Informação a Sua Majestade sobre o sucedido no Maranhão em fevereiro de 1684," BPE, Cod. CXV (2-11), fols. 77r–80v; and Bettendorf, "Informação dos missionários da companhia de Jesus do estado do Maranhão hoje assistentes nesta corte," 1685, BPE, Cod. CXV (2-11), fols. 84r–86v; and Wermers, "O estabelecimento," 528–530 and 553.

29. "Capítulo tercero: misión de los Omaguas, Jurimaguas, Aysuares . . . y otras naciones desde Napo hasta el Río Negro," undated and unsigned document, BPE, Cod. CXV (2-15), no. 10, 20r–37r.

30. "Capítulo tercero: misión de los Omaguas, Jurimaguas, Aysuares . . . y otras naciones desde Napo hasta el Río Negro," undated and unsigned document, BPE, Cod. CXV (2-15), no. 10, 23r.

31. "Ninguna esperanza hay de que tomen con empeño su alivio alegando que las cajas reales no están para gastos y que es muy difícil el remitir gente a países tan distantes y clima tan puesto al de la sierra." "Capítulo tercero: misión de los Omaguas, Jurimaguas, Aysuares . . . y otras naciones desde Napo hasta el Río Negro," undated and unsigned document, BPE, Cod. CXV (2-15), no. 10, fols. 57r.

32. Tamar Herzog, "La empresa administrativa y el capital social: los Sánchez de Orellana (Quito, siglo XVIII)," in Juan Luis Castellano, ed., *Sociedad, administración y poder en el siglo XVIII. Hacia una nueva historia institucional* (Granada: Universidad de Granada, 1996), 381–396, on 382–384 and 289–290 and Tamar Herzog, "¿Letrado o teólogo? Sobre el oficio de la justicia a principios del siglo XVIII," in Johannes Michael Scholz, ed., *Fallstudien zur spanischen und portugiesischen Justiz (16.–20. Jahrhundert)* (Frankfurt: Vittorio Klostermann, 1994), 697–714. On the Sánzhez de Orellana more generally see Tamar Herzog, *Upholding Justice: State, Law and the Penal System in Quito* (Ann Arbor: University of Michigan Press, 2004), 72–88, 111, 136–138, 144, 149, and 178.

33. Requerimiento of father Fritz to Joseph Antunes da Fonseca, 20.4.1697, and the response he received on 22.4.1697, both attached to consulta of the conselho ultramarino, Lisbon, 12.11.1697, AHU_ACL_CU_013, cx. 4, d. 340.

34. "Relação da jornada do Solimões e Río Negro por Frei Vitoriano Pimentel," dated 7.9.1705 and reproduced in João Renôr F. de Carvalho, "Presença e permanência da ordem do Carmo no Solimões e no Rio Negro no século XVIII, in *Das reduções latino-americanas às lutas indígenas actuais: IX simpósio latino-americano do CEHILA, Manaus 29.7 a 1.8.1981* (São Paulo: Ed. Paulinas, 1982), 175–190, on 181–190. Also see Wermers, "O estabelecimento."

35. "Sobre los términos de estas misiones": Rodríguez Castelo, *Diario del padre Fritz*, 132.

36. Juan Bautista Santa María Mayor to Samuel Fritz, Yurimaguas, 26.12.1707, and letter of Sebastián Luis Abad, both included in the information supplied by Father Francisco Ruiz and debated in Quito in 1708, AGI, Quito 158, fols. 6r–7v.

37. Alexandre de Souza Freire to Juan Bautista Julian, Pará 12.12.1729, AGI, Quito 158.

38. Dionisio de Alcedo to Alexandre de Souza Freire, Quito, 3.4.1731 and 23.5.1731; letter of the procurator of the missions in Mainas and Marañón to the president of Quito, Quito 28.5.1731, and vista fiscal and consulta, 20.10.1732, all in AGI, Quito 158. See also Dionisio Alcedo y Herrera to Alexandre de Souza Freire, Quito 28.5.1731 AGI, Quito 374.

39. Juan Bautista Julián to the governor of Pará, La Laguna, 5.10.1730, attached to João de Abreu de Castelo Branco to the king, Belém, 18.9.1739, AHU_ACL_CU_013, cx. 22, d. 2082.

40. "Certidão dos capítulos do regimento referente aos limites de ocupação dos territórios pelos missionários portugueses e espanhóis," Belém, 18.10.1731, AHU_ACL_CU_013, cx.13, d. 1207.

41. "Para dejar de esta manera ajustados los límites y poner fin a los disturbios que de algún tiempo a esta parte pasaron entre los vasallos de ambas majestades." Melchior Mendes, La Laguna, 6.9.1732, AGI, Quito 158, fols. 13r–v.

42. "Porque para la dicha averiguación no se hallaba persona autorizada para intervenir de parte de la corona de Castilla en la división y demarcación legítima de estas tierras." This Jesuit response to Mendes was also reproduced in Juan Bautista Julián to the governor of Pará, La Laguna, 8.9.1732, AGI, Quito 158, fols. 14r–15v. See also Requerimiento made by Juan Bautista Julián to Melchior Mendes, AGI, Quito, 158, fols. 16r–v.

43. Dionisio Alcedo y Herrera to Souza Freire, Quito, 3.4.1731 and 23.5.1731, attached to João de Abreu de Castelo Branco para to the king, Belém, 18.9.1739, AHU_ACL_CU_013, cx. 22, d. 2082. See also Dioniso Alcedo y Herrera to Pablo Maroni, Quito, 28.5.1733, followed by the information supplied by Pablo Maroni on 13.6.1733, AGI, Quito 158, fols. 29r–30r and 31r–32v; and the response of the viceroy, Lima, 14.4.1733, AGI, Quito 158, fols. 26r–28v.

44. Requerimiento of Andrés de Zárate to Joseph Ferreira de Mello, San Ignacio de los Pebas, 24.1.1737, AGI, Quito 158, fols. 144r–v; and information

given by Father Andrés de Zárate, Madrid, 28.8.1739, AGI, Quito 158. See also Almeida, *A formação*, 38.

45. "Ofício respondendo a pretensão dos padres castelhanos em ampliar os seus domínios na fronteira do Grão Pará," Belém, 28.11.1737, AHU_ACL_ CU_013, cx. 20, d. 1920.

46. Royal orders dated 5.3.1732 and 8.5.1732 to the governor of São Paulo Conde de Sarzedas, ANTT, Papéis do Brasil, Cod. 6, fols. 27r and 7r; "Ofício respondendo a pretensão dos padres castelhanos em ampliar sus domínios na fronteira do Grão Pará," 28.11.1737, AHU_ACL_CU_013 cx. 20 d. 1920; "Parecer do conselho ultramarino ao rei sobre as novas missões que os padres castelhanos da companhia de Jesus e os religiosos do Carmo têm realizado no Estado do Maranhão," Lisbon, 6.3.1739, AHU_ACL_CU_009, cx. 25, d. 2554; Marco António de Azevedo Coutinho to Francisco Pedro de Mendonça Gorjão, Lisbon, 15.9.1748, reproduced in Reis, *Limites e demarcações*, vol. 2, 113–116, on 114–115; and António Rolim de Moura Tavares to Diogo de Mendonça Corte Real, Vila Bela, 20.3.1757, AHU_ACL_CU_010, cx. 09, d. 543.

47. "Os padres da companhia das províncias de Itália sem titulo nem permissão alguma ocupavam muitas terras sobre o rio da Prata da repartição deste reino, com tal poder e violência que se opunham a castelhanos e portugueses." "Papel que fés o Marquês de Fronteira," in "Pareceres do Exmo. Marquês de Fronteira conselheiro de estado sobre as diferenças que houve entre as cortes de Lisboa e Madrid sobre a fundação de Nova Colónia," probably dated 1680, BPE, Cod. CXVI (2-12), no. 1, fols. 4r–8r, on fol. 7r.

48. "Noticia e justificação do titulo e boa fé com que se obrou na Nova Colónia do Sacramento," anonymous undated (c. 1681), BA, Ms. 51-VI-48, fols. 117r–146r, on fol. 141. See also Eduardo Neumann, "Fronteira e identidade: Confrontos luso-guarani na Banda Oriental 1680–1757," *Revista Complutense de Historia de América* 26 (2000): 73–92, on 76 and 83.

49. Thomé Joaquim da Costa Corte Real to António Rolim de Moura, Lisbon, 22.8.1758, APMG, CMG-SG, Livro C-18, Estante-01, letter 2, fols. 19r–29v, fols. 19r–v.

50. "Informe e justificação jurídica do uso de armas de fogo pelo índios, apresentados pelos jesuítas do Paraguai," 1639, reproduced in Cortesão, *Jesuítas e Bandeirantes*, 302–314; "Relación y carta del Pedro de Orduña del avance de indios al fuerte portugués y victoria que ganaron en 7.8.1680"; "Copia de la certificación auténtica que don Baltasar García Ros sargento mayor del presidio de Buenos Aires dió sobre las operaciones y servicios de los cuatro mil indios de guerra," Buenos Aires, 15.6.1705; and "Relación de lo que hicieron los indios que tienen a su cargo los religiosos de la Compañía de Jesús . . . en servicio de su majestad . . . años 1704–5," undated and anonymous; all in ANC/S, Jesuitas, vol. 197, pieza 1, fols. 2r–5v; pieza 3, fols 15r–16v; and pieza 7, fols. 43r–53v. See also Mörner, *The Political and Economic Activities*, 118–120 and 147–148; and Constancio Eguía Ruiz, "El espíritu militar de los jesuitas en el antiguo Paraguay español, *Revista de Indias* 5(16) (1944): 266–319.

51. Information by Father Andrés de Zárate, Madrid, 28.8.1739, AGI, Quito 158; and cédula of 7.8.1679, reproduced in cédula real of 12.9.1628; and "relación

de los agravios que hicieron algunos vecinos y moradores de la villa de San Pablo," Bahia, 10.10.1629; all reproduced in *Campaña del Brasil*, vol. 1, 75–76.

52. "Consiguieron los portugueses el quedar hechos dueños de aquellos países sin contradicción, porque los padres de la compañía española no defendían el país, sino principalmente las almas de aquellas naciones que tenían a su cargo y como en la retirada de los que los habitaban tenían logrado completamente su intento, cesaba el motivo que les subministraba justa causa de oponerse a los designios de los portugueses y así desde entonces empezaron éstos a establecerse como absolutos dueños en aquellas tierras." Juan and Ulloa, *Disertación histórica*, 161–162.

53. "Petición de respuesta a la que presentó el padre Diego de Ureña procurador . . . en el pleito que tenemos con los padres dominicos," 19.5.1684, ARSI, Manuscripta antiquae societatis pars I. assistentiae et provinciae, Provincial nr. et Quito n. 18, fols. 14r–v; "Expediente promovido por don Pedro Estevan Dávila gobernador de las provincias del Río de la Plata con los padres jesuitas," AGI, Charcas 28, R. 4, N. 49; "Información de la enemiga y aversión que don Alonso de Mercado y Villa Corta tiene a la compañía de Jesús," Santiago del Estero, 1661, ANC/S, Jesuitas, vol. 194, no. 6, fol. 95r; "Memorial impreso presentado al supremo consejo de Indias por el provincial de la compañía Jaime Aguilar en defensa de sus misiones," 1730, and "Memorial impreso presentado al supremo consejo de Indias por el procurador Gaspar Rodero en defensa de las misiones del Paraguay," 1743, both in ANC/S, Jesuitas, vol. 193, nos. 5 and 6; and the council of Belém to the king, Belém, 12.4.1657, AHU_ACL_ CU_013, cx. 2, d. 106. See also Prien, "O papel dos jesuítas, 238–240; and Dauril Alden, *The Making of an Enterprise: The Society of Jesus in Portugal, Its Empire and Beyond, 1540–1750* (Stanford: Stanford University Press, 1996), 21–23.

54. "Pedro Vermudo de la Compañía de Jesús procurador general en esta corte de las provincias de las Indias," undated manuscript (c. 1673), ANC/S, Jesuitas, vol. 194, pieza 7, fols. 104r–106v.

55. Pedro de Cevallos to Ricardo Wall, San Borja, 15.2.1759 and 30.11.1759 (who thought the Jesuits were responsible) and Marqués de Valdelirios to Pedro de Cevallos, San Nicolás, 9.1.1760 (who disagreed), all reproduced in *Campaña del Brasil*, vol. 2, 267–270, 275–277, and 286–293. See also José María Mariluz Urquijo, "Clima intelectual rioplatense de mediados del setecientos. Los límites del poder real," in Maziel, *De la justicia*, 15–55, 30–34; José María Mariluz Urquijo, "La historiografía rioplatense sobre el Tratado de Madrid (1750–1850)," in *El Tratado de Tordesillas y su época*, vol. 3, 1637–1651; Félix Becker, "La guerra guaranítica desde una nueva perspectiva: Historia, ficción e historiografía," *Boletín Americanista* 32 (1982): 7–37; Juan Molina Cortón, "El tratado de límites de 1750 y la intervención jesuita," *Cuadernos de investigación histórica* 16 (1995): 199–223; and Quarleri, *Rebelión y guerra*, 16–19.

56. "Ruegan los padres misioneros de los indios Guaranís al padre confesor del rey considere algunos cargos de la conciencia de su majestad que resultan de la ejecución del real tratado [de 1750]," unsigned and undated, ANC/S, Jesuitas, vol. 197, fols. 109r–110v; and Joseph Cardiel, "Declaración de la verdad

contra un libelo inflamatorio impreso en portugués contra los padres jesuitas misioneros del Paraguay y Marañón," Pueblo de Borja, 14.9.1758, BRAH/M, 9-1663: Colección Mata Linares, Tomo 8, fols. 1–35.

57. "Breve y exacto diseño de la justicia del tratado de límites celebrado entre las majestades Católica y Fidelísima en 13.1.1750," anonymous, 20.6.1760, AMN, 0115, Ms. 0124/004, fols. 152v–153r and 164v.

58. Félix Feliciano da Fonseca, "Relação do que aconteceu aos demarcadores portugueses e castelhanos," Lisbon, post-1753, 5–6, cited in Domingues, *When the Amerindians Were Vassals*, 193; "Nicolás Ñenguirú's Letter to the Governor of Buenos Aires (1753)," reproduced and translated in Kenneth Mills and William B. Taylor, eds., *Colonial Spanish America: A Documentary History* (Wilmington, DE: Scholarly Resources, 1998), 263–267; and the letters reproduced in Barbara Ganson, *The Guaraní under Spanish Rule in the Río de la Plata* (Stanford: Stanford University Press, 2003), 191–199.

59. "Informe de Baltasar Maziel al gobernador Bucareli," in Maziel, *De la justicia*, 201–204; Joseph Cardiel, "Declaración de la verdad contra un libelo inflamatorio impreso en portugués contra los padres jesuitas misioneros del Paraguay y Marañón, Pueblo de Borja, 14.9.1758," BRAH/M, 9-1663: Colección Mata Linares, Tomo 8, fols. 1–35; "Copia de una carta respuesta que dio don Juan del Campo y Cambroneras castellano . . . a don Alexandre de Bique capitán europeo . . . en ocasión que le comunicó un librito portugués con el título 'Relación abreviada de la república que los religiosos jesuitas de las provincias de Portugal y España establecieron en los dominios ultramarinos de las dos monarquías . . . ,' 20.8.1758," BA, Ms. 20.208; "El gobernador [Francisco Bucareli] da cuenta de algunas noticias relativas a la conducta y carácter de don Miguel de la Rocha," Buenos Aires, 1769, ANC/S, Jesuitas, vol. 161, pieza 5, fols. 61r–66v; and Francisco de Paula Bucareli y Ursua to the consejo de Indias, 14.4.1768, AGN/BA, IX.32.1, Exp. 4.

60. Francisco Bucareli y Ursua to Conde de Aranda, Buenos Aires, 6.9.1767, ANC/S, Jesuitas, vol. 160, pieza 1, fols. 1r–2v.

61. Contemporary literature on these questions is enormous. See, for example, "Relazione abbreviata della repubblica che i Gesuiti della provincia di Portogallo e di Spagna hanno stabilita ne domini che le due sopradette corone possiedono nel America," undated, anonymous, ASV, Fondo Gesuiti, vol. 2; *Relation abrégée concernant la république que les religieux, nommes jésuites, des provinces de Portugal et d'Espagne, ont établie dans les pays et domaines d' outre-mer de ces deux monarchies et de la guerre qu'ils ont excitée et soutenue contre les armées espagnoles et portugaises* (Amsterdam: Aux Depans de la Compagnie, 1758); Jean-Baptiste Bourguignon d'Anville, *Le gouvernement du Paraguay sous les Jésuites. Ouvrage ou l'on expose les moyens que les Jésuites ont employés pour maintenir leur royauté dans le Paraguay* (Madrid, 1771); and *I gesuiti accusati e convirti di spilorceria* (Venezia: Gino Bottagrissi, 1760). Defending Jesuit innocence was "Verdad desnuda oprimida contra la calumnia artificiosamente divulgada," undated, anonymous, BPE, Cod. CXVI (2-12) no. 19-1; and "Protesto anônimo de um padre da companhia. . . . a acusação de infidelidade ao rei," Asunción, 10.5.1653, reproduced in Cortesão, *Jesuítas e bandeirantes no Itatim*, 113–119.

62. Maria Regina Celestino de Almeida, "Os Vassalos d'El Rei nos confins da Amazônia. A colonização da Amazônia Ocidental, 1750/1798," *Anais da Biblioteca Nacional* 112 (1992): 63–85, 68.

63. "Copia de algunos capítulos de la carta instructiva que el teniente general don Francisco Bucareli y Ursua dejó a su partida a estos reinos al mariscal de campo don Juan José de Vertiz," 15.8.1770, ANC/S, Jesuitas, vol. 160, pieza 18, fols. 82r–200r, fol. 84v.

64. "Traducción al castellano de la carta original que escribió Antonio de Silveira Peyxoto," 14.9.1770; declaration of Antonio Silveira, Pueblo de Candelaria, 25.10.1770; and Francisco Bruno de Zabala to Joseph de Vertiz, Pueblo de Candelaria, 25.10.1770, all in AGN/BA, IX.4.3.6.

65. Joseph de Andonaegui to Luis García de Vivar, Buenos Aires, 10.1.1750, AGN/BA, IX.3.8.2; and Francisco Xavier de Mendonça Furtado to João Pedro da Câmara, Lisbon, 2.5.1767, APMG, CMG-SG, Livro C-18, Estante-01, letter 15, fols. 45r–v.

66. Manuel Fernández to Nicolás Arrendondo, 5.9.1791 and 7.9.1791, AGN/BA, IX.1.4.3.

67. Francisco Feijo y Noguera to Juan Joseph de Vertiz, Pergamino, 8.5.1772, and the declaration of Felipe Baquero, Buenos Aires, 13.5.1772, AGN/BA, IX.1.5.6.

68. "Oponerse y contener a los portugueses que como vecinos quieren introducirse o puede lo estén ya." "Capítulo cuarto del interrogatorio por que fue examinado el regular expulso Carlos Abrisi," ANQ, FE 30, vol. 83, no. 3226, fols. 80r–275v, fol 87r–v.

69. AGN/BA, IX.23.2.4 and IX.23.2.5, contain information regarding such suspicions.

70. On Carmelite perceptions of this conflict, see Manuel María Wermers, *A ordem carmelita e o Carmo em Portugal* (Lisbon: União Gráfica, 1963), 213–246, on 230 and 245; Andre Prat, *Notas históricas sobre as missões carmelitanas no extremo norte do Brasil, séculos XVII e XVIII* (Recife: Convento do Carmo, 1941), 30–42; Eduardo Hoornaert, "As missões carmelitanas na Amazônia (1695–1755)," in *Das reduções latino-americanas às lutas indígenas actuais: IX simpósio latino-americano do CEHILA, Manaus 29.7 a 1.8.1981* (São Paolo: Ed. Paulinas, 1982), 161–174; Emanuelle Boaga, *Como pedras vivas . . . para ler a história e a vida do Carmelo* (Rome: Litografia Principe, 1989), 204; and Wilmar Santin, "Missões carmelitas nos rios Negro e Solimões," *Carmelus* 55 (2008): 59–87, 59–60.

71. Consulta of the consejo de Indias, Madrid, 13.6.1715, AGI, Quito 103, doc. 4, fols. 15r–26v; and "Relación del estado de las misiones del Marañón o Mainas a cargo de la compañía de Jesús por Andrés de Zárate," Quito, 30.10.1735, AGI, Quito 158. The ordinances of the Carmelites of Maranhão and Pará, dated 1728, partially confirmed these image: AGOC, VM/CV 1714–1740, II Maranhão, Commune I, doc. 3. Similar prohibitions repeated in 1737: AGOC, VM/CV 1714–1740, II Maranhão, Commune I, unnumbered document, dated 21.10.1737. So did the reports of fray António de Araujo, 10.9.1735 and fray Tomas Jordão, 12.9.1743, AGOC, VM/CV 1741–1752, II Maranhão, Commune I, unnumbered documents.

72. Requirement of Antonio de Ade, Carmelite, reproduced by Joseph Pinheiro Marques on 21.12.1707 and included in the information supplied by Father Francisco Ruiz, AGI, Quito 158, fols. 5r–4v; and "Relação da jornada do Solimões e Rio Negro por Frei Vitoriano Pimentel," 7.9.1705, reproduced in Carvalho, "Presencia e permanência," on 181–190.

73. Thomé Joaquim da Costa Corte Real to António Rolim de Moura, Lisbon, 7.7.1757 and 22.8.1758, APMG, CMG-SG, Livro C-18, Estante-01, letter 1, fols. 9–17v, fol. 17r, point 20, and letter 2, fols. 19r–29v, fol. 21r; and Aloysio Conrado Pfeil to the Jesuit general in Rome, Colégio São Alexander, Pará, 27.2.1691, ARSI, Manuscripta antiquae societatis pars I. assistentiae et provinciae, Bras. 9, fols. 361–368v, point 8, fols. 365v–366r, fol. 366r. See also Mörner, *The Political and Economic Activities*, 61 and 89; and Leandro Tormo Sanz, "Las diferencias misionales a uno y otro lado de la línea," in *El tratado de Tordesillas y su proyección*, vol. 2, 81–92, on 84.

74. "Si la indita religión carmelitica es la fecunda madre que en sus hijos da, y ha dado, en todos siglos al mundo tantos otros soles que con las luces de su santidad, sabiduría, doctrina y celo han ilustrado el firmemente de la iglesia." The author also suggested that the Carmelite "también ejerce de médico con los dolientes, de ameno padre con los menesterosos, de juez con los delincuentes y de aventajado maestro con los ignorantes." Certificate of Carlos Bretano, San Joaquín de Omaguas, 1.6.1746, copied by António Jose Ribeiro, apostolic notary in Lisbon, AGOC, VM/CV 1741–1752, II Maranhão, Commune I.

75. "Lista dos padres jesuítas missionários que servirão na província jesuítica de Quito," 1755, AHU_ACL_CU_071, cx. 1, d. 13; Francisco Xavier de Mendonça Furtado to Sebastião José, Pará, 28.11.1757, AHU_ACL_CU_013, cx. 43, d. 3927; and Petitions of Giuseppe da Natividade and André de Piedade, dated 1744 and 1745, AGOC, VM/CV 1741–1752, II Maranhão, Commune I, unnumbered documents. See also Alden, *The Making of an Enterprise*, 267–271; Mörner, *The Political and Economic Activities*, 168–169; Molina Cortón, "El tratado de límites," 208; Ganson, *The Guaraní*, 31; Almeida, *A diplomacia portuguesa*, vol. 1, 56–57; P. Lázaro de Aspurz, *La aportación extranjera a las misiones españolas del patronato regio* (Madrid: Consejo de la Hispanidad, 1946); Pierre Delattre and Edmond Lamalle, "Jésuites wallons, flamands, français missionnaires au Paraguay, 1608–1767," *Archivum Historicum Societatis Iesu* 15 (1946): 98–176; and Miguel Batllori, "Algunos aspectos internacionales de la compañía de Jesús en el Nuevo Mundo" and "Los jesuitas en el Brasil. La aportación italiana," both in his *Del descubrimiento a la independencia. Estudios sobre Iberoamérica y Filipinas* (Caracas: Universidad Católica Andrés Bello, 1979), 77–84 and 85–100.

76. Consulta of the conselho ultramarino, Lisbon, 12.11.1697, AHU_ACL_CU_013, cx. 4, d. 340; Rodríguez Castelo, *Diario del padre Fritz*, 86 and 110; "Relação da jornada do Solimões e Rio Negro por Frei Vitoriano Pimentel," dated 7.9.1705, reproduced in Carvalho, "Presencia e permanência," 185; and Juan Bautista Julián to the governor of Pará, La Laguna, 5.10.1730, AHU_ACL_CU_013, cx. 22, d. 2082.

77. Ángel Sanz Tapia, *El final del Tratado de Tordesillas. La Expedición del virrey Cevallos al Río de la Plata* (Valladolid: V Centenario del Tratado de

Tordesillas, 1994); Guedes, "A cartografia da delimitação," 26–27; and Renata Malcher de Araújo, *As Cidades da Amazónia no século XVIII*. *Belém, Macapá e Mazagão* (Porto: FAUP, 1998), 19–38 and 67. The "replacement" of Jesuit expertise with scientific expertise is studied in Nicholas Richard, "Une géographie post-jésuite au XVIIIe siècle," in Félix de Azara, *Voyages dans l'Amérique Méridionale, 1781–1801* (Rennes: Presses Universitaires de Rennes, 2009), vii–lxiv.

78. Domingues, *When the Amerindians Were Vassals;* and Almeida, "Os Vassalos d'El Rei," 65 and 68. Although nothing similar to the Portuguese *Directório* was implemented in Spanish territories, it is nevertheless clear that similar processes of secularization, centralization, and assimilation did take place at around the same time or perhaps a few decades later: Guillermo Wilde, *Religión y poder en las misiones de guaraníes* (Buenos Aires: Editorial SB, 2009), 265–267. The passage from an ecclesiastic to a secular discourse on the "other" is studied in Guillermo Wilde, "Orden y ambigüedad en la formación territorial del Río de la Plata a fines del siglo XVIII," *Horizontes antropológicos* 9(19) (2003): 105–135, on 109–112.

79. ANQ, FE 106, 6342-1, fols. 178r–217r; and Lázaro de Ribera to Santiago Liniers, San Nicolás de los Arroyos, 25.4.1808, AGI, Estado leg. 80, no. 107/4.

80. Diego de Alvear y Ponce, "Diario de la segunda partida de demarcación de límites entre los dominios de España y Portugal," 1783, BNL, C414; Vicente Aguilar y Jurado and Francisco Requena, "Historia de las demarcaciones de límites en la América entre los dominios de España," 1777, AMN, Ms. 283; "Diario da viagem que. . . . Francisco Xavier de Mendonça Furtado . . . a fês o Rio Negro," reproduced in Reis, *Limites e demarcações,* vol. 2, 276–290; and "Relación de viaje que de la capital de Santa Fe de Bogotá . . . hizo a las montañas de los Andaquines y misiones de los ríos Caqueta y Putumayo . . . don Sebastián Joseph López Ruiz," Santa Fe, 30.9.1783, AMRE/MRE/R/G.1.2.2, G-47, no. 18, fols. 62r–83r. See also Manuel Lucena Giraldo, *Ilustrados y bárbaros. Diario de la exploración de límites al Amazonas (1782)* (Madrid: Alianza Editorial, 1991).

81. Jorge Juan and Antonio Ulloa were naval officers charged by the king of Spain to accompany the French scientific mission that visited the viceroyalty of Peru between 1736 and 1744. In 1749 they authored *Disertación histórica y geográfica sobre el meridiano de demarcación* (Madrid: Instituto Histórico de la Marina, 1972). See also Luis J. Ramos Gómez, *El viaje a América (1735–1745) de los tenientes de navío Jorge Juan y Antonio Ulloa y sus consecuencias literarias* (Madrid: CSIC, 1985); Luis J. Ramos Gómez, *Época, génesis y texto de las Noticias Secretas de América de Jorge Juan y Antonio de Ulloa* (Madrid: CSIC, 1985); Antonio Lafuente and Antonio Mazuecos, *Los caballeros del punto fijo: Ciencia, política y aventura en la expedición geodésica hispanofrancesa al virreinato del Perú en el siglo XVIII* (Madrid: CSIC, 1987); and Herzog, *Upholding Justice,* 221–226.

82. Correspondence between Antonio de Ulloa and the Marqués de la Regalía, AGS, Marina 712, fol. 151; and "Notas sobre la disertación geográfica e histórica sobre el meridiano de demarcación entre las coronas de España y

Portugal impresa por orden de su majestad por Jorge Juan y Antonio de Ulloa, Madrid, año de 1748 o 1749" and a note to Julián de Arriaga, San Lorenzo, 15.10.1775, both in AHN, Estado leg. 4546, no. 1. See also Luis J. Ramos Gómez, "Jorge Juan y Antonio de Ulloa y el meridiano de Tordesillas: La disertación histórica y geográfica (1747–1776), in *El Tratado de Tordesillas y su época*, vol. 3, 1561–1592.

83. Flynn Roller, "River Guides," 111–112. The original report, titled "memória," can be found in Arquivo Histórico do Itamaraty in Rio de Janeiro, lata 288, Mç. 5, pasta 5. See also Graça Almeida Borges, "Entre a diplomacia e a cartografia: O 'tratado' de Francisco de Seixas e a soberania portuguesa na América," in Márcia Motta, José Vicente Serrão, and Marina Machado eds., *Em terras lusas: Conflitos e fronteiras no Império Português* (Rio de Janeiro: Universidade Federal Fluminense, 2013), 55–80.

84. Juan and Ulloa, *Disertación histórica*, 10. See also Neil Safier, *Measuring the New World: Enlightenment Science and South America* (Chicago: University of Chicago Press, 2008); and Wilson Martins, "Um agente secreto da coroa portuguesa na Amazônia: Alexandre Rodrigues Ferreira (1756–1815)," *Bulletin des Etudes Portugaises et Brésiliennes* 46–47 (1987): 171–183.

85. Francisco Requena to José García de León y Pizarro, 17.12.1783, AHN, Estado 4677-1, no. 7.

86. Joseph García de León Pizarro to Antonio Caballero y Góngora, 18.4.1784, Juan Joseph de Villalengua to José de Gálvez, Quito, 18.6.1784, and Francisco Requena to José García de León Pizarro, Egas, 17.12.1783, all in AHN, Estado 4677-1, no. 5.

87. Wilde, *Religión y poder*, 267 and 287–290; and Elisa Frühauf Garcia, "De inimigos a aliados: Como parte dos missionários repensou o seu passado de conflitos com os portugueses no contexto das tentativas de demarcação do tratado de Madri," *Anais de História de Alémmar* 8 (2007): 123–137.

88. The interrogatory elaborated by Juan Francisco Gómez de Villajufre y de Arce, 26.5.1775, and the declarations that followed it, ANQ, FE 30, vol. 83, no. 3226, fols. 80r–275v; Francisco Requena to Manuel da Gama Lobo de Almeida, 10.10.1791, AHN, Estado 4611; Joseph Dibuja to Diogo Luís de Barros e Vasconcelos, Quito, 24.2.1776, AHU_ACL_CU_013, cx. 76, d. 6348; and Manuel da Gama Lobo de Almada to Martinho de Melo e Castro, Fortaleza da Barra do Rio Negro, 22.7.1791, AHU_ACL_CU_020, cx. 16, d. 608.

89. Joaquín Alos to Nicolás Arrendondo, Asunción, 19.9.1791, AHN, Estado 4387, no. 5. Also see "Autos formados a consecuencia de una real cédula para que se informe a su majestad sobre la conducente a la provincia de Mainas," ANQ, FE 30, vol. 83, no. 3226, fols. 80r–275v, fols. 87r–v; declarations collected in the village of San Joachim de Omagua on 26.5.1775, ANQ, FE 30, vol. 83, no. 3226, fols. 80r–275v, fols. 95v–107v; and Juan Francisco Gómez de Arce to Joseph Dibuja, Omagua, 12.10.1775, ANQ, FE 30, vol. 83, no. 3226, fols. 80r–275v, fols. 108r–113r. On how the Portuguese responded, see, for example, Feliz José Souza to Francisco José Teixeira, Forte el príncipe de la Vera, 23.11.1784, AHN, Estado 4436, no. 10.

90. Francisco Rodrigues to the Governor of Pará, Barcelos, 24.4.1765, APEP, Cod. 151, doc. 131. See also Joaquim Tinoco Valente, Barcelos, 5.12.1764,

APEP, Cod. 155, doc. 9. The relationship between controlling (or anihilating) Indians and territorial acquisition was studied in Rafael Chabouleyron and Vanice Siqueira de Melo, "Indios, engenhos e currais na fronteira oriental do estado do Maranhão e Pará (século XVII)," in Márcia Motta, José Vicente Serrão, and Marina Machado eds., *Em terras lusas: Conflitos e fronteiras no Império Português* (Rio de Janeiro: Universidade Federal Fluminense, 2013), 231–259.

91. Information supplied by Joachin Fernández de Bustos, ANQ, FE 111, vol. 264, doc. 6492, fols. 167r–240r. See also Wilde, *Religión y poder*, 296; and Elisa Frühauf Garcia, *As diversas formas de ser índio. Políticas indígenas e políticas indigenistas no extremo sul da América portuguesa* (Rio de Janeiro: Arquivo Nacional, 2009).

92. "Informação de Francisco Caldeira Castelo Branco Lara para que se averigúe acerca das questões que apresenta," Pará, 10.11.1618, AHU_ACL_CU_009, cx. 1, d. 21; petition of Melchor Ruiz del Mármol, 1681, ANQ, Gobierno 7, Exp. 5 de 5.5.1681; petition of Manuel de Laviano, Quito, 14.5.1711, ANQ, FE 9, vol. 22, no. 701, fol. 71r; Bernardo Pereira de Berredo to the king, Belém, 10.8.1721, AHU_ACL_CU_009, cx. 13, d. 1316; petition of Pablo Noa, ANQ, Indígenas 42 Exp. 25 de 2.11.1729; petition of Felipe Romero, discussed in the audiencia of Quito on 17.5.1754, ANQ, Gobierno 17, Exp. 4 de 9.5.1754; Diego de Sala to Francisco Bucareli y Ursua, Buenos Aires, 5.7.1768 and 3.9.1768, AGN/BA, IX.11.5.6; Luis de Albuquerque de Melo Pereira e Cáceres to Martinho de Melo e Castro, Vila Bela, 25.5.1773, AHU_ACL_CU_101, cx. 17. d. 1026; and the city council of Rio Grande de São Pedro to the king, Viamão, 23.9.1771, AHU_ACL_CU_019, cx. 2, d. 171. See also Hal Langfur, "Moved by Terror: Frontier Violence as Cultural Exchange in Late-Colonial Brazil," *Ethnohistory* 52(2) (2005): 255–289; and Martha Bechis, "Ángulos y aristas de la guerra por las vacas en los comienzos del siglo XVIII: 'Divertimentos' asesinatos y rivalidades jurisdiccionales," in *Piezas de etnohistoria del sur sudamericano* (Madrid: CSIC, 2008), 53–80.

93. Richard Slatta, "Spanish Colonial Military Strategy and Ideology," in Donna J. Guy and Thomas E. Sheridan, eds., *Contested Grounds: Comparative Frontiers on the Northern and Southern Edges of the Spanish Empire* (Tucson: University of Arizona Press, 1998), 83–96; Guillermo Boccara, "Génesis y estructura de los complejos fronterizos euro-indígenas. Repensando los márgenes americanos a partir (y más allá) de la obra de Nathan Wachtel," *Memoria Americana* 13 (2005): 21–52; Hal Langfur, *The Forbidden Lands: Colonial Identity, Frontier Violence, and the Persistence of Brazil's Eastern Indians, 1750–1830* (Stanford: Stanford University Press, 2006), 24–30; Sara Ortelli, *Trama de una Guerra conveniente. Nueva Vizcaya y la sombra de los apaches (1748–1790)* (Mexico-City: Colegio de México, 2007); Martha Bechis, "La participación de la capitanía general de Chile y del virreinato del Río de la Plata en la génesis de la "nación Pehuenche," in *Piezas de etnohistoria*, 141–164; and Christophe Giudicelli, " 'Identidades' rebeldes. Soberanía colonial y poder de clasificación: sobre la categoría calchaquí (Tucumán, Santa Fe, siglos XVI–XVII)," in Alejandra Araya and Jaime Valenzuela, eds., *América colonial. Denominaciones, clasificaciones e identidades en América colonial* (Santiago: PUCC/Universidad de Chile, 2010), 137–172.

94. Decree of Pedro Melo de Portugal, Buenos Aires, 20.10.1797, BRAH/M, 9-1666, fols. 35r–36v.

95. Manuel Fernández to viceroy Arredondo, 7.9.1791, AGN/BA, IX.1.4.3. See also Almir Diniz de Carvalho Júnior, "Índios cristãos. A conversão dos gentios na Amazônia portuguesa (1653–1769)" (Ph.D. diss., Universidade Estadual de Campinas, 2005), 41 and 54.

96. "Por este meio acresceram a coroa e estados seus porque os que conseguiram ver a felicidade desta empresa, não só com os olhos em o céu, senão também em terra tem por certo que com ela se acabou de conquistar o Estado do Maranhão, porque com os Ingaybas por inimigos seria o Pará de qualquer nação estrangeira que se confederasse com eles, e com os Ingaybas por vassalos e por amigos fica o Pará seguro e impenetrável a todo o poder estranho." Bettendorff, *Crônica da missão*, 143. See also Almeida, "Os Vassalos d'El Rei," 70; Barbara Ann Sommer, "Negotiated Settlements: Native Amazonian and Portuguese Policy in Para, Brazil, 1758–1798" (Ph.D. diss., University of New Mexico, 2000); Mary Karasch, "Rethinking the Conquest of Goias, 1775–1819," *Americas* 61(3) (2005): 462–492; and Nádia Farage, *As muralhas dos sertões. Os povos indígenas no rio Branco e a colonização* (São Paulo: Paz e Terra, 1991).

97. Diogo de Mendonça Corte Real to Francisco Xavier de Mendonça Furtado, Lisbon, 1.6.1756, AHU_ACL_CU_020, cx. 1, d. 44; information sent by Felipe Sturm, Boca rio Tacutu, 19.11.1775, AHU_ACL_CU_013, cx. 75, d. 6279, also reproduced in APEP, Cod. 294, doc. 7, pp. 25–27; and João Pereira Caldas to Martinho de Melo e Castro, Barcelos, 21.6.1785, AHU_ACL_CU_020, cx. 9, d. 380.

98. "Passaporte del capitam geral de Mato Grosso João de Albuquerque de Mello Pereira e Cáceres," 29.7.1791, AHN, Estado 4548.

99. João Martins Barrosto to Luís Antônio de Sousa, Iguatemi, 30.1.1771, AHU_ACL_CU_023-01, cx. 27, d. 2553.

100. Luís Antônio de Sousa to Martinho de Melo e Castro, São Paulo, 21.4.1771, AHU_ACL_CU_023-01, cx. 27, d. 2553.

101. "Lembrando-me daquela celebre reposta que um embaixador de Marrocos deu na corte de Paris a quem lhe notou haver oferecido ao rei umas poucas peles de onça e de marroquim, ce n'est pas, lhe disse ele, la quantité ni la qualité de ces présents qu'il faut regardé; c'est l'impression qu'ils portent de l'hommage et des respects que je vins rendre au monarque à qui je les présente. Tout ce qu'il-y-a de plus précieux est au-dessous de la grandeur du Roy." Luís Antônio de Sousa to Martinho de Melo e Castro, São Paulo, 21.4.1771, AHU_ACL_CU_023-01, cx. 27, d. 2553.

102. On how European records can be read to rescue a native voice, see the powerful reconstruction in Daniel K. Richter, *Facing East from Indian Country: A Native History of Early America* (Cambridge, MA: Harvard University Press, 2001), for example, on 150.

103. "Notícias da voluntária redução de paz da feroz nação do gentio Mura nos anos de 1784, 1785 e 1786," *Boletim de Pesquisa da CEDEAM* 3(5) (1984): 17–87. Similar suspicions may have been directed at other groups too: Chabouleyron and Siqueira de Melo, "Indios, engenhos e currais," 244–245.

104. "Porque não sendo isto obra de um dia, pouco a pouco, com brandura e com rigor, poderão chegar ao ponto desejado." João Baptista Mardel to João Pereira Caldas, Nogueira, 26.7.1785, in "Notícias da voluntária redução de paz da feroz nação do gentio Mura nos anos de 1784, 1785 e 1786," *Boletim de Pesquisa da CEDEAM* 3(5) (1984): 17–87, on 45. See also João Pereira Caldas to João Baptista Mardel, Barcellos, 4.4.1786, in the same journal on 62–63.

105. "Tratados que deberá observar con este superior gobierno el cacique Callfilqui," AGN/BA, BN 189, Exp. 1877; "Instrumento judicial hecho en el río de los Engaños de las noticias que dieron los indios infieles Omaguaes," AHN, Estado 4500/1; Joseph Dibuja to Jose de Gálvez, Quito, 18.7.1776 and 16.4.1777, ANQ, FE 37, vol. 102, no. 3754-16, fols. 29r–32v, and ANQ, FE 40, vol. 108, no. 3855-15, fols. 31r–35v.

106. "Ordenanzas de Nueva Población," reproduced in Francisco Morales Padrón, *Teoría y leyes de la conquista* (Madrid: Ediciones cultura hispánica, 1979), 489–518, art. 138–148 on 515–518; and Bernardo de Vargas Machuca, *Milicia y descripción de las Indias* (Madrid: Victoriano Suárez, 1892 [1599]), vol. 2, book 4, 12–13. An English translation of this book is available as Bernardo de Vargas Machuca, *The Indian Militia and Description of the Indies*, ed. Kris Lane (Durham, NC: Duke University Press, 2008).

107. "Excmo. señor gobernador y capitán general . . . doy parte como llegaron al pueblo de San Fernando dos caciques principales de nación Moscovi," 1771, ANC/S, Jesuitas, vol. 159, pieza 7, fols. 35r–37v.

108. "Si verdaderamente desean establecerse en el lugar de los Remolinos, de esta jurisdicción, y si es su ánimo abrazar la santa fe de Jesús Cristo, y guardar en todo tan santa religión, como así mismo observan una firme paz con la provincia, sus estantes y habitantes y con cuantos cristianos habiten esos parajes y naveguen el río a cuyas márgenes se han de establecer" and "Es forzoso se instruyan de las obligaciones a que quedan afectos en correspondencia de la amistad y paz que les promete la provincia de sus contribuciones y costos, a fin de que en ningún tiempo se rompa ésta y sea perpetua": "Tratado entre el cacique Etasurim y el gobernador y capitán general de Asunción, Ángel Ernando de Pinedo, Asunción, 1.6.1776," reproduced in Lidia R. Nacuzzi, "Los cacicazgos del siglo XVIII en ámbitos de frontera de Pampa-Patagonia y el Chaco ," in Mónica Quijada, ed., *De los Cacicazgos a la ciudadanía. Sistemas políticos en la frontera, Río de la Plata, Siglos XVIII–XX* (Berlin: Gebr. Mann Verlag, 2001), 23–77, apéndice IV, 74–77, on 74 and 76.

109. Vargas Machuca, "The Defence of Western Conquests," in *The Indian Militia*, 248; Manuel Bernardo de Melo de Castro to Francisco Xavier de Mendonça Furtado, Pará, 9.4.1763 and 20.6.1763, AHU_ACL_CU_013, cx. 54, d. 4913 and d. 4948; "Declaración de tres indios que acaban de llegar desertados con cuatro chinas del Río Pardo, 10.4.1775," AGN/BA, IX.4.3.7; and Monteiro de Noronha, *Roteiro da viagem*, point 74 on 42. See also Gabriel Darío Taruselli, "De conchabados a bandidos: Alianzas y traiciones en el mundo rural bonaerense durante el siglo XVIII," unpublished paper presented in the V Jornadas de Investigadores del Departamento de Historia, 2–3 septiembre de 2004, Mar del Plata, Argentina.

110. "Que vivan con más cuidado y vigilancia al cumplimiento de su obligación para que en lo sucesivo no sean sorprendidos tan vilmente de esta canalla." Diego de Sala to Francisco Bucareli y Ursua, Buenos Aires, 5.7.1768, AGN/BA, IX.11.5.6.

111. These two last options were mentioned in Lázaro de Ribera to José de Espínola, Santa Rosa, 28.1.1797, AGI, Estado 81, n. 15 (1b); and "Presentación a Lázaro de Ribera, gobernador intendente de Paraguay por los oficiales vecinos y comandantes de las tropas auxiliares," undated, AGI, Estado 81, n. 15 (1a).

112. The negotiations between the "cacique infiel Cumbay" and Jorge Michel in 1806, AGN/BA, IX.24.04.06, fol. 6r; and Francisco Xavier de Mendonça Furtado to António Rolim de Moura, Lisbon, 18.6.1761, APMG, CMG-SG, Livro C-18, Estante-01, letter 5, fols. 32r–35r, fols. 34r–v.

113. "Y no conformándose en la práctica de todo lo que contienen, después de haberles esforzado y persuadido a su condescendencia, los hará retirar a su campo en señal de rompimiento y los castigará con la mayor severidad posible para su escarmiento." "Capítulos que debe proponer Manuel Pinazo a los indios aucas para convenir en el paz que solicitan, Buenos aires, 8.5.1770," reproduced in Nacuzzi, "Los cacicazgos," apéndice II, 70–71, on 71.

114. "Só por ações se percebe pretenderem descer." The director of Vila de Serpa dated 24.9.1786 in "Notícias da voluntária redução de paz da feroz nação do gentio Mura nos anos de 1784, 1785 e 1786," Boletim de Pesquisa da CEDEAM 3(5) (1984): 17–87, on 84–85.

115. José Antonio Maravall, La teoría española del estado en el siglo XVII (Madrid: Instituto de Estudios Políticos, 1944), 321–330 and 358–359; and Jose-Manuel Pérez Prendes Muñoz de Arraco, "Los criterios jurídicos de Cristóbal Colón," in "J. M. Pérez Prendes Muñoz de Arraco, Pareceres (1956–1998)," ed. Magdalena Rodríguez Gil, special issue, Revista de historia del derecho 7 (1999) (2): 1035–1062, on 1045–1046.

116. The requirement, used by Spaniards in the sixteenth century, informed Indians of papal donation and, requesting that they "consider what we have said to you, and that you take the time that shall be necessary to understand and deliberate upon it," nonetheless demanded complete compliance. Failure to do so would result in Spaniards threatening that they would "powerfully enter into your country, and shall make war against you in all ways and manners that we can, and shall subject you to the yoke and obedience of the church and their highnesses; we shall take you and your wives and your children, and shall make slaves of them." In these citations, I use the translation included in John H. Parry and Robert G. Keith, eds., New Iberian World: A Documentary History of the Discovery and Settlement of Latin America to the Early 17th Century (New York: Times Books, 1984), vol. 1, 288–290.

117. Abelardo Levaggi, Paz en la frontera. Historia de las relaciones diplomáticas con las comunidades indígenas en la Argentina (siglos XVI–XIX) (Buenos Aires: Universidad del Museo Social Argentino, 2000); Abelardo Levaggi, Diplomacia hispano-indígena en las fronteras de América. Historia de los tratados entre la monarquía española y las comunidades aborígenes (Madrid: Centro de Estudios Políticos y Constitucionales, 2002); Eugenia A. Néspolo, "Los tratados escritos con las sociedades indígenas en los bordes del río Salado durante el siglo

XVIII. Un análisis desde el derecho de gentes," *Memoria Americana. Cuadernos de etnohistoria* 12 (2004): 237–276; and Carlos Lázaro Ávila, "Conquista, control y convicción: El papel de los parlamentos indígenas en México, el Chaco y Norteamérica," *Revista de Indias* 59(217) (1999): 645–673.

118. Joseph Dibuja to José de Gálvez, Quito, 18.7.1776, ANQ, FE 37, vol. 102, n. 3754-16, fols. 29r–32v; Manuel Guzmán to Feliz José de Souza, Exaltación, 21.9.1784, AHN, Estado 4436; "Certificado de Don Manuel Mariano de Echeverría," ANQ, Gobierno 24, Exp. 9 de 14.7.1771, fols. 3r–5r; "Requerimento do índio principal da aldeia de Mortigura da nação Aruaquizes Apolinário Rodrigues para o rei," before 9.3.1757, AHU_ACL_CU_013, cx. 42, d. 3841; negotiations between the "cacique infiel Cumbay" and Jorge Michel, AGN/BA, IX.24.04.06, fol. 4r; and João Martins Barrosto to Luís Antônio de Sousa, Iguatemi, 30.1.1771, AHU_ACL_CU_023-01, cx. 27, d. 2553.

119. Bettendorff, *Crônica da missão*, 56; and ANQ, Criminales 156, Exp. 6 de 9.10.1793. See also Taruselli, "De conchabados a bandidos"; and Carvalho, "Lealdades negociadas," 227–228 and 233.

120. Petition of the Jesuit Pedro Joseph Melanesio, 8.10.1751, ANQ, FE 15, vol. 42, no. 1583, fols. 135r–6v; and Cristovão da Costa Freire to the king, Belém, 15.3.1712, AHU_ACL_CU_013, cx. 6, d. 482. See also Cecilia Sheridan, "Social Control and Native Territoriality in Northeastern New Spain," in Jesús F. De la Teja and Ross Frank, eds., *Choice, Persuasion, and Coercion: Social Control on Spain's North American Frontier* (Albuquerque: University of New Mexico Press, 2005), 121–148, on 125–129; and Langfur, *The Forbidden Lands*, 217–225.

121. Manuel Fernández to Nicolás Arredondo, 5.9.1791, AGN/BA, IX.1.4.3.

122. Marqués de Avilés to Joseph Francisco de Amigorena, Santiago de Chile, 14.3.1797, and Marqués de Sobremonte to Nicolás Arrendondo, 15.5.1792, both in AGN/BA, IX.11.4; Pedro Antonio Cervino, Buenos Aires, 25.6.1804, AGN/BA, BN 189, Exp. 1882; "Autos de don Anotnio de la Peña sobre informe a España," Quito, 11.7.1771, ANQ, Gobierno 24, Exp. 9 de 14.7.1771; and Conde de São Miguel to the secretary of state Diogo de Mendonça Corte Real, Vila Boa, 12.12.1755, AHU_ACL_CU_008, cx. 13, d. 775.

123. João Maia da Gama to the king, São Luís de Maranhão, 9.7.1726, AHU_ACL_CU_009, cx. 15, d. 1525.

124. "Tratado entre el gobernador Urizar y los Lules," reproduced in José Miranda Borelli, "Tratados de paz realizados con los indígenas en la Argentina (1597–1875)," *Suplemento antropológico* 19(2) (1984): 233–284, on 245–246.

125. Manuel Fernández to Nicolás Arredondo, 10.11.1791, AGN/BA, IX.1.4.3; and Juan Francisco de Ecala to Marqués de Avilés, Frontera del Monte, 7.10.1799, AGN/BA, IX.1.4.6.

126. Bettendorff, *Crônica da missão*, 140–141.

127. "No haríamos mucho caso de dios ni del rey cuando la palabra que les habíamos dado en nombre de ambos la habíamos quebrantado sin dar ellos motivo alguno." Joseph Vaguer to Juan José Vertiz, Fuerte de San Joseph, 29.6.1770, AGN/BA, IX.1.5.2. See also Conde de dos Arcos to the king, Vila Boa, 10.2.1751, AHU_ACL_CU_008, cx. 6, d. 466.

128. "No hay cosa que más altere al indio conquistador, que quebrarle las condiciones y palabras y no cumplírselas, con las cuales se han sujetado al dominio y vasallaje." Vargas Machuca, *Milicia y descripción*, vol. 2, book 4, 57. In the text, I used the translation published in Vargas Machuca, *The Indian Militia*, 158–159. Also see 49–50 and 52–57.

129. The interrogatory and the declarations of Fernando de Santillán and Jorge Ichel in AGN/BA, IX.23.2.5, Cuaderno 1, fols. 23v–24v and 27r–v.

130. Petition of Pedro Antonio Cervino, Buenos Aires, 25.6.1804, AGN/BA, BN 189, Exp. 1882.

131. "Presentación a Lázaro de Ribera ... por los oficiales, vecinos y comandantes de las tropas auxiliares," undated, AGI, Estado 81, n. 15 (1a).

132. Abílio da Costa Brochado, "O problema da guerra justa em Portugal," *Rumo. Revista de cultura portuguesa* 1 (1946): 41–59; Beatriz Perrone-Moisés, "A guerra justa em Portugal no séc. XVI," *Revista da SBPH* 5 (1989/90): 5–10; Alida C. Metcalf, "The Entradas of Bahia of the Sixteenth Century," *The Americas* 61(3) (2005): 373–400; Márcia Eliane Alves de Souza e Mello, "Desvendando outras Franciscas: Mulheres cativas e as ações de liberdade na Amazônia colonial portuguesa," *Portuguese Studies Review* 13(1) (2005): 1–16; Márcia Eliane Alves de Souza e Mello, *Fé e império. As juntas das missões nas conquistas portuguesas* (Manaus: Universidade Federal do Amazonas, 2007); António Manuel Hespanha, "Luís de Molina e a escravização dos negros," *Análise social* 25 (2001): 937–960; and Marcocci, *A consciência de um império*, 281–333.

133. Conde de Sabugosa to the king, Bahia, 23.6.1726 and 18.5.1734, AHU_ACL_CU_005, cx. 27, d. 2468, and cx. 47, d. 4220; Rodrigo César de Meneses to the king, Cuiabá, 28.3.1728, AHU_ACL_CU_010, cx. 1, d. 24; Luís Barbosa de Lima to the king, Pará, 2.10.1732, AHU_ACL_CU_013, cx. 14, d. 1329; and João de Abreu de Castelo Branco to António Guedes Pereira, Belém, 9.9,1738, AHU_ACL_CU_013, cx. 21, d. 1982.

134. "Sendo nossos confederados e amigos recebendo todo ... em nossas terras, casas e fazendas com toda afabilidade socorrendo de todo o necessário que por eles nos era pedido e debaixo desta aliança terem feito grandes extorsões, mortes e roubos." Inácio Coelho da Silva to the regent prince, Pará, 20.4.1679, AHU_ACL_CU_013, cx. 2, d. 178.

135. João de Maia da Gama to the king, Belém, 23.10.1726, AHU_ACL_CU_013, cx. 10, d. 863.

136. "Parecer do frei Clemente de São Joseph, comissário provincial de Santo Antônio e membro da junta das missões," in *Autos da devassa contra os índios Mura do Rio Madeira e nações do Rio Tocatins (1738–1739)*, introd. Adélia Engrácia de Oliveira, transcip. Raimundo Martins de Lima (Manaus: Universidade do Amazonas, 1986), 97–111; and Bettendorff, *Crônica da missão*, 217–218.

137. Pedro Puntoni, *A guerra dos bárbaros. Povos indígenas e a colonização do sertão nordeste do Brasil, 1760–1720* (São Paulo: Universidade de São Paulo, 2000), 77–81.

138. "Ley ... de 9.4.1655 sobre os índios do Maranhão," *Anais da Biblioteca Nacional* 66(1): 25–28; and "Instruções régias públicas e secretas para Francisco Xavier de Mendonça," in d'Azevedo, *Os jesuítas no Grão Pará*, 348–356, note F.

139. Draft of "Instruções do secretário de estado Martinho de Melo e Castro para o governador e capitão-geral de São Paulo Luís Antônio de Sousa," Lisbon, 22.4.1774, AHU_ACL_CU_023-01, cx. 29, d. 2661.

140. The move from "conquest" to "pacification" was enshrined in the "Ordenanzas de Nueva Población" of 1573, reproduced in Morales Padrón, *Teoría y leyes*, 489–518, that in article 20 prohibited the use of war and in article 29 instructed that discoveries not be called "conquests" because they should be carried out with "peace and charity." Most of these rules were reproduced in the *Recopilación de Indias*, the main legal compilation of colonial legislation, book 4, title 1, laws 6 and 10. De jure prohibited, de facto, some wars did take place: petition of the Jesuit Pedro Joseph Melanesio, 8.10.1751, ANQ, FE 15, vol. 42, no. 1583, fols. 135r–6v; petition of Miguel Hernández Bello, Quito, 13.7.1979, ANQ, FE 150, vol. 343, no. 8216, fols. 44r–47v; letter of Juan Jose de Sarden to the viceroy, Fuerte de Monte, 4.11.1780, AGN/BA, IX.1.4.6; and letter to Luis García de Vivar, Buenos Aires, 16.9.1754, AGN/BA, IX.3.8.2. See also Silvio Zavala, *Los esclavos indios en Nueva España* (Mexico City: El Colegio Nacional, 1967); David Block, *Mission Culture on the Upper Amazon: Native Tradition, Jesuit Enterprise, and Secular Policy in Moxos, 1660–1880* (Lincoln: University of Nebraska Press, 1994), 33; Cecilia Sheridan, *Anónimos y Desterrados. La contienda por el "sitio que llaman de Quauyla," XVI–XVIII siglos* (Mexico City: CIESAS, 2000), 17 and 77–78; and Paul Wojtalewicz, "The Junta de Missões/Junta de Misiones: A Comparative Study of Peripheries and Imperial Administration in Eighteenth-Century Iberian Empires," *Colonial Latin American Review* 8(2) (1999): 225–240.

141. Their petition to the governor, undated, and letter of Lázaro de Rivera to José de Espínola, Santa Rosa, 28.1.1797, AHN, Estado 3410, no. 13.

142. "Atendiendo que el bárbaro no sólo se ha hecho dueño de los dominios sino también se ha excedido a destruir los vasallos y sus haciendas . . . con la más sangrienta persecución": petition of Rafael Torrico, Laguna, 17.1.1805, in AGN/BA, IX.23.2.5, Cuaderno 1, fols. 42r–45r, fols. 43r–v; Diego Velasco to Ramón Pizarro, La Laguna, 19.1.1805; Ramón Pizarro to Marqués de Sobremonte, La Plata, 25.1.1805; Vicente Rodriguez Romano, La Plata, 7.7.1808, AGN/BA, IX.23.2.5, Cuaderno 1, fols. 45v–123v, and Cuaderno 8 (unnumbered).

143. On how peace and war could coincide and how they were both related to conversion, see also Marcocci, *A consciência de un império*, 252–265.

144. Ramón García Pizarro to Marqués de Sobremonte, La Plata, 25.8.1806, AGN/BA, IX.24.4.6, Exp. 39; Pedro Antonio Cervino, Buenos Aires, 25.6.1804, AGN/BA, BN 189, Exp. 1882; "Expedición para contener las irrupciones de los indios infieles de las fronteras de la cordillera de los Sauces," AGN/BA, IX.24.4.8, Exp. 50; Joaquin Alos to Nicolás Arrendondo, Asunción, 19.9.1791 and 19.1.1793, AHN, Estado 4387, no. 4, and Estado 4548; and Martín Boneo to Joaquín de Aosmino, Asunción, 14.10.1790, BRAH/M, 9-1663, fols. 36–41.

145. "Tratados que deberá observar con este superior gobierno el cacique Callfilqui," AGN/BA, BN 189, Exp. 1877, partly reproduced in Levaggi, *Paz en la frontera*, 135; and Levaggi, *Diplomacia hispano-indígena*, 240–241.

146. "Tratado entre el gobernador Urizar y los Malbalaes," reproduced in Borelli, "Tratados de paz," 243–244; Francisco Coelho de Carvalho to the king, 28.2.1624, AHU_ACL_CU_009, cx. 1, d. 79; and "Carta Patente de principal," given by Francisco Xavier de Mendonça Furtado on 6.10.1752, petitions of Ignacio Coelho, Francisco de Souza de Menezes, and Luís de Miranda to the king, all three dated 15.3.1755, and Sebastião José de Carvalho e Mello to the conselho ultramarino, 15.3.1755, all cited in Mauro Cezar Coelho, "De guerreiro a principal: Integração das chefias indígenas à estrutura de poder colonial, sob o Diretório dos índios (1758–1798)," in *Actas do congresso internacional "Espaço Atlântico de Antigo Regime: Poderes e Sociedades," Lisboa 2 a 5 Novembro de 2005,* 6, available at http://cvc.instituto-camoes.pt/eaar/coloquio/comunicacoes/mauro_cezar_coelho.pdf. See also Farage, *As muralhas dos sertões,* 160–163 and 170.

147. Neil L. Whitehead, "Tribes Make States and States Make Tribes: Warfare and the Creation of Colonial Tribes and States in Northeastern South America," in R. Brian Ferguson and Neil L. Whitehead, eds., *War in the Tribal Zone: Expanding States and Indigenous Warfare* (Santa Fe, NM: School of American Research Press, 1992), 127–150; Guillaume Boccara, "Antropología política en los márgenes del Nuevo Mundo. Categorías coloniales, tipologías antropológicas y producción de la diferencia," in Christophe Giudicelli, ed., *Fronteras movedizas. Clasificaciones coloniales y dinámicas socioculturales en las fronteras americanas* (Mexico-City: CEMCA, 2010), 103–135, on 119–120; Christophe Giudicelli, "¿'Naciones' de enemigos? La identificación de los indios rebeldes en la Nueva Vizcaya (siglo XVII)," in Salvador Bernabéu Albert, ed., *El gran norte mexicano. Indios, misioneros y pobladores entre el mito y la historia* (Seville: CSIC, 2009), 27–57; Alexandra V. Roth, "The Xebero "indios amigos"? Their Part in the Ancient Province of Mainas," in María Susana Cipolletti, ed., *Resistencia y adaptación nativas en las tierras bajas latinoamericanas* (Quito: Abya-Yala, 1997), 107–122; Garcia, *As diversas formas,* 138–139 and 227–265; and Puntoni, *A guerra dos bárbaros,* 60–61, 68–69, and 77.

148. Francisco Vitoria, "De Indis (1539)," reproduced and translated in Anthony Pagden and Jeremy Lawrance, eds., *Francisco de Vitoria: Political Writing* (Cambridge: Cambridge University Press, 1991). See also Anthony Pagden, "Dispossessing the Barbarian: The Language of Spanish Thomism and the Debate over the Property Rights of the American Indians," in David Armitage, ed., *Theories of Empire, 1450–1800* (Aldershot: Ashgate-Variorum, 1998), 159–178; Anthony Pagden, *Lords of All the World: Ideologies of Empire in Spain, Britain, and France, c.1500–c.1800* (New Haven, CT: Yale University Press, 1995), 46–62, on 47–49; Rolena Adorno, *The Polemics of Possession in Spanish American Narrative* (New Haven, CT: Yale University Press, 2007); Joshua Castellino and Steve Allen, *Title to Territory in International Law: A Temporal Analysis* (Aldershot: Ashgate, 2003), 42–55; and Christopher Tomlins, *Freedom Bound: Law, Labor, and Civic Identity in Colonizing English America, 1580–1865* (New York: Cambridge University Press, 2010), 115–120, 131–134, 143, and 148.

149. Martin Kintzinger, "From the Late Middle Ages to the Peace of Westphalia," in Bardo Fassbender and Anne Peters, eds., *The Oxford Handbook of the History of International Law* (Oxford: Oxford University Press, 2012), 608–627,

613, and 618; and Marti Koskenniemi, "Histories of International Law: Dealing with Eurocentrism," *Rechtsgeschichte* 19 (2011): 152–176. See also Robert A. Williams, *The American Indian in Western Legal Thought: The Discourses of Conquest* (Oxford: Oxford University Press, 1990), 6–7; and Lauren Benton and Benjamin Straumann, "Acquiring Empire by Law: From Roman Doctrine to Early Modern European Practice," *Law and History Review* 28(1) (2010): 1–38.

150. Andrew Fitzmaurice, "Discovery, Conquest, and Occupation of Territory," in *The Oxford Handbook of the History of International Law*, 840–861, 841; and Fitzmaurice, *Sovereignty, Property, and Empire, 1500–2000* (Cambridge: Cambridge University Press, 2014).

151. Paolo Marchetti, *De Iure Finium. Diritto e confine tra tardo medioevo ed età moderna* (Milan: Giuffrè Editore, 2001), 73–4, 96–111, and 185–181; and Castellino and Allen, *Title to Territory*, 29–89.

152. Thomas More, *Utopia*, trans. Gilbert Burnet (Dublin: R. Reilly, 1737 [1516]), 60–61.

153. Alberico Gentili, *De Iure Belli libri tre*, trans. John C. Rolf (Oxford: Clarendon Press, 1933; modern reprint of the 1612 edition [1588]), book 1, chapter 17, 80–81.

154. Hugo Grotius, *The Freedom of the Seas or the Right Which Belongs to the Dutch to Take Part in the East Indian Trade*, trans. Ralph van Deman Magoffin (New York: Oxford University Press, 1916 [1609]), chapter 2, 11–12, chapter 5, 24–30, 34, and 39, and chapter 7, 47–60; and Grotius, *On the Law of War*, book 2, chapter 2, 4, 11, and 17, and chapter 4, 1–3 and 8–9.

155. Pufendorf, *Of the Law of Nature*, book 4, chapter 4, 1, 2, 4, 6, 9, and 13, and chapter 6, 3 and 4 and chapter 12, 7–9 and 11. Also see Olivecrona, "Appropriation," 216–217.

156. Emilio Bussi, *La formazione dei dogma di diritto private nel diritto commune (diritti reali e diritti di obbligazione)* (Padova: Cedam, 1937), 22–30; and Paolo Grossi, *Il dominio e le cose. Percezioni medievali e moderne dei diritti reali* (Milan: Guiffrè, 1992).

157. "Y verdaderamente para las islas y tierras que hallaron por ocupar y poblar de otras gentes, o ya porque nunca antes las hubiesen habitado o porque si las habitaron se pasaron a otras y las dejaron incultas, no se puede negar que lo sea y de los más conocidos por el derecho natural y de todas las gentes, que dieron este premio a industria y quisieron que lo libre cediese a los que primero lo hallasen y ocupasen y así se fue practicando en todas las provincias del mundo, como a cada paso nos lo enseña Aristóteles, Cicerón, nuestros jurisconsultos y sus glosadores" and "los lugares desiertos e incultos quedan en la libertad natural y son del que primero los ocupa en premio de su industria": Solórzano y Pereira, *Política Indiana*, book 1, chapter 9, points 13–14 and 18–19 on 90–92.

158. Nuix, *Reflexiones imparciales*, 138–144.

159. Botella Ordinas, "¿Era inevitable 1808?"; Eva Botella Ordinas, "Debating Empire, Investigating Empires: British Territorial Claims against the Spaniards in America, 1670–1714," *Journal for Early Modern Cultural Studies* 10(10) (2010): 142–168; and Eliga H. Gould, "Entangled Histories, Entangled

Worlds: The English-Speaking Atlantic as a Spanish Periphery," *American Historical Review* 112(3) (2007): 764–786, on 770–772.

160. Nuix, *Reflexiones imparciales*, 145–149.

161. John Locke, *Two Treatises of Government* (London: Black Swan, 1698), second treaty, chapter 5, points 27–51, especially points 31–32. Locke's treatises were studied by many. I found the following most useful: C.B. MacPherson, *The Political Theory of Possessive Individualism: Hobbes to Locke* (Oxford: Clarendon Press, 1962); and James Tully, *A Discourse on Property: John Locke and His Adversaries* (Cambridge: Cambridge University Press, 1980). See also Paulo Grossi, *An Alternative to Private Property: Collective Property in the Juridical Consciousness of the 19th Century*, trans. Lydia Cochrane (Chicago: University of Chicago Press, 1981); J.M. Neeson, *Commoners: Common Right, Enclosure, and Social Change, England, 1700–1829* (Cambridge: Cambridge University Press, 1993), 15–109 and 313–319; Laura Brace, "Husbanding the Earth and Hedging out the Poor," in A.R. Buch, John Mclaren, and Nancy E. Wright, eds., *Land and Freedom: Law, Property Rights, and the British Diaspora* (Burlington, VT: Aldershot 2001), 16–17; Laura Brace, *The Idea of Property in Seventeenth-Century England: Tithes and the Individual* (Manchester: Manchester University Press, 1998), 164; James Warren Springer, "American Indian and the Law of Real Property in Colonial New England," *American Journal of Legal History* 30(1) (1986): 25–58, 45–46; James Muldoon, *Canon Law, the Expansion of Europe and World Order* (Aldershot: Ashgate, 1998), chapters 4 and 6; and Tamar Herzog, "Did European Law Turn American? Territory, Property and Rights in an Atlantic World," in Thomas Duve and Heikki Pihlajamäki, eds., *New Horizons of Spanish Colonial Law: Contributions to Transnational Early Modern Legal History* (Frankfurt: Vittorio Klostermann-Max Planck, forthcoming).

162. "El hombre, después de haber disputado con las fieras el domino de la naturaleza sujetó las unas a obedecer el imperio de su voz y obligó a las demás a vivir escondidas en la espesura de los montes, y cómo rompiendo con su ayuda los bosques y malezas que cubrían la tierra, supo enseñorearla y hacerla servir a sus necesidades" and "el oficio del labrador es luchar a todas horas con la naturaleza, que de suyo nada produce sino maleza, y que sólo da frutos sazonados a fuerza de trabajo y cultivo": Gaspar Melchor de Jovellanos, "Informe de la Sociedad Económica de Madrid al Consejo de Castilla en el Expediente de la Ley Agraria," Madrid, 1795, reproduced in Gaspar Melchor de Jovellanos, *Escritos Económicos*, ed. Vicent Llombart (Madrid: Real Academia de Ciencias Morales y Políticas, 2000), 185–359, 304, and 381.

163. Barbara Arneil, *John Locke and America: The Defense of English Colonialism* (Oxford: Clarendon, 1996), 16. See also Wilcomb E. Washburn, "The Moral and Legal Justifications for Dispossessing the Indians," in James Morton Smith, ed., *Seventeenth-Century America: Essays in Colonial History* (Chapel Hill: University of North Carolina Press, 1959), 15–32, on 23–24; Wilbur R. Jacobs, *Dispossessing the American Indian: Indians and Whites on the Colonial Frontier* (New York: Charles Scriber's Sons, 1972), 111; John E. Kicza, "Dealing with Foreigners: A Comparative Essay Regarding Initial Expectations and Interactions between Native Societies and the English in North America and the Spanish in Mexico," *Colonial Latin American Historical Review* 3(4) (1994): 381–

397, on 389 and 392; George Raudzens, "Why Did Amerindian Defense Fail? Parallels in the European Invasions of Hispaniola, Virginia and Beyond," *War in History* 3(3) (1996): 331–352, on 343–344; Jean M. O'Brien, *Dispossession by Degrees: Indian Land and Identity in Natick, Massachusetts, 1650–1790* (Cambridge: Cambridge University Press, 1997), 6–7; Bernard W. Sheehan, *Savagism and Civility: Indians and Englishmen in Colonial Virginia* (Cambridge: Cambridge University Press, 1980), 5; and Stuart Banner, "Why *Terra Nullius?* Anthropology and Property Law in Early Australia," *Law and History Review* 23(1) (2005): 95–131.

164. Tully, *A Discourse on Property*, 65–68, 80, and 100; and Paschal Larkin, *Property in the Eighteenth Century with Special Reference to England and Locke* (New York: Howard Fertig, 1969), 53–66.

165. José Calvet de Magalhães, *História do pensamento económico em Portugal da idade-média ao mercantilismo* (Coimbra: Boletim de Ciências Económicas, 1967), 3–4 and 11; and Manuel J. Rodríguez Puerto, "Derecho natural, propiedad y utilidad en el humanismo jurídico," *Ius Fugit* 5–6 (1996–1997): 491–503 and 510–525, on 499–500 and 518.

166. Ignacio de la Concha y Martínez, *La "presura." La ocupación de tierras en los primeros siglos de la reconquista* (Madrid: CSIC, 1946); and Virgínia Rau, *Sesmarias medievais portuguesas* (Lisbon: Presença, 1982 [1946]), 34–35.

167. By mentioning "art," contemporaries probably referred to the need to use the land to its best potential or, as a modern discourse would have it, to "improve it"; "Acrescentar et amuchiguar et fenchir la tierra fue el primero mandamiento que Dios mando al primero home et mugger depues que los hubo fechos" (law 1); "Acrescentando et criando el pueblo su linaje et labrando la tierra et sirviendose della asi como diximos en las leyes antes desta, son dos cosas que por se amuchigua la gente et se puebla la tierra segunt Dios mando. Mas aun hi ha otra cosa que deben facer los homes para ser el mandamiento complido, et esto es que se apoderen et sepan ser señores della. Et este apoderamiento viene en dos guisas: la una es arte et la otra fuerza. Ca por seso deben los homes conocer la tierra y saber para qué será más provechosa et adobarla et endereszarla por mestria segunt aqueso, et non la deben despreciar deciendo que non es buena; . . . et faciendo esto se apoderaran de la tierra, et servirse han de las cosas que son en ella . . . segunt mandamiento de Dios" (law 6): Siete Partidas, Partida II, title 20, laws 1 and 6.

168. Rau, *Sesmarias medievais*, 87; and Carmen Margarita Oliveira Alveal, "Converting Land into Property in the Portuguese Atlantic World, 16th–18th century" (Ph.D. diss., John Hopkins University, 2007), chapter 1.

169. Royal obligation was to "cuidar de que cada uno labre su tierra, y que la labre bien, porque también conviene a la república, cuyo curador es vuestra majestad . . . y aunque no sea en España toda la tierra de vuestra majestad . . . lo es por lo universal para dirección de los dominios particulares a pública utilidad . . . que toda la tierra fue de la república originalmente y si se repartió a cada uno, fue de intento y para comodidad de la labor y se dió para que la labrasen como en enfiteusis, como dije que nos la dió dios, cuyos mayorales son los reyes." Pedro de Valencia, cited in Carmelo Viñas y Mey, *El problema de la tierra en la España de los siglos XVI–XVII* (Madrid: CSIC, 1941), 164. See also

Thomas Kenneth Niehaus, "Population Problems and Land Use in the Writing of the Spanish Arbitristas: Social and Economic Thinkers, 1600–1650" (Ph.D. diss., University of Texas at Austin, 1976); Manuel Martín Rodríguez, *Pensamiento económico español sobre la población*. *De Soto a Matanegui* (Madrid: Pirámide, 1984); Maravall, *Estado moderno*, vol. 2, 325–339; and David E. Vassberg, "The Tierras Baldías: Community Property and Public Lands in 16th Century Castile," *Agricultural History* 48(3) (1974): 383–401, on 384–385 and 393–394.

170. Melchor de Jovellanos, *Informe de la Sociedad Económica*, 8 and 12–13. See also Viñas y Mey, *El problema de la tierra*, 164 (citing Juan de Mariana, *De rege et regis institutione* [Toledo: Apud Petrum Rodericum typo. Regium, 1599]) and 147.

171. Magalhães, *História do pensamento económico*, 11, 137–139; Armando de Castro, *O pensamento económico no Portugal moderno (de fins do século XVIII a começos do século XX)* (Lisbon: Ministério da Cultura e da Ciência, 1980), 38–40; and José Vicente Serrão, "O pensamento agrário setecentista (pré-fisiocrático): Diagnósticos e soluções propostas," in José Luís Cardoso, ed., *Contribuições para a história do pensamento económico em Portugal* (Lisbon: Dom Quixote, 1988), 23–50. See also Richard Drayton, *Nature's Government: Science, Imperial Britain, and the "Improvement" of the World* (New Haven, CT: Yale University Press, 2000), 50–51.

172. ANTT, Cortes, Mç. 13, fols. 21–22.

173. Francisco de Peralta, "Relación de lo que han informado los corregidores . . . acerca del remedio que se tendrá para la conservación de la labranza y crianza," undated manuscript (seventeenth century?) BNE, Ms. 9372, fols. 31r–40v; and *Pragmática en que se declara los que han de ser hermanos de la Mesta y en la forma que pueden traspasar y vender las dehesas* (Madrid: Juan de la Cuesta, 1609). See also Márcia Maria Menendes Motta, *Direito à terra no Brasil. A gestação do conflito 1795–1824* (São Paulo: Alameda Casa Editorial, 2009), 28–45.

174. Tamar Herzog, "Terres et déserts, société et sauvagerie. De la communauté en Amérique et en Castille à l'époque moderne," *Annales HSS* 62(3) (2007): 507–538, on 525–528. See also Vicente Palacio Atard, *Las "nuevas poblaciones" andaluzas de Carlos III: Los españoles de la ilustración* (Córdoba: Monte de Piedad y Caja de Ahorros de Córdoba, 1989); Jordi Olivera Samitier, *Nuevas poblaciones en la España de la ilustración* (Barcelona: Fundación Caja de Arquitectos, 1998); and Juan Helguera Quijada, "Los despoblados y la política de colonización del reformismo ilustrado en la cuenca del Duero," in *Despoblación y colonización del Valle del Duero, siglos VIII–XX, IV Congreso de Estudios Medievales* (Ávila: Fundación Sánchez Albornoz, 1995), 375–411.

175. "Pues ni han tenido ni tienen ni pueden tener por el orden regular en ellas más utilidad, que lo que pudieran figurarse en unas posesiones situadas en los espacios imaginarios." Nicolás de Arriquibar, *Recreación política. Reflexiones sobre el amigo de los hombres en su tratado de población considerando con respecto de nuestros intereses* (Vitoria: Tomás de Robles y Navarro, 1779), 236.

176. "Un reino podría formarse de sólo estos desiertos espantosos y su reconquista sería más gloriosa, útil y segura, que la de países distantes." Arriqui-

bar, *Recreación política*, 235. See also Joaquín Navarros, "Plan de repoblación para el lugar de Zarapuz en el reino de Navarra," 1778, ARSEMAP 25/11.

177. Tamar Herzog, "Colonial Law and 'Native Customs': Indigenous Land Rights in Colonial Spanish America," *The Americas* 63(3) (2013): 303–321.

178. Latin American *composiciones* were studied by many. See, for example, Cristina Torales Pacheco, "A Note on the Composiciones de Tierra in the Jurisdiction of Cholula, Puebla (1591–1757)," in Arij Ouweneel and Simon Miller, eds., *The Indian Community of Colonial Mexico: Fifteen Essays on Land Tenure, Corporate Organizations, Ideology, and Village Politics* (Amsterdam: CEDLA, 1990), 87–102; and Donato Amado Gonzáles, "Reparto de tierras indígenas y la primera visita y composición general, 1591–1595," *Histórica* 22(2) (1998): 197–207. Also see *Recopilación de Indias*, book 4, title 12, laws 15–21. Their operation vis-à-vis native communities was exemplified in petition of Salvador Ango Pilainlade Salazar cacique, Otavalo, 3.12.1692, ANQ, Tierras 18, Exp. 15.12.1692, fol. 1v; and petition of Juan Guaytara, cacique, Quito, 15.3.1712, ANQ, Tierras 34, Exp. 15.3.1712, fols. 2r–v.

179. Vânia Maria Losada Moreira, "Nós índios, índios nós senhores de nossas ações . . . Direito de domínio dos índios e cristandade em conflito (vila de Nova Benavente, capitania do Espíritu Santo, 1795–1798)," in Márcia Motta, José Vicente Serrão, and Marina Machado eds., *Em terras lusas: Conflitos e fronteiras no Império Português* (Rio de Janeiro: Universidade Federal Fluminense, 2013), 231–259. See also Carlos Castilho Cabral, *Terras devolutas e prescrição* (Rio de Janeiro: Jornal do Comércio, 1943), 38, and Manuela Carneiro da Cunha, *Os direitos do índio. Ensaios e documentos* (São Paulo: Editora Brasiliense, 1987), 32 and 58–63.

180. "Voto do padre Antonio Vieira . . . sobre o governo espiritual e temporal dos índios do Brasil," Bahia, 12.7.1694, BA, 51-V-45, fol. 5r; "Voto do padre Antonio Vieyra sobre as dúvidas dos moradores de São Paulo a cerca da administração dos índios," 12.7.1694, BA, 51-V-45, fols. 5r–10r; "Informação do modo com que foram tomados e sentenciados por cativos os índios do ano de 1655 feita pelo p. Antonio Viera," BA, 49-IV-23, fols. 115r–136r, fol. 116v. Some of these opinions were reproduced in Vieira, *Escritos históricos e políticos*, 429–444.

181. Márcia Maria Menendes Motta, *Nas fronteiras do poder: Conflito e direito à terra no Brasil de meados do século XIX* (Rio de Janeiro: Arquivo Público do Estado do Rio de Janeiro, 1998); Motta, *Direito à terra no Brasil*, 15–16 and 81 and 129; Márcia Maria Menendes Motta, "The Sesmarias in Brazil: Colonial Land Policies in the Late Eighteenth Century," *E-Journal of Portuguese History* 3(2) (2005); Ruy Cirne Lima, *Pequena história territorial do Brasil: Sesmarias e terras devolutas* (Brasília: ESAF, 1988); Nelson Nozoe, "Sesmarias e apossamento de terras no Brasil colônial," *Revista Economia* 7(3) (2006): 587–605; José Ribamar Bessa Freire e Márcia Fernanda Malheiros, *Os Aldeamentos Indígenas do Rio de Janeiro* (Rio de Janeiro: EDUERJ, 1997), 67–68 and 70; Alveal, "Converting Land," chapter 5.

182. Patricia Seed, *American Pentimiento: The Invention of Indians and the Pursuit of Riches* (Minneapolis: University of Minnesota Press, 2001); and John

H. Elliott, *Empires of the Atlantic World: Britain and Spain in America, 1492–1830* (New Haven, CT: Yale University Press, 2006).

183. Langfur, *The Forbidden Lands*, 42–47, 68, and 170; Amy Turner Bushnell, "'None of These Wondering Nations Has Ever Been Reduced to the Faith': Mission and Mobility on the Spanish-American Frontier," in James Muldoon, ed., *The Spiritual Conversion of the Americas* (Gainesville: University Press of Florida, 2004), 142–168, on 142; and Christophe Giudicelli, "La raya de los pulares: Institution d'une frontière indienne coloniale au sein du Valle Calchaquí (1582–1630)," in Jimena Paz Obregón Iturra, Luc Vapdevila, and Nicolas Richard, eds., *Les indiens des frontières coloniales. Amérique australe, XVIe siècle/temps présent* (Rennes: Presses Universitaires de Rennes, 2011), 27–57. See also A.J.R. Russel-Wood, "Frontiers in Colonial Brazil: Reality, Myth and Metaphor," in Paula Covington, ed., *Latin American Frontiers, Borders, and Hinterlands: Research Needs and Resources* (Albuquerque: General Library—University of New Mexico, 1990), 26–61, on 36–54; and Herzog, "Terres et déserts."

184. Carlos de Araújo Moreira Neto, "Índios e fronteiras," *Revista de Estudos e Pesquisas* (Brasilia) 2(2) (2005): 79–87; and Daniel Clayton, "The Creation of Imperial Space in the Pacific Northwest," *Journal of Historical Geography* 26(3) (2000): 327–350, 334.

185. "Ruegan los padres misioneros de los indios guaranís al padre confesor del rey considere algunos cargos de la conciencia de su majestad que resultan de la ejecución del real tratado [de 1750]," anonymous and undated, ANC/S, Jesuitas, vol. 197, fols. 109r–110v; and Baltasar Maziel, "Informe de Baltasar Maziel al gobernador Bucareli," Buenos Aires, 19.10.1769, reproduced in Maziel, *De la justicia*, 201–204

186. "El derecho natural de los indios . . . a los bienes inmuebles adquiridos con su propio trabajo y la propia industria, en la tierra donde ellos nacieron y poseyeron de tiempo inmemorial sus antepasados y abuelos." Manuel Arnal, "Injusticia de la causa paraguaya," trans. Cayetano Bruno and reproduced in Maziel, *De la justicia*, 187–200, on 189.

187. Félix Feliciano da Fonseca, "Relação do que aconteceu aos demarcadores portugueses e castelhanos," Lisbon, post-1753, pp. 5–6, cited in Domingues, *When the Amerindians Were Vassals*, 193; and "Estos papeles dan noticia con más extensión del estado en que se hallaba la expedición de los pueblos el día 15.2.de este año," BPE, Cod. CXVI (2-12), no. 16.

188. "Riduzione di tatto e di ragione," undated anonymous manuscript, ASV, Fondo Gesuiti, vol. 4, point 2.

189. Luís António de Souza to Carlos Morphy, São Paolo, 17.7.1771, AGN/BA, IX.4.3.6.

190. "Se reintegraron a esta provincia por derecho de reversión todos aquellos campos, como que son vasallos de nuestro monarca y señor natural y han prestado palabra de fidelidad y subordinación." Joaquín de Alós to Nicolás Arredondo, Asunción 8.2.1792, AHN, Estado 4555, no. 9-42, fol. 5.

191. Juan Carlos Bazán, "Examen jurídico y discurso historial sobre . . . los confines de los reinos de Castilla y Portugal . . . en el Río de la Plata," undated, BNE, Ms. 3042, fols. 42r–101v, fol. 96r.

192. "Primeramente, que por cuanto ocupan estos territorios que han poseído sus antepasados en los cuales como criados en ellos gozan de buena salud ... se les ha de dejar y mantener en dicha posesión, que han tenido, sin despojarlos de ellas, por dárselas a otros nacionales." Levaggi, *Paz en la frontera*, 82.

193. "Que como manteniendo su majestad a todos los indios ... en la posesión de las tierras que comprenden, ha conservado siempre sobre éstas el dominio alto que como a soberano dueño de todo le corresponde." Ibid., 152.

194. "Considerándose con derecho a los terrenos que hacen la confluencia de dichos ríos ... cedieron en la posesión de ellos para el establecimiento del mismo fuerte." Ibid., 163.

195. "Sobre las hostilidades de los indios chiriguanos de la cordillera de Sauces por parte de las fronteras de Tomina en el distrito de la intendencia de Charcas 1805," AGN/BA, IX.23.2.5, Cuaderno 1, for example, the investigation that took place in Pueblo Real de San Pedro Larabuco on 3.1.1805, including the interrogatory and the declarations of Fernando de Santillán, fols. 23v–24v, and Jorge Ichel, fols. 27r+v.

196. "Respecto a que la extensión de estas campañas es dilatada, y que franquea su utilidad, a todas las naciones de indios que las pueblan sin perjuicio de nuestros usuales territorios, siempre que se contengan en los que les son a ellos proporcionados." Levaggi, *Paz en la frontera*, 127.

197. " 'Para cuando hayan dado buenas pruebas de su fiel vasallaje al rey ... observando buen correspondencia con todos los españoles." Jerónimo Matorras on 29.7.1774, reproduced in Nacuzzi, "Los cacicazgos," apendix III, 71–74, on 71.

198. Consulta of the conselho ultramarino, Lisbon, 12.2.1716, AHU_ACL_CU_013, cx. 6, d. 515; "Instrução da Rainha para D. António Rolim de Moura," Lisbon, 19.1.1749, APMG, Livro C-03, Doc. 01, fols. 3–8, fol. 6, point 19; consulta of the conselho ultramarino, Lisbon, 8.2.1731, ahu_acl_cu_023-01, cx. 7, d. 756; and João de Abreu Castelo Branco to the king, Pará, 16.1.1746, AHU_ACL_CU_013, cx. 28, d. 2676. Similar Spanish perceptions are described in Joaquín Alos to Nicolás Arrendondo, Asunción del Paraguay, 26.10.1792, AHN, Estado 4548; and Lázaro de Rivera to José de Espínola, Santa Rosa, 28.1.1797, AHN, Estado 3410, no. 13.

199. "Por derecho natural y común el dominio de las cosas se adquiere al primo capiente el cual por cédulas y leyes municipales de estos reinos está mandado guardar a sus pobladores y particularmente a los indios para que se les conserve la posesión de aquellas tierras que hubiesen estado ocupando sus mayores o los gentiles de quienes proceden, sin perturbar a los sucesores que hubiesen recibido la católica enseñanza de nuestra verdadera fe y la sujeción a nuestro soberano, con los recomendables privilegios que a no se hallare que hubiesen estado ocupando tierras algunas o las despoblasen los bárbaros siguiendo su ciega idolatría y huyendo el reducirse al gremio cristiano y sujeción de los católicos y gloriosos reyes de España y se poblasen otros convertidos aún que estos no hubiesen ocupado tierras algunas": Protector de Indios, ANQ, Tierras 47, Exp. of 1735, fol. 2v.

200. "Creo que V.E. no quiere en este lugar hacer dependiente el dominio de la corona portuguesa en una ocupación privativa porque si tal fuese su mente y la tácita consecuencia que envuelven aquellas palabras, además de ser opuestas a los principios del derecho público y de las gentes, que sólo requieren una ocupación general, que puerta no abriría que a todas las naciones para entrar por los vastos dominios de la corona Española, muchos de los cuales sólo están ocupados por sus antiguos y silvestres habitadores?" Lazaro de Ribera de Cayetano Pinto de Miranda Montenegro, Vila Bela, 30.6.1797, the response of his Spanish counterpart dated Asunción, 7.9.1797, and his second letter, Mato Grosso, 21.11.1797, all in AGN/BA, IX.4.4.1. A second copy can be found in AHN, Estado 3410, no. 13. The citation is from the letter dated 21.11.1797.

201. "Ni puede ser otra cosa porque si el fin principal de esta conquista es propagar el evangelio a más de no ser decente a nuestra corte la reducción a límites, sería estrechar la puerta a la civilización queda a conocer al enemigo las ventajas de nuestra religión." Boifacio Biscarra to the president of the audiencia, Lagunas, 19.1.1805, AGN/BA, IX.23.2.5, Cuaderno 1, fols. 45v–48r, on fol. 47r.

202. "Los hombres necesitados a fijar alguna residencia en la tierra, para poder cultivarla y alimentarse de ella, se vieron también precisados a marcar y señalar la área que ocupaban para precaverse de que otros no se introdujesen y apoderándose de ella les privasen de los frutos y productos que les pertenecen. He aquí el origen de las fronteras . . . resulta de las reglas antecedentes que para ocupar un país y reducirlo a propiedad nacional la ocupación debe ser justa y racional. Si no lo fuese sería un desojo y los ocupantes llevando consigo el carácter de tiranos y usurpadores no podrían ampararse del derecho de gentes, porque serían acreedores a ser tratados como ladrones y bandidos por los habitantes de las naciones circunvecinas . . . el derecho de ocupación pura está reglado por los principios de la inmutable justicia natural, que a nadie le es dado traspasar. La naturaleza ha criado la tierra para que los hombres la cultiven y se sustenten de ella. No habiendo producido nada en vano ha dado derecho a todos para ocuparla y distribuírsela con moderación y justicia, sin daño de otros; pues que el globo tiene extensión y capacidad bastante para que ninguna sociedad quede sin alguna parte . . . ninguna nación debe ocupar un espacio tan dilatado de tierras que ella no sea capaz de poblar y cultivar. En tal caso es manifiesto que perjudicaría a otros la ocupante, privándoles del lugar necesario para su población y que para alimentar su ambición frustraría los fines de la naturaleza y su autor, haciéndose refractaria del derecho natural y autorizando con el hecho a sus vecinos para que se opusiesen a la usurpación que se haría a todo el género humano . . . por las mismas razones los pueblos que están en sus confines estrechados pueden poblar y ocupar algún terreno que se halla inculto y desierto entre tribus salvajes que ni lo necesitan ni lo cultivan ni lo ocupan y poseen permanentemente o con residencia fija . . . es en virtud de este principio que se justifica la ocupación que hace el gobierno y los habitantes de nuestro país de los terrenos despoblados que hay fuera de las antiguas fronteras, y por los cuales se suelen encontrar tribus errantes de salvajes que sin fijar residencia ni domicilio en un lugar determinado pretenden el

señorío de tales parajes, recorriéndolos con sus chozas, las cuales mudan de una parte a otra . . . por vivir de este modo no cultivan la tierra como es consiguiente, ni quieren tener arraigo alguno; viven sólo del robo." Antonio Sáenz, *Instituciones elementales sobre el Derecho Natural y de Gentes* (Buenos Aires: Facultad de Derecho y Ciencias Sociales, 1936 [1822]), 178–182.

203. Frederick Jackson Turner, "The Significance of the Frontier in American History," in *The Frontier in American History* (New York: Dover Publications, 1996) [1920], 7–26.

204. "Porque en lo substancial se llaman fronteras todas las tierras incógnitas ocupadas por los bárbaros y nuestras pertenencias siguen siempre extendiéndose con la población de nuevas misiones y de las estancias que se van estableciendo más adelante por el interés de los buenos pastos y fértiles terrenos, como siempre se ha ejecutado desde la pacificación de este continente." Letter of the president of the audiencia de La Plata to the viceroy, La Plata, 25.1.1805, AGN/BA, IX.23.2.5, fol. 123r. Miguel Télez Menses to Marqués de Sobremonte, San Rafael, 8.12.1806, AGN/BA, IX.11.4.5, includes a similar vision of the frontier.

205. "A la espada y el compás, más y más y más y más." This saying appears in the counter front page of Bernado de Vargas Machuca's Milicia y descripción de las Indias (first edition) published in Madrid by Pedro Madrigal in 1599.

206. Herzog," The Meaning of Territory"; and Jeremy Adelman and Stephen Aron, "From Borderlands to Borders: Empires, Nation-States, and the Peoples in between in North American History," *American Historical Review* 104(3) (1999): 814–841, on 815 and 838. See also Bartolomé Clavero, "Original Latin American Constitutionalism," *Rechts Geschichte* 16 (2010): 25–28.

PART II *Defining European Spaces*

1. Mattoso, *Identificação;* and José Mattoso, ed., *A História de Portugal* (Lisbon: Círculo de Leitores, 1994 and 1995), vols. 2–4. See also António Henrique Oliveira Marques, *History of Portugal* (New York: Columbia University Press, 1972), vols. 1 and 2.

2. Cordero Torres, *Fronteras hispánicas*, 97–112; Rodríguez López, *La consolidación;* and J. Torres Fontes, "La evolución de las fronteras peninsulares durante el gran avance de la Reconquista (c.1212–c.1350)," in *Historia de España Menéndez Pidal* (Madrid: Espasa, 1990), vol. 13 (1), xiii–lvi.

3. Ladero Quesada, "La formación," most particularly on 449–457; Rita Costa Gomes, "A construção das fronteiras," in Francisco Bethencourt and Diogo Ramada Curto, eds., *A memória da nação* (Lisbon: Livraria Sá da Costa Editora, 1991), 357–382, on 371; and Andrade, *A construção*.

4. Ladero Quesada, "Reconquista," 689; and Manuel Martínez Martínez, *Olivenza y el tratado de Alcañices* (Olivenza: Ayuntamiento de Olivenza, 1997), 9. While some have asserted that the border was formed in the thirteenth century and thus is the oldest in Europe, others have pointed out that all conflicts that occurred since were unimportant: Braga, *Um espaço, duas monarquias*, 103, citing Romero Magalhães. However, recent historiography has divided the evolution of the frontier into three stages: the reconquest, the treaties, and the

contiendas. It has argued that the last stage was the longest and, despite common belief, that it had brought about substantial changes: Martín Martín, "La tierra de las 'contiendas.'"

5. Sahlins, *Boundaries;* and José María Imízcoz Beunza, "De las fronteras de la comunidad a las redes de la nación: construcción de identidades y de exclusiones en la vieja Europa," in Natividad Planas and Michel Bertrand, eds., *Les sociétés de frontière. De la Méditerranée à l'Atlantique* (xvie-xviie siècle) (Madrid: Casa de Velázquez, 2011), 107–124.

6. Marchetti, *De Iure Finium*, 96–180. See also Manoel de Almeida Sousa, *Tractado pratico e critico de todo o direito emphyteutico* (Lisbon: Impressão Regia, 1814), vol. 2, nos. 1222–1223, 1227, and 1230, on 279–283; and Thomaz, *Observações sobre o discurso*, 39–44 and 95–102. By the end of the eighteenth century, these notions were defended as natural and thus international law: Vattel, *The Law of Nations*, book 2, chapter 11.

7. Letter of Badajoz, 15.4.1601, AHME, TP 1584/82, vol. 1, fol. 190r. See also its letter dated 30.7.1614, AHME, TP 1587/82, vol. 4, fol. 27r. The king, however, suggested that such toleration was not advisable: Royal order, Lisbon, 31.10.1603, AHME, TP 1586/82, vol. 4, fol. 147.

8. Consulta of the consejo de estado, 4.4.1701, which reproduced the opinion of the council of Castile in "El Consejo de Estado con oficio del enviado de Portugal sobre los daños que los vecinos de La Guardia recibían de los portugueses de Seixas," Madrid 10.3.1701, AHN, Estado leg. 1778, Exp. 15; also reproduced in "Con consulta del de Castilla sobre los daños que los vecinos de La Guardia experimentaban de los portugueses de Seixas," Madrid, 4.4.1701, AHN Estado leg. 1788, Exp. 18.

9. The consejo de estado on 5.6.1696 in AGS, Estado 4042. Somewhat similar were the opinions of the consejo de estado on 26.3.1697 in AGS, Estado 4043, and of the consejo de Castilla on 7.5.1594, AGS, CRC leg. 480, Exp. 2.

10. "El Consejo de Estado con la carta de V.M. se ha servido remitirle del gobernador de Badajoz y comandante interino de Extremadura sobre los excesos cometidos por portugueses en aquella frontera y prisión que había hecho de diez de ellos," Madrid, 26.12.1716, AHN, Estado leg. 1791, Exp. 51; and "El consejo de estado con carta del gobernador de Badajoz . . . sobre los excesos cometidos por portugueses y prisión que había hecho de diez de ellos," 26.12.1716, AHN, Estado leg. 1768, Exp. 32. Similar was also the report sent by the council of Tui, 24.11.1784, AMAE/M, Tr 132/002 (1720/1792), no. 0207/2. The same attitude was taken by locals in 1799, when some fifty-four armed Portuguese penetrated Spanish territory, taking wheat and rye: The Duque de Frias to Mariano Luis de Urquijo, Lisbon, 23.5.1799, and Luis de Pinto de Souza to the Duque, Lisbon, 22.5.1799, in "Portugal. Excesos cometidos por los portugueses en el lugar de Vindóla, corregimiento de Ledesma, y en otros pueblos de la frontera. Año de 1799," AHN, Estado leg. 4444.

11. Thomaz, *Observações*, 38 and 44.

12. "Instrucciones para la formación de itinerarios y reconocimientos de la frontera de Portugal y Extremadura," 1797, AGMM, 5-3-4-2; Domingo

Antonio Taboada to Juan Ignacio de Ochoa, San Marín, 40.4.1757, AHMLC, RA (en organización), número provisional 1091; Joseph Gabriel, "Descripción geográfica . . . desde la plaza de Badajoz por la frontera de Portugal y provincias confiantes de Castilla, 25.4.1801," AGMM, 5-5-7-11; "Ofício do Conde de Oeiras dirigido ao Conde de Lippe enaltecendo as qualidades de conhecedor das fronteiras de Castela," Lisbon, 9.8.1762, AHM/DIV/4/1/23/021; Pedro Folque, Caetano Paulo, and José Dias, "Projecto da defesa do terreno anexo a fronteira de Espanha que decorre entre o ribeiro de Maravão," (1797), AHM/DIV/3/01/02/03; "Descrição topográfica das comarcas fronteiras da província de Minho oferecida a Real Sociedade Marítima de Lisboa por Custodio José Gomes de Villasoas," 3.12.1800, and "Instrução geral relativa ao reconhecimento de toda a fronteira e costas marítimas do reino," 28.7.1802, both in AHM/DIV/4/1/14/11; and "Instrucción dada a los ingenieros destinados al levantamiento del plano de la frontera de Galicia confinante con Portugal por el ingeniero en jefe Francisco Villarroel, Tui, año de 1801," AGMM, 3-1-7-1.

13. Costa, *Corografia portuguesa*, vol. 1, iii; Pedro Moreau, "Proyecto y reconocimiento de las fronteras Extremadura, Castilla la Vieja con el reino de Portugal," San Lorenzo el Real, 16.11.1735, AGMM, 5-5-5-15, fol. 4r; and Joseph de Gabriel, "Relación detallada de la clase y número de los ríos, arroyos y torrentes, sus puentes y direcciones de los caminos de los pueblos desde la plaza de Badajoz y provincia confinantes," 20.3.1801, AGMM, 5-5-7-10.

14. "Instrucción dada a los ingenieros destinados al levantamiento del plano de la frontera de Galicia confinante con Portugal por el ingeniero en jefe Francisco Villarroel, Tui, año de 1801," AGMM, 3-1-7-1. See also Rui Miguel C. Branco, "Da carta topográfica do reino à carta chorographica do reino. Políticas e modelos cartográficos em Portugal (1788–1852)," *Penélope* 26 (2002): 31–59, on 31; and Rui Miguel C. Branco, *O mapa de Portugal. Estado, território e poder no Portugal de oitocentos* (Lisbon: Livros Horizonte, 2003), 85–89.

15. The bibliography on these issues is particularly large. See, for example, Niehaus, *Population Problems*; Martín Rodríguez, *Pensamiento económico español*; and Herzog, "Terres et déserts."

16. *Real provisión . . . en que se contiene el fuero de población de la nueva villa de Encinas . . . provincia de Extremadura con inserción de las once reglas generales de población establecidas para los despoblados de la propia provincia a consulta del consejo, año 1779* (Madrid: Imprenta de Pedro Marín, 1779), available in AHN, Consejos 4084. See also Felipe Lorenzana de la Puente, "Extremadura, siglos XVII–XVIII. La frontera como condicionante político," *Revista de Extremadura* 7 (1992): 49–70.

17. Historians have affirmed that the state of both Extremadura and Alentejo was greatly affected by the proximity of the frontier: Vieira, *Centros urbanos*, 250–255; Sancha Soria, *La guerra de restauración*; Cortés Cortés, *Militares y Guerra*, 17–24; Cosme, *Elementos para a história*, 131–133; and Fonseca, "The Municipal Administration," 6. Contemporaries tended to agree: Silveira, "Racional discurso"; and Domingos Vandelli, "Memoria sobre a agricultura

deste reino e das suas conquistas," in *Memorias económicas da Academia Real das Ciências de Lisboa para o adiantamento da agricultura, das artes e da industria em Portugal e suas conquistas* (Lisbon: Oficina da Academia Real das Ciências, 1789), vol. 1, 164–175.

18. "Reconocimiento y visita de la frontera de Castilla y Portugal . . . por el coronel e ingeniero en jefe Pedro Moreau y en segundo Juan Amador Courter en presencia y con asistencia del ilustrísimo Felipe Dupuy comandante general de esta provincia, Ciudad Rodrigo, 12.7.1735," AGMM, 5-5-5-14, fols. 3r–v.

19. "Un reino podría formarse de sólo estos desiertos espantosos y su reconquista sería más gloriosa, útil y segura, que la de países distantes." Arriquibar, *Recreación política*, 235.

20. Herzog, "Colonial Law."

21. Paolo Grossi, "La proprietà nel sistema privatistico della seconda scolastica," in Paolo Grossi, ed., *La seconda scolastica nella formazione del diritto privato moderno. Incontro di studio. Atti* (Milan: Giuffrè Editore, 1973), 117–222; and António Manuel Hespanha, "O jurista e o legislador na construção da propriedade burguesa," *Análisis social* 61 (1980): 211–236. See also Teofilo F. Ruiz, "Fronteras: De la comunidad a la nación en la Castilla bajo medieval," *Anuario de estudios medievales* 27(1) (1997): 23–42.

22. On these points, see also Albert Silbert, *Le Portugal méditerranéen à la fin de l'Ancien Régime* (Paris: SEVPEN, 1966), vol. 1, 166–171; and Eusebio Medina García, "Orígenes históricos y ambigüedad de la frontera hispano-lusa (La Raya)," *Revista de estudios extremeños* 62(2) (2006): 713–723, on 717.

23. "La corte y el ejército de España estaban en la mayor ignorancia sobre Portugal que parecían tan extranjeros como lo habría sido uno del Nuevo Mundo." "Memoria militar sobre Portugal," AHN, Estado leg. 4389.

24. These rumors led the governor to complain in 1703 that he was asked three times the same question and that he had affirmed twice already that there were absolutely no incidents in Galicia: "El consejo de estado con carta del príncipe de Barbanzón satisfaciendo al informe que se le pidió," Madrid, 29.3.1703, AHN, Estado leg. 1765, Exp. 44. The governor suggested that "debe creer que la larga distancia que hay hasta Lisboa habrá confundido las noticias que da Capicelatro [the Spanish ambassador in Lisbon] pues él ha procurado siempre la unión entre unos y otros": "El consejo de Estado al señor Conde de Frigiliana . . . con motivo de lo que el Príncipe de Barbanzón ha informado cuanto a las refriegas que se ha supuesto hubo por aquella frontera entre castellanos y portugueses," Madrid, 5.4.1703, AHN, Estado leg. 1790, Exp. 105. See also the acuerdo of the consejo de estado, 8.2.1703, AHN, Estado leg. 1790, Exp. 8; and "El consejo de estado con carta del Marquéz de Villadarias informando de las refriegas que se dijo haber habido por la parte de Ayamonte entre castellanos y portugueses, Madrid, 3.2.1703," AHN, Estado leg. 1765, Exp. 20.

25. A. J. R. Russel-Wood, "Frontiers in Colonial Brazil: Reality, Mythi and Metaphor," in Paula Covington, ed., *Latin American Frontiers, Borders, and Hinterlands: Research Needs and Resources* (Albuquerque: General Library–University of New Mexico, 1990), 26–61.

26. Luigi Nuzzo, "A Dark Side of Western Legal Modernity: The Colonial Law and Its Subjects," *Zeitschrift für Neuere Rechtsgeschichte* 33(3/4) (2011): 205–222, on 206–207.

27. "El consejo de estado con consulta del de Castilla sobre las diferencias que se han suscitado entre vecinos del lugar de Río Manzanas del reino de Castilla y los de Guadramil del de Portugal," Madrid, 28.9.1701, AHN, Estado leg. 1788, Exp. 52; and "El consejo de estado con consulta suya y dos del de Castilla, que la una acompaña otra del de Guerra sobre las diferencias que hay entre vecinos de los lugares de Río Manzanas y Santa Cruz del reino de Castilla y los de Guadramil del de Portugal," Madrid, 3.11.1701, AHN, Estado leg. 1778, Exp. 53.

28. Anthony Pagden, *The Fall of Natural Man: The American Indian and the Origins of Comparative Ethnology* (Cambridge: Cambridge University Press, 1982), 200; and "Vitoria on the Justice of the Conquest," reproduced in Parry and Keith, *New Iberian World*, vol. 1, 290–323, point 22.

29. Luigi Nuzzo, *Il linguaggio giuridico della conquista. Strategie di controllo nelle Indie Spagnole* (Naples: Jovene Editore, 2004), 214–215; and Pagden, *The Fall of Natural Man*, 97–98.

30. Adriano Prosperi, "'Otras Indias': Missionari della contrarriforma tra contadini e selvaggi," in *America e apocalisse e altri saggi* (Pisa: Istituti editoriali e poligrafici internazionali, 1999), 65–87; Jennifer D. Selwyn, *A Paradise Inhabited by Devils: The Jesuit's Civilizing Mission in Early Modern Naples* (Aldershot: Ashgate 2004), 17, 95–96, 127, and 131; Dominique Deslandres, "Mission et altérité. Les missionnaires français et la définition de l'autre au XVIIe siècle," *Proceedings of the French Colonial Historical Society* 18 (1992): 1–13, on 1, 6, and 9–11; and Dominique Deslandres, "*Exemplo aeque ut verbo:* The French Jesuit's Missionary World," in John W. O'Mally, Gauvin Alexander Bailey, Steven J. Harris, and T. Frank Kennedy, eds., *The Jesuits: Cultures, Sciences, and the Arts, 1540–1777* (Toronto: University of Toronto Press, 1999), 258–273, on 258, 261, and 266. See also Herzog, "Can You Tell."

31. Lewis, "The Closing"; Richard E. Sullivan, "The Medieval Monk as Frontiersman," in William W. Savage and Stephen I. Thompson, eds., *The Frontier: Comparative Studies* (Norman: University of Oklahoma Press, 1979), vol. 2, 25–49; and Robert Bartlett, *The Making of Europe: Conquest, Colonization, and Cultural Change, 950–1350* (Princeton, NJ: Princeton University Press, 1993).

CHAPTER 3   *Fighting a Hydra*

1. "Carta a respeito dos direitos de pastagens entre as terras vizinhas de Portugal e Castela," 11.9.1290, ANTT, Gavetas, XVIII, 3-22, pp. 299–301. Alongside Serpa and Noudar, Moura was granted by King Alfonso X to his daughter Beatriz, the Portuguese consort queen. Whether this donation implied the seizure of private, seigniorial rights or it was meant to establish royal jurisdiction is still under debate. However, most historians agree that the Treaty of Alcañices (1297) settled this issue, declaring the three villages Portuguese. A copy of the donation, dated 4.3.1283, can be found in ACDC, Cx. 20, 70-657, suplemento no. 595, fols. 71r–72r. On the privileges of Noudar

before it became Portuguese, see notarial certificate dated 25.4.1304 [1267], ACDC, Cx. 20, 70-657, suplemento no. 595, fols. 44v–45r. The early stages of this conflict were studied in Florentino Pérez-Embid, *La frontera entre los reinos de Sevilla y Portugal* (Seville: Ayuntamiento de Sevilla, 1975).

2. "Doação de Noudar à Ordem de Avis," ANTT, Chancelarias Régias (Dinis), Liv. 3, fol. 47; "Composição feita entre os moradores de Moura e Arronches, 15.5.1304," ANTT, Gavetas, III, 5-13; "Informação pela qual constava que os procuradores de el-rei d. Dinis tinham estado presentes na contenda entre o concelho de Sevilha e Arronches de Castela com os de Moura e Noudar, 1.6.1311," ANTT, Gavetas, XVIII, 7-12; and "Inquirição feita a respeito dos termos dos conselhos de Sevilha e de Arroches e dos concelhos de Moura e Noudar, 3.11.1346," ANTT, Gavetas, XX, 14-1.

3. Luis Adão da Fonseca, "Fronteiras territoriais e memórias históricas: o caso da Comenda de Noudar da Ordem de Avis," in Ricardo Izquierdo Benito and Francisco Ruiz Gómez, eds., *Las órdenes militares en la península ibérica* (Cuenca: Universidad de Castilla-La Mancha, 2000), vol. 1, 655–681.

4. "Carta de composição entre os moradores das vilas de Moura e Aroche para que hajam de vizinhar uns com os outros," 1314, ANTT, Gavetas, III, 5-13.

5. "Carta pela qual el-rei Dinis dava poder a Aparício Domingues e a João Lourenço para verificarem as contendas a respeito dos termos do concelho de Aroche e o concelho de Noudar e Moura," Lisbon, 9.9.1315, ANTT, Gavetas, XVIII, 3-23.

6. "Processo que Gomes Martins e João Lourenço fizeram por causa da contenda sobre os termos entre Moura e Aroche e Noudar e Monsaraz," 24.2.1332, ANTT, Gavetas, XVII, 9-8. An additional copy of this document is found in "Registro dos privilégios, leis e liberdades dos moradores da vila de Noudar," ACDC, Cx. . 20, 70-657, suplemento no. 595, fols. 49v–74v.

7. Historians placed this older demarcation in the 1270s: Francisco García Fitz, "Conflictos jurisdiccionales, articulación territorial y construcciones militares a finales del siglo XIII en el alfoz de Sevilla: La Sierra de Aroche," *Archivo Hispalense* 230 (1992): 25–51, on 40–42.

8. "Inquirição feita a respeito dos termos dos conselhos de Sevilha e de Arroches e dos concelhos de Moura e Noudar," 3.11.1346, ANTT, Gavetas, XX, 14-1, citation on fol. 3v; and "Instrumento pelo qual constava que os procuradores de Moura e Noudar tinham ido a aldeia de São Veríssimo para aí determinarem as dúvidas que havia entre os termos de Moura e de Sevilha e de Aroche," 1.3.1353, ANTT, Gavetas, XVIII, 5-31.

9. "Adiamento por 10 anos da demanda entre o concelho de Moura e a vila de Noudar sobre a divisão dos termos destes lugares," 1427, ANTT, Ordem de Avis-Papéis diversos e Tombo das comendas, Mç. 10, no. 849.

10. María Antonia Carmona Ruiz, "La explotación ganadera en la frontera luso-española: La 'contienda' de Moura, Nódar, Aroche y Encinasola," *Revista da faculdade de letras. História* 15(10) (1998): 242–257, 249–252.

11. In the early 1420s, the Conde de Linhares, comendador de Noudar, was collecting documentation regarding the border and his rights: ACDC, Cx. 20, 70-657, suplemento no. 595, fol. 75r. In 14.5.1491, a demarcation took

place: ANTT, Chancelaria de Dom Sebastião e Dom Henrique, privilégios, Liv. 13, fol. 265; and ANTT, Gavetas, XIV, 5-23.

12. "Instrumento de vários documentos e de uns artigos pertencentes à inquirição que se tirou a respeito da contenda entre Portugal e Castela sobre as demarcações e termos das vilas de Nodar e Moura com Ancinasola e Aroche," 22.2.1493, ANTT, Gavetas, XVIII, 2-1; "Inquirição que se tirou a respeito do termo de Noudar e de Ansina Sola," 20.2.1493, ANTT, Gavetas, XV, 23-8; and "Inquirição que se tirou a respeito da aldeia de Barrancos que Castela dizia per sua, mas que era pertença de Portugal," 16.3.1493, ANTT, Gavetas, XIV, 5-2. See also ANTT, Gavetas, XIV, 5-7 and 5-21.

13. "Concordata do rei Manuel com o rei de Castela para que nomeassem cada um o seu representante para resolver as dúvidas da contenda entre as terras de Moura e Noudar e Aroche e Sevilha," 29.8.1504, ANTT, CC, parte II, Mç. 8, doc. 116. See also "Autos sobre términos entre la villa de Aroche y la de Mora en el Reino de Portugal," AGS, CCA, Diversos 42, doc. 29, fols. 140r–143v.

14. "Auto de inquirição a respeito da vinda dos castelhanos aos termos de Moura para lavrar e semear," 2.11.1510, ANTT, Gavetas, XIV, 5-13.

15. Declaration of João Fernandes Bacias in "Auto de inquirição a respeito da vinda dos castelhanos aos termos de Moura para lavrar e semear," 2.11.1510, ANTT, Gavetas, XIV, 5-13.

16. "Carta que escrivou João da Fonseca, juiz de fora de Moura . . . em que da conta como na vila de Moura tem havido varias contendas com os castelhanos," Moura, 12.6.1517, ANTT, CC, parte I, Mç. 22, no. 9; "Inquirição que se tirou a respeito dos limites entre a vila de Moura e a de Arronches," 1528, ANTT, Gavetas, XIV, 5-9; "Carta da câmara de Moura representando ao rei as violências que os moradores de Ansina Sola, reino de Castela fazem naquela vila," Moura, 27.4.1538, ANTT, CC, parte I, Mç. 61, doc. 57; "Autos da demarcação da vila de Moura," 29.7.1537, ANTT, Gavetas, XIV, 7-2; and "Autos principiados en 11.12.1537 . . . para arreglar los términos de la villa de Mora, de Portugal con los de Encinasola y Aroche, de España," AMS, Sección I: Archivo de Privilegios, Carpeta 94, Exp. 320.

17. "Processo da contenda de Moura com Ansina Sola e Aroche acerca de suas confrontações e outras coisas," 12.3.1544, ANTT, Gavetas, XVIII, 8-2; and "Sentença dada a respeito da demarcação das vilas de Arronches, Moura y Encinasola," 1542, ANTT, Gavetas, XVIII, 9-8. See also "Copia de la ejecutoria que se guarda en el Archivo de la villa de Aroche por la cual se declara la concordia hecha en el año de1542," AGMM, 5-3-4-4. The 1542 accord was reproduced in Máximo Ramos y Orcajo, *Dehesa de la Contienda. Origen, historia y estado actual. Derechos de Aroche, Encinasola y Moura. Proyectos de división* (Lisbon: Typographia Franco-Portuguesa, 1891 [1890]), 27–69. Negotiations in 1542 left traces in letters of Luís Afonso and Pedro de Mascarenhas to the Portuguese king, 14.8.1542, 25.9.1542, and 16.10.1542, ANTT, CC, parte I, Mç. 72, docs. 88, 120, and 138. Some of these questions are also treated in CC, parte I, Mç. 75, doc. 95, and parte II, Mç, 240, doc. 29, and in Gaveta, XVII, 8-1, and XVIII, 2-19. See also "Visto da sentença de liquidação sobre os danos que os moradores das vilas de Moura, Aroche, Encinasola e Figueira fizeram

uns aos outros," 1543, ANTT, CC, parte I, Mç. 74, doc. 44; "Carta e declaração para as pessoas que o imperador Carlos V mandava para determinar os limites das vilas de Moura, Aroche e Enzina Sola," 21.6.1543, ANTT, Gavetas, XVIII, 2-19; "Carta de perdão de certas mortes que el-rei d. João III deu aos moradores das vilas de Moura, Aroche e Ansina Sola," 1543, ANTT, Gavetas, XVII, 8-1; and "Amojonamiento con Portugal," 1550, AMA, leg. 435.

18. As early as 1589 and repeatedly since, no other documentary evidence was invoked to justify the entitlements of the three villages: "Contienda. Informaciones y diligencias que hace por comisión de SM . . . sobre la dehesa que se llaman la Contienda y se encuentra entre Encinasola, Aroche y Mora," San Lorenzo, 9.5.1589, AMAE/M, Tr 282/003, no. 0431; "Extracto de la información hecha por el asistente de Sevilla . . . acerca de la pertenencia de la propiedad de la dehesa de La Contienda," Seville, 7.8.1589, in AMAE/M, Tr 282/002, no. 0431; Antonio de Gaber, "Relación que individualmente se expresa puerto por puerto los ríos, arroyos, barrancos y mojones que dividen . . . la línea de demarcación que divide España y Portugal," 24.7.1750, AGMM, 5-3-4-4 and 3-5-2-3, point 2. This last document was transcribed in María Cristina Hevilla, "Reconocimiento practicado en la frontera de Portugal por el ingeniero militar Antonio Gaber en 1750," *Biblio 3W. Revista bibliográfica de geografía y ciencias sociales* 6(335) (2001), available at http://www.ub.es/geocrit/b3w-335.htm#N_1. See also petition of Francisco Javier Tinoco y Castillo to Godoy, Príncipe de la Paz, 6.9.1801, AMAE/M, Tr 283/004, no. 0431, and the anonymous summary of his allegations, San Idelfonso, 17.9.1801, AMAE/M, Tr 283/004, no. 0431.

19. The activities of Moura are described, for example, in the petition of Cristóbal de Santiago, undated, inserted with the records of 1701, AMA, AC, leg. 9, council meeting 7.10.1797, and the various "Autos de posse que a camara de notável villa da Moura tomou da contenda," dated 30.4.1798, 11.5.1799, 24.5.1801, 5.6.1802, 11.5.1803, 5.4.1804, and 31.5.1805, AMM, B/A/01/014, fols. 26r, 56r, 79r–v, 125r–v, and 176r, and AMM, B/A/01/013, fols. 65v–66v, on fols. 66r, 89v, and 152r. Evidence for the involvement of Aroche can be found, inter alia, in "El concejo de Encinasola con el concejo de Aroche," 1625, AHPS, RA, 233/1 (nueva numeración: 29298), fols. 667v–668r; "Autos de la contienda," corresponding to 1711, 1723, 1727, 1728, 1729, 1732, and 1734, in AMA, leg. 453, and AMA, AC, leg. 12; "Autos contra los lusitanos en la Contienda por cortes, año de 1727," AMA, leg. 1133; council meeting dated 26.8.1747, AMA, AC, leg. 14; and "Denuncia sobre rompimiento de tierras en la dehesa de la Contienda contra . . . vecinos de Encinasola," 1765, AMA, leg. 1143. Because of the frequency of its interventions, the activities of Encinasola left abundant records. See, for example, council meetings dated 12.2.1697, 1.2.1680, 4.10.1689, 14.9.1692, 12.2.1697, 1.2.1698, 10.12.1731, 20.12.1732, 28.2.1733, 21.12.1734, 13.12.1735, 21.12.1736, 21.12.1737, 19.12.1741, 22.12.1742, 22.12.1743, 29.12.1744, 22.12.1745, 17.12.1747, 17.12.1748, 22.12.1749, 4.12.1750, 2.3.1751, 20.4.1754, and 22.11.1755, AME, AC, legs. 3, 6, 7, 8, 9, and 10; and "Causa escrita de daños causados en la dehesa de la Contienda contra los vecinos de la villa de Aroche, » 1757, AME, leg. 228.

20. The practice of *ramoneo*, the cutting of the smallest branches of trees in order to feed animals when pasture was scarce was mentioned in María Anto-

nia Carmona Ruiz, *Usurpaciones de tierras y derechos comunales en Sevilla y su "tierra" durante el siglo XV* (Madrid: Ministerio de Agricultura, Pesca y Alimentación, 1995), 65.

21. Encinasola's council meeting, 29.3.1767, AME, AC, leg. 13; decree of the municipal judge of Aroche, dated 4.10.1711, and the proceedings that followed it, in AMA, leg. 1132; opinion of Francisco Vázquez Banda, procurator of Aroche, in "Denuncia contra Eugenio González Barbudo," Aroche, 12.3.1754, AMA, leg. 453, fols. 5r–6v; and declaration of Josef Noguera, Encinasola, 22.9.1787, in "Causa de denuncia, 1787," AME, leg. 749. These clarify, among other things, that there was a market for stolen and counterfeit certificates and that the three communities often discussed the proper proceedings to recognize individuals as citizens. On local citizenship and usage rights, see Herzog, *Defining Nations,* 17–42.

22. El Conde de Frigiliana to the consejo de estado, Madrid, 3.12.1696, and the consejo de estado, Madrid, 8.1.1697, both in AGS, Estado leg. 4043; "El Consejo de Estado con un oficio del enviado de Portugal," Madrid, 13.5.1700, AHN, Estado leg. 1766, Exp.63; "El Consejo de Estado con consulta del de Castilla sobre instancia del envido de Portugal en orden a la controversia suscitada entre la villa de Encinasola de estos reinos y la de Moura del de Portugal," Madrid, 2.5.1700, AHN, Estado leg. 1766, Exp.60; and "El Consejo de Estado con consulta del de Castilla sobre instancia del enviado de Portugal," Madrid, 17.6.1700, AHN, Estado leg. 1781, Exp. 16.

23. Council meeting dated 23.9.1757, AMA, AC, leg. 15; letter of Jose Antonio de Olivéria Damásio to Luís da Cunha Manuel, Beja, 16.2.1761, AHM/DIV/1/06/23/01; and Josef Adrian Leal, representing Emanuel Patricio Janeiro and others, citizens of Moura, AME, leg. 228, fols. 14r–19v. On 22.1.1760, for example, the visit to La Contienda began with an affirmation that the three villages have the *same* faculty to punish, imprison, and proceed against those who contravened the concordata: council meeting on that date, AME, AC, leg. 11.

24. This might have been a recent development as evidence dated 1625 and 1641 suggested that Aroche and Moura initially adhered to the original mandate that made La Contienda Spain for Spaniards, Portugal for the Portuguese: "El concejo de Encinasola con el concejo de Aroche," 1625, AHPS, RA, 233/1, fols. 667v–668r; and "Capítulos que deram os procuradores da villa de Moura nas cortes ... de 1641," petition no. 9, ANTT, Cortes, Mç. 12, fols. 141r–142r and 146v. This last document was reproduced in João Cosme, *Elementos para a história do Além-Guadiana português (1640–1715)* (Mourão: Câmara Municipal de Mourão, 1996), 249–250.

25. "Encinasola, año de 1787. Causa de denuncia contra varios vecinos y ganados del lugar de Barrancos reino de Portugal," AME, leg. 228.

26. "Auto del cabildo para que se pase a evacuar ciertas diligencias del real servicio," Encinasola, 6.3.1785, in "Papeles y documentos relativos ... al famoso pleito ... por Francisco Méndez de nación portugués, vecino de Barrancos," AME, leg. 228, fols. 1r–4v; Council of Encinasola, 9.3.1785, AME, leg. 228, fols. 5v–6v, and the declaration of witnesses that followed on fols. 7r–9v; petitions of Blas de Andrade for the council of Encinasola, AME, leg.

228, fols. 25r–28r, 29r–30v, and 31r–36r; certificate of Ambrosio González Lechuga, dated 10.8.1785, AME, leg. 228, fols. 44r–49v; "Autos sobre el cordón hecho en la raya de Portugal en virtud de real orden, año de 1786," AME, leg. 739, decree dated 23.9.1787; and the declaration of Joseph Marques Novalio in "Causa de denuncia, 1787," AME, leg. 749. See also Miguel Ángel Melón Jiménez, *Los tentáculos de la hidra. Contrabando y militarización del orden público en España (1784–1800)* (Madrid: Sílex, 2009), 171, 213–215, and 231.

27. Petition of Encinasola, undated, AME, leg. 228, fols. 55r–72r, on fols. 57r and v. Although this was to become the most insistent portrayal of Barrancos as a safe haven for criminals, claims that such was the case were already present in the early seventeenth century, when lawyers working for Aroche suggested that Barrancos was a place where "the most wicked men" *(hombres más facinerosos)* of both Spain and Portugal found refuge *(se recogen)*: "Por el concejo, justicia y regimiento de la villa de Aroche en el pleito con la villa de Encinasola," undated (1631?), AMA, leg. 1131, articulo 4, fol. 224r. In 1734, 1757, and 1760 Barrancos was again identified as a fortress for smugglers: Council meetings 19.9.1757 and 22.1.1760 and letter of Aroche to Encinasola, dated 26.9.1757, AME, AC, leg. 11. Among other things, this portrayal might have originated in the fact that in the fifteenth century Noudar was declared "couto de homiziados," that is, a place that welcomed condemned criminals as settlers. This privilege that dated to 1424 was confirmed continuously in the sixteenth century and again in 1673: João Augusto Espadeiro Ramos, "Fronteira e relações de poder. Noudar e Barrancos no Antigo Regímen" (M.A. thesis, Universidade de Évora, 2012), 17–18. See also Margarida Garcez Ventura, "Os coutos de homiziados nas fronteiras com o direito de asilo," *Revista da Faculdade de Letras. História* serie II 15(1) (1998): 601–626.

28. Two "proceso verbal de denuncia," dated 1798 and 1797, both in AME, leg. 228.

29. Possession taking dated 8.6.1686, ACDC, Cx. 19, 67-635, no. 2628.

30. Aroche's council meetings dated 26.6.1760, 12.11.1762, and 27.1.1779, AMA, AC, leg. 15 and 16; and Encinasola's council meetings dated 26.7.1760 and 14.12.1762, AME, AC, leg. 11 and 12. See also petition of both councils dated 10.12.1768, reproduced in royal order dated Madrid, 29.11.1780, and the annexed documentation, all in "Testimonio y demás diligencias sobre la tasación de granos y su cobranza de la dehesa de la contienda," AMA, leg. 453; council meeting, 5.5.1798, the letters exchanged between Moura, Aroche, and Encinasola, and the meeting that took place at La Tomina on 29.9.1798, AMM, B/A/01/013, fols. 91r–92v and 100v–102v.

31. "Memorial de Francisco Javier Tinoco y Castillo to Godoy, Príncipe de la Paz, dated Fregenal, 6.9.1801, AMAE/M, Tr 283/004, no. 0431; report of the audiencia, Seville, 30.6.1789, and vista fiscal, undated, both in AME, leg. 228, fols. 88r–93r and fols. 94r–95v. See also the anonymous summary of Tinoco's allegations, dated San Idelfonso, 17.9.1801, AMAE/M, Tr 283/004, no. 0431.

32. Francisco Rojas y Soto to the Intendant General of Extremadura, 10.3.1800, in "Diligencias practicadas sobre la dehesa de La Contienda, año de

1802," AMAE/M, Tr 283/003, no. 0431; letter of Manuel Rada, Ayamonte, 3.10.1802, AMAE/M, Tr 283/003, no. 0431; and the anonymous memo dated Aranjuez, 19.1.1803, and directed to the Príncipe de la Paz, AMAE/M, Tr 283/004, no. 0431.

33. These questions are described in AMAE/M, Tr 283/004, no. 0431; and AMAE/M, Tr 282/002, no. 0431. Part of the discussion between the two commissioners was reproduced in Ramos y Orcajo, *Dehesa de la Contienda*, doc. no. 1, on 71–75.

34. Opinion of Bartolomé de Rada y Santander, 7.11.1803, and cited in a summary inserted in AMAE/M, Tr 282/002, no. 0431.

35. Letter of Francisco Fersen dated 26.6.1804 and cited in a summary (undated); the king to Francisco Fersen, Madrid, 5.7.1804, cited in a summary (undated); and royal decision dated 18.6.1805 and directed to Joseph Gabriel, mentioned in another undated summary; all of which are included in AMAE/M, Tr 282/002, no. 0431.

36. Undated petition by Aroche and royal response dated 6.7.1804, cited in a summary (undated) inserted in AMAE/M, Tr 282/002, no. 0431. Somewhat similar was the appeal of the representatives of Encinasola, 16.7.1802, in ibid. The Spanish commissioner attested in 1804 that "Algunos granjeros y dueños de ganado tanto de la villa de Aroche en España como de la de Mora en Portugal, acostumbrados a disfrutar de la dehesa de La Contienda como si fuera propia, recelosos de las providencias que puedan producir la actual empresa de demarcación de límites repugnan la partición de dicho terreno, los de Aroche no se atreven a manifestar abiertamente su modo de pensar, los del partido de Mora lo propalan sin rebozo y es positivo que unos y otros están de acuerdo; estos últimos por medio de sus diputados han intrigado en Lisboa y obtenido subrepticiamente la orden indicada de 10.10.1803 relativa a la división de La Contienda por la mitad y es igualmente cierto que su verdadera pretensión es que el terreno subsista en el estado de contienda para cuyo efecto dirigen sus intrigas a que el asunto se vuelva un pleito ordinario interminable": letter of Francisco Fersen dated 26.6.1804 and cited in a summary (undated) inserted in AMAE/M, Tr 282/002, no. 0431.

37. Inventory dated 11.2.1808, ACDC, Cx. 18, 66-633, no. 944; letters of Aroche to Moura dated 6.9.1808, Encinasola to Aroche, 16.9.1808, 21.9.1808, and 23.10.1808, Aroche to Encinasola, 27.10.1808, and Moura to Aroche, 9.9.1808 and 19.9.1808, all in AMA, leg. 453; letters of Aroche to Encinasola 11.9.1808, 19.9.1808, and 20.9.1808, Encinasola to Aroche, 16.10.1808, and related documents, in "Autos formados en virtud de oficio del ayuntamiento de la villa de Aroche sobre el aprovechamiento de la dehesa de la Contienda,1808," AME, leg. 228.

38. "Florencio López Regalado y consortes, vecinos de Encinasola . . . sobre el repartimiento de tierras de la Contienda, 1813," AHPS, 565/5.

39. "Autos formados en virtud de oficio del ayuntamiento de la villa de Aroche sobre el aprovechamiento de la dehesa de la Contienda, 1808," AME, leg. 228. See also Pérez-Embid, *La frontera*, 153–157; Ramos y Orcajo, *Dehesa de la Contienda*, 9–10 and 77–99; and Félix Sancha Soria, "Los archivos municipales de Aroche y Encinasola como fuentes para el estudio de la Contienda,"

Actas de las I Jornadas Transfronterizas sobre la Contienda hispano-portuguesa (Aroche: Escuela Taller Contienda, 1996), vol. 1, 53–69, on 61–62.

40. "Merece particular mención la dehesa llamada de la Contienda; es un terreno fertilísimo . . . propio de las villas de Moura en Portugal, Encinasola y Aroche y los habitantes de estas poblaciones no sólo aprovechan con sus ganados los pastos y bellota, sino que también siembran lo que mejor les parece, causándose en esto el deterioro del arbolado . . . este terreno ni pertenece a España ni a Portugal. Las municipalidades de las tres villas expresadas tienen en el mismo . . . la jurisdicción y cuando alguna de ellas ha tratado de cortar aquellos abusos se han suscitado contestaciones de difícil y grave resolución que sólo fuera dado determinar de conformidad de ambos gobiernos": Pascual Madoz, *Diccionario geográfico estadístico-histórico de España y sus posesiones de ultramar* (Madrid: Tipográfico Literario Universal, 1847), vol. 2, 591.

41. Ramos y Orcajo, *Dehesa de la Contienda*, 16.

42. "Don Fidel Seviano y Calzada en nombre de los ayuntamientos de Aroche y Encinasola . . . contra la demanda del ministerio de hacienda hecha 12.10.1903 por la que se declara enajenable la dehesa de la Contienda," AME, leg. 23; and James Sidaway, "Signifying Boundaries: Detours around the Portuguese-Spanish (Algarve/Alentejo-Andalucía) Borderlands," *Geopolitics* 7(1) (2002): 139–164, 149.

43. *Convenio de límites entre España y Portugal de 29 de junio de 1926* (Lisbon: Imprensa Nacional, 1928), preamble and art. 7, 13, and 14. This treaty was translated to English and published as "Spain and Portugal: Boundary Convention Signed at Lisbon, 29.6.1926," *League of Nations-Treaty Series* 105 (1863) (1928).

44. "El concejo de Encinasola con el concejo de Aroche," 1603, AHPS, RA, 282/1; "El concejo de Encinasola con el concejo de Aroche," 1625, AHPS, RA, 233/1; "Ejecutorias ganadas por esta villa a la de Aroche en la real audiencia de Sevilla," AME, leg. 236; "Memorial ajustado . . . del pleito que el consejo de Encinasola sigue contra el consejo de Aroche," "Pretensión de las partes sobre el conocimiento de los delitos . . . que cometen los vecinos de Encinasola en el término de Aroche," and "Por el concejo, justicia y regimiento de la villa de Aroche en el pleito con la villa de Encinasola," all three in AMA, leg. 1131; and a draft of a summary of these lawsuits, untitled, undated, and unsigned, AMA, leg. 448.

45. The procurator of Aroche, undated, in "El concejo de Encinasola con el concejo de Aroche, 1625," AHPS, RA, 233/1, fols. 756r–757r. See also "Juan Garcia Ronquillo en nombre de Aroche y del consejo de Moura," in "Ejecutorias ganadas por esta villa a la de Aroche en la real audiencia de Sevilla," AME, leg. 236.

46. Council meeting dated 23.9.1757, AMA, AC, leg. 15.

47. Alvará dated 15.3.1684 and related documents, ACDC, Cx. 19, 67-635, no. 2676; and petition of the Duque dated 9.1.1692, ACDC, Cx. 19, 67-635, no. 2696. The decree that dispossessed the Conde de Linhares, which was dated Lisbon 31.12.1642, can be found in BNP, Ms. Cx. 201, Doc. 115. Also see ANTT, Chancelaria da Ordem de Avis, Liv. 17, fols. 410v, 411, and 460. It is possible that the heirs of the Duque de Linares s (son of the Conde de Linhares) con-

tested this result, requesting in the 1690s the devolution of the *comenda* to their family: Ramos, "Fronteira e relações," 48–49.

48. Order dated Lisbon, 10.11.1674, and the proceedings that followed in Noudar in 4.12.1675 and the following days, ACDC, Cx. 19, 68-648, no. 2598. These developments were also mentioned in ANTT, Chancelaria da Ordem de Avis, Liv. 17, fols. 5v and 114v.

49. Indirect evidence for these proceedings can be found in the first page of AME, AC, leg. 3, book 1688. They were also mentioned in the letter of Manuel de Torres to Juan de Elizondo, Seville, 13.10.1716, AHN, leg. 1768, Exp. 12; and "Resumen . . . de todo lo ocurrido hasta el día de la fecha sobre las controversias entre vasallos de S.M. de la villa de Encinasola y de los del rey de Portugal del Castillo de Nodar y lugar de Barrancos" (c. 24.10.1716), in "El Consejo de Estado con un resumen . . . de lo ocurrido . . . sobre la demarcación de límites entre la villa de Encinasola de este reino y el Castillo de Nodar y lugar de Barrancos del de Portugal," Madrid, 24.10.1716, AHN, Estado leg. 1768, Exp. 17. See also "El Consejo de Estado, con carta del Marqués de Capecelatro diciendo ejecutará lo que se le ha ordenado cuanto a la dependencia de la villa de Encinasola," Madrid, 1.12.1716, AHN, Estado leg. 1768, Exp. 30. The question whether "renovation" was the same as "innovation," as Encinasola argued, was discussed in other cases too. For example, "El concejo de San Cibrián de Ardón con el concejo de Zillanueva sobre apeo y amojonamiento de los límites de los términos de ambos concejos, 1762–66," RCV, PC, Pérez Alonso (OLD) 326/4.

50. Proceedings dated 19.3.1676, ACDC, Cx. 19, 68-648, no. 2598.

51. Possession taking dated 8.6.1686, ACDC, Cx. 19, 67-635, no. 2628.

52. ACDC, Cx. 19, 68-648, no. 2598.

53. Demarcation dated 31.1.1688, ACDC, Cx. 19, 68-644, nos. 2690 and 2630; demarcation carried out 19.1.1688 to 20.1.1688, in "Autos do tombo e medição e demarcação da defeza da Ruciana," 15.7.1702, ACDC, Cx. 20, 70-658, no. 6214, fols. 21r–32r; and letter of Seville to the Marqués de Grimaldi, dated 18.2.1716, in "El Consejo de Estado con una carta de la ciudad de Sevilla y otras que cita de la villa de Encinasola sobre haber pasado portugueses a hacer nuevo deslinde de términos en ella," Madrid, 15.2.1703, AHN, Estado leg.1790, Exp. 26.

54. "Provisão para o Duque comendador das comendas de Noudar e Barrancos para a medição, demarcação e tombo dos bens da comenda (1700)," ANTT, Chancelaria da Ordem de Avis, Liv. 22, fol. 65; and "Autos do tombo e mediação e demarcação da defeza da Ruciana," 15.7.1702, ACDC, Cx. 20, 70-658, no. 6214.

55. The council of Encinasola, 14.11.1693, 5.6.1694, 9.6.1697, 19.6.1702, and 23.12.1702, and its letter to the judge demarcating the territory, dated 23.12.1702, in "Autos do tombo e mediação e demarcação da defeza da Ruciana," 15.7.1702, ACDC, Cx. 20, 70-658, no. 6214, fols. 11r–15r, 32r–33r, 43r–45r, 70v–71r, 77r–v, and 78r–v.

56. "No obstante que al Duque de Cadaval se le informó siniestramente cuanto a que mediante haber sobornado la villa a dicho juez quedó perjudicada su encomienda en gran parte de tierra que se agregó [Encinasola] a su término":

Letter of Encinasola, in "El Consejo de Estado con una carta de la ciudad de Sevilla y otras que cita de la villa de Encinasola sobre haber pasado portugueses a hacer nuevo deslinde de términos en ella," Madrid, 15.2.1703, AHN, Estado leg. 1790, Exp. 26.

57. "Provisão para o duque comendador das comendas de Noudar e Barrancos para a medição, demarcação e tombo dos bens da comenda," 1700, ANTT, Chancelaria da Ordem de Avis, Liv. 22, fol. 65.

58. "El Consejo de Estado con una carta de la ciudad de Sevilla y otras que cita de la villa de Encinasola sobre haber pasado portugueses a hacer nuevo deslinde de términos en ella," Madrid, 15.2.1703, AHN, Estado leg. 1790, Exp. 26.

59. "El Consejo de Estado con carta de la ciudad de Sevilla . . . sobre lo ejecutado por portugueses contra los límites de ambos reinos y jurisdicción de la villa de Encinasola," Madrid, 18.3.1716, AHN, Estado leg. 1791, Exp. 89. These complaints led to an order to investigate the case: "Don Manuel de Torres regente de Sevilla . . . sobre la averiguación de los confines entre Castilla y Portugal por parte de Encima Sola," Seville, 13.10.1716, AHN, Estado leg. 1768, Exp. 12; the council of Encinasola, 20.7.1716, AME, AC, leg. 4; and letter of Manuel de Torres to Juan de Elizondo, Seville, 13.10.1716, AHN, Estado leg. 1768, Exp. 12.

60. "Provisão ao Duque de Cadaval para tombar as terras da sua comenda de Noudar e Barrancos (1716)," ANTT, Chancelaria da Ordem de Avis, Liv. 24, f. 77 and the council of Encinasola, 20.4.1716, AME, AC leg. 4.

61. "Resumen . . . de todo lo ocurrido hasta el día de la fecha sobre las controversias entre vasallos de S.M. de la villa de Encinasola y de los del rey de Portugal del Castillo de Nodar y lugar de Barrancos" (circ. 24.10.1716), in "El consejo de estado . . . sobre la demarcación de límites entre la villa de Encinasola de este reino y el Castillo de Nodar y lugar de Barrancos del de Portugal," Madrid, 24.10.1716, AHN, Estado leg. 1768, Exp. 17. See also "El consejo de estado, con carta del Marqués de Capecelatro diciendo ejecutará lo que se le ha ordenado cuanto a la dependencia de la villa de Encinasola," Madrid, 1.12.1716, AHN, Estado leg. 1768, Exp. 30.

62. "Si la dificultad que pueda ocurrir en esto es la influencia del Duque de Cadaval por el interés en su encomienda podrá dar a entender que no tiene dificultad el que las tierras que tocaren a su encomienda queden pendientes de ella, aunque estén en territorio de Castilla, pues no solo en esta encomienda se verifica esta práctica": El consejo de estado in its consulta, dated 24.10.1716, AHN, Estado leg. 1768, Exp. 17.

63. "El consejo de estado con carta del Marqués de Capecelatro dando cuenta de lo que le expresa aquel secretario de estado sobre la dependencia de Encinasola," Lisbon, 28.1.1717, AHN, Estado leg. 1773.

64. Petition of the council of Moura, 2.3.1673, and related documents, ANTT, Casa do Infantado, Mç 1059; and two certificates dating 1st and 2nd of March, 1691, in ACDC, Cx. 19, 68-648, no. 2595. See also ACDC, Cx. 19, 68-648, nos. 2640, 2598, 2599, 2691, and 2714, and Cx. 20, 69-653, nos. 4032, 4139, 4144, and 3648.

65. The council of Moura on 2.3.1673, royal letter dated 12.4.1673, and opinion of the judge, 2.2.1764, in "Moura 1665–1677," ANTT, Casa do Infantado, Mç. 1059. See also ACDC, Cx. 19, 68-648, no. 2598.

66. Petition of the Duquesa de Cadaval, dated 26.2.1812, decision of the judge and administrator (corregedor) of Avis, dated 17.9.1820, and proceedings against Jose Damiel, resident of Santo Aleixo (Moura) by the officers of the comenda, dated 28.9.1825, all in ACDC, Cx. 19, 68-648, nos. 2641, 2751, and 2599, and Cx. 18, 66-629, no. 2048. On the episodes dated 1594, see "Parecer do desembargo do paço sobre o desacato havido na comenda de Noudar por causa dos marcos que o Conde de Linhares ali colocou," 8.6.1594, reproduced in João dos Santos Ramalho Cosme, *O Alentejo a Oriente d'Odiana (1600–1640). Política, sociedade, economia e cultura* (Lisbon: Cosmos, 1994), 217–218; and "Instrumento de justificação sobre a demarcação da vila de Noudar, 1593," ANTT, CC, Parte III, Mç. 22, Doc. 52. See also Ramos, "Fronteira e relações," 29–34.

67. These processes happened on the same side of the border or across it. The example of Seville, Aroche, and Encinasola demonstrated how they functioned within the same kingdom. A somewhat similar example of undivided territory among communities that were rearranging their relations was "El concejo y vecinos de la villa de Alcazarén con el de Mojados sobre deslinde y amojonamiento de la raya divisoria, 1807," RCV, PC, Fernando Alonso (OLV) 608/3.

68. "Auto de inquirição a respeito da vinda dos castelhanos aos termos de Moura para lavrar e semear," 2.11.1510, ANTT, Gavetas, XIV, 5-13.

69. "Juan Garcia Ronquillo en nombre de Aroche y del consejo de Moura," in "Ejecutorias ganadas por esta villa a la de Aroche en la RA de Sevilla," AME, leg. 236; and the procurator of Aroche, undated, in "El concejo de Encinasola con el concejo de Aroche, 1625," AHPS, RA, 233/1, fols. 756r–757r.

70. Council meetings dated 26.6.1760, 12.11.1762, and 27.1.1779, AMA, AC, leg. 15 and 16; and council meetings, 26.7.1760 and 14.12.1762, AME, AC, leg. 11 and 12. See also petition of both councils dated 10.12.1768, reproduced in royal order dated Madrid, 29.11.1780, and the annexed documentation in "Testimonio y demás diligencias sobre la tasación de granos y su cobranza de la dehesa de la contienda," AMA, leg. 453.

71. Ramos, "Fronteira e relações," 42–44.

72. "Carta a respeito dos direitos de pastagens entre as terras vizinhas de Portugal e Castela," 11.9.1290, ANTT, Gavetas, XVIII, 3-22.

73. Manuel González Jiménez, "Conflictos fronterizos en la sierra de Aroche. El pleito de Barrancos (1493)," *Actas das I jornadas de história medieval do Algarve e Andaluzia* (Loulé: Câmara Municipal de Loulé, 1987), 349–359; Carmona Ruiz, "La explotación ganadera," 248–249; Félix Sancha Soria, *La guerra de restauración portuguesa en la Sierra de Aroche (1640–1645)* (Huelva: Diputación de Huelva, 2008), 44; and Cosme, *O Alentejo*, 33–34, 37, and 55. See also José Luis Martín Martín, "La tierra de las 'contiendas': Notas sobre la evolución de la raya meridional en la edad media," *Norba. Revista de historia* 16 (1996–2003): 277–293, on 292.

74. João Luís de Lima e Silva de Sousa, "Contendas entre vilas e seus termos na fronteira portuguesa nos séculos XIII–XVI," *Boletim do Instituto Histórico da Ilha Terceira* 37 (1979): 41–59, 43; García Fitz, "Conflictos jurisdiccionales," 38 and 47–50; Carmona Ruiz, *Usurpaciones de tierras*, 45–46 and 52–53; Carmona Ruiz, "La explotación ganadera," 242–245; and Sancha Soria, *La guerra de restauración*, 69.

75. María Antonia Carmona Ruiz, *La ganadería en el reino de Sevilla durante la baja edad media* (Seville: Diputación de Sevilla, 1998), 375 and 456–457; Carmona Ruiz, *Usurpaciones de tierras*, 53 and 75. On *comunidad de pastos* more generally, see David E. Vassberg, *Tierra y sociedad en Castilla. Señores, "poderosos" y campesinos en la España del siglo XVI* (Barcelona: Crítica, 1986), 83–89.

76. Records dating from the 1680s demonstrate that, by that time, Noudar no longer existed, as the representative of the Duque de Cadaval who took possession of it in 1686 remarked that "where in old time" *(antiguamente)* various houses and a castle had been located, all that remained were some defenses and a church. Barrancos, on the contrary, was thriving: Possession taking dated 8.6.1686, ACDC, Cx. 19, 67-635, no. 2628. This process of abandonment might have begun in the mid- to late fifteenth century, when it became clear that Noudar might have military functions but Barrancos was the economically more active part. In 1527–1532 Barrancos had seventy-three inhabitants while Noudar six; in 1580 the numbers were 145 and twelve; in 1708, 350 and fifty; and in 1798, 265 and seven: Ramos, "Fronteira e relações," 20–21 and 36–40.

77. Fonseca, "Fronteiras territoriais"; Carmona Ruiz, "La explotación ganadera," 253; González Jiménez, "Conflictos"; and Amândio Jorge Morais Barros, "Uma contenda a norte da 'contenda' (alguns aspectos das relações fronteiriças entre Portugal e Castela na idade média)," *Revista da faculdade de letras. História* 15(1) (1998): 323–364, 330–331. Spanish immigration to Barrancos might have continued into the 1800s: María Victoria Navas Sánchez-Élez, "El río Guadiana lazo de unión entre España y Portugal: El caso de su margen izquierda," *Actas de las I Jornadas Transfronterizas sobre la Contienda hispano-portuguesa* (Aroche: Escuela Taller Contienda, 1996), vol. 1, 85–98, on 95.

78. "Inquirição que se tirou a respeito da aldeia de Barrancos que Castela dizia ser sua, mas que era pertença de Portugal," 16.3.1493, ANTT, Gavetas, XIV, 5-2.

79. Two treaties were signed in Tordesillas on June 4, 1494. The most famous dealt with the division of the Atlantic into spheres of potential expansion by drawing an imaginary line from pole to pole. It was accompanied by a second treaty that divided the fairly well-known yet still partially to be possessed maritime routes and lands in Africa. On the two treaties, see Luís Adão da Fonseca, "Portugal e o Mediterrâneo, entre Castela e Marrocos. A formação da fronteira marítima nos séculos XIV–XV e a noção de espaço político descontínuo," *População e sociedade* 17 (2009): 53–60, on 53 and 55. Both treaties might have had an antecedent in the Treaty of Alcáçovas (1479) in which, inter alia, Portugal retained its control over certain parts of Africa already or potentially under its power and Spain received the Canary Islands *ganadas y por ganar:*

"Tratado de paces entre las coronas de Castilla y de Portugal firmado en Toledo a 16.3.1480," *Boletín de la Real Academia de la historia* 38 (1901): 325–329,
cláusula VIII, on 327. Mainly centering on routes to Africa, this treaty did not
settle westward navigation, which is why Tordesillas was required. The coin-
cidence between the proceeding at Barrancos and the treaties might have not
been fortuitous: the commissioner sent by the Portuguese monarch to investigate Barrancos was also empowered to solve not only this conflict but also all
others that existed between Spain and Portugal, including their jurisdiction in
Africa. His power included the following: "Praticar e assentar, concordar e
formar tudo o que a ele parece razão e justiça assim sobre a terra que jaz entre
os cabos de Bojador e de Nam; como isso mesmo sobre as pescarias que fazem
e vão e enviam fazer os naturais e súbditos dos sobreditos rei e rainha de
Castela . . . que faz entre os ditos cabos de Nam e de Bojador que é terra e mar em
que assim pelas bulas dos Santos Padres como pela nova capitulação e reforma-
ção das pazes se não pode tratar negociar nem pescar sem nossa autoridade e
especial licença sob certas penas nas ditas bulas e capitulação conteúdas. E
outrossim lhe damos mais o dito poder e autoridade que possa assentar, com-
por, concordar e capitular tudo o que a ele dito doutor parece razão e justiça
acerca das Enxovias que são em terra d'Africa do que é da nossa conquista dos
reinos de Fez e cousas que de tudo o que dito é dependem e a forem anexas e
conexas for dito facto consentido, outorgado e firmado, assentado e capitalado
seja firme, estável e duradoiro para sempre. E prometemos por nossa fé real de
o havermos por rato e gato e de o guardarmos inviolavelmente e de nunca em
tempo algum irmos contra ele em parte nem em todo em juízo nem fora dele
directa nem indirecta por nos nem por outrem sob obrigação de todos nossos
bens asi da coroa dos nossos reinos como patrimoniais que para ela obrigamos
e especialmente hipotecamos." Power of the Portuguese king to Doctor Vasco
Fernandes, Lisbon, 3.2.1492, in "Inquirição que se tirou a respeito do termo de
Noudar e de Ansinasola," 20.2.1493, ANTT, Gavetas, XV, 23-8.

80. The Portuguese judge leading the investigation suggested that they
were "no good friends of these kingdoms, aggravating rather than supporting
it" (*são castelhanos e pouco amigos do proveito destes reinos e fazem mais perda nestes
reinos que proveito*): "Instrumento de vários documentos e de uns artigos pertencentes à inquirição que se tirou a respeito da contenda entre Portugal e Castela
sobre as demarcações e termos das vilas de Nodar e Moura com Anzina Sola e
Aroche," 22.2.1493, ANTT, Gavetas, XVIII, 2-1, reproduced in GTT, vol. 8,
52–105, on 68.

81. "Relação do que sucedeu na vila de Moura e seu termo no ano de 1641,"
reproduced in Cosme, *Elementos para a história*, 331–342, on 332–333. The
original can be found in BNP, Res. Cod. 6687.

82. Miguel de Noronha was one of several important Portuguese noblemen who chose this road and whose betrayal—as portrayed by the Braganza
propaganda—was both undeniable and colossal. He had been governor of
Tangier (1624–1628) and viceroy of India (1629–1635) and was related to the
Marqués de Villarreal and the Duque de Caminhas, two prominent men who
were convicted of treason and executed by João. In return to his allegiance to

Philip, he secured a title for his firstborn (the first Duque de Linares) and several potentially lucrative administrative posts, and was allowed to call himself not only Conde de Linhares, as was his previous title, but also Conde-Marqués de Villareal. Yet contemporaries suspected that these achievements faded in relation to what he had lost in the process. He might have agreed, suggesting in his various testaments that most of his estate remained in Portugal and that since 1640 he could no longer use it, having remained in Castile "without even one maravedí." He confessed not knowing what had happened to Noudar and Barrancos yet, in his undated petition for annual income from the king he explained that "the Portuguese have burned and depopulated his estates as had been seen in Barrancos, along the border in Extremadura" (*quemando los portugueses y despoblando mis lugares como se ha visto en Barrancos raya de la Extremadura*). Having spent 1637–1642 in Madrid first as a member and then as the president of the Council of Portugal and having been considered for the office of viceroy of Brazil, he reassumed in 1642 a military career, commanding galleys in Italy and Spain until his death on April 1656. Information on the Conde de Linhares can be found in Anthony Disney, "On Attempting to Write an Early Modern Biography: My Encounter with the Life of Dom Miguel de Noronha, Fourth Count of Linhares (1588–1656)," *Indica* 29(2) (1992): 89–106; Anthony Disney, *The Portuguese in India and Other Studies, 1500–1700* (Burlington, VT: Ashgate, 2009), chapters 7, 9, and 12; Bouza Álvarez, "Entre dos reinos," 84–87 and 100–101; and Fernando J. Bouza Álvarez, *Papeles y opinión: Políticas de publicación en el siglo de oro* (Madrid: CSIC, 2008), 131–133. Miguel de Noronha left several testaments: AHPM protocolo 4786, fols. 210r–296v and 483r–509v, for example, fols. 484v, 492r–v, and 504r. See also the petition of Fernando de Noronha, his firstborn, to the council of Castile and its consulta dated 22.10.1670, AHN, consejo 7180/39; and "Relación de servicios de don Miguel de Noroña," ACEDAL. I would like to thank the Duque de Abrantes for sending me a copy of this document. Contemporaries suggested that "Ao Linhares satisfizeram, deixando-o chamar Conde de Gijon, pequeno lugar de Astúrias, nas ribeiras do mar Cantábrico; da qualidade não tirou mais que a verdade de se manifestar por neto de Dom Affonso, antigo Conde de Gijon, filho de Dom Henrique o bastardo, honra que ninguém lhe duvidava antes, nem invejou depois, em cujo troco perdeu em Portugal vinte mil cruzados de renda, bons lugares, e nobres comendas": Francisco Manoel de Mello, *Tácito português*, eds. Afrânio Peixoto, Rodolfo Garcia, and Pedro Calmon (Rio de Janeiro: Bedeschiimprimiu, 1940), 97.

83. The council of Encinasola, 28.6.1641, 30.6.1641, and 12.7.1641, AME, AC, leg. 1, fols. 26r–28v. These versions found support in reports by the inhabitants of Santo Aleixo, a hamlet of Moura, who suggested that there were indications that during the war Barranqueños gave "secret messages" to Castilians: this report dated 1644 was cited in Bento Caldeira, *Aldeia heroica (Santo Aleixo da Restauração)* (Lisbon: Colibrí, 1997), 27. Similar suggestions were made by Luís de Meneses, *História de Portugal Restaurado* (Lisbon: João Galvão, 1679), vol. 1, 216.

84. On the local character of the Portuguese independence war, see, for example, Freitas, *O combatente*, 266–269; and João Cosme, "A solidariedade e a

conflitualidade na fronteira portuguesa do Alentejo (séculos XIII–XVIII),"
População e Sociedade 6 (2000): 83–100, on 90.

85. These hopes might have been frustrated. In 1642, Moura complained that because of the war its inhabitants could not use this territory at all: "Item e memorial das defezas e propriedades que estão perdidas no termo desta vila que se não cultivam nem aproveitam por razão das guerras," ANTT, Cortes, Mç 12, fols. 169r–170v; also reproduced in Cosme, *Elementos para a história*, 266–286.

86. Freitas, *O combatente*, 266–269; and Cosme, "A solidariedade," 90.

87. "Capítulos que deram os procuradores da vila de Moura nas cortes . . . de 1641," petition no. 9, ANTT, Cortes, Mç. 12, fols. 141r–142r and 146v. This document was reproduced in Cosme, *Elementos para a história*, 249–250.

88. Declaration of Pedro López Catano and Esteban Martín de Castro in "Encinasola, año de 1787. Causa de denuncia contra varios vecinos y ganados del lugar de Barrancos reino de Portugal," AME, leg. 228, fols. 19v–22v and 87r–90r. See also certificate of Encinasola, 8.10.1788 on fols. 81r–83v; and notarial certificate dated 13.9.1787 and the various notifications that the audiencia of Seville sent on February 1790, in "Causa de denuncia, 1792," AME, leg. 749. In the mid-eighteenth century, natives of Encinasola formed the largest group in Barrancos: Ramos, "Fronteira e relações," 133.

89. ANTT, Tribunal do Santo Ofício, Habilitações, Mç. 165, Doc. 4036, fols. 1, 2, 8, 100, and 108–114.

90. Carmona Ruiz, "La explotación ganadera," 250–252.

91. "Auto que se fez a respeito da demarcação entre Portugal e Galiza por mandado de el-rei d. João III," Vinhais, 1.6.1538, ANTT, Gavetas, XIV, 5-15.

92. "Los vecinos de Barcia de Mera Manuel Mosquera y consortes contra Manuel Antonio de Otero escribano sobre exceso, 1795," ARG, RA 9144/26.

93. Several certificates by Ambrosio González Lechuga, dated August 1785, AME, leg. 228, fols. 40v–43v; council meeting, 5.5.1798, the letters exchanged between Moura, Aroche, and Encinasola, and the meeting that took place at La Tomina on 29.9.1798, AMM, B/A/01/013, fols. 91r–92v and 100v–102v; and "Autos formados en virtud de oficio del ayuntamiento de la villa de Aroche sobre el aprovechamiento de la dehesa de la Contienda, 1808," AME, leg. 228. La Tomina, currently in ruin, was founded in the 1680s and, in 1709, was granted to the Congregação dos Clérigos Regulares dos Doentes, whose main task was to take care of the moribund.

94. These confrontations were described in multiple records, all in AME, leg. 228, for example, council meeting 9.3.1785, fols. 5v–6v, and the declaration of witnesses that followed on fols. 7r–9v; and "Papeles y documentos relativos . . . al famoso pleito . . . por Francisco Méndez de nación portugués, vecino de Barrancos," AME, leg. 228.

95. ANTT, Tribunal do Santo Ofício, Habilitações, Mç. 165, doc. 4036, fols. 75 and 81–82. See also Ramos, "Fronteira e relações," 147–148.

96. "El consejo de estado con consulta suya y dos del de Castilla . . . sobre las diferencias que hay entre vecinos de los lugares de Rio Manzanas y Santa Cruz del reino de Castilla y los de Guadramil del de Portugal," Madrid, 3.11.1701, AHN, Estado leg. 1778, Exp. 53; and "El consejo de estado con consulta del de

Castilla sobre las diferencias que se han suscitado entre vecinos del lugar de Rio Manzanas del reino de Castilla y los de Guadramil del de Portugal," Madrid, 28.9.1701, AHN, Estado leg. 1788, Exp. 52.

97. The conde de Frigiliana al consejo de estado, Madrid, 3.12.1696, and the consejo de estado, Madrid, 8.1.1697, both in AGS, Estado leg. 4043; "El consejo de estado con consulta del de Castilla sobre instancia del enviado de Portugal en orden a la controversia suscitada entre la villa de Encinasola de estos reinos y la de Moura del de Portugal," Madrid, 2.5.1700, AHN, Estado leg. 1766, Exp. 60; consulta of the consejo de Castilla, Madrid, 17.6.1700 and 17.4.1697, both summarized in "El Consejo de Estado con consulta del de Castilla sobre instancia del enviado de Portugal," Madrid, 17.6.1700, AHN, Estado leg. 1781, Exp. 16; "El Consejo de Estado con un oficio del enviado de Portugal," Madrid, 13.5.1700, AHN, Estado leg. 1766, Exp. 63; "El Consejo de Estado . . . sobre la demarcación de límites entre la villa de Encinasola de este reino y el Castillo de Nodar y lugar de Barrancos del de Portugal," Madrid, 24.10.1716, AHN, leg. 1768, Exp. 17; and "El Consejo de Estado con carta del Marqués de Capecelatro dando cuenta de lo que le expresa aquel secretario de estado sobre la dependencia de Encinasola," Lisbon, 28.1.1717, AHN, Estado leg. 1773.

98. "El monasterio de Melón con Gonzalo Ojea vecino del lugar de Perdices sobre apropiar el coto de Villamayor al reino de Portugal, 1573," ARG, RA 569/13; and "Los vecinos de Alcobazas (Portugal) Bartolomé Domingues y consortes con los vecinos de Azoreira . . . sobre comunes en Allariz (Ourense)," 1631, ARG, RA 2501/8. Similar was also "Juan das Agras con vecinos de Castro Liveiro sobre pastos, 1594," ARG, RA 26601/27.

99. Ambrosio Spinoza, procurator of Encinasola on 19.6.1697, in "Autos do tombo e mediação e demarcação da defeza da Ruciana," 15.7.1702, ACDC, Cx. 20, 70-658, no. 6214, fols. 43v–45r. The Mesa da Consciência e Ordens was a court charged with overseeing matters related to the church, the military orders, and the universities. Among other things, it administered the three military orders (Orders of Christ, of Avis, and of Santiago) incorporated in 1551 to the Portuguese crown. According to the procurator, if the duke wanted to appeal a decision taken in the ordinary style and form by a judge, he had to address an ordinary appeal court, not the Mesa.

100. "Los vecinos del lugar de Bousenses . . . sobre excesos en deslinde de los montes de los Vidos a pedimento de los vecinos del lugar de Canvedo (Portugal), 1753," ARG, RA 9135/9.

101. "Instrumento de vários documentos e de uns artigos pertencentes à inquirição que se tirou a respeito da contenda entre Portugal e Castela sobre as demarcações e termos das vilas de Nodar e Moura com Anzina Sola e Aroche," 22.2.1493, ANTT, Gavetas, XVIII, 2-1; and "Inquirição que se tirou a respeito do termo de Noudar e de Ansina Sola," 20.2.1493, ANTT, Gavetas, XV, 23-8.

102. Royal decree, Lisbon, 9.10.1603, ANTT, Chancelaria de Filipe II, Doações, Liv. 10, fol. 299. The conflict in 1603 and 1605 is briefly mentioned in a letter Manuel de Torres wrote to Juan de Elizondo, Seville 13.10.1716, AHN, Estado leg. 1768, Exp. 12; and "Resumen . . . de todo lo ocurrido hasta el día de la fecha sobre las controversias entre vasallos de S.M. de la villa de Encinasola

y de los del rey de Portugal del Castillo de Nodar y lugar de Barranco" (c. 24.10.1716), in "El consejo de estado . . . sobre la demarcación de límites entre la villa de Encinasola de este reino y el Castillo de Nodar y lugar de Barrancos del de Portugal," Madrid, 24.10.1716, AHN, Estado leg. 1768, Exp. 17.

103. Ramos, "Fronteira e relações," 27.

104. Carmona Ruiz, *Usurpaciones de tierras*, 134, identified the conflict as involving "Campo de Gamos," also called "La Contienda." Nevertheless, contemporary documents suggested that the two were not identical or at least that they were gradually distinguished. On how the contested area first grew and then contracted see García Fitz, "Conflictos jurisdiccionales," 44.

105. The archives of Aroche and Encinasola were burned to the ground during the war of Portuguese Independence, and in the 1690s Moura complained that its archives were hardly legible: council of Encinasola, 14.11.1693, 5.6.1694, 9.6.1697, 19.6.1702, and 23.12.1702, and its letter to the judge demarcating the territory dated 23.12.1702, in "Autos do tombo e mediação e demarcação da defeza da Ruciana," 15.7.1702, ACDC, Cx. 20, 70-658, no. 6214, fols. 11r–15r, 31r–33r, 43r–45r, 70v–71r, 77r–v, and 78r–v; "Alvará autorizando a vila de Moura a copiar o seus arquivos," Lisbon, 2.8.1697, reproduced in Cosme, *Elementos para a história*, 379–380; and copy of an undated letter of Moura to Aroche and the deliberations of Aroche on 7.7.1699, AMA, AC, leg. 9.

106. Carmona Ruiz, "La explotación ganadera," 242.

107. It is therefore not surprising that historians have done so, too, studying the conflict between Aroche, Encinasola, Moura, Serpa, and Noudar until the 1540s as if nothing important had transpired since: José Avelino da Silva e Matta, "Annaes de Moura ou apontamentos históricos para a topographia mourense," 1855, AMM, 193–202; Sebastião Lopes Calheiros Meneses, *Noticia sobre a contenda de Moura. Alguns documentos. Conclusões. Nota de 19.9.1805, tratado de 14.10.1542 que se tem denominado a concordata. Planta da contenda de Moura* (Lisbon: Imprensa Nacional, 1889), 3; Pérez-Embid, *La frontera*; and Navas Sánchez-Élez, "El río Guadiana," 94.

108. These questions were endlessly treated in contemporary letters, pamphlets, and essays. I found the following most useful: Francisco de Peralta, "Relación de lo que han informado los corregidores de Castilla la Vieja y Nueva, La Mancha, Extremadura y Andalucía acerca del remedio que se tendrá para la conservación de la labranza y crianza," undated manuscript, BNE, Ms. 9372, fols. 31r–40v; Arriquibar, *Recreación política;* "Discursos políticos del Marqués de Monte-Real ministro del Consejo de Castilla" (undated, ca. 1752–1769), BPR, Ms. II/3496, discurso 12, fols. 36v–38v, the city of Cáceres on 31.5.1800, in "Proyecto de población de la nominada villa de Balbanera en la provincia Extremadura," AHN, Consejos 4060, for example, on fols. 224v–225r; Antonio Henriques da Silveira, "Racional discurso sobre a agricultura, e população da província de Alem-Tejo," and José Ignacio da Costa, "Agronómica relativa ao concelho de Chaves," both in *Memorias económicas da Academia Real das Sciencias de Lisboa para o adiantamento da agricultura, das artes e da industria em Portugal e suas conquistas* (Lisbon: Oficina da Academia Real das Ciências, 1789), vol. 1, 41–122 and 351–398. See also Castro, *O pensamento económico*, 38–40; and Serrão, "O pensamento agrário."

109. Paradoxically, when the Royal Mesta *(honrado concejo de la mesta)*, the official body charged with overseeing long-distance grazing, was created in the thirteenth century, it was viewed as a modernizing agent because it privileged the commercialization of wool and long-distance trade over local production and a subsistence economy. However, in the seventeenth and eighteenth centuries, it was reimagined as a conservative institution and, for reformers, became the symbol of the "barbarian laws" that "preferred sheep to men" and the enemy of progress. The main problem was that the rules vindicated by the Mesta prohibited enclosure and placed restrictions on proprietors who could not freely enjoy their land. Thereafter, it became responsible for the agricultural backwardness of Spain and economic decline more generally: Melchor de Jovellanos, *Informe de la Sociedad Económica*, 5–6, 23–24, and 148. Several manuscripts presented to Madrid's Sociedad de Amigos del País in 1777 and included in ARSEMAP, leg. 15, Exp. 1, also discussed these issues, as did the famous Pedro Rodríguez de Campomanes, *Memorial ajustado del expediente de concordia que trata el honorable Concejo de la Mesta con la diputación general del reino y provincia de Extremadura*, introduced by Miguel Ángel Melón Jiménez (Cáceres: Caja de Extremadura, 2006 [1783]). See also Javier M. Donézar Diez de Ulzurrun, *Riqueza y propiedad en la Castilla del Antiguo Régimen* (Madrid: Ministerio de Agricultura, Pesca y Alimentación, 1996), 160–171; and Gonzalo Anes, "Agricultura y ganadería en el siglo de las luces," in *Cultivos, cosechas y pastoreo en la España Moderna* (Madrid: Real Academia de la Historia, 1999), 93–104.

110. "Nota apresentada pelo conde del Campo de Alange embaixador de sua majestade católica dirigida ao governo de sua alteza real o príncipe regente, 19.9.1805," reproduced in Meneses, *Noticia sobre a contenda*, 31–36, on 34.

111. Isabel Testón Núñez, Carlos Sánchez Rubio, and Rocío Sánchez Rubio, *Planos, guerra y frontera. La raya luso-extremeña en el Archivo Militar de Estocolmo* (Mérida: Gabinete de Iniciativas Transfronterizas-Junta de Extremadura, 2004), 8.

112. José Cornide, *Descripción circunstanciada de la costa de Galicia y raya por donde confina con el inmediato reino de Portugal, hecha en el año de 1764*, ed. X.L. Axeitos (A Coruña: Edición do Castro, 1991 [1764]), 151.

113. "Composição feita entre as vilas de Marvão e Valência de Alcântara," 12.12.1313, ANTT, Gavetas, XV, 23-5. See also Possidónio Mateus Laranjo Coelho, *Terras de Odiana. Medobriga, Ammaia, Armenha, Marvão* (Marvão: Câmara Municipal de Castelo de Vide e Marvão, 1984), 86–91.

114. "Demarcação feita por inquirição entre a vila de Marvão e a vila de Valença de Castela," 8.2.1455, ANTT, Gavetas, XIV, 5-1; "Carta testemunhável a respeito das dúvidas dos termos entre Marvão y Valença," Marvão, 20.1.1488, ANTT, Gavetas, XVIII, 5-29; and "Autos de vistorias que fizeram judicialmente os oficiais das câmaras das vilas de Marvão e Valença, sobre as demarcações e divisões dos termos destas duas vilas," 22.9.1519, ANTT, CC, parte II, Mç. 84, doc. 163. The accord became permanent in 1585 and was again ratified in 1682: "Treslado dos compromissos das nobres villas de Marvão y Valencia." I would like to thank Juan Carlos Corchero Ramajo, consejal

de cultura of the city council of Valencia de Alcántara for sending me a copy of this document.

115. Council meetings, 6.8.1763 and 20.8.1763, AMVA, LC 1763, fols. 120r–v and 128r–129v; and records of a joint meeting of the councils of both municipalities dated 18.8.1763 and reproduced in CMM, 01-057, Vereações 1763–1764, fols. 25r–v.

116. Council meeting, 23.2.1725, AMVA, LC 1725, fols. 28r–29r.

117. Council meeting, 7.12.1805, AMVA, LC 1805, fols. 168r–v.

118. In 1758, for example, the council of Valencia suggested that Spanish custom guards (*guardas del resguardo de la renta*) could not apprehend horses belonging to Marvão, which pastured in the territory of Valencia: letter of Ramón de Larumbes dated Badajoz, 7.5.1758, copied into the records of the council meeting, 19.5.1758, AMVA, LC 1758, fols. 92r–96r. Similarly, they intervened in 1760 and 1766 to ensure the liberation of goats and their shepherds: council meeting, 2.12.1760, AMVA, LC 1760, unnumbered page; and council meeting, 11.12.1766, AMVA, LC 1766, fols. 111r–112v.

119. José Baptista Barreiros, "Delimitação da fronteira luso-espanhola," *O distrito de Braga. Boletim Cultural de Etnografia e História* 3(3) Fasic. I–II (1964): 1–97, 21.

120. Council meeting, 24.6.1868, CMM, 01-113, Vereações 1868, fols. 24r–25r.

121. Antonio de Gaber, "Relación que individualmente se expresa puerto por puerto los ríos, arroyos, barrancos y mojones que dividen . . . la línea de demarcación que divide España y Portugal," 24.7.1750, AGMM, 5-3-4-4 and 3-5-2-3, point 2; and notes dated Badajoz 21.7.1750, most probably authored by Antonio de Gaber and included in "Copia de los papeles citados en esta relación," AGMM, 5-3-4-4, note 1. These documents were transcribed in Hevilla, "Reconocimiento practicado."

122. "Esta circunstancia, las tradiciones de los mayores del país y otras inferencias fundadas que expresara a su tiempo inspiran fuertes presunciones de que esta dehesa fue primitivamente de España y es una usurpación violenta de los fronterizos portugueses, cuya época se pierde en la obscuridad de los tiempos según parece fue una resulta de las porfiadas y continuadas guerras durante los reinados de la reina doña Isabel de Castilla y sus antecesores en que las expediciones contra los moros . . . distrajeron la atención de la superioridad de este rincón de tierra de tan poca atención al parecer": "Borrador y expediente de La Contienda," anonymous and undated manuscript probably authored by the Spanish commissioner Francisco Fersen, in AMAE/M, Tr 282/002, no. 0431, Part III. See also his letter dated 26.6.1804 and cited in a summary (undated) inserted in AMAE/M, Tr 282/002, no. 0431.

123. Letter of Joseph Gabriel to Pedro Cevallos, Badajoz, 16.2.1805, and accompanying documents, AMAE/M, Tr 133/003, no. 0207.

124. The same book also vindicated Serpa as a Spanish municipality because alongside Moura, Cáceres, Badajoz, and Trujillo, it belonged to Castile as late as 1294: copy of the relevant pages from that book, authenticated by Manuel de Silva, notary, Badajoz, 9.2.1805, in AMAE/M, Tr 133/003, no. 0207.

125. Ramos y Orcajo, *Dehesa de la Contienda*, 14.

126. Allegations made on 4.7.1802 by Encinasola, in "Diligencias practica-das sobre la dehesa de La Contienda, año de 1802," AMAE/M, Tr 283/003, no. 0431.

CHAPTER 4   *Moving Islands in a Sea of Land*

1. "Resumen de lo que ha pasado en la raya de Galicia entre gallegos y portugueses sobre la pertenencia de una isla sita en el río Miño que llaman de Berdoejo o Caldelas," AHN, Estado leg. 872.

2. "Copia da petição que deu em Lisboa el reitor da companhia de Jesus da cidade de Coimbra," and "Lo que respondió el abad de Caldelas cuando el corregidor de la comarca de Viana le citó," both in AHN, Estado leg. 1752, Exp. 20.

3. Letter of Duque de Uceda, La Coruña, 24.12.1684, AHN, Estado leg. 872.

4. Letter of the Portuguese ambassador, Madrid, 4.8.1684, reproduced in "El consejo de estado con un papel del enviado de Portugal sobre el embarazo que se ofrece en las fronteras de Galicia," Madrid, 17.8.1684, AHN, Estado leg. 1752, Exp. 18.

5. "En consejo de estado, con carta del Duque de Uceda y papeles que envía sobre una controversia entre gallegos y portugueses tocante a la pesca del Miño," Madrid, 11.11.1684, AHN, Estado leg. 1752, Exp. 19. The council continued to uphold this position the following year: its consulta dated 27.1.1685, AHN, Estado leg. 1752, Exp. 20.

6. "En consejo de estado, con carta del Duque de Uceda y papeles que envía sobre una controversia entre gallegos y portugueses tocante a la pesca del Miño," Madrid, 11.11.1684, AHN, Estado leg. 1752, Exp. 19; and letter of Duque de Uceda, La Coruña, 24.12.1684, AHN, Estado leg. 872.

7. Joseph de Faria to the Conde de Chinchón, Madrid, 10.2.1691, in "El consejo de estado con una memoria del enviado de Portugal sobre que las jus-ticias de Tui ejercen jurisdicción en una isleta del reino de Galicia que pertenece a la corona de Portugal," Madrid 17.7.1691, AHN, Estado leg. 1771, Exp. 2. See also consulta of the consejo de estado dated 21.7.1691, AHN, Estado leg. 1771, Exp. 1; and "Informação sobre a insola de Verdoejo sita no rio Minho a qual pertence à coroa de Portugal," undated and unsigned, AHN, Estado leg. 872-2, and the attached documentation, dated 1694.

8. Jacinto de Aruz Ossorio to the king, Tui, 18.6.1691, and the judicial proceedings attached dated Tui, 14.5.1691, in "El consejo de estado con una consulta y carta del alcalde de la ciudad de Tui sobre excesos que cometen portugueses en aquella jurisdicción," Madrid, 21.6.1691, AHN, Estado leg. 1771, Exp. 1.

9. "Al Conde de Puñonrrostro y obispo de Tui," draft of letters dated 17.6.1691 and 21.6.1691, AHN, Estado leg. 872; Manuel de Semanat to the King, Lisbon, 31.7.1691 and 21.8.1691, and the responses of the Portuguese minister of foreign affairs, dated 31.7.1691 and 18.8.1691, all in AHN, Estado leg. 872.

10. Anselmo Gómez de la Torre to the consejo de estado, Tui, 4.10.1691, and the documents attached, AHN, Estado leg. 872.

11. Conde de Puñonrrostro, La Coruña, 28.10.1691, AHN, Estado leg. 872.

12. "El consejo de estado con una memoria del enviado de Portugal," 15.7.1693, AHN, Estado leg. 872; "El consejo de estado con un resumen de todo lo que ha pasado en la raya de Galicia entre portugueses y gallegos," 10.9.1693, AHN, Estado leg. 872; and draft of the consulta of 10.9.1693, AHN, Estado leg. 872.

13. "El licenciado don Gabriel Tavares, relator de la real audiencia de este reino dará a continuación de este decreto relación del pleito que litiga en dicha audiencia el colegio de padres de la compañía de Coimbra en el reino de Portugal con el abad de Caldelas," La Coruña, 22.8.1694, and "El consejo de estado con carta del Conde de Palma y relación que acompaña del pleito pendiente en la audiencia de La Coruña," 7.9.1694, both in AHN, Estado leg. 872. A copy of the documents presented by the monastery can be also found in MNE, LH, Cx. 1 (no. 1118), fols. 529r–534r.

14. "El Consejo de estado con dos cartas de don Manuel Semanat y papeles que remitió," 29.7.1694, and the attached documents, AHN, Estado leg. 872; and "Informação sobre a insola de Verdoejo sita no rio Minho a qual pertence à coroa de Portugal," anonymous undated manuscript in AHN, Estado leg. 872.

15. "Cabeza de proceso y testigos ante Diego Iñigom juez ordinario sobre que el juez ordinario del coto de San Fins rompió la jurisdicción de SM," Tui, 13.7.1695, and "El consejo de estado con carta de la ciudad de Tui, una consulta suya (de 7.9.1694) y otra de Castilla sobre la pertenencia de la isla de Caldelas o Berdoejo," 9.2.1696, both in AHN, Estado leg. 872, which also contains numerous other representations made by the city of Tui, its bishop, and the governor of Galicia. "Ni verisímilmente parece puede haberle [pleito] sobre esta isla en la audiencia de La Coruña porque siendo la duda sobre si esta isla toca al reino de Portugal o al de Galicia no parece que tribunal de ningún reino pueda ser competente para esta determinación": Consulta of the consejo de Castilla, undated, AHN, Estado leg. 872.

16. Letter of Manuel de Semanat, Lisbon, 14.2.1696, AHN, Estado leg. 872.

17. Letter of the audiencia of Galicia to the King, 4.10.1695, AHN, Estado leg. 872; consulta of consejo de Castilla dated 20.2.1696 and reproduced partially in "El consejo de estado con consulta del de Castilla y carta de don Manuel de Semanat," 17.3.1696, AHN, Estado leg. 872.

18. Letter of the ambassador dated Madrid, 8.5.1696, included in the information sent by the Conde de Frigiliana to the King, Madrid, 8.5.1696, and his letter of 22.10.1696, both in AGS, Estado 4043; and consultas of the consejo de estado, 10.7.1696, 25.9.1696, and 13.11.1696, AGS, Estado 4042 and 4043. The Marqués de Villafranca and the Marqués de Mancera, for example, insisted that examining the situation of the island and the river were "very essential circumstances" (circunstancias muy esenciales) in the decision-making process: their opinion in the consulta of 13.11.1696, AGS, Estado 4043.

19. In March 1696, for example, the council studied the representation of the kingdom of Galicia and the city of Tui, requesting that the conflict would

be at last resolved: Petition by Miguel de Araujo, diputado del Reino de Galicia and consulta of the consejo de estado, 25.9.1696, and representation of the city of Tui, 26.5.1696, AGS, Estado 4043.

20. Article 5 of the 1715 Utrecht treaty determined: "Las plazas, castillos, ciudades, lugares, territorios y campos pertenecientes a las dos coronas, así en Europa como en cualquiera parte del mundo se restituirán enteramente y sin reserva alguna; de suerte que los límites y confines de las dos monarquías quedarán en el mismo estado que tenían antes de la presente guerra. Y particularmente se volverán a la corona de España las plazas de Alburquerque y la Puebla con sus territorios . . . y a la corona de Portugal el castillo de Noudar con su territorio, la isla de Verdejo y el territorio y Colonia de Sacramento." Cantillo, *Tratados*, 165–166.

21. Marqués de Risbourg to Miguel Fernández Durán, La Coruña, 3.5.1716, an anonymous note inserted in the above documentation indicating the response given to the governor in 13.5.1716, "El consejo de estado con dos cartas del Marqués de Risbourg," Madrid, 12.9.1716, the Marqués de Risbourg to the Marqués de Grimaldi, La Coruña 2.8.1716 and Auto de cabeza de proceso," Tui, 18.6.1716, and the following declarations, AHN, Estado leg. 1769, Exp. 46. Copies of many of these documents can also be found in AHN, Estado leg. 1791, Exp. 107, and AHPP, AMT, LA 1716, Asign. 837, fols. 117r–122r.

22. José Baptista Barreiros, "Delimitação da fronteira luso-espanhola," *O distrito de Braga. Boletim Cultural de Etnografia e História* 2, fasc. I–II (1964): 83–170, 79, 82–84, 88–90, and 138 (hereafter Barreiros, "Delimitação da fronteira" [1964a]).

23. "Treaty of Boundaries between Spain and Portugal . . . 1864," in *Treaties Series: Treaties and International Agreements Registered or Filed and Recorded with the Secretariat of the United Nations* (New York: United Nations, 1991), vol. 1288, II-906, on 243–261, art. 1, p. 245, and annex I on 262–265.

24. "El Conde de Frigiliana dice como los portugueses se han apoderado de la isla de Verdoejo," Madrid, 30.4.1696, a text authored by the Portuguese ambassador in Madrid, and "Resumen de lo que ha pasado en la raya de Galicia entre gallegos y portugueses sobre la pertenencia de una isla sita en el río Miño que llaman de Berdoejo o Caldelas," AHN, Estado leg. 872. See also "Traslado do enfezamento em fateusim perpetuo feito a Leonel de Abreu de Regalados," testament of the abbot of the monastery dated 27.1.1540, and "Translado da posse da ínsua de Verdoejo dada a dona Maria mulher de Leonel d'Abreu em seu filho," 5.12.1548, MNE, LH, Cx. 1 (no. 1118), fols. 529r–230r, 530v–531v, and 533r–534r.

25. Pedro Gómez (Gomes) de Abreu was one of the first Portuguese nobles to take this road. His arrival in Madrid was celebrated and he was awarded the title of Conde de Regalados. Although he died soon after (in 1642), he continued to symbolize both extreme loyalty and extreme treason, depending on who was speaking: José Augusto Carneiro, *Notícia histórica e genealógica dos Abreus de Regalados, apresentada à Academia Real das Ciências de Lisboa* (Barcellos: Typographia Barcellense de Augusto Soucasaux, 1905), 13–14, 28–30, and 87–91; Celia Rodríguez de Maribona y Álvarez de la Viña, Marquesa de Ciadoncha, "Los caballeros portugueses en las órdenes militares españolas," *Arquivo*

histórico de Portugal 5(1) (1943): 237–330, 275–276, 289–291, and 294–295; Conde de Ericeira, *História de Portugal restaurado*, ed. António Álvaro Dória (Porto: Livraria Civilização Editora, 1945 [1710]), vol. 1, 149; and Luis Vilar y Pascual, *Diccionario histórico, genealógico y heráldico de las familias ilustres de la monarquía española* (Madrid: Imprenta de D.F. Sánchez, 1859), vol. 1, 395–406. The genealogy of the family in the 1640s is included in AHN, Caballeros-Calatrava, Exp. 1062, expediente of Gaspar Gómez de Abreu.

26. Anselmo de la Torre to the consejo de estado, 4.10.1691, and the proceeding in Tui on 8.9.1691, AHN, Estado leg. 872; and "Auto de cabeza de proceso," Tui, 18.6.1716, and the following declarations, reproduced in AHN, Estado leg. 1769, Exp. 46. Copies of this documentation are also found in AHN, Estado leg. 1791, Exp. 107, and AHPP, AMT, LA 1716, Asign. 837, fols. 117r–122r. María de Abreu e Noronha, granddaughter of Leonel de Abreu, married Fernando de Sotomayor, Conde de Crecente and Señor de Cala de Soutomayor in Galicia, thereafter uniting the Abreu with the Sotomayors: Costa, *Corografía portugueza*, vol. 1, 245–246.

27. "¿Cómo fue la intrusión de portugueses en la isla que llaman de Caldelas 23 o 24 años ha y cómo se les consintió y disimuló la introducción en ella o si hubo reclamación de los interesados Falcones?," Consulta of the consejo de estado, 12.9.1716, AHN, Estado leg. 1769, Exp. 46. Another copy of this consulta is found in AHN, Estado leg. 1791, Exp. 107.

28. Francisco Castro Viejo to the Marqués de Astorga, La Guardia, 29.4.1699, and the information elaborated in La Guarda, 24.4.1691, attached to "El consejo de estado con consulta suya y otra del de Castilla sobre las vejaciones que padecen los vecinos de la Guardia causados por los de Seixas, jurisdicción de Portugal," Madrid, 15.1.1700, AHN, Estado leg. 1781, Exp. 2; "El consejo de estado con una memoria del enviado de Portugal sobre que las justicias de Tui ejercen jurisdicción en una isleta del reino de Galicia que pertenece a la corona de Portugal," Madrid 17.7.1691, AHN, Estado leg. 1771, Exp. 2; "El señor Conde de Frigiliana para que pase oficio de queja con el enviado de Portugal sobre las molestias causadas a los vecinos de la Guarda por los de Seixas, jurisdicción de Portugal," Madrid, 23.1.1700, AHN, Estado leg. 1766, Exp. 43; Diego de Manrique Corte Real, Madrid, 4.3.1701, in "El consejo de estado con oficio del enviado de Portugal sobre los daños que los vecinos de La Guardia recibían de los portugueses de Seixas," Madrid, 10.3.1701, AHN, Estado leg. 1778, Exp. 15; and "Consulta del de Castilla sobre los daños que los vecinos de La Guardia experimentaban de los portugueses de Seixas," Madrid, 4.4.1701, AHN, Estado leg. 1788, Exp. 18.

29. "El consejo de estado con carta del Duque de Uceda y papeles que envía sobre una controversia entre gallegos y portugueses tocante a la pesca del Miño," Madrid, 11.11.1684, AHN, Estado 1752, Exp. 19.

30. Until 1381, the area between the Minho River and Lima in today's Portugal was under the jurisdiction of the diocese of Tuy: Maria Filomena Andrade, "Entre Braga e Tui: Uma fronteira diocesana de duzentos (o testemunho das inquirições)," *Revista da faculdade de Letras. História* serie II, 15(1) (1998): 77–98; and José Luis Martín Martín, "Problemas de límites en las diócesis vecinas de Castilla y Portugal en la Edad Media," in Klaus Herbers, Fernando

López Alsina, and Frank Engel, eds., *Das begrenzte Papsttum. Spielräume päp-stlichen Handelns Legaten—delegierte Richter- Grenzen* (Berlin: De Gruyter, 2013), 169–196.

31. Bartolus de Saxoferrato, *Tractatus Tyberiadis seu de fluminibus: Liber 1–3: De alluvione, de insula, de alveo; Tractatus de insigniis et armis* (Turin: Bottega d'Erasmo, 1964), also available in abbreviated form at http://lafogonera. blogspot.com.es/2007/11/de-insula-brtolo-de-sassoferrato-1313.html.   See also Nordman, *Frontières de France*, 114–121; and Marchetti, *De Iure Finium*, 185–191. On the reception of *ius commune* in Spain and Portugal, see José María Font Rius, "La recepción del derecho romano en la península ibérica durante la edad media," *Recueil des mémoires et travaux publiés par la Société d'Histoire du Droit et des Institutions des Anciens Pays de Droit Écrit* 6 (1967): 85–104; and Bartolomé Clavero, *Institución histórica del derecho* (Madrid: Marcial Pons, 1992), 55–56.

32. Siete Partidas, Partida III, title 28, laws 26, 27, and 28.

33. Emmer de Vattel, *The Law of Nations or the Principles of Natural Law Applied to the Conduct and to the Affairs of Nations and of Sovereigns*, trans. Charles Fenewick (Washington, DC: Carnegie Institution of Washington, 1916 [1758]), book 1, chapter 22, 102.

34. "Copia de la representación hecha por Don Joseph Quintana sobre poner corriente y navegable el estero o caño que desde la playa de Ayamonte corre hasta la de San Miguel y Barra del Terrón," Ayamonte, 8.9.1741, in "Copia de los papeles citados en esta relación perteneciente al estero navegable o brazo del río Guadiana en la Playa de Ayamonte," AGMM, 5-3-4-4; Antonio de Gaber, "Relación en que distintamente y por partes se explican los puertos que sirven de demarcación y línea que divide los reynos de España y Portugal en la Provincia de Andalucía," AGMM, 5-3-4-4; letter of Joseph Quintana Cevallos, Ayamonte, 24.11.1764, Palacio to Joseph Quintana, Madrid, 7.12.1764, and a memo authored by the Marqués de Grimaldi, Palacio, 10.12.1764, in "1764 asuntos de pesca," AGS, SMA, 0264. Connecting what happened in the Miño with what transpired in Ayamonte was "El consejo de estado con carta de don Domingo Capecelatro," Madrid, 19.12.1702, AHN, Estado leg. 1755, Exp. 44.

35. "Actas de la comisión mixta compuesta de los comisarios de los gobiernos de España y Portugal para esclarecer . . . la propiedad y dominio del islote formado recientemente en la desembocadura del Guadiana," Villa Real de San Antonio, 12.6.1840, AMN, Ms. 1800, Miscelánea doc. 29, fols. 80r–89r. At stake was also distinguishing man-made from natural changes: see, for example, "Expediente sobre el río Miño, 1757," AGS, SGU 3376, and the map 20/97 that accompanied it. Contemporaries thus insisted that changes that affected rights had to be "natural," not man-made *(mutaciones que naturalmente y sin industria alguna producen las circunstancias del terreno y aguas)*: "1764 asuntos de pesca," AGS, SMA, 0264.

36. Letter of Sebastián Rubin to Félix Oneille, Valença do Minho, 24.2.1773, AMAE/M, Tr 132/002 (1720/1792), no. 0207/2; letter of João de Almeida e Melo to the Marqués de Pombal, Porto, 29.7.1773, and the letter of the juiz de fora of Barea that accompanied it, dated 7.7.1773, both in AHM/DIV/1/06/38/01.

37. The Marquês de Pombal to João de Almada de Tello, Lisbon, 4.8.1773, AHM/DIV/1/11/02/12, doc. 2, pp. 14–15.

38. "Al Marqués de Casatremanes, San Lorenzo 21.10.1773" and "Extracto sobre la dependencia del Monte de la Magdalena," AMAE/M, Tr 132/002 (1720/1792), no. 0207/2.

39. "Treslado da certificação da Torre do Tombo da demarcação de o concelho de Lindozo com el reino de Galiza," in "Documentos sobre a demarcação de limites entre a Hespanha e Portugal, 1803," AHM/DIV/4/1/10/10.

40. Suzanne Daveau, "Caminhos e fronteira na Serra da Peneda. Alguns exemplos nos séculos XV e XVI e na actualidade," *Revista da Faculdade de Letras—Geografia*, serie I, 19 (2003): 81–96, on 87.

41. José Francisco Barbosa Pereira to Aires de Sá e Melo, 17.3.1778, AHM/DIV/1/09/01/35.

42. The ambassador to the Conde de Floridablanca, Aranjuez, May, 1779, AMAE/M, Tr 132/002 (1720/1792), no. 0207/2.

43. Conde de Floridablanca to Pedro Martin Cermeño, Aranjuez, 19.5.1779, and the responses of the latter, La Coruña, 29.5.1779 and 21.7.1779, AMAE/M, Tr 132/002 (1720/1792), no. 0207/2.

44. The Portuguese ambassador to the Conde de Floridablanca, Madrid, 4.12.1779; Floridablanca's answer dated Palacio, 9.12.1779; "sumario respectivo a las contiendas que han habido entre portugueses residentes en Lindoso y Gallegos y que resulta de ella conviene la demarcación," 27.6.1780; and order sent to Pedro Martin Cermeño, Aranjuez, 3.5.1780; all in AMAE/M, Tr 132/002 (1720/1792), no. 0207/2; and complaint of the Portuguese ambassador, 18.5.1803, summarized in "Extracto del expediente," AMAE/M, Tr 132/001 (1754/1807), no. 0207/1.

45. Pedro Martin Cermeño to the Conde de Floridablanca, La Coruña, 10.3.1789, and the attached information before the ordinary judge of Trasportela, 18.1.1789, AMAE/M, Tr 132/002 (1720/1792), no. 0207/2; Antonio Feliz de Contreiras da Silva to the queen, Porto, 10.11.1789, MNE LH, Cx. 6 (no. 1123), fols. 83r–85v; Pedro Martin Cermeño to the Conde de Floridablanca, La Coruña, 8.4.1790, AMAE/M, Tr 132/002 (1720/1792), no. 0207/2, the judicial information that accompanied it, Trasportela, 10.3.1790; and David Calder to Luis Pinto de Sousa Coutinho, Viana, 24.6.1790, AHM/DIV/1/11/02/12. See also draft of an answer to the Portuguese ambassador, 5.11.1791, with the judicial investigation carried out in Trasportela on 23.9.1791, AMAE/M, Tr 132/002 (1720/1792), no. 0207/2; Juan Antonio Bringas to Pedro Martin Cermeño and "El caballero Carvallio e Sampayo to the Conde de Aranda," 22.3.1792, AMAE/M, Tr 132/002 (1720/1792), no. 0207/2; "Extracto del expediente," "Al señor Conde del Campo de Alange," Aranjuez, 10.4.1804, "Según minutas del 16,17 y 18 de Julio 1804," undated and anonymous manuscript, and Conde del Campo de Alange to Pedro Cevallos, Lisbon, 21.4.1804, AMAE/M, Tr 132/001 (1754/1807), no. 0207/1; and complaint of the Portuguese ambassador, 18.5.1803, summarized in "Extracto del expediente," AMAE/M, Tr 132/001 (1754/1807), no. 0207/1.

46. Pedro Martin Cermeño to Floridablanca, La Coruña, 10.3.1789, and the attached information before the ordinary judge of Trasportela, 18.1.1789, AMAE/M, Tr 132/002 (1720/1792), no. 0207/2.

47. Letters of Luis Pinto de Souza to José Pedro de Câmara, Viana, 30.4.1789, and Luís Pinto de Souza to João de Souza, Lisbon, 11.9.1789, AHM/DIV/1/11/02/12, doc. 4, p. 15, and doc. 6, pp. 20–22.

48. António Feliz de Contreiras da Silva to the queen, Porto, 10.11.1789, MNE, LH, Cx. 6 (no. 1123), fols. 83r–85v.

49. Pedro Martin Cermeño to Floridablanca, La Coruña, 8.4.1790, AMAE/M, Tr 132/002 (1720/1792), no. 0207/2, and the judicial information that accompanied it, Trasportela, 10.3.1790; and David Calder to Luis Pinto de Sousa Coutinho, Viana, 24.6.1790, AHM/DIV/1/11/02/12; draft of an answer to the Portuguese ambassador, 5.11.1791, with the judicial investigation carried out in Trasportela on 23.9.1791, AMAE/M, Tr 132/002 (1720/1792), no. 0207/2; and Juan Antonio Bringas to Pedro Martin Cermeño and "El caballero Carvallio e Sampayo to the Conde de Aranda," 22.3.1792, AMAE/M, Tr 132/002 (1720/1792), no. 0207/2; complaint of the Portuguese ambassador, 18.5.1803, summarized in "Extracto del expediente," AMAE/M, Tr 132/001 (1754/1807), no. 0207/1.

50. The Portuguese ambassador suggested, for example, that in 1803 Spaniards might have collected wood and destroyed beehives only in order to ascertain their possession and usage rights: complaint of the Portuguese ambassador, 18.5.1803, summarized in "Extracto del expediente," AMAE/M, Tr 132/001 (1754/1807), no. 0207/1. In 1807 the Portuguese commissioners nevertheless insisted "O que tem sido a causa de moverem os ambiciosos fronteiros galegos sanguinolentas desordens pretendendo com estas obstinadamente usurpar pelo direito da força o que por justiça lhe não deve pertencer": Joaquim José de Almeida and Raymundo Valeriano to the king, Viana do Minho, 14.9.1807, MNE, LH, Cx. 2 (no. 1119), fols. 70r–75r, on fol. 70r.

51. Spaniards, however, attested that the priest requested that they show charity to their Portuguese neighbors, sharing the land with them: draft of an answer to the Portuguese ambassador, 5.11.1791, with the judicial investigation carried out in Trasportela on 23.9.1791, AMAE/M, Tr 132/002 (1720/1792), no. 0207/2; and Juan Antonio Bringas to Pedro Martin Cermeño and "El caballero Carvallio e Sampayo to the Conde de Aranda," 22.3.1792, AMAE/M, Tr 132/002 (1720/1792), no. 0207/2; "Extracto del expediente" and "Al señor Conde del Campo de Alange," Aranjuez, 10.4.1804, "Según minutas del 16,17 y 18 de Julio 1804," undated and anonymous manuscript, and Conde del Campo de Alange to Pedro Cevallos, Lisbon, 21.4.1804, AMAE/M, Tr 132/001 (1754/1807), no. 0207/1.

52. Luis Pinto de Souza to Joseph Pedro da Câmara, Viana, 30.4.1789, and "Memoria do embaixador do Portugal sobre as desordens ultimamente cometidas pelos vassalos de s.m. católica nos domínios del s.m. fidelíssima," Madrid, 26.6.1789, AMAE/M, Tr 132/002 (1720/1792), no. 0207/2, royal response to the ambassador, Madrid, 14.7.1789, AMAE/M, Tr 132/002 (1720/1792), no. 0207/2; and Pedro Martin Cermeño to the conde de Floridablanca, La Coruña, 21.7.1789, 12.8.1789, and 6.10.1789, AMAE/M, Tr 132/002 (1720/1792), no. 0207/2. See also the complaint of the governor of the castle of Lindoso, dated 7.2.1791, and Diogo de Carvalho e Sampayo to the Conde de Floridablanca, Aranujez, 21.5.1790, AMAE/M, Tr 132/002 (1720/1792), no. 0207/2.

53. Ventura Caro, Orense, 18.4.1791, Conde de Floridablanca to the Portuguese ambassador, San Lorenzo, 20.10.1791, Juan Antonio Bringas to Pedro Martin Cermeño, and "El caballero Carvallio e Sampayo to the Conde de Aranda," 22.3.1792, all in AMAE/M, Tr 132/002 (1720/1792), no. 0207/2.

54. "Extracto del expediente," "Al señor Conde del Campo de Alange," Aranjuez, 10.4.1804, "Según minutas del 16,17 y 18 de Julio 1804," undated and anonymous manuscript, and Conde del Campo de Alange to Pedro Cevallos, Lisbon, 21.4.1804, AMAE/M, Tr 132/001 (1754/1807), no. 0207/1. See also proceedings in Villar, 15.7.1802, attached to the letter of Julián de Araujo to Pedro Cevallos, El Ríos, 21.8.1802, AMAE/M, Tr 133/004, no. 0207.

55. "Certificación dada por el escribano de cámara Manuel de Carranza," mentioned in an "extracto" included in AMAE/M, Tr 132/001 (1754/1807), no. 0207/1.

56. "Al señor Conde del Campo de Alange," Aranjuez, 10.4.1804, AMAE/M, Tr 132/001 (1754/1807), no. 0207/1.

57. Pedro Cevallos to the Conde de Campo de Alange, 6.11.1806, and Tomas de Rifa to Pedro Cevallos, Verin, 16.10.1806, "Copia traducida del portugués" of the letter of Raymundo Valeriano da Costa Correa to Tomás de Rifa, Cuartel de Lindozo, 27.6.1806, Tomás de Rifa to Pedro Cevallos, Orense, 15.7.1807, "Extracto del expediente," "Conforme la resolución puesta en la anterior se pasa oficio en 9.4 al embajador de Portugal," and a draft of a letter dated Palacio, 20.7.1806, AMAE/M, Tr 132/001 (1754/1807), no. 0207/1. See also Raymundo Valeriano da Costa to Antonio de Araujo Azevedo, undated (1806), MNE, LH, Cx. 1 (no. 1118), fols. 340r–341r; Tomás Rifa and Manuel de Otermin, "Reflexiones . . . después de haber examinado en concurrencia de los señores comisionados . . . por s.m. fidelísima don Raymundo Valeriano de Costa Correa y don Joaquim Josef de Almeida los puntos por dónde éstos pretenden avanzar la línea divisoria," Compostela, 27.6.1807, MNE, LH, Cx. 2 (no. 1119), fols. 65r–69r; and Joaquim Jose de Almeida and Raymundo Valeriano to the king, Viana do Minho, 14.9.1807, MNE, LH, Cx. 2 (no. 1119), fols. 70r–75r, on fol. 70r. The 1538 *tombo* was reproduced in MNE, LH, Cx. 1 (no. 1118), fols. 327 and 333r–337r.

58. "El juiz ordinário João Domingues Duoro al senhor doutor corregedor da comarca de Viana," Lindozo, 25.8.1821, MNE, LH, Cx. 1 (no. 1118), fols. 319r–320v; and undated, anonymous memo in Portuguese, MNE, LH, Cx. 6 (no. 1123), fols. 77r–80v.

59. "Desde muy antiguo han engendrado y mantienen cada día más vivos y tenaces los sentimientos de odiosa rivalidad y de discordia que animan recíprocamente a los vecinos de Lindoso y a los de esta parte del Cabril, con notable prejuicio de sus intereses bien entendido, afrenta de la civilización europea, aflicción de españoles y portugueses honrados y manifiesto descrédito de la suprema autoridad de ambos gobiernos:" "Copia de proyecto de memoria sometido a la superior aprobación del secretario de estado y del despacho," reproduced in Barreiros, "Delimitação da fronteira" (1964a), 144. See also Barreiros, "Delimitação da fronteira luso-espanhola," *O distrito de Braga. Boletim Cultural de Etnografía e História* 3(3), Fasic. I–II (1964): 1–97, 43 and 45–68 (hereafter Barreiros, "Delimitação da fronteira" [1964b]).

60. Instructions to Raimundo Valeriano da Costa Correa and Joaquim José de Almeida, the Portuguese commissioners, Lisbon, 9.9.1806, Barreiros, "Delimitação da fronteira" (1964b), doc. 70, 42, which argued that demarcation must be "a mais justa que for possível, e mais natural, e conveniente."

61. "Treaty of Boundaries between Spain and Portugal . . . 1864," in *Treaties Series*, vol. 1288, II–906, on 243–261, art. 4 on 245–246.

62. Pedro Martin Cermeño to the Conde de Floridablanca, La Coruña, 10.3.1789, and the attached judicial information before the ordinary judge of Trasportela, 18.1.1789, both in AMAE/M, Tr 132/002 (1720/1792), no. 0207/2.

63. Isabel M.R. Mendes Drumond Braga, "A fronteira difusa entre Trás-os-Montes e a Galiza ou as povoações místicas de Santiago, Rubiães e Meãos," *Brigantia, Revista de Cultura* 17(3/4) (1997): 3–13, 11, note 42; and Cornide, *Descripción circunstanciada*, 150.

64. "Extracto del expediente," "Al señor Conde del Campo de Alange," Aranjuez, 10.4.1804, "Según minutas del 16,17 y 18 de Julio 1804 . . . Excmo. señor," undated and anonymous manuscript, and Conde del Campo de Alange to Pedro Cevallos, Lisbon, 21.4.1804, AMAE/M, Tr 132/001 (1754/1807), no. 0207/1.

65. Herzog, *Defining Nations*.

66. Letter of Joseph Bernardino Romero Figueroa to the Conde de Floridablanca, El Ríos, 15.1.1789, AMAE/M, Tr 132/002 (1720/1792), no. 0207/2; letters of Julián de Araujo to Pedro Cevallos, El Ríos, 21.8.1802 and 11.11.1803, AMAE/M, Tr 133/004, no. 0207, and Tr 132/001 (1754/1807), no. 0207/1; letter of Julián Araujo to Pedro Cevallos, El Ríos, 4.1.1804, AMAE/M, Tr 132/001 (1754/1807), no. 0207/1; and letter of Galcevan Villalba to Pedro Cevallos, La Coruña, 22.11.1802, AMAE/M, Tr 133/004, no. 0207.

67. Ventura Caro to the Conde de Floridablanca, La Coruña, 21.1.1792, and the investigation carried out on 12.10.1791, attached, AMAE/M, Tr 133/003, no. 0207.

68. Letter of Diego, bishop of Cartagena to the Marqués de Ensenada, 1.4.1753, and undated and unsigned petition by the citizens of Tejera, AMAE/M, Tr 132/001 (1754/1807), no. 0207/1; Antonio Arada to the Cardinal de Molina, Puebla, 21.11.1743, Cardinal de Molina to Marqués de Villarias, Madrid, 8.12.1743, royal decision, communicated by the Marqués de Lara to the Marqués de Villarias, Madrid, 29.4.1745, the answer of the Portuguese minister of foreign affairs, undated and unsigned (original and its translation in Spanish), letters of the Marqués de la Candia to the Marqués de Villarias dated Lisbon, 8.6.1745 and 17.8.1745, royal order to the Marqués de la Candia, San Idelfonso, 16.9.1745, and a note dated 8.9.1745, signed by the Marqués de Lara, in "Año de 1742 hasta 1746—Portugal límites. Correspondencia con el Marqués de la Candia sobre límites y pastos del lugar de la Tejera, jurisdicción de la Puebla de Sanabria, reino de Castilla con los vecinos de Soutelo del reino de Portugal," AMAE/M, Tr 133/004, no. 0207; letter of the Marquéz de Ouvizal, San Idelfonso, 28.8.1784, AMAE/M, Tr 132/002 (1720/1792), no. 0207/2; letter of Joseph António do Valle to Manuel Jorge Gómez de Sepúlveda, Bragança, 31.7.1784, undated representation of the interested parties to the governor, and the judicial information that followed (Bragança, 30.7.1784), AMAE/M, Tr 132/002, no. 0207.

69. Letter of Felipe Jorge Montexino to Francisco António Real, Tejera, 16.1.1757, in "Año de 1742 hasta 1746—Portugal límites. Correspondencia con el Marqués de la Candia sobre límites y pastos del lugar de la Tejera, jurisdicción de la Puebla de Sanabria, reino de Castilla con los vecinos de Soutelo del reino de Portugal," AMAE/M, Tr 133/004, no. 0207.

70. The Spanish ambassador to Lisbon reported on such rumors circulating at the Portuguese court: Joseph Caamaño to the Conde de Floridablanca, Lisbon, 3.4.1791, AMAE/M, Tr 132/002 (1720/1792), no. 0207/2.

71. "Auto que el rei mandara fazer pelo ouvidor da Galiza e o corregedor da comarca de Beira respeito dos limites entre Portugal e Galiza, 16.3.1540," ANTT, Gavetas, XIV, 5-12. See also Luis Manuel García Maña, *La frontera hispano-lusa en la provincia de Ourense* (Ourense: Boletín Avriense, 1988), 42; and Isabel Vaz de Freitas Cardoso, "Viver e conviver em terras raianas na idade média," *Revista da faculdade de letras. História* 15(10) (1998): 476–482.

72. "Vivem misturados galegos e portugueses, hunos metidos por outros e não acerta divisam entre hunos nem outros, somente uma casa de Portugal jaz metida entre as de Galiza e as de Galiza entre as de Portugal": cited in Braga, "A fronteira difusa," 8; and in Isabel M.R. Mendes Drumond Braga, *Um espaço, duas monarquias (interrelações na península ibérica no tempo de Carlos V)* (Lisbon: Universidade Nova de Lisboa, 2001), 113–114. See also João Gonçalves da Costa, *Montalegre e terras de Barroso. Notas históricas sobre Montalegre freguesias do concelho e região de Barroso* (Montalegre: Câmara Municipal de Montalegre, 1987), 134–143.

73. AHN, Estado leg. 1785-26, include many references to these episodes.

74. "El consejo de estado con carta del Marqués de Capecelatro . . . en orden a que se le restituya el Castillo de Piconcha y tres lugares que les pertenecen en los confines de Galicia," Madrid, 3.8.1717, AHN, Estado leg. 1773. See also draft of a decision dated 19.8.1717, "El consejo de estado con oficio del embajador de Portugal instando en la restitución del Castillo de Piconcha con tres lugares que nombra y supone pertenecen a aquel reino," Madrid, 19.8.1717, and the copy dated 15.6.1716 of a 1538 [1518] concordant regarding the three places, all in AHN, Estado leg. 1785, Exp. 26.

75. AHCB, FDE, N.N.G. 1312, Ms. 1504, fols. 166r–171v.

76. "Auto de reconhecimento da serventia do ofício d'escrivão das honras do termo de Montalegre em que entram os três lugares mistos Santiago, Rubiães, e Meãos de como pertencia a sereníssima Casa e Estado de Bragança," 5.8.1730, MNE, LH, Cx. 1 (no. 1118), fols. 639r–641v.

77. "Auto de posse do couto misto dos lugares de Santiago de Rubiães, Rubiães, e Meãos que en 4.6.1756 tomou o desembargador Antonio Paes Teixeira Cabral ouvidor da comarca da cidade de Bragança em nome da sereníssima senhora dona Maria Princesa do Brasil e Duquesa de Bragança," MNE, LH, Cx. 1 (no. 1118), fols. 642r–643r; and possession taking of the castle of Piconha by Miguel Pereyra de Barros, 6.10.1788, AHCB, FDE, N.N.G. 1312, Mss. 1504, fol. 3r.

78. Catastro de Ensenada, San Juan de Randin, 1753, AGS, CE, RG, L217, 075, fols. 73r–86r, 74r.

79. "Tem a liberdade de se constituírem espanhóis ou portugueses, bebendo um copo de vinho a saúde do Monarca de quem querem ser vassalos, e

depois com esta mesma cerimonia vão erigir dois lares na casa que andem hab-
itar para assim escaparem aos procedimentos, que de qualquer dos reinos se
quisera ter contra eles, fugindo ora para este ora pra aquele lar oposto as justiças
que os buscam": Diogo Inácio de Pia Manique a Aires de Sá, Lisbon, 27.3.1786,
reproduced in J. R. Dos Santos Júnior, "Povoações mistas da raia trasmontano-
galaica e inquérito que ás mesmas fez em 1786 o corregedor e provedor da comarca do Porto Francisco de Almada e Mendonça," in *Quarto Congresso celebrado
na cidade do Porto de 18 a 24 de Júnio de 1942* (Porto: Imprensa Portuguesa,
1943), vol. 8, 404–425, on 406. See also Conde de Floridablanca to Conde de
Fernan Nuñes, San Lorenzo, 15.11.1785, reproduced in ibid., on 409–410.

80. Joseph Caamaño to the Conde de Floridablanca, Lisbon, 3.4.1791,
AMAE/M, Tr 132/002 (1720/1792), no. 0207/2; Diogo Inácio de Pia Manique to
Aires de Sá, Lisbon, 27.3.1786, the certificate of the Manoel Jose Gomes Pereyra,
Santiago de Rubiães, 24.12.1785, and Conde de Floridablanca to Conde de Fer-
nan Nuñes, San Lorenzo, 15.11.1785, all reproduced in Dos Santos Júnior, "Po-
voações mistas," 405–410. The term "rebels" was mentioned in the report of
Francisco de Almada e Mendonça, Porto, 7.1.1786, on p. 412. See also Barreiros,
"Delimitação da fronteira" (1964a), 124 and 139.

81. "Demarcação feita em 17.7.1538 da vila de Montalegre, dos castelos de
Portello e de Piconha e das aldeãs anexas que são Santiago de Rubiães, Rubiães, Meãos, e Tourein que partem com a Galiza," MNE, LH, Cx. 1 (no.
1118), fols. 626r–632v.

82. José Maria Amado Mendes, *Trás-os-Montes nos fins do século XVIII segundo um manuscrito de 1796* (Lisbon: Fundação Calouste Gulbenkian, 1995),
403–404.

83. Certificate by Julián de Castro y Rodríguez, MNE, LH, Cx. 3 (no.
1120), fols. 125r–129r, mostly on fol. 128r.

84. On similar developments regarding foreigners, see Herzog, *Defining
Nations*, 82–91.

85. Declaration of witnesses reproduced in Barreiros, "Delimitação da
fronteira" (1964a), 123; and opinion of José María Ozorio Cabral, dated
2.10.1859, the petition of 20.12.1857 of the residents of the three villages, and
dispatches of 31.12.1825, 6.6.1826, and 13.5.1826, all in MNE, LH, Cx. 1 (no.
1118), documents 10, 11, 5, 6, and 7.

86. Undated, anonymous memo in Portuguese, MNE, LH, Cx. 6 (no. 1123),
fols. 77r–80v; and memo elaborated by Luz Augusto Pinto de Joveral, Madrid,
12.3.1858, MNE, LH, Cx. 3 (no. 1120), fols. 104r–105r, on fols. 104v–105r.

87. "Treaty of Boundaries between Spain and Portugal . . . 1864," in *Treaties
Series*, vol. 1288, II–906, on 243–261, arts. 7, 8, 11, and 27 on 246–247 and 251.

88. In the nineteenth century, the three communities shared one archive
to which each had a key, and three keys were required to open it. Inside it
were many illegible papers in both Spanish and Portuguese (*abriéndose han
reconocido un montón de papeles y legajos de más o menos folios en idioma español y
portugués*) mainly concerned with disagreements between the Conde de
Monterrey and the Duque de Braganza: certificate of Julián de Castro y Rodríguez, MNE, LH, Cx. 3 (no. 1120), fols. 125r–129r, mostly on fol. 128r;
report elaborated by Luz Augusto Pinto de Joveral, Madrid, 12.3.1858,

MNE, LH, Cx. 3 (no. 1120), fols. 104r–105r; and representation by the junta and councilors of the parish of San Martinho de Pedroso, district of Villareal, Conselho de Montalegre, on 10.6.1857, MNE, LH, Cx. 3 (no. 1120), fols. 115r–117r.

89. Present-day historians affirm that the process might have happened on the inverse: the three communities that were already under the House of Braganza might have appealed to the Conde de Monterrey in order to free themselves of this subjection: García Maña, *La frontera hispano-lusa*, 34–39.

90. "A sombra de antigos direitos feudais sem obedecer a lei de espécie alguma; ora são portugueses ora espanhóis, segundo as circunstâncias ou origem; outras vezes não são nem uma nem outra cousa": report elaborated by Luz Agusto Pinto de Joveral, Madrid, 12.3.1858, MNE, LH, Cx. 3 (no. 1120), fols. 104r–105r, on fols. 104r–v.

91. Abelardo Levaggi, "La propiedad medieval ante la codificación moderna," *Iacobus. Revista de estudios jacobeos y medievales* 13–4 (2002): 447–466, 452; and Kathleen Davis, *Periodization and Sovereignty: How Ideas of Feudalism and Secularization Govern the Politics of Time* (Philadelphia: University of Pennsylvania Press, 2008), 23–47.

92. MNE, LH, Cx. 1 (no. 1118), doc. no. 10, signed by twenty-two residents of Rubiás, ten of Santiago, and twenty-five of Meaus.

93. "Os moradores das três povoações de Santiago, Rubiães e Meãos que formam o antiquíssimo couto denominado misto," Couto Mixto, 2.7.1862, MNE, LH, Cx. 3 (no. 1120), fols. 88r–v.

94. Representation by the junta and councilors of the parish of San Martinho de Pedroso, 10.6.1857, MNE, LH, Cx. 3 (no. 1120), fols. 115r–117r. See also "António Joaquim Gonçalves Pereira, administrador do concelho pede certificado sobre los autos de força nova da junta da paroquia de freguesia de São Martinho de Padrozo, Couto Mixto," 8.4.1859, MNE, LH, Cx. 3 (no. 1120), fols. 118r–122v.

95. Braga, "A fronteira difusa," 11, note 42; and Cornide, *Descripción circunstanciada*, 150.

96. The "pueblos promiscuos" were studied in García Maña, *La frontera hispano-lusa*, 110–115.

97. Undated, anonymous memo in Portuguese, MNE, LH, Cx. 6 (no. 1123), fols. 77r–80v; and a memo elaborated by Luz Agusto Pinto de Joveral, Madrid, 12.3.1858, MNE, LII, Cx. 3 (no. 1120), fols. 104r–105r, on fols. 104v–105r. See also Melón Jiménez, *Los tentáculos de la hidra*, 119.

98. Barreiros, "Delimitação da fronteira," (1946a), 122; Jorge Dias, *Rio de Onor. Comunitarismo Agro Pastoril* (Porto: Instituto de Alta Cultura, 1953), 43–78; and Joaquim Pais de Brito, *Retrato de aldeia com espelho* (Lisbon: Dom Quixote, 1996), 27–39.

99. José Luís Martín Martín, "Conflictos luso-castellanos," 265, citing ANTT, Leitura Nova, Paces, fols. LXII–LXIIII.

100. "Estes aldeões, são mui pouco civilizados, e vivem de um modo excepcional deixando de satisfazer a alguns deveres para com a sua nação, como por exemplo, não concorrer para o serviço militar . . . nas contribuições directas, não seguiam pelo rol que dá a autoridade, mas por arbítrios entre eles, apon-

tando a soma exigida": cited in Brito, *Retrato de aldeia*, 34. The rest of the citations are on 36.

101. The answer of the Portuguese minister of foreign affairs, undated and unsigned (original and its translation in Spanish), in "Año de 1742 hasta 1746—Portugal límites. Correspondencia con el Marqués de la Candia sobre límites y pastos del lugar de la Tejera, jurisdicción de la Puebla de Sanabria, reino de Castilla con los vecinos de Soutelo del reino de Portugal," AMAE/M, Tr 133/004, no. 0207.

102. Adriano Vasco Rodrigues, "Relações históricas entre Guarda e Salamanca," *Revista Altitude* ano III, 2 série, nos. 7–8 (1982–1983): 5–13; Julieta Araújo, "Relações de fronteira na idade média: a transumância," *Revista da faculdade de letras. História* 15(10) (1998): 230–240; Rui Cunha Martins, "O jogo de escalas hispano-português," in Carlos de Ayala Martínez, Pascal Buresi and Philippe Josserand, eds., *Identidad y representación de la frontera en la España medieval (siglos XI–XIV)* (Madrid: Casa de Velázquez-Universidad Autónoma de Madrid, 2001), 75–87; Rui Rosado Vieira, *Centros urbanos no Alentejo fronteiriço. Campo Maior, Elvas e Olivença (de inícios do século XVI a meados do século XVII)* (Lisbon: Livros Horizonte, 1999), 46; and Braga, *Um espaço, duas monarquias.*

103. His delcaration dated 1803 in "Auto das demarcações de Villanho e Teixeira que por inquirições de Portugal e Castela se determinarão," 24.4.1500, AHM/DIV/4/1/10/10, fol. 3.

104. "y tener estos repúblicos en la raya los que se casan y avecindan sólo con el cuerpo que el corazón los tienen siempre en la patria": letter of Salvador Martínez de Castro, Tabagón 15.11.169,1 in "El consejo de estado con una memoria del enviado de Portugal sobre que las justicias de Tui ejercen jurisdicción en una isleta del reino de Galicia que pertenece a la corona de Portugal," Madrid 17.7.1691, AHN, Estado leg. 1771, Exp. 2.

105. García Maña, *La frontera hispano-lusa*, 12; Fonseca, "Fronteiras territoriais"; Testón Núñez, Sánchez Rubio, and Sánchez Rubio, *Planos, guerra y frontera*, 8; and Cosme, "A solidariedade" 97. José Luis Martín Martín, "Conflictos luso-castellanos," 273, argues instead that the frontier had multiple facets: it was sometimes defined, sometimes confused, but always unstable. The political powers attempted to control it, but the human groups that inhabited these regions and their interests in protecting their pasturing or agricultural rights were usually the reason that explained confrontations.

106. Francisco Xavier Lardizabal to Luis da Cunha Manuel, 23.8.1760, AHM/DIV/1/06/17/36.

107. Braga, *Um espaço, duas monarquias*, 106–114 and 372–375.

108. Antonio Gaber, "Relación en que distintamente y por partes se explican los puertos que sirven de demarcación y línea que divide los reynos de España y Portugal en la Provincia de Andalucía," in "Varios reconocimientos practicados en diversos tiempos en la frontera de Portugal, 1750," AGMM 5-3-4-4; Manuel del Olmo. "Memoria sobre las diferentes calidades de tierra que hay en Extremadura revista examinada y después acordada por la clase de agricultura," Badajoz, 16.4.1776, ARSEMAP, leg. 8, no. 12; and "Plan de campaña contra Portugal (1767)," "Memoria militar sobre Portugal," and "Informe

del brigadier Cermeño Pedro, director de ingenieros al Conde de Aranda," 13.7.1768, AHN, Estado leg. 4389.

109. "Ningún convenio celebrado por los gobiernos respectivos ha señalado antes de ahora la línea de separación de los dos territorios; la cual se halla entretanto determinada tan sólo por los amojonamientos privados de los pueblos que sirven a la vez de deslinde de la propiedad particular de cada uno y de indicación del alcance de la jurisdicción soberana de las dos naciones": "Instruções dadas aos comissários de sua majestade católica encarregados da demarcação da frontera entre Espanha e Portugal," Madrid, 18.11.1854, reproduced in Luiz Teixeira de Sampayo, ed., *Compilação de elementos para o estudo da questão de Olivença (perda desta praça e diligências para a reaver)* (Lisbon: Associação dos Amigos do Arquivo Histórico-Diplomático do Ministério dos Negócios Estrangeiros, 2001), 231–234, on 231.

110. The current relations and possible integration between Tuy and Valença were analyzed in Filipe Lima, "As dinâmicas territoriais no espaço de fronteira na fachada atlântica peninsular: a eurocidade Valença/Tuy," *Cuadernos: Curso de Doutoramento en Geografia* 4 (2012): 75–86.

111. "Valença será espanhola até que as urgências voltem a abrir," "Bandeiras espanholas en Valença contra fecho do SAP," and readers' comments, *El público de Portugal*, 6 and 7 April 2010. *El público* is a national daily, published since 1990, and is the second largest Portuguese newspaper.

112. "Banderas española para protestar por los recortes sanitarios en Portugal," "Manifestación 'española' en la localidad portuguesa de Valença," "Para esto, más nos valdría ser gallegos," "Estamos dispuestos a ir a Lisboa con las Banderas," "Cinco pueblos de Portugal piden usar un hospital de Vigo," "Donde se funda la raya," and "Bandeiras espanholas," and readers' comments, *El País*, 5, 7, 8, and 9 April 2010. *El País* is the largest Spanish national daily, founded 1976.

Conclusion

1. Luc Boltanski and Laurent Thévenot, *On Justification: Economies of Worth*, trans. Catherine Porter (Princeton, NJ: Princeton University Press, 2006 [1987]). See also François Eymard-Duvernay, Olivier Favereau, André Orléan, Robert Salais, and Laurent Thévenot, "Pluralist Integration in the Economic and Social Sciences: The Economy of Conventions," *Post-Autistic Economic Review* 34(30) (2005): article 2.

2. Herzog, *Defining Nations*, 166–169; and Bartolomé Clavero, "Lex Regni Vicinioris. Indicio de España en Portugal," *Boletim da faculdade de direito de Coimbra* 58(1) (1983): 239–298.

3. Andrade, *A construção*, 98.

4. "Tombo dos propios e direitos do concelho desta villa de Serpa feito por mandado de sua magestad pellos licenceado Bartolomeu Castel Branco," 1625, AHMS, A/1E-0, fols.196r–197r.

5. The original version reads: "um tombo é uma descrição de bens, e direitos; daqueles se declara a medida e confrontação, destes a natureza e origem. Um tombo pois não é mais que uma lembrança do que se fez, com o fim de ficar

constando autenticamente para o futuro; e em consequência tudo quanto ali se acha escrito, não merece maior crédito depois disso, do que tinha antes de lá se escrever. Se um auto por tanto foi mal feito, uma medição errada, uma declaração contra a verdade; auto, mediação e declaração ficam sempre e eternamente mal feitos, errados e mentirosos, como eram antes de se lançarem no tombo." Thomaz, *Observações*, 143. See also 124–135; João Pedro Ribeiro, *Observações históricas e criticas para servirem de memorias ao systema da diplomática portugueza* (Lisbon: Typografia da Academia das Ciências de Lisboa, 1798), 56; Sousa, *Tractado pratico*, vol. 2, nos. 1214 and 1217, on 275–276; and Alberto Carlos de Menezes, *Pratica dos tombos, e medições, marcações dos bens da coroa, fazenda real, bens das ordens militares ou comendas* (Lisbon: Imp. Regia, 1819).

6. Victor Prescott and Gillian D. Triggs, *International Frontiers and Boundaries: Law, Politics, and Geography* (Leiden: Martinus Nijhoff, 2008), 7.

7. Antonio Sáez-Arace, "Constructing Iberia: National Traditions and the Problems of a Peninsular History," *European Review of History* 10(2) (2003): 189–202.

8. Sidaway, "Signifying Boundaries," 144–145; and Xosé-Manoel Múñez, "The Iberian Peninsula: Real and Imagined Overlaps," in Tibor Frank and Frank Hadler, eds., *Disputed Territories and Shared Pasts: Overlapping National Histories in Modern Europe* (Basingstoke: Palgrave, 2010), 329–348.

9. Already in 1767 some Spaniards complained against Spanish belief that Portugal could never resist its hegemony: "Memoria militar sobre Portugal" (1767), AHN, Estado leg. 4389.

10. Víctor Martínez-Gil, *El naixement de l'iberisme catalanista* (Barcelona: Curial, 1997).

11. One notable exception is Marcocci, *A consciência de um império.*

12. Clavero, "Lex Regni Vicinioris."

13. "Informação do Conselho Ultramarino sobre os serviços prestados por D. Francisco Rodrigues Salvaterra, castelhano de nação, no período de 1649 a 1660," Lisbon, post-1660, AHU_ACL_CU_015, cx. 7, d. 622; and "Requerimento de um castelhano que servia desde 1619 nas armadas na guerra de Pernambuco," Pernambuco, 18.9.1650, AHM/DIV/2/1/1/3.

14. Manuel de Melo Godinho Manso to the king, São Paulo, 29.8.1724, AHU_ACL_CU_023-01, cx. 4, d. 419; Manoel Rodrigues Torres to the king, Cuiabá, 20.8.1740, AHU_ACL_CU_101, cx. 2, d. 136; Manoel Rodrigues Torres to Luíz Mascarenhas, Cuiabá, 20.8.1740, AHU, MT, Cx. 2, d. 136; Carlos Morphi to Julián Arriaga, Asunción 22.9.1770, AGI, Buenos Aires, 539, cited in Carvalho, "Lealdades negociadas," 530; and Juan de Escandón, cited in Quarleri, *Rebelión y guerra*, 192, note 33.

15. Osório, *O império português*, 65; David Graham Sweet, "A Rich Realm of Nature Destroyed: The Middle Amazon Valley, 1640–1750" (Ph.D. diss., University of Wisconsin, 1974), vol. 1, 301–313; and Arthur Cezar Ferreira Reis, "Estrangeiros na Amazónia no período colonial," *Ocidente. Revista Portuguesa* 64(299) (1963): 185–190.

16. Fernando Costas Castillo, "informe sobre el estado del comercio de España y Portugal . . . a los directores generales de rentas del reino," Badajoz, 9.4.1769, Biblioteca Municipal de Olivenza, manuscrito, fols. 26r–38r.

17. "Se han visto infinitos ejemplares de dispensas de dicho tiempo por especial gracia de los reyes de España en donde se entiende genéricamente por españoles los portugueses, como patrios de una misma península, religión y costumbres y que para este merecimiento y consentimiento son entre todos reputados y tenidos por de una misma nación sin diferencia alguna, a respecto de la que ha para con las demás naciones en las cuales este asentada y practicada la gran diferencia de extranjeras absolutamente diversas." "Razón ... que puede ofrecer sobre concesiones de naturaleza de estos reinos," anonymous and undated, AGS, GJ 873. In 1797, Rafael Atúnez y Acevedo suggested that the Portuguese were "true Spaniards" *(verdaderamente españoles):* Rafael Antúnez y Acevedo, *Memorias históricas sobre la legislación y gobierno del comercio de los españoles con sus colonias en las Indias Occidentales* (Madrid: De Sancha, 1797), 270–272.

18. Ana Cristina Nogueira da Silva and António Manuel Hespana, "A identidade portuguesa," in José Mattoso, ed., *História de Portugal* (Lisbon: Círculo de Leitores, 1993), vol. 4, 19–37. See also Cardim, *Portugal Unido y separado.*

19. Karen Ordahl Kupperman, *Indians and English: Facing off in Early America* (Ithaca: Cornell University Press, 2000), advocates the need for historians of colonial America to be more attuned to development in English historiography related to social and cultural issues. On the tendency to consider changes among Indians but ignore those that have occurred among Europeans, see, for example, Gregory H. Nobles, *American Frontiers: Cultural Encounters and Continental Conquest* (New York: Hill and Wang, 1997), 19–56.

20. David Armitage, "Three Concepts of Atlantic History," in David Armitage and Michael J. Braddick, eds., *The British Atlantic World, 1500–1800* (Basingstock: Palgrave, 2002), 11–27.

21. Gurminder K. Bhambra, "Historical Sociology, International Relations and Connected Histories," *Cambridge Review of International Affairs* 23(1) (2010): 127–143; and Sanjay Subrahamanyam, *Mugals and Franks: Explorations in Connected History* (New Delhi: Oxford University Press, 2011).

22. Pedro Cardim, Tamar Herzog, José Javier Ruiz Ibáñez, and Gaetano Sabatini, eds., *Polycentric Monarchies: How Did Early Modern Spain and Portugal Achieve and Maintain a Global Hegemony?* (Brighton: Sussex Academic Press, 2012).

23. John H. Elliott, *History in the Making* (New Haven, CT: Yale University Press, 2012), 175–183.

24. The governor and captain general of Galicia on 7.4.1681, reproduced by Antonio Eiras Roel ed., *Actas de las juntas del reino de Galicia* (Santiago de Compostela: Xunta de Galicia, 1994), vol. 10, document 108-D; and unsigned and undated report in AHN, Estado leg. 4389, no. 5. Similar concerns were also expressed in the letter of Pedro Cermeño to the Conde de Aranda, 13.7.1768, AHN, Estado leg. 4389, no. 6.

25. Article 5 of the 1715 treaty determined the following: "Las plazas, castillos, ciudades, lugares, territorios y campos pertenecientes a las dos coronas, así en Europa como en cualquiera parte del mundo se restituirán enteramente y sin reserva alguna; de suerte que los límites y confines de las dos monarquías quedarán en el mismo estado que tenían antes de la presente guerra. Y

particularmente se volverán a la corona de España las plazas de Alburquerque y la Puebla con sus territorios en el estado en que se hallan al presente, sin que su majestad portuguesa pueda pedir cosa alguna a la corona de España por las nuevas fortificaciones que ha hecho aumentar en dichas plazas; y a la corona de Portugal el castillo de Noudar con su territorio, la isla de Verdejo y el territorio y Colonia de Sacramento." Cantillo, *Tratados*, 165–166.

26. "Ofício dos plenipotenciários Portugueses em Viena, dirigido ao Marquês de Aguiar," Viena, 24.11.1814, "Nota de Pedro Cevallos, secretário de estado espanhol para o Marquês de Aguiar," Madrid, 28.11.1814, and "ofício de José Luís de Sousa ao Marquês de Aguiar," Madrid, 14.12.1814, all reproduced in Sampayo, *Compilação de elementos*, 57–60, 63–67, and 93–97.

27. António Manuel Hespanha, "Antigo Regime nos trópicos? Um debate sobre o modelo político do Império colonial português," in João Fragoso and Maria de Fátima Gouvêa, eds., *Na trama das redes* (Rio de Janeiro: Civilização Brasileira, 2010), 43–94.

28. Jorge Cañizares-Esguerra, *Puritans Conquistadors: Iberianizing the Atlantic, 1550–1700* (Stanford: Stanford University Press, 2006); and Gould, "Entangled Histories." See also Lauren Benton, *Law and Colonial Cultures: Legal Regimes in World History, 1400–1900* (Cambridge: Cambridge University Press, 2002).

29. Elliott, *History in the Making*, 205–207.

30. Nicholas P. Canny, "The Origins of Empire: An Introduction," in *The Origins of Empire*, 1–33, on 24–25; Linda Colley, *Britons: Forging the Nation, 1707–1837* (New Haven, CT: Yale University Press, 2005 [1992]), 132–133; Mark L. Thompson, " 'The Predicament of Ubi': Locating Authority and National Identity in the Seventeenth-Century English Atlantic," in Elizabeth Mancke and Carole Shammas, eds., *The Creation of the British Atlantic World* (Baltimore: Johns Hopkins University Press, 2005), 71–92, 87; J. M. Rodríguez-Salgado, "Christians, Civilised and Spanish: Multiple Identities in Sixteenth-Century Spain," *Transactions of the Royal Historical Society* 8 (1998): 233–251, on 239–240 and 244; Henry Kamen, *Empire: How Spain Became a World Power, 1492–1763* (New York: Harper Collins, 2003), 331–333; and Irene Silverblatt, *Modern Inquisitions: Peru and the Colonial Origins of the Civilized World* (Durham, NC: Duke University Press, 2004), 19–20. See also Edward W. Said, *Culture and Imperialism* (New York: Vintage Books, 1994), 35 and 42.

31. Herbert E. Bolton, "The Epic of Greater America," *American Historical Review* 38(3) (1933): 448–474. Although often interpreted as including a plea for a comparative history of the Americas, this piece, which reproduces the address that Bolton, then president of the American Historical Association, gave members, advocated the study of an America that would not be divided by national units. Criticizing such stands was Lewis Hanke, ed., *Do the Americas Have a Common History? A Critique of the Bolton Theory* (New York: Alfred A. Knopf, 1964).

32. Bernard Bailyn and Philip D. Morgan, *Strangers within the Realm: Cultural Margins of the First British Empire* (Chapel Hill: University of North Carolina Press, 1991).

33. Colin Steele, *English Interpreters of the Iberian New World from Purchas to Stevens (1603–1726)* (Oxford: Dolphin Book, 1975); and Fitzmaurice, *Sovereignty*.

34. Patricia Seed, *American Pentimento: The Invention of Indians and the Pursuit of Riches* (Minneapolis: University of Minnesota Press, 2001). James Lang, *Conquest and Commerce: Spain and England in the Americas* (New York: Academic Press, 1975), stresses the differences between a Spanish empire based on conquest and an English one based on commerce. Robert A. Williams, *The American Indian in Western Legal Thought: The Discourses of Conquest* (Oxford: Oxford University Press, 1990), distinguishes a Spanish Catholic discourse on empire from a Protestant one. More recently, Christopher Tomlins argued that England had developed a particular discourse that, contrary to other European nations, increasingly focused its attention "on the possession of territory to the exclusion of its inhabitants" and thus "elevated land over people as the primary object of the colonizer's attention": Tomlins, *Freedom Bound*, 132–133. According to him, there was therefore a move from pan-European discussions (in the sixteenth century) to an English particularism (in the seventeenth century).

35. John H. Elliott, *Empires of the Atlantic World: Britain and Spain in America, 1492–1830* (New Haven, CT: Yale University Press, 2006).

36. Ken MacMillan, *Sovereignty and Possession in the English New World: The Legal Foundation of Empire, 1576–1640* (Cambridge: Cambridge University Press, 2006), 4–14. See also Elliott, *Empires of the Atlantic World*, 185.

37. Elliott, *Empires of the Atlantic World*; and Cañizares-Esguerra, *Puritans Conquistadors*.

38. Locke, *Two Treatises*, second treaty, chapter 5, points 27–51, especially points 31–32.

39. Solórzano y Pereira, *Política Indiana*, book 1, chapter 9, points 12 and 13. The original version reads: "y verdaderamente para las islas y tierras que hallaron por ocupar y poblar de otras gentes, o ya porque nunca antes las hubiesen habitado o porque si las habitaron se pasaron a otras y las dejaron incultas, no se puede negar que lo sea y de los más conocidos por el derecho natural y de todas las gentes, que dieron este premio a industria y quisieron que lo libre cediese a los que primero lo hallasen y ocupasen y así se fue practicando en todas las provincias del mundo, como a cada paso nos lo enseña Aristóteles, Cicerón, nuestros jurisconsultos y sus glosadores" and "los lugares desiertos e incultos quedan en la libertad natural y son del que primero los ocupa en premio de su industria." In the seventeenth century, *industria* was identified as "the diligence and easiness in which one does something with less work than others." With a comparative perspective in mind, it designated those who knew better and performed better: Sebastián de Covarrubias Orozco, *Tesoro de la lengua castellana o española*, ed. Felipe C. R. Maldonado (Madrid: Editorial Castalia, 1995 [1611]), 666. It is possible, however, that by the mid-eighteenth century it came to designate simply "a mastery or an ability in any art or profession": Real Academia Española, *Diccionario de autoridades* (Madrid: Editorial Gredos, 1990 [1732]), vol. 2, 257.

40. Jacobs, *Dispossessing the American Indian*, 111; and Arneil, *John Locke and America*, 16 and 21.

41. On conversations across empires, see, for example, April Lee Hatfield, "Spanish Colonization Literature, Powhatan Geographies, and English Perceptions of Tsenacommacah/Virginia," *Journal of Southern History* 69(2) (2003): 245–282; and Gould, "Entangled Histories."

42. Wesley Frank Craven, "Indian Policy in Early Virginia," *William and Mary Quarterly*, 3rd series, 1(1) (1944): 65–82, 74–77; and Gregory Evans Dowd, *War under Heaven: Pontiac, the Indian Nations, and the British Empire* (Baltimore: Johns Hopkins University Press, 2002).

43. Richard White, *The Middle Ground: Indians, Empires, and Republics in the Great Lakes Region, 1650–1815* (Cambridge: Cambridge University Press, 1991); and Kupperman, *Indians and English*.

44. Charles Gibson, "Conquest, Capitulation, and Indian Treaties," *American Historical Review* 83(1) (1978): 1–15. See also Lawrence Kinnaird, Francisco Blanch, and Navarro Blanche, "Spanish Treaties with Indian Tribes," *Western Historical Quarterly* 10(1) (1979): 39–48. To date, the affirmation that the contrary might be true is mainly focused on the cases of Chile and Argentina.

45. Francis John Ebert, "The Anglo-French Boundary Dispute in Colonial New York from 1713–1763" (M.A. thesis, Stanford University, 1947), 2–6, 12–13, 16–17, 22–28, 49–50, 55–59, 67, 70–71, and 84; W. Stitt Robinson, *The Southern Colonial Frontier, 1607–1763* (Albuquerque: University of New Mexico Press, 1979), 25, 188–190, 193–197, and 202–225; Thompson, "'The Predicament of Ubi,'" 87–91; and Kathleen DuVal, *The Native Ground: Indians and Colonists in the Heart of the Continent* (Philadelphia: University of Pennsylvania Press, 2006), 7–8.

46. On how raids on Spanish mission Indians not only supplied labor but also were meant to diminish Spain's claims and weaken its hold, see, for example, Alan Gallay, *The Indian Slave Trade: The Rise of the English Empire in the American South, 1670–1717* (New Haven, CT: Yale University Press, 2002), 197.

47. Already in 1953, Roy Harvey Pearce, *Savagism and Civilization: A Study of the Indian and the American Mind* (Baltimore: John Hopkins University Press, 1967 [1953]), stressed the importance of conversion to the English colonists and the territorial implications that it could carry.

48. Sheehan, *Savagism and Civility*, 1; Arneil, *John Locke and America*, 14, 30–31, and 38–39; and Stuart Banner, *How the Indians Lost Their Land: Law and Power on the Frontier* (Cambridge, MA: Harvard University Press, 2005), 7.

49. Arneil, *John Locke and America*, 9; Vattel, *The Law of Nations*, book 1, chapters 7, on 37–38. See also Botella-Ordinas, "Debating Empire."

50. Solórzano y Pereira, *Política Indiana*, book 1, chapter 9, point 24, on 93; and Nuix, *Reflexiones imparciales*, 145–149.

51. MacMillan, *Sovereignty and Possession*, 10–14, 17–48, and 178–207; Fitzmaurice, *Sovereignty*; and Anthony Pagden, "Law, Colonization, Legitimation, and the European Background," in Michael Grossberg and Christopher Tomlins, eds., *The Cambridge History of Law in America* (Cambridge: Cambridge

University Press, 2008), 1–31.See also James Muldoon, "John Marshall and the Rights of Indians," in Renate Pieper and Peer Schmidt, eds., *Latin America and the Atlantic World: El Mundo Atlántico y América Latina (1500–1850). Essays in Honor of Horst Pietschmann* (Koln: Böhlau Verlag, 2005), 67–82, on 80–82.

52. G. Zeller, "Histoire d'une idée fausse," *Revue de synthèse* 11–12 (1936): 115–131; and Nordman, *Frontières de France*, 10–11.

53. Michiel Baud and Willem Van Schendel, "Toward a Comparative History of Borderlands," *Journal of World History* 8(2) (1997): 211–242, 237–240; Michiel Baud, "Fronteras y la construcción del estado en América Latina," in Gustavo Torres Cisneros et al., *Cruzando Fronteras. Reflexiones sobre la relevancia de fronteras históricas simbólicas y casi desaparecidas en América Latina* (Quito: Ediciones Abya-Yala, 2004), 41–86, 69; and Prescott and Triggs, *International Frontiers*, 52.

54. Daniel Nordman, "Problématique historique: Des frontières d'Europe aux frontières du Maghreb (XIXe siècles)," in *Profils du Maghreb. Frontières, figures et territoires (XVIIIe–XXe siècle)* (Rabat: Université Mohammed V, 1996), 25–39, on 29.

55. On somewhat similar issues, see Graham Burnett, *Masters of All They Surveyed: Exploration, Geography, and a British El Dorado* (Chicago: University of Chicago Press, 2000), mainly 258–264.

56. Benton and Straumann, "Acquiring Empire," 35.

57. *Ius Commune* jurists also argued that these doctrines, which they elaborated, belonged to *ius gentium:* Marchetti, *De Iure Finium*, 218–222.

58. Clifford Geertz, "Local Knowledge: Fact and Law in Comparative Perspective," in *Local Knowledge: Further Essays in Interpretive Anthropology* (New York: Basic Books, 1983), 167–234.

59. Rose, *Property and Persuasion*, 5–6 and 169–270.

60. Tamar Herzog, "Nombres y apellidos: ¿cómo se llamaban las personas en Castilla e Hispanoamérica durante la época moderna?," *Jahrbuch für Geschichte von Staat, Wirtschaft und Gesellschaft Lateinamerikas* 44 (2007): 1–36; and Herzog, "Colonial Law."

61. Jesús Vallejo, *Ruda Equidad, Ley Consumada. Concepción de la Potestad Normativa (1250–1350)* (Madrid: Centro de Estudios Constitucionales, 1992).

62. Carl Schmitt, *The Nomos of the Earth in the International Law of the Jus Publicum Europaeum*, trans. G. L. Ulmen (New York: Telos Press, 2003 [1950]).

63. Norman Hill, *Claims to Territory in International Law and Relations* (London: Oxford University Press, 1945), 81–90; Alexander B. Murphy, "Historical Justifications for Territorial Claims," *Annals of the Association of American Geographers* 80(4) (1990): 531–548, on 532 and 544–545; Yehuda Z. Blum, *Historical Titles in International Law* (the Hague: Martinus Nijhoff, 1965), 9–21; and Tamar Meisels, *Territorial Rights* (Dordrecht: Springer, 2005), 25–46.

64. Michael R. Radclift, *Frontiers*, 27–30. See also Richard Tuck, "The Making and Unmaking of Boundaries from the Natural Law Perspective," in Allen Buchanan and Margaret Moore, eds., *States, Nations, and Borders: The Ethics of Making Boundaries* (Cambridge: Cambridge University Press, 2003), 143–170, on 157–158.

65. Suzanne Lalonde, *Determining Boundaries in a Conflicted World: The Role of Uti Possidetis* (Montreal: McGill–Queen's University Press, 2002), 18–23; and Castellino and Allen, *Title to Territory*, 29–89. See also Jorge I. Domínguez with David Mares, Manuel Orozco, David Scott Palmer, Francisco Rojas Aravena, and Andrés Serbin, "Boundary Disputes in Latin America," *Peaceworks* (Washington, DC: Unites States Institute of Peace, 2003), 21.

66. Raúl A. Molina, "Los conflictos de límites y las primeras misiones diplomáticas en archivos nacionales y extranjeros," *Historia* (Buenos Aires) 8(29) (1962): 20–53. See also Alberto Marin Madrid, "Las fronteras entre Chile y Argentina," *Revista chilena de historia y geografía* 156 (1988): 76–107, 79; Juan Jones Parra, "Proceso histórico para la fijación de nuestras fronteras," *Cultura universitaria* 54 (1956): 10–40, 13; José María Egas, *El principio del uti possidetis americano y nuestro litigio de fronteras con el Perú* (Guayaquil: Imprenta Municipal, undated), 9. For a comparative perspective, see Tetz Rooke, "Tracing the Boundaries: From Colonial Dream to National Propaganda," in Inga Brandell, ed., *State Frontiers: Borders and Boundaries in the Middle East* (London: I. B. Tauris, 2006), 123–139; and Michel Foucher, *L'invention des frontières* (Paris: Fondation pour les Études de Défense Nationale, 1986), 179–183.

67. Herzog, "The Meaning of Territory."

Acknowledgments

To the archivists who assisted me in different places and times, most particularly Inmaculada Nieves Gálvez, archivist of Encinasola and Aroche (as well as many other municipalities in the province of Huelva); Catarina Bucho Machado, former archivist of Marvão; and Isabel Aguirre, of the Archivo General de Simancas—all of whom went out of their way to be kind and helpful.

To Miguel de Castro Cancella de Abreu and Bernardo Sá Nogueira, who gave me permission to consult the archives of the House of Cadaval in Lisbon; José Manuel Zuleta y Alejandro, Duque de Abrantes, who sent me documentation from the Archives of the House and Estates of the Dukes of Abrantes and Linares; Vasco Luis S. de Quevedo Pessanha, who allowed me to use the library at the Quinta do Ferro; and Esther Bertoletti, who facilitated access to a copy of the Resgate CD file collection.

To the Guggenheim Foundation, the University of Chicago, Stanford University, Fundación Séneca (Región de Murcia), and the research project titled "Las fronteras del Imperio español (1659–1812). Procesos de definición, formas de ocupación del espacio, y sistemas de control del territorio" (HAR2010-17797), for helping defray the costs of the research and writing.

To Fernando Bouza, Miguel Ángel Melón, Luis Alfonso Limpo Píriz, Heather Flynn Roller, António Casaca, João Antonio Botelho Lucidio, Manfredi Merluzzi, Donatella Montemurno, Juan Francisco Pardo Molero, Ângela Barreto Xavier, and João Ramos, for supplying me with vital references and with copies of certain documents; to

Anthony Disney, who facilitated information regarding the Count of Linhares; to Lucca Scalia, who helped with (odd) Latin texts; to José Carlos Vilardaga, Gabriel Darío Taruselli, Guida Marques, Carmen Margarita Oliveira Alveal, Paulo Possamai, João Augusto Espadeiro Ramos, and Antonio Terrasa Lozano, who allowed me to read and cite their unpublished work; and to Jaime E. Rodríguez and Anthony Pagden, who, as readers for Harvard University Press, phrased some of my thoughts much better than I did.

To the members of Columnaria (www.redcolumnaria.com), a scholarly network created in 2004 to encourage communication and collaboration among researchers interested in the Iberian worlds, for constantly challenging me to overcome national and nationalistic historiographies and search for an analysis that—like the network itself—is focused on specific locations but has a wider history in mind.

To my historian friends Richard White, Emma Rothschild, Simona Cerutti, Serge Gruzinski, Cécile Vidal, Laurence Fontaine, Nathan Wachtel, Carmen Bernand, Zacarías Moutoukias, Aude Argouse, António Manuel Hespanha, Iris Kantor, Jose Javier Ruiz Ibáñez, Pedro Cardim, Mafalda Soares da Cunha, Ângela Barreto Xavier, Stuart B. Schwartz, Carla Rahn-Phillips, Bernard Lavalle, and Rodrigo Bentes Monteiro, who discussed different aspects of this book with me; and in loving memory of Mónica Quijada Mauriño.

To Ruth MacKay, Juan Pro Ruiz, António Manuel Hespanha, and Elizabeth Amann, who read this text and gave me wonderful advice.

To David Nirenberg and Gaetano Sabatini for having listened and responded so wisely and so frequently.

And, above all, to Yuval Erlich, who continues to guide my way, and to Alexander and Daniel, who were born together with this book and grew up alongside it. I still owe the Chuchususis an answer as to why the Spaniards and the Portuguese fought so much over (sometimes) so little. All I can hope is that they remember this inquiry with awe when they are adults and when the memory of this book and of their mother is otherwise extremely dim.

Index

Note: Page numbers followed by *f* indicate figures.

Abreu, Leonel de, 201, 357n26
Abreu, Pedro Gómez de, 201–202, 356n25
Abreu e Noronha, María de, 357n26
Acuña, Father Cristóbal, 52–53
Afonso Henriques, king, 189
Agency, 5, 15, 143, 173–174, 222, 262
Aggression, 8, 39, 44; Fritz and Portu-
    guese, 82; Indians and, 108–109; Jesuits
    and, 87. *See also* Violence
Agriculture, usage and property rights
    concerns, 73, 121–123, 260–261; in
    disputed Iberian border areas, 152–154,
    156, 159, 166–167, 176, 178–179, 185,
    187, 207–209, 220, 225, 234, 338n20
Alcañices, Treaty of, 4, 136–137, 242,
    335n1
Alentejo, 141, 149, 241, 333n17
Alfonso X el Sabio, king of Castile, 189,
    335n1
Aljubarrota, battle of, 240
Alliances, 12–13; with indigenous people,
    85, 98–99, 102–105, 109, 114
Almeida, 235
Alvares, Joham, 9
Amazon basin: Jesuits and, 77, 80,
    91–92; 1630s expedition to interior
    of, 50–55
Amazon River, Fritz and, 76
Animals. *See* Grazing

Annes, Gonçalo, 9
Aragon, 56–58, 60, 252
Aroche, territorial disputes (1290–1955),
    149–160; claims about immemorial
    possession, 181–190; coveted object
    and, 178–179; parties to, 164–174,
    176
Arredondo, Nicolás, 30
Artificial borders, 2, 4, 7, 31, 260–261
As Casas dos Montes, 177
Asunción, governor of, 104
Atlanic history, 253–255
Aviz, order of, 149–151, 160, 163,
    169–171, 173–174
Ayamonte, Marquis of, 59
Azores, 17, 27, 28f

Badajoz, 63, 85, 139, 189
Bandeirantes, 36, 36–37, 66–67
Barbarians, 259; indigenous people as, 71,
    101–109, 112, 129–130; peasants as, 14;
    Portuguese and, 22
Barbosa de Luna, Pedro, 57
Barcia de Mera, 173
Barrancos, territorial disputes (1290–1955),
    149, 155–156, 161–165, 238, 340n27;
    claims about immemorial possession,
    181, 184–187; coveted object and, 179;
    parties to, 165–174, 176

Belém do Pará, 50–54, 85, 91
Benavente, Count of, 235
Bettendorff, João Felipe, 54, 59–60, 61, 64, 125, 160, 170
Border commission, 185, 199, 236
Border stones, 8, 150, 152, 159, 161–164
Bousés, 177
Braer, Wenceslao, 82
Braganza, Duke of, 57–64, 136, 170–171, 223–225
Braganza, House of, 227, 231–232, 233, 235, 253
Brazil, Portuguese uprising and, 60–63, 65–66
Burden of proof, possession and, 35

Cabo Verde Islands, 17–19, 27, 28f
Cabril River, 210, 212–213, 216–217
Caciques (native chiefs), 90, 104, 108, 113–114
Cadaval, Duke of, 158, 160–164, 169, 174, 177
Caldelas, abbot of, 192–194, 196–197, 200, 202, 205–206
Camaydevena, Mariano, 95–96
Cambedo, 177, 234
Camões, Luis de, 241
Campo de Gamos, 149–151, 153, 160–162, 164–166, 171–173, 178–179, 180f, 220, 351n104
Canon law, 125, 260, 264
Canosa (island), 204, 208–209, 238
Carmelites, 74, 81–85, 90–92
Carrillo, Martin, 57
Chaves, 220, 234
Christianity, 4, 22, 57, 136, 163, 251; conversion and, 70–86, 97–98, 101–104, 108, 114, 258–259; New Christians, 66. See also Carmelites; Jesuits; Reconquest
Civility, 22
Colonia de Sacramento, 26, 31, 38, 42–44, 47–48, 59, 61, 75, 77, 254
Colonialism, 4, 10–11, 14, 113; British, 255–260; indigenous rights not seen as detriment to European expansion, 126–131; indigenous rights seen as conditional, 123–126; natural law theories of possession and use, 117–123; revision of, 256–260
Compostela, 210, 212, 214, 218–219

Comunidad de montes y pastos, 167
Concordia, 153, 176, 185, 224–225
Connected history, 250–253, 255–260
Conquest, 111; pacification and, 321n40
Consent, implied by silence, 8, 34, 37–48, 139–140, 203, 237
Contendas, 237–238
Contraband, 5, 34, 52, 66, 139, 155, 174, 234
Conversion, to Christianity, 97–98, 101–104, 108, 114, 258–259; used for civic/political ends, 70–86
Coria, bishop of, 57
Correrías (forays), 111
Cotrim, Filipe de Matos, 52
Council of State (Spain): mixed and promiscuous villages and, 227; Verdoejo and, 193, 195–196, 198, 199, 200, 204
Council of the Indies, 39, 53, 75–76, 61–62, 80, 83
Couto misto (mixed places). See Mixed and promiscuous villages (1518–1864)
Cultivation. See Agriculture
Cumbres de San Bartolomé, 167, 168, 169
Customary law, 251, 264
Customs administration, 3, 139, 209, 229, 233
Customs and traditions, 21, 142, 144, 207, 236, 251, 256

Demarcation: Campo de Gamos and, 149–150, 152–153, 160–164, 173, 177, 179, 185; Colonia de Sacramento and, 43–44; Fritz and, 73, 81–82; Indians and European expansion, 129–130; informal, but limiting of activities, 9; Magdalena/Lindoso Mountains and, 211–217, 223; Pará and, 54, 84; Spain and Portugal and, 48–49, 67. See also Tombos
Diplomacy, 15, 20, 94, 132, 139; ambassadors' roles in, 76, 83–85, 154, 158, 164, 173–177, 192, 194–195, 197–198, 211, 227, 244; diplomatic history, 260–262; documentation and, 29–30; laymen and 45, 47; negotiations on borders, 2–3, 46–47, 157–158; negotiations with Indians, 95–96, 102–104, 106, 112–113

Discovery, and claims of possession, 26, 34, 40, 50–54, 67, 75, 116, 131, 292n98
Dispossession, of indigenous people, 108, 111, 120, 128, 245
Dúvidas, 237–238

Ecclesiastical tithes, 165, 192–194, 196–198, 200–207
El Ríos, 220
Elvas, 64, 85, 139
Encinasola, territorial disputes (1290–1955), 149–165, 238; claims about immemorial possession, 181–189; coveted object and, 178–179; parties to, 165–177
Enslavement, of indigenous people, 34, 36–37, 53, 61, 75, 111–112
Entradas (incursions), 111
Ethnogenesis, 114, 248
European tradition, South American territorial divisions and, 25–69, 46f; papal bulls, treaties, and formal documents and, 25–33; possession and intention, 33–37; possession and lack of opposition, 37–48; possession and legal doctrines of Roman law, 25–26; vassalage and, 48–68, 289n80, 295n119
Expediciones (expeditions), 111
Expert witnesses, Jesuits as, 75–76
External borders, 2, 7, 13–14, 141, 146–148, 260–261
Extremadura, 64, 141, 241, 333n17

Falcón de Ulloa, Rodrigo Antonio (Marquis of Bendaña), 194, 195, 196, 202, 203
Faria y Sousa, Manuel, 57
Fernandes, Joam, 9
Feudal past, remnants of in mixed and promiscuous villages, 232–234
1516 accord, 164–165
1542 accord, 153–156, 158–159, 166–168, 171, 174, 178–179, 182–183, 187, 189
Figueroa Altamirano, Juan Solano de, 189
Fishing rights, Verdoejo and, 192, 200–201, 204, 207–208
Foreigners, 56–57, 61, 92, 130, 139–140, 187, 220, 233
Forgetfulness and memory, 5, 9, 14, 122, 140, 181, 237, 244, 265

Freedom, 95, 106, 115, 117–118, 264
Fregenal, 167–168
Friars of the Temple, 151
Fritz, Father Samuel, 78–83, 86, 91, 92
Fronteira, Marquís of, 86
Fronterizos, 9, 144–146, 184, 188, 213, 241, 248

Gaber, Antonio de, 187–188
Galicia: audiencia of, 196–198, 204, 205, 227; governor of, 145, 334n24
Gentili, Alberico, 117
Gift-giving, New World alliances and, 97–104, 107
Global history, 255–256
Grazing, usage and property rights concerns, 7, 9, 33–34, 124, 283n31, 352n109; in disputed Iberian border areas, 138, 141, 148, 151–153, 156–157, 167–168, 171, 173, 178–179, 183–185, 187, 207–209, 215, 219–222, 225, 234, 238
Great Britain, colonialism and, 255–260
Grotius, Hugo, 34, 117–118, 284n36
Guadiana River, 209–210
Guadramil, 176

Hespanha, António Manuel, 255
Hispanic customary law, 251
Hispanic monarchy, Portugal as equal participant in, 56–57
Hispanism, 249–250
Historia eclesiástica de la ciudad y obispado de Badajoz (Figueroa Altamirano), 189
Historical rights to land, deconstructing of, 264–267
Hospitallers, 149, 151, 173–174

Iberian Peninsula, complex history of contested areas on, 135–148, 147f, 249–253; coveted objects and claims about rights and possession, 177–190; examples from 1290–1955, 149–165; examples from 1290–1955, parties to, 165–177; internal versus external frontiers and, 146, 148; possession and divine order versus human agency, 143–146; possession, intentions, and response to incursions, 139–142
Iguatemi River, 36, 48, 99

Immemorial rights and possession: legality and, 140, 142–144, 192–193, 207, 213–220, 263; precariousness of, 254; specific places and, 141–143, 181–190; tithes and, 196. *See also* Forgetfulness and memory

Improvement of land, territorial rights and, 73, 120–126, 157, 245, 255–260, 266

Independent villages. *See* Promiscuous villages

Indigenous people, of South America, 70–133; documentation of claims, 94–95; inter-indigenous feuds and, 107–108; issues of salvation versus territorial denomination, 86–93; religious conversion used for civic purposes, 70–86; rights as conditional rights, 123–126; rights not seen as determinant to European expansion, 126–131; war and peace and, 97, 104–107, 109–115, 117, 386n116

Infidels, 33–37, 53, 90, 104, 128

Informants, possession and ability to protest, 38–39

Intention, to establish rights, 34–37, 48, 118, 140, 148

Inter Caetera. See Papal bulls

Inter-indigenous feuds, 107–108

Internal borders, 7, 13–14, 141, 146–148, 260–261

"Islands of occupation," 1, 7, 42, 137, 260

Ius Commune doctrines, 116, 123, 207–208, 247

Jaime II, king of Aragon, 150

Jesuits: conversion of indigenous people and competition between countries, 71–75; expulsions of, 89–90, 199; issues of salvation versus territorial denomination, 86–93; legal and political advice given by, 75–86; Paulistas and, 67; possession and intentions, 35–37

Juan, Jorge, 94

Junta das Missões, 109–110

Juridical doctrine, 8, 18–19, 25, 35, 45–49, 116, 246. *See also* Silence

Juris et de jure, 140

"Justice and reason" *(justicia y razón)*, 198, 208, 245

Just wars, 109–115, 121, 125, 265

Kings, and border negotiations, 2–10, 43–44, 136–138, 175–184

La Contienda, 149, 152–161, 166, 172, 174, 178–179, 180*f*, 181–183, 187–189, 220, 226, 232, 351n104

Lama, 220

Lamadarcos, 234

Land grants. See *Sesmarias*

La Plata, audiencia of, 112

La Rossiana, 151, 162, 178, 179, 220

La Tejera, 8–9, 238

La Tomina, convent of, 174

Law: versus practice, 262–264; usage rights and, 1–9. *See also* Natural law

Law of nations, 22, 35, 47, 78, 112, 127, 129, 187, 257, 260

Law of Nations (Vattel), 208

Legal presumption, converting silence into consent. *See* Silence, as implied consent

Lei das Sesmarias (1375), 121–122

Lemos, House of, 231

Letters, in interplay of action and reaction in South America, 44–45, 47–48

Lindoso. *See* Magdalena/Lindoso Mountains (1773–1864)

Lindoso Castle, military commander of, 219

Linear borders, 2, 7, 260

Linhares, Count of, 63, 165, 166, 170, 174, 347n82

Locke, John, 120–121, 124, 257

Longue durée, 13, 135

Loyalty, to monarchs and country, 59–66, 169–170, 201; Jesuits and, 89, 92

Madrid, Treaty of (1750), 5, 20, 27, 31–32, 73, 127; Indian resistance to, 77, 88–90

Magdalena/Lindoso Mountains (1773–1864), 191, 210–233; claims, 222–223; coveted object and, 221–222; history of issues and confrontations, 210–218; parties, 218–221

Mainas and Quijos, governor of, 79, 80

Manín, 210, 218–219, 220, 234

Maps: preparation of Old World maps, 141; Treaty of Tordesillas and disputes over meridian, 17–19, 21, 27, 28*f*, 29, 30–31, 77

Maranhão, 50, 98

Marvão, 184–186, 353n18

Mato Grosso, governor of, 74

Meaus. *See* Mixed and promiscuous villages (1518–1864)

Medina Sidonia, Duke of, 59

Memory. *See* Forgetfulness and memory

Mendes de Morais, Francisco Xavier, 94–95

Mendes, Francisco, 174–175, 176

Mendes y Moraes, Belchior, 84

Meridian, dispute over location of and zone of influence, 17–19, 21, 27, 28f, 29, 30–31, 77

Mesa da Consciência, 162, 163, 177, 350n99

Middle Ages: doctrines and, 25, 115–116; Iberian Peninsula's complex history and, 135, 138, 144, 148, 189, 249

Military commanders, 35–36, 41–42, 45, 78, 89, 99, 103–104, 131

Military orders, 136, 163, 350n99. *See also* Aviz, order of; Hospitallers; Templars

Miño River, 192–195, 197–198, 204, 207–209

Missionaries, and roles in territorial possession, 1, 12, 70–75, 87–88, 92, 95–97, 99, 103, 109–110. *See also* Carmelites; Fritz; Jesuits

Mixed and promiscuous villages (1518–1864), 191, 223–236; issues, confrontations, and self-selection of country, 223–230; parties, privileges, and claims, 231–236

Moluccas, 17–19

Moncloa, Count of, 79–80

Monforte, 220

Montalegre, 223, 226, 233

Monterrey, Count of, 223, 224–225, 227

Monterrey, House of, 231

More, Thomas, 117

Motherland–offspring paradigm, reversal of, 11–12

Moura, territorial disputes (1290–1955), 149–161, 164–165; claims about immemorial possession, 181–184, 186–189; coveted object and, 179; parties to, 165–169, 171, 173–174

Mura Indians, 102–103

Muslims, 4, 121, 136, 167, 250

Napo River, 50–51, 54, 82, 84–85

Natural borders, 2, 7, 31, 208, 217, 218, 223, 260–261

Natural law, 3–4, 22, 35, 41, 45, 257–260, 263; indigenous rights as conditional rights, 123–126; indigenous rights not seen as detriment to European expansion, 126–131; occupation and use of vacant places, 117–123; Roman law and private and political space, 114–117

Negotiations, with Indians, 95–96, 102–104, 103, 112–113; *praticas*, 98–104

New Christians, 66

Noronha, Miquel de. *See* Linhares, Count of

Not-yet-subjected Indians, 71, 95, 107

Noudar, territorial disputes (1290–1955), 140, 149–152, 153, 158, 160–165, 254; claims about immemorial possession, 181, 183–187; coveted object and, 178–179; parties to, 165–171, 174, 176

Nueva Planta decrees, 242

Occupation: "islands of occupation," 1, 7, 42, 137, 260; natural law and use of vacant places, 117–123. *See also* Possession entries

Olivares, Count-Duke of, 60

Olivença, 15, 241

Omaguas, 19

Ordenanzas de Nueva Población (1573), 106–107

Overseas Council (Conselho Ultramarino, Portugal), 83, 86, 111

Pacification: from "conquest" to, 111, 321n40; and not-yet-subjected Indians, 71, 95, 107; versus punishment, 113

Pagans, 72–73, 88, 97, 107, 259

Papal bulls, 17, 19, 26–27, 68, 73–75, 82, 85

Paraguay, 66–67, 74, 87, 89, 104, 111–112; governor of, 38–39, 48

Pará, 39, 50–51, 78, 81–86, 98

Paris, Treaty of (1763), 20

Parliaments, natives and, 104

Pasturing. *See* Grazing

Paulistas, 36–37, 65–68, 86–87, 111

Peace: dangers of, 7, 42, 45, 47, 246; indigenous people and war versus, 97,

Peace *(continued)*
104–107, 109–115, 117, 386n116; lack of
protest and possession of territory, 42
Pereira de Castro, Gabriel, 57
Peres, Jódoco, 78
Pfiel, Aloísio Conrado, 77–79
Philip II, king of Spain, 19, 48–50,
57–64, 65–66, 125, 160, 170–171
Philip IV, king of Spain, 65
Philip V, king of Spain, 66
Picoña, castle of, 140, 223, 227–228,
231
Pires, Alvaro, 9
Portello, castle of, 231
Possession, Iberian Peninsula territorial
division and: divine order and human
agency, 143–146; immemorial rights
and, 141–143, 181–190; understanding
of incursions, 139–141
Possession, South American territorial
division and, 68; intention to appropri-
ate territory and, 33–37; legal doctrines
of Roman law and, 25–26; property and
persuasion, 284n36; silence and lack of
opposition and, 37–48, 46f
Praticas, 98–104
Prescription, 9, 116, 118–119, 123, 165
Presumption, 35, 45, 106, 139–140, 188
Private property: concepts and concerns,
3–4, 116–117, 122, 138, 143, 172–173,
221–222, 265; Verdoejo and, 201–203
Promiscuous villages. *See* Mixed and
promiscuous villages (1518–1864)
Property rights, private and public spaces
and, 114–117
Protest, failure to protest taken as
consent, 34, 37–42, 237, 246
Public domain concerns, 123, 165, 174
Puebla de Sanabria, 220
Pufendorf, Samuel, 34, 118, 119

Quito, 39, 76, 79–85, 124; audiencia of,
50–54, 80, 82

Ramoneo, 154, 338n20
Raya (division), 30, 48, 176, 188
Raymundo, Duke of Aveiro, 63
Realengos (royal lands), 214, 219–220
Reconquest, 4, 121, 136, 250
Recopilación de Indias, 56
Refertas, 237–238

Regalado, House of, 201–203, 205
Resende, Mendo Afonso de, 239
Resettlement, of indigenous people, 70,
128–129
Restauração. See War of Portuguese
Independence
Rihonor (Rio de Onor), 235, 236
Río Grande de San Pedro, 41, 45, 47
Rio Jacuy, 47
Riomanzanas, 176
Rio Pardo, 47
River, change in course of. *See* Miño
River
River Plate territory, 18, 19, 29, 283n31
Rodrigues, Pedro, 9, 238
Roman law, 33–35, 251, 260, 262–263;
possession and, 25–26; private and
political space and, 114–117
Rose, Carol M., 284n36
Rubiás. *See* Mixed and promiscuous
villages (1518–1864)
Rumors: Braganza uprising and, 59,
60–61; Iberian borders and, 145, 169,
200–221, 334n24; Jesuits and Portu-
guese territories, 85, 90; lack of
information about settlements and
aggression, 37–38, 44; native rights
and, 127

Salazar, Alonso Pérez de, 54
Sánchez de Orellana, Juan Bautista, 80,
83, 92
San Fins, Jesuit monastery of, 192, 194,
196–197, 199, 200, 201, 205
San Idelfonso, Treaty of (1777), 5, 20, 27,
31, 32
Santa Rosa, 111–112
Santa Teresa, Domingo de, 91–92
Santiago. *See* Mixed and promiscuous
villages (1518–1864)
São Luís, 109
Sauces, 112
Saxoferrato, Bartolus de, 207
Schmitt, Carl, 264
Secularization of the missions, 93
Serpa, territorial disputes (1290–1955),
149–151; claims about immemorial
possession, 181, 187; parties to, 165,
168, 173
Sesmarias, 121–122, 125
Siete Partidas, 121–122

Silence, as implied consent, 8, 34, 37–48, 139–140, 203, 237; presumption and, 106–107, 318n116
Slavery. *See* Enslavement
Slave trade, 61, 67, 94
Smugglers, 210, 216
Solórzano Pereira, Juan de, 119, 124, 257
Sotomayor, Fernando de, 357n26
Soutelinho, 234
South America, as contested territory, 17–23; history of relations between European kingdoms, 55–68. *See also* European tradition, South American territorial divisions and

Tapuias Indians, 109
Teixeira, Pedro, 50–52, 54, 64, 81
Téllez-Girón, Juan Francisco Pacheco, 195
Templars, 149, 151, 173–174
Temple, friars of, 151
Terra nullius, 132, 245
Territorial formation, in Europe and Americas: claim-making, usage rights, law and conflict over, 6–10; colonial history, improvement, and indigenous people, 255–260; complexity of process, 243–249; deconstructing border formations, 260–262; deconstructing contentious past and historical rights to land, 264–267; historians and, 1–6; reconstructing law and practice, 262–264; research methodology, 10–12; revision of intertwined Iberian histories, 249–253
Tithes. *See* Ecclesiastical tithes
Tombos, 149, 194, 196, 247–248, 263
Tordesillas, Treaty of (1494), 5, 6, 25, 29, 30, 73–74, 169–170, 346n79; disputes over meridian, 17–19, 21, 27, 28f, 29, 30–31, 77; vassalage issues and, 48, 50–51
Trasportela, 213, 214, 218–219
Trás-os-Montes. *See* Mixed and promiscuous villages (1518–1864)
Treason and traitors, 170, 240; Barranqueños and, 170; Braganza and, 60, 63–64; Indians and, 70; Valença and, 240

Treaties: among Europeans, 4–8, 17–20, 25–33, 43–51, 73–77, 88–89, 94, 127, 136–137, 140, 154, 159, 163, 195, 198–200, 205, 254; conceived of as method to guarantee peace, 30; with Indians, 258–266. *See also specific treaties*
Treatises on Government (Locke), 120–121
Tremeberes Indians, 109
Tuy, 193–197, 200, 203, 240

Ulloa, Antonio, 94
Union and disunion of Spain and Portugal (1580–1640): complications of, 7, 140; emigration issues and, 55–57; Portugal's sovereignty and political crisis after 1640, 57–64, 136; Verdoejo and, 197, 202–203, 206, 240, 241
Usage rights, 7, 138–139, 155–160, 166–167, 179, 187, 189, 205, 214, 222, 236. *See also* La Contienda
Uti possidetis principle, 265–266
Utrecht, Treaty of (1715), 20, 31, 32, 43, 48, 163, 198–199, 205, 254

Vacant places, occupation and, 117–123
Valdelirios, Marquis of, 74
Valença do Minho, 193, 200, 240
Valencia de Alcántara, 184–186, 353n18
Vassalage, 22, 30, 34, 35; religious conversion and, 70–86; territory and establishment of loyalty, 48–68, 289n80, 295n119
Vattle, Emmer de, 208
Verdoejo (1683–1863), 140, 191, 240, 254; claims of acquired versus natural rights, 206–210; coveted object and, 203–206; issues of, 192–200; parties, 200–203
Vieira, António, 71–72
Vilar de Perdizes, 234
Vilariño, 234
Villameá, 234
Villarinho, 8–9, 238
Vinhais, 173
Violence, 8, 68, 140, 210; as strategy, 11–13, 109–113, 184, 186. *See also* War
Vitoria, Francisco de, 115, 146

War: acquisition of territory and, 13, 20, 32; just wars, 109–115, 121, 125, 265; Indians and, 97, 104–107, 109–115, 117, 318n116; peace and dangers to territory, 7, 42, 45, 47, 246; peace and war as strategies, 13, 131–132. *See also* Violence; *specific wars*

War of Castilian succession (1475–1479), 167

War of Portuguese Independence, 51, 60, 64, 140, 162, 170, 171, 193–195, 202, 204, 227

War of Spanish Succession, 57, 163, 199, 206, 227

Westphalia, peace of (1648), 3

Zaragoza, Treaty of (1529), 18, 29, 154

Zonal borders, 2, 7, 260